Ford/Southampton Studies in North/South Security Relations

Managing editor: Dr JOHN SIMPSON
Executive editor: Dr PHIL WILLIAMS

Superpower competition and crisis prevention in the Third World

Ford/Southampton Research Project 'North/South Security Relations',
University of Southampton

Principal Researchers:
Professor P. A. R. CALVERT
    Dr J. SIMPSON
    Dr C. A. THOMAS
    Dr P. WILLIAMS
    Dr R. ALLISON

While the Ford Foundation has supported this study financially, it does not necessarily endorse the findings. Opinions expressed are the responsibility of their authors.

Other titles in this series include:

Superpower competition and crisis prevention in the Third World

edited by

ROY ALLISON and PHIL WILLIAMS

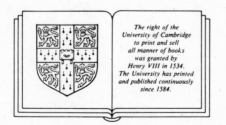

The right of the
University of Cambridge
to print and sell
all manner of books
was granted by
Henry VIII in 1534.
The University has printed
and published continuously
since 1584.

Cambridge University Press

CAMBRIDGE

NEW YORK   PORT CHESTER   MELBOURNE   SYDNEY

Published by the Press Syndicate of the University of Cambridge
The Pitt Building, Trumpington Street, Cambridge CB2 1RP
40 West 20th Street, New York NY 10011, USA
10 Stamford Road, Oakleigh, Melbourne 3166, Australia

First published 1990

Printed in Great Britain at The University Press, Cambridge

British Library cataloguing in publication data
Superpower competition and crisis prevention
in the Third World. – (Ford/Southampton
studies in north/south security relations)
1. Great powers. Foreign relations with
developing countries
2. Developing countries. Foreign relations
with great powers
I. Allison, Roy   II. Williams, Phil, 1948–
III. Series
327

Library of Congress cataloguing in publication data
Superpower competition and crisis prevention in the Third World /
edited by Roy Allison and Phil Williams
        p.   cm. – (Ford/Southampton studies in North/South security
relations).
Includes index.
ISBN 0–521–36280–6
1. Developing countries – Foreign relations.   I. Allison, Roy
II. Williams, Phil, 1948–   III. Series.
   D887.S87 · 1989
327′.091724 – dc 20   89–31512   CIP

ISBN 0 521 36280 6

Contents

Contents

Notes on contributors

Dr Roy Allison is currently a lecturer in Soviet defence and international security in the Centre for Russian and East European Studies, University of Birmingham. He is author of *Finland's Relations with the Soviet Union, 1944–84* and *The Soviet Union and the Strategy of Nonalignment in the Third World*.

Dr Roger Barnett is presently Director of Strategic and Maritime Studies at National Security Research, Inc. He retired from the United States Navy in 1984 at the grade of captain. One of the crafters of the US Navy's Maritime Strategy, he also has expertise in Soviet and US national strategy, terrorism, simulation and wargaming and arms control. He has served as an Adjunct Professor in the National Security Studies programme in the Graduate School at Georgetown University since 1981.

Dr Geoff Berridge is a lecturer in politics at Leicester University. Author of *Economic Power in Anglo-South African Diplomacy* and co-editor of *Diplomacy at the UN*. Dr Berridge visited South Africa for research purposes in 1979 and 1982. He has also written widely on broader issues in international relations.

Dr Shahram Chubin is currently at the Graduate Institute of International Studies in Geneva. He was formerly on the staff of the International Institute of Strategic Studies (London); his most recent publication is *Iran and Iraq at War* (with Charles Tripp). His other books include *The Persian Gulf: The Role of the Outside Powers*, and *Iran's Foreign Relations*. He has written extensively on regional conflicts, including articles in *Survival* and *Politique Etrangère*. Dr Chubin is a graduate of Oberlin College and Columbia University and has taught at universities in the US and Europe.

Stuart Croft is currently a lecturer in the Department of Politics, University of Birmingham. He has researched on Anglo-American policy towards Germany from 1945 to 1954 and has written articles and book chapters on 'The Westland

Helicopters Crisis', 'US Policy Towards the Middle East', 'European Reaction to SDI', and 'British Assessments of the Conventional Balance'. He has written a Faraday Paper and is author of an Adelphi Paper on Western Europe and SDI.

Dr Robert O. Freedman is Peggy Meyerhoff Pearlstone Professor of Political Science and Dean of Graduate Studies at the Baltimore Hebrew College. He is author of *Economic Warfare in the Communist Bloc: A Study of Soviet Economic Pressure Against Yugoslavia, Albania and Communist China* and *Soviet Policy Toward the Middle East since 1970.* Dr Freedman is also editor of *World Politics and the Arab–Israeli Conflict; Soviet Jewry in the Decisive Decade 1971–1980; The Middle East since Camp David;* and *The Middle East since the Israeli Invasion of Lebanon.*

Professor Alexander L. George is Stuart Professor of International Relations at Stanford University. He is the author of *Woodrow Wilson and Colonel House* (with Juliet L. George), *Deterrence in American Foreign Policy* (with Richard Smoke), *Presidential Decision Making in Foreign Policy, US–Soviet Rivalry: Problems of Crisis Prevention* (with others), *Force and Statecraft* (with Gordon A. Craig), and is co-editor of *US–Soviet Security Cooperation.*

Dr Derek Leebaert is a managing director of the Washington, D.C.-based computer systems integration company, Future Technology, Inc. He has also taught national security policy since 1985 in the Pentagon's Senior Officer Program. Dr Leebaert was a founding editor of Harvard's *International Security* in 1976.

Dr Robert Litwak directs the International Security Studies Programme at the Woodrow Wilson International Center for Scholars in Washington, D.C. He is a former Research Associate at the International Institute for Strategic Studies in London and Fellow of Harvard University's Center for International Relations. His publications include *Détente and the Nixon Doctrine* and *Security in the Persian Gulf: Sources of Inter-State Conflict.* Dr Litwak was a participant in the US–Soviet academic exchange during 1986 and spent three months at the Soviet Academy of Sciences' Institute of Oriental Studies in Moscow.

Dr P. Saravanamuttu is a lecturer in the Department of Politics, University of Southampton, specialising in foreign policy analysis, the international politics of the Third World and security problems of Southeast Asia.

Dr Peter Shearman is a lecturer in the Department of Government, University of Essex, specialising in the Soviet Union. He is co-editor of *US and Soviet Foreign Policies in the Middle East and Central America* and author of a Chatham House Paper on *The Soviet Union and Cuba.*

Dr Joanna Spear is a lecturer in the Department of Politics at Sheffield University. Her Ph.D. examined the conventional arms transfer policies of the Carter and Reagan administrations. A version of this is to be published under the title *Carter, Reagan and Arms Sales*. Publications include 'Belief Systems and Foreign Policy: the Cases of Carter and Reagan' in R. Little and S. Smith (eds.), *Belief Systems and International Relations*.

Dr Phil Williams is Senior Lecturer in International Relations, Department of Politics, University of Southampton, and currently Head of the International Security Programme, The Royal Institute of International Affairs (Chatham House). He is author of *Crisis Management, The Senate and US Troops in Europe, US Troops in Europe*, and co-author of *Contemporary Strategy*. He is also co-author of a Chatham House book entitled *Superpower Détente: A Reappraisal*, published in September 1988. In addition, Phil Williams has contributed articles to many journals including *Survival, International Affairs, Washington Quarterly* and *Politique Internationale*.

Acknowledgements

It is impossible to produce a book of this kind without incurring debts to a great many people. We would particularly like to thank the Ford Foundation for its generous support for the Southampton project on North–South Security of which this is one of the core studies. Enid Schoettle, especially, has been a constant source of encouragement to the project members and we are appreciative of her efforts.

Perhaps our greatest debt as editors is to Professor Alexander George, who not only provided the inspiration for the study of superpower competition in the Third World, but agreed to contribute to this volume. His own pioneering work in the field of superpower rivalry offered a model which this volume seeks to emulate, albeit in a more modest way.

We would also like to thank colleagues at Southampton for their advice, support and friendship. John Simpson, Caroline Thomas, Peter Calvert and Paikiasothy Saravanamuttu, the other members of the Ford Project, have contributed in many ways to this volume.

The chapters contained in this volume are substantially revised and updated versions of papers presented initially at a conference held in Guernsey in March 1987. The participants at that conference contributed numerous insights and ideas, many of which have been incorporated into the present volume. We are particularly grateful to Kenneth Waltz, Joseph Frankel, Randall Forsberg, Marc Williams, Ken Booth, Aswini Ray, Matin Zuberi, Avi Shlaim, Mark Hoffman, Nancy Adler and Nicholas Wheeler for their contributions. Our special thanks go to Darryl Howlett who not only contributed many ideas but made a very efficient conference officer, and to David Dunn who displayed a rare degree of skill and dedication in his task as rapporteur.

Elizabeth Schlamm was a major source of strength and encouragement throughout the conference and in the subsequent preparation of the volume. All her organisational and diplomatic skills, and especially those related to the prevention and management of crises, are enormously appreciated. She was ably assisted in the preparation of the manuscript by Joanne Fluck who typed several of the chapters and by Holly Porteous who helped in the final compilation of the chapters. We would also like to thank all our contributors for their cooperation and to thank Michael Holdsworth of Cambridge University Press for his help and patience.

I Superpower competition and crisis prevention in the Third World

Roy Allison and Phil Williams

SOURCES OF SUPERPOWER COMPETITION

Competition between the United States and the Soviet Union in the Third World is inevitable and endemic. It is rooted in their broader adversarial relationship, is sustained by indigenous developments in Asia, Africa and Latin America which encourage external involvement in regional politics, and is intensified by both fear and ambition. The temptations for military involvement are frequent and, on some occasions at least, irresistible. Intervention in regional conflicts, whether direct or indirect, may offer considerable opportunities for geopolitical advancement; nonintervention, in contrast, may provide such advantages to the adversary that it can appear as the most futile and damaging kind of self-denying ordinance.

The pervasiveness of superpower competition in the Third World reflects the structural basis of Soviet–American relations. In a world dominated by two great powers, rivalry is not only unavoidable, it is also both intensive and extensive. Even the existence of uncommitted nations, and the emergence in the 1960s of the Nonaligned Movement opposed to the ethics and expressions of East–West competition and bloc politics, could not prevent the superpower competition generating its own momentum. As Kenneth Waltz has noted, 'In a bipolar world there are no peripheries. With only two powers capable of acting on a world scale, anything that happens anywhere is potentially of concern to both of them. Bipolarity extends the geographic scope of both Powers' concern.'[1] Although there is something of an exaggeration in this – as it is possible to distinguish between vital and less important interests in the Third World – it helps to explain why the superpowers, having consolidated their military blocs in Europe, adopted a zero-sum vision of political developments in the developing countries during the 1950s and 1960s.

The structural imperative for conflict is intensified by perceptual and ideological factors, with neither superpower accepting the need to circumscribe the extent of its involvement outside the central military alliances in Europe. One of the most important of these perceptual factors is each superpower's self-image. Soviet–American competition is sustained partly by the sense of mission that is inherent in each side's vision of itself. The superpowers even share a sense of obligation to promote certain values and ideals – albeit very different ones. They champion divergent principles, provide incompatible social and economic models to be emulated, and offer inspiration, encouragement and support for rival governments and for competing political and ideological movements. Each is convinced of the rightness of its cause; each believes the other to be the source of turmoil and instability or of repression and reaction. Indeed, each acts with a sense of moral rectitude, not to say self-righteousness, that makes it oblivious to the similarities between its own behaviour and that of the adversary. Ideology has engendered feelings of moral absolutism which have discouraged restraint or collaboration, especially when it has been believed that the adversary will eventually collapse into internal crisis.

It is hardly surprising, therefore, that the superpower competition is also perpetuated by conflicting Soviet and American views about the legitimacy of involvement or intervention in the developing countries. In addition to the predictable assumption that one's own actions are legitimate while those of the adversary are not, the issue of what is or is not permissible has also been influenced by shifts in both the balance of power and in the balance of opportunities for exercising that power. The result has been that the incentives for restraint, let alone collaboration, have rarely been symmetrical. At different junctures, the superpowers have differed considerably in their ability and willingness to intervene in the Third World: constraints on one side have offered opportunities for the other. Yet there has also been a long-term shift: the Western powers were dominant in the Third World during the 1950s and 1960s and – in spite of earlier Soviet efforts to cultivate the leaders of the newly independent states – were not seriously challenged by the Soviet Union until the 1970s. This shift was also reflected in the increasingly global character of the struggle. For a quarter of a century after the Second World War, superpower disputes in the Third World were largely confined to regions contiguous to the Soviet Union or its one-time ally, China; in the 1970s more distant theatres engaged the mutual interests of the superpowers, damaging *détente* and threatening to draw Moscow and Washington into direct military confrontation.

This may have been inevitable. Both superpowers perceived the Third World as a proving ground, as an arena where revisionist political aspirations could be promoted or opposed, and where ideologies would clash without the immediate and obvious dangers attendant upon any attempt to change the status quo in

Europe. Furthermore, the Third World itself has provided a relatively permissive and attractive environment for superpower competition. In contrast to Europe where the demarcation between the blocs was delineated very clearly, the Third World seemed to hold out far greater possibilities for making gains at the expense of the adversary. Many Third World states are themselves highly fragmented or polarised. Consequently, a change in foreign-policy alignment could very easily follow shifts in the internal power balance. In these circumstances, the superpowers had considerable incentive for meddling in the internal affairs of Third World states.

If the possible gains were considerable, however, concern over potential losses also loomed large in Soviet and American calculations. It is hardly surprising, therefore, that the US and the Soviet Union have responded to indigenous developments in the Third World and have become drawn into intra-regional disputes where their direct interests have been marginal, but where their concern over the potential influence of the adversary has been paramount. At times the superpowers have appeared to define their interests in terms of excluding the presence or minimising the influence of the adversary. There exists a tendency in Washington and, to a lesser extent, in Moscow to ascribe Third World instability to external agency, and both governments have been reluctant to renounce their initial political investment in a state or region, treating it not in terms of the intrinsic interests involved (which have often been marginal if not trivial) but in terms of credibility, prestige, status and the like.[2] The result of this has been that the superpowers have engaged in a series of pre-emptive, preventive and reactive commitments in certain regions of the Third World. When one power gains access to military facilities or achieves a position of influence, there are strong pressures for countervailing action by the adversary. Military facilities may assist contingency planning for hostilities. Once established, however, bases frequently take on their own rationale. Maintaining a presence ceases to be a means to security and becomes an end in itself.

This has provided opportunities for superpower clients to exercise varying degrees of reverse influence on their patrons and to impede the process of superpower military extrication from regional conflict or instability: the vulnerability of the strong to the collapse of the weak should not be underestimated. This also explains why the transfer of arms to friendly and client states has been fraught with difficulties. The superpowers could all too easily be dragged into direct confrontation. In spite of the attendant dangers, however, it is not certain that Moscow and Washington will be able completely to avoid 'competitive engagement'.

Part of the reason for this can be found in the divergent historical experiences and the objectives of the superpowers in the Third World. The United States and other Western powers were globally preponderant in the first postwar decades as the result of an extensive basing network and the political heritage of colonialism. Washington sought essentially to contain Soviet influence in Eurasia and exclude it from other regions while maintaining the broad structure of political and military relations between developing and Western states, subject to the gradual process of decolonisation. These goals were accompanied by the perceived need to maintain the credibility of American power. The post-Stalin Soviet leadership, however, sought to break the USSR out of its continental mould and to mobilise the uncommitted Third World states into an anti-Western coalition. This strategy aimed at the acquisition of Third World allies through support for national liberation struggles and the military denial of Third World regions to the Western powers. As a revisionist state the Soviet Union saw little merit in the political stability of Third World states, contending that such stability was merely an expression of the structural intervention of Western power in the political and economic fabric of the new states. Indeed, for the USSR, a desirable global order would follow revolutionary upheaval on a massive scale. Soviet theorists maintained that this outcome could be retarded or hastened but not prevented – and that it would be prefigured by the growing power of socialist states. Such thinking reveals once again the ideological dimension of superpower competition.

Yet, even though ideological fervour on both sides has encouraged the view that superpower interests are inherently incompatible, it has not prevented Washington and Moscow from acknowledging a mutual interest in avoiding direct confrontation. Indeed, as well as the pressures for conflict in Soviet–American relations, there are also incentives for collaboration – if only to ensure that their competition does not get out of hand.

INCENTIVES FOR COLLABORATION IN CRISIS PREVENTION

Until the 1970s the asymmetrical strategic relationship between Washington and Moscow discouraged serious efforts to collaborate in advance to reach explicit understandings designed to avoid superpower confrontation in the Third World. Even so, there was tacit acceptance of the idea of asymmetrical intervention: when the United States was involved in local or regional conflict, the Soviet Union stood on the sidelines. Moscow might assist its proxies with arms supplies, but was careful not to get directly involved. Perhaps even more important, Soviet reticence reflected Soviet weakness and vulnerability, not only at the strategic level but also in terms of its negligible military presence outside the socialist bloc: the United States had a virtual monopoly on global power projection. The incentives for formal collaboration, therefore, were minimal. Indeed, Khrushchev tried to compensate for Soviet weakness by cultivating an image of belligerence – and even in the Soviet Union was subsequently accused of 'adventurism'. With the exception of the Cuban Missile Crisis, however, he took great care to avoid direct confrontation with the United States in the Third World. His threats during the Suez crisis were bluffs made in awareness of US opposition to the Anglo–French invasion; he failed to take any action against American bases in Pakistan in connection with the U–2 crises; and even in the Missile Crisis he withdrew once American determination was manifest.[3] At the same time Khrushchev made clear that, in spite of implicit understandings about Eastern and Western Europe, 'spheres of influence' thinking was unacceptable in relation to the Third World where it appeared as a 'policy of imperialism . . . a most inveterate colonial policy'.[4]

After Khrushchev's downfall, Soviet policy in the Third World became even more obviously risk averse. Adventurism was eschewed in favour of a steady build-up of nuclear forces designed to replace Soviet strategic inferiority by at least some form of parity with the United States. At the same time, Moscow remained acutely aware of the limitations on its military capacity to influence Third World developments through direct intervention. This, of course, did not preclude indirect assistance to liberation struggles like that in Vietnam. Indeed, this assistance was very attractive, in that it contributed to American misfortunes without risking direct military confrontation. This pattern of opportunism was to continue in Soviet policy during the 1970s. Yet this was not immediately apparent. As the superpowers moved towards *détente* so they began to discuss the possibility of an explicit code of conduct which would enable them to avoid confrontation in the Third World.

This attempt to establish a set of formal understandings in relation to Third World conflict and instability stemmed from both a common interest in avoiding direct confrontations and a coincidence of very different and ultimately incompatible Soviet and American interests. The primary incentive for collaboration remained the potential costs of confrontation. Indeed, to the United States, the dangers inherent in Soviet–American confrontations were underlined by the Soviet attainment of strategic parity. As in earlier years, however, the Soviet Union accepted that, in relation to the United States and its allies, the use of force would pose acute dangers of escalation and create unacceptably high risks of large-scale and probably uncontrollable military conflict. In 1972 the Soviet specialists V. Zhurkin and Ye. Primakov viewed with alarm the possibility of 'an expansion of local military crises', since this was attached to 'the greatest probability of their development into a nuclear conflict, particularly taking into account the unusually broad contemporary system of mutual obligations, political guarantees and military links'. At the same time they

5

noted that such escalation exerted 'a growing restraining influence' on an aggressor, which may hold it back from 'a rapid transition to an "active stage" of a military clash'.[5]

During the cold war the superpowers had meticulously refrained from authorising violence against each other's military forces. The Soviet attainment of parity and the build-up of Soviet power projection capabilities did nothing to alter this *fundamental rule of prudence*.[6] As a leading Soviet civilian strategist acknowledged, 'the main thing . . . is not merely to extinguish military conflicts after the hostilities have started, but to prevent the emergence of the sources of war, to defuse the explosive situations before they break out'.[7] An added incentive for the Soviet Union to do this was the danger that confrontation with the United States would encourage Washington to develop a Sino–American axis directed against Moscow. The Soviet aim in *détente* was not only to avoid such an outcome but, if possible, to create an anti-Chinese condominium.

Although the superpowers were in broad agreement on the dangers of Soviet–American confrontations, their attempts to preclude crises reflected underlying differences which resulted in rather selective efforts to regulate their competition. The United States still wished to proscribe Soviet activity outside the Eurasian heartland where Moscow had historically staked out its interests. For the United States, *détente* – and the code of conduct for the Third World which accompanied it – was an attempt to get the Soviet Union to accept a degree of restraint that amounted to 'self-containment'.[8] Washington denounced Soviet efforts to project influence globally as inconsistent with *détente*. This reflected the limits on American involvement imposed as a result of the domestic disillusionment with the Vietnam War. For the Soviet Union, however, *détente* was partly about equality and partly about making the world safer for Soviet–American competition to continue. The Soviet Union wished to avoid direct superpower confrontation or armed conflict but emphasised that within this constraint there would be no end to the class struggle and that Moscow would continue to support wars of national liberation.

The United States was concerned with prohibiting Soviet military intervention in the Third World, and consequently had a much more extensive concept of 'crisis' than a Soviet leadership concerned only with avoiding situations which, in its judgement, contained a serious risk of war between the superpowers.[9] Whenever tempting opportunities arose for Moscow to change the correlation of forces in its favour, and to do so safely then, in its view, military assistance was legitimate. Indeed, although Soviet leaders were aware of the danger and unpredictability of crises, during the early 1970s they seemed to become somewhat more sanguine about the prospects of military escalation from local conflicts in the Third World. Soviet military officials judged that the USSR had not only a greater capacity than ever before for military intervention in the Third World but also a greater ability to keep the conflict localised.[10] At the same time, Soviet military doctrine began to recognise the utility of a wide range of conventional and specialised forces for the projection of power. Soviet leaders saw no reason to impose restraints on the military activities of Cuba or other close confederates involved in Third World conflicts. The United States, however, took a very different view. In fact, the superpowers had not only divergent but contradictory views about what was permissible behaviour under *détente*. Although this was to undermine the efforts at collaboration, it did not prevent Moscow and Washington from embarking upon them.

ATTEMPTS AT COLLABORATION

The superpower summits of 1972 and 1973 witnessed an attempt by the superpowers to establish understandings designed to regulate the competition which they acknowledged as an inescapable feature of their relationship. As George Breslauer has put it, they attempted to move from 'confrontational competition' to 'collaborative competition' and to replace improvisation in crises by a more explicit effort to avoid crises.[11]

The Basic Principles Agreement or BPA (see Appendix 1) signed at the Moscow Summit was a serious, if badly flawed, attempt by the superpowers to establish rules of behaviour which, according to Kissinger in a press conference in Kiev just after the Summit, would mark the 'transformation from a period of rather rigid hostility to one in which, without any illusions about the differences in social systems, we would try to behave with restraint and with a maximum of creativity in bringing about a greater degree of stability and peace'.[12] In 1973 the BPA was reinforced by an Agreement on the Prevention of Nuclear War (see Appendix 2).

In the declarations of 1972 and 1973 the superpowers pledged to act so as to prevent situations developing which might cause 'a dangerous exacerbation of their relationship' and provoke military confrontations. At the same time, Moscow and Washington agreed to refrain from the threat or use of force against each other and against each other's allies. In addition, if situations arose involving the risk of nuclear conflict, they were to 'engage in urgent consultations with each other and make every effort to avert this risk'. Finally, the superpowers committed themselves to exercise restraint in their relationship, and acknowledged that efforts by either side to obtain 'unilateral advantage at the expense of the other, directly or indirectly', were incompatible with this notion of restraint.[13]

These principles reflected an attempt to specify the kind of restraints appropriate to *détente*. Yet it is far from clear that both parties perceived them as an agreed code of conduct applicable to the Third World. The commitments themselves were ambiguous, and were described by Alexander George as a 'quasi-agreement'.[14] Notions such as restraint are inherently imprecise, and the obligations imposed were uncertain, offering considerable scope for differences in interpretation. At the same time, the stringency of the accords in demanding that both refrain from unilateral advantage, meant that there would be considerable opportunity for recriminations and for allegations 'that the understandings were being violated and that detente was being betrayed.'[15]

In the event each side interpreted the 1972 and 1973 accords to suit itself, applying them selectively on the basis of strategic convenience or political expediency. Furthermore, both felt it necessary to subordinate the accords to interests and objectives related more directly to the competitive aspect of their relationship. The United States, for example, worked to exclude the Soviet Union from the Middle East – but because this was done through diplomacy rather than force did not see it as inconsistent with the prohibition on attempts to obtain unilateral advantage. For its part, the Soviet Union would not accept that the accords placed any restriction on support for national liberation struggles.

In view of all this, it seemed rather over-ambitious to characterise what were, in effect, vague mutual understandings as a binding code of conduct with legal force. Nevertheless, Washington claimed that rules had been established which effectively precluded the introduction of outside military forces into Third World conflicts and which mandated each power to respect the spheres of influence of the other. In fact, in many regions in the Third World it was impossible to demarcate spheres of influence with sufficient clarity to act as an unequivocal guide to action. Consequently, both powers continued to compete vigorously, especially where conditions on the ground seemed to presage a favourable outcome.

In a sense, therefore, both superpowers defected from a cooperative approach to Third World crises. The United States' defection came in the Middle East where Kissinger's attempt to obtain unilateral advantage through skilful diplomacy designed to exclude Soviet influence from the region was remarkably successful. Furthermore, in Angola in 1975, both sides became involved in a competitive game, and one which the CIA described as having all the characteristics of an action–reaction phenomenon.[16] Throughout the spring and summer of 1975 the United States supported UNITA and the FNLA as vigorously as the Soviet Union was supporting the MPLA. It was only after the introduction of the Cubans as Soviet proxies that Kissinger alleged that the competition was inconsistent with *détente* – a charge that became even more strident when the US Congress, fearful of being dragged into another Vietnam, banned further US assistance.

The Soviet Union was not convinced. In retrospect, it is clear that, at a time when the tide of national liberation in the Third World favoured the Soviet Union's revolutionary aspirations, Moscow would not accept the status quo in terms of spheres of influence defined by the United States. In the view of one Soviet specialist, Kissinger's attempt to reach agreement with the USSR on a division of spheres of influence reflected 'Washington's inability to do anything practical in Angola to create a pro-American regime there'. The formulation of the Sonnenfeldt Doctrine in December 1975 was interpreted as an expression of Kissinger's new approach 'by officially recognising Eastern Europe as the sphere of influence of the Soviet Union, to try to confirm Western Europe, Africa and Latin America as the indisputable sphere of influence of the United States'. Soviet identification with the national liberation struggle, it was observed, meant that such a division of the world could not be acceptable to the USSR.[17]

This is not to suggest that Moscow was reckless. In the Horn of Africa, for example, the Soviet Union obtained geopolitical advantage but was careful to respect the territorial integrity of Somalia. Nevertheless, the scale and extent of Soviet involvement in the Third World during the 1970s suggests that the agreements of 1972 and 1973 did not significantly constrain Moscow. Yet the difference between Soviet and American behaviour was not in the extent to which they observed the injunctions of the crisis prevention accords. Both sides were guilty of violating the rules in pursuit of what Keohane has termed 'myopic self-interest'.[18] The difference was simply that the Soviet Union seemed to be much more successful in ensuring that it obtained favourable outcomes from Third World instability.[19]

In these circumstances, the failure of collaboration was inevitable. The comprehensive scope of the agreements of 1972 and 1973 and the ambitious nature of their injunctions combined with the uncertain benefits and continued distrust between the superpowers to discredit the whole enterprise. This outcome was made all the more likely by the implicit, but incorrect, assumption that each of the superpowers was in complete control of its allies. Even if the accords of 1972 and 1973 had succeeded in restricting superpower intervention-ary activities to respective, mutually agreed spheres of influence, this would have met hostility and even resistance from Third World states. The establishment of *competition free zones* was anathema to the majority of Third World states since it implied either the unilateral domination of one superpower or a Soviet–American condominium in which the distinct interests of the Third World would be sacrificed to the superpower concerns over crisis avoidance. Consequently, American interest in the application of spheres of influence to Third World regions in the 1970s was strenuously opposed by regional Third World organisations and by the Non-Aligned Movement. Equally significantly, Sadat's decision to go to war against Israel in 1973 was designed in large part to ensure that the impasse between the Arab states and Israel was not frozen into immobility as a result of Soviet and American concerns with regulating and moderating their competition.

The Soviet Union, too, was reluctant to subscribe to American ideas about competition-free zones. The Soviet interpretation of the Basic Principles and Prevention of Nuclear War Agreements can be understood much more in terms of *free competition but crisis controlled zones*. This was more acceptable to Third World opinion since it smacked far less of condominium or unilateral domination. It also offered Third World states greater room for manoeuvre and some opportunity to play off the superpowers against each other. For the Soviet Union, however, the importance of such an interpretation lay primarily in the fact that it implied equality as well as restraint. With the attainment of strategic parity, the Soviet Union felt entitled to equal influence with the United States in dealing with disputes or instability in strategically important regions.

The emphasis on Soviet superpower status, however, did not mean that the Soviet Union was oblivious to the need for restraint. The accords were seen as a means of controlling superpower competition in ways which minimised the risk of military, and especially nuclear, confrontation. One Soviet specialist described the Basic Principles Agreement as the outcome of Soviet–American efforts directed at averting and regulating dangerous situations. He applauded the supporters of a 'constructive approach' in American policy who gave significance to the realisation of prophylactic measures which would contribute to averting international conflicts and crises and the reduction of the threat of war. He observed that both powers assumed the obligation through the 1972 agreement 'to display restraint in mutual relations and to regulate [*uregulirovat'*] differences of view by peaceful means'.[20] Ironically this view of the agreement as a means to regulate competition by dampening down escalatory risks may have encouraged Soviet activism in the Third World – after all *détente* effectively made the confrontation less dangerous. Yet the Soviet Union was still risk averse in its behaviour, and adhered strictly to the fundamental rule of prudence which demanded not only that the superpowers eschew the use of force against each other but also avoid situations liable to result in violence. This was reflected in, and reinforced by, another accord signed in Moscow in 1972 in which the superpowers agreed to take measures to prevent incidents 'on and over the high seas'. Risk limitation also characterised other aspects of Soviet Third World policy. Soviet leaders selected opportune moments and targets for their interventionary actions so as to minimise the likelihood of an American response. Where possible, they preferred indirect action through proxy or friendly governments which could act as buffers and permit the USSR to extricate itself quickly and easily in the event of unexpected American resistance.[21] The paradox, however, was that precisely because these avenues were available, Moscow was unwilling to accept the broader asymmetrical restraints on Soviet activism that Washington consistently sought to impose.

The basic divergence of approach between the superpowers not only undermined the agreements of 1972 and 1973 but also made it impossible to go beyond these to establish a more ambitious crisis-prevention regime. An option which was attractive to the Third World was the idea of formally acknowledged *mutual no-go zones*, that is, Third World regions from which all forms of superpower security activities are excluded. Such a zone would effectively prevent both unilateral and competitive superpower interventions. The problem, however, was that establishment of a zone generally required an asymmetry of sacrifice. Consequently Soviet proposals for the creation of such zones in areas where the Soviet presence was negligible were regarded as disingenuous. The notion of an Indian Ocean zone of peace sponsored by Third World states, for example, received declaratory Soviet support but failed to receive the active support of the United States.

This somewhat selective approach to the regulation of Soviet–American rivalry in the 1970s was also evident in the attitudes of both superpowers towards arms limitation techniques. The superpowers in the late 1960s, of course, had agreed to establish a nuclear non-proliferation regime to reduce the dangers of uncontrolled conflict in the Third World. This regime was maintained throughout the 1970s despite Soviet complaints that Washington was exerting insufficient pressure on certain of its allies to prevent proliferation. It proved very difficult to extend this to conventional arms transfers. While there were certain tacit restraints accepted by both superpowers, these were not translated into more formal prohibitions. A working group was established between the superpowers in 1977 to discuss international arms transfers, but no substantial progress was achieved. Although Carter and Brezhnev expressed continued interest in the idea when they met at Vienna in June 1979 they were unable to take it any further as a result of the demise of *détente*. Indeed, it is hard to escape the conclusion that throughout the 1970s the superpowers were more interested in using arms transfers as a tool of competition than as a means of collaboration. Furthermore, by the end of the decade the opportunities for collaboration had disappeared almost completely – at least temporarily. Six months after the Vienna Summit, Soviet–American relations had reverted to cold war. Although the Soviet invasion of Afghanistan in December 1979 was the proximate cause of this shift, American animosity towards the Soviet Union had been increased by what many Americans interpreted as an unrestrained Soviet geopolitical offensive which, in the judgement of policy-makers like Brzezinski, made a mockery of the rules of the game established in the early 1970s. Afghanistan was seen simply as the culmination of Soviet policies which were ruthlessly opportunist and based upon the desire to seek maximum unilateral advantage wherever this could be done with impunity.

INCENTIVES FOR COLLABORATION TO AVOID CRISES IN THE 1980s

Soviet intervention in Afghanistan in December 1979 ushered in a more confrontational period in superpower relations in which the United States went at least some way towards ridding itself of the 'Vietnam syndrome' and became more activist. The dominant American mood in the early 1980s opposed ill-defined constraints on US actions in the Third World: Moscow had shown throughout the 1970s that it wanted free competition, although this remained subject to the need to avoid dangerous crises. The Reagan Administration was happy to engage in more active competition. By increasing defence spending, committing itself to a 600-ship Navy and refurbishing American strategic power, it hoped to be able to compete from strength. The Soviet gains of the late 1970s were challenged as illegitimate and the Administration enunciated what became known as the Reagan Doctrine which postulated American support for revolutionary struggles against Marxist governments in the Third World. Thrown on the defensive, Moscow began to reassess its military commitments to regional clients. In addition, Soviet spokesmen urged restraint in regional conflicts, proposed collaborative arrangements for volatile areas, and condemned the reassertion of American power and will in the Third World.

In spite of the American rhetoric and the enunciation of concepts such as 'horizontal escalation' which appeared to be the antithesis of the traditional preoccupation with managing crises and localising conflict, the fundamental rule of prudence between the superpowers still applied. It remained an overriding interest of both Moscow and Washington to avoid being drawn into direct confrontation. For this reason, Moscow evinced greater interest in security arrangements to regulate and mitigate competition with the United States in regions such as the Persian Gulf where the risks of confrontation remained high.

One consideration underlying this change of approach seems to have been a careful assessment of the dangers resulting from the resurgence of the United States. In the late 1970s and early 1980s there was no consensus among Soviet military specialists on issues of horizontal and vertical escalation. Some upheld Khrushchev's earlier belief in the inevitability of escalation from local conflict which involved the superpowers to nuclear war, while others saw escalation as having a relatively low probability even in these circumstances and continued to advocate Soviet power projection in local conflicts to combat the export of 'counter-revolution'. There was broad agreement in Moscow, however, that new

American-sponsored military groupings in the Third World could precipitate broader conflict, and from about 1981 Soviet political authorities and civilian specialists began to reconsider Soviet interventionism in the Third World. In effect they agreed with those military figures who were concerned about the escalatory potential of regional conflicts.[22] Starting from this premise, a number of non-military specialists increasingly emphasised the need for superpower cooperation to avert crises. This emphasis on collaboration, which had been a persistent strain in the writings of certain Soviet analysts in the 1970s, was derived from the premise that conflicts involving the two world social systems were most likely to be sparked off by wars in which the forces of imperialism attempted to suppress national liberation movements. In 1981 Trofimenko summed up the collaborative strain in Soviet thinking in pragmatic language. He accepted that 'the continuing stormy events in the Third World' generated by the process of development among the new states 'will develop against the background of the continuing competition between the two systems . . . for influence on its course and outcome'. In his view it was only 'an unbiased and business-like approach of all non-local forces to the political settlement of acute crisis situations that can ensure their not leading to the military involvement of great powers, to another world war'.[23]

The escalation dangers inherent in conflict in the Third World were analysed later in the 1980s in a Soviet specialist study on the political content of contemporary war. The authors drew attention to a tendency for wars between developed capitalist and underdeveloped countries to expand. This, in turn, raised the danger of the transformation of such wars into region-wide armed conflicts, which in turn could be transformed into world war. The use of tactical nuclear weapons was regarded as the main catalytic factor which could result in the threshold between regional and global war being crossed. According to this study the likelihood of escalation depends on the character of the states involved in hostilities. Conflicts among *developing* countries do not pose such a danger in themselves. Conflicts between advanced Western and Third World states are potentially escalatory. Aggression by Western states against individual 'socialist' countries outside the Warsaw Pact (such as Vietnam, Laos, North Korea and Cuba) is fraught with the danger of escalation to world war, but may be contained within the limits of a local war. Finally, aggression against the 'socialist community' at large would inevitably lead to global war.[24] The perception of risks inherent in this hierarchy of conflict appears to provide strong incentives for Soviet leaders to collaborate with their American counterparts to preclude the escalation of local and regional conflicts into direct Soviet–American confrontation.

The Soviet reappraisal of its activities in the Third World can also be understood as a learning process. Soviet leaders had consistently repudiated the notions of linkage enunciated by both Kissinger and Brzezinski; yet the experience of the 1970s had shown the difficulties of compartmentalising Soviet–American competition in the Third World from the central strategic relationship. American assessments which saw heightened Soviet activism as a result of Soviet nuclear advantage made the linkage very explicit. Furthermore, this linkage contributed significantly to the demise of *détente*, as was perhaps most apparent in Brzezinski's claim that 'SALT Two was buried in the sands of the Ogaden'.[25] Although the Soviet Union had asserted that the *détente* process was irreversible, the *de facto* collapse of *détente* revealed otherwise. Furthermore, American perceptions of the illegitimacy of Soviet actions in Asia, Africa and Central America, provided a receptive environment within the US for a resurgence of American military power and the reinvigoration of regional coalitions.

This trend was all the more disturbing for Moscow because by the early 1980s it had acquired a range of political and military assets in the Third World, usually in volatile regions or weak and unstable states, which transformed the Soviet Union from a revisionist power into a more status quo oriented actor. The Reagan Doctrine sought to exploit these new vulnerabilities and placed Moscow on the defensive by threatening to undermine Soviet political and military outposts outside the core socialist bloc. It was not surprising, therefore, that the categories used by Soviet analysts of Third World security became more traditional, legal and stability oriented. The depth of Soviet concern was highlighted by the way in which some specialists speculated on the possible neutralisation of crucial Third World regions.[26]

Another consideration which encouraged a downgrading of the ideological elements in Soviet foreign policy towards the Third World was a growing awareness of the financial and economic costs of regional ventures and of subsidies to client states. The geopolitical gains of the 1970s had, in many cases, become the economic drains of the 1980s. As economic retrenchment became a priority of Soviet policy towards developing countries, an autarkist strain in Soviet thinking became increasingly evident. Soviet analysts began to criticise the tendency of Third World states to engage in regional arms races, since these were costly for all concerned including superpower patrons – and potentially escalatory. Disenchantment gradually spread in the Soviet Union over the cost of the war in Afghanistan, as it became clear that the analogies with the Czechoslovak intervention of 1968 (which had been discernible in the initial intervention) were less appropriate than analogies with the American experience in Vietnam.

Although Moscow was becoming more pragmatic in its approach to the Third

World, the Reagan Administration remained fixated with the Soviet threat to American interests. The President and his key advisers imposed a bipolar framework on the Third World, seeing it as little more than an arena for superpower competition. The inherent complexities and pluralism of Third World issues were overlooked in favour of a more simplistic approach which saw any gain for one superpower as resulting automatically in a loss for the other. Furthermore, the new assertiveness in US policy seemed to suggest that United States policy-makers were less risk averse than their Soviet counterparts in the early 1980s. Part of this, of course, was simply intended to clarify American interests in the Third World. The Carter Doctrine, specifying that the United States had vital interests in the Persian Gulf, which it was prepared to use force to protect, was intended to prevent any miscalculation by the Soviet Union and avert a direct clash with Soviet forces. Yet this was also indicative of the fact that the United States was moving, if only incompletely, beyond the Vietnam syndrome. Increasing emphasis was placed on a capacity for rapid deployment in Third World contingencies and, in 1983, the Rapid Deployment Force which had been created under Carter became United States Central Command. Furthermore, there was a new willingness to use force in the Third World – as was evident in the intervention in Grenada and the retaliatory strike on Libya, which took place regardless of Soviet advisers in that country.

For all this, the Vietnam syndrome was not superseded by a new enthusiasm for Third World ventures. There was tension between the desire to ensure that the United States avoided further humiliations like the Iran hostage crisis – which required a willingness to use force – and the concern that the use of force would once again result in prolonged stalemate with highly divisive domestic consequences. This was evident in the way in which opposition developed to the deployment of American marines in Lebanon as part of a peacekeeping effort. It was also apparent in November 1984 when Secretary of Defense Weinberger enunciated a set of conditions which, in his view, had to be met before the United States should resort to military force. These included the likelihood that public support could be mobilised and maintained and, perhaps most important of all, the possibility that victory could be achieved. This set Weinberger in opposition to Secretary of State George Shultz, who believed that a United States willingness to resort to force was essential to the success of American diplomacy. The implication of this is that the contrast with the Carter Administration, when the reluctance of the United States to become involved militarily in the Third World had been all pervasive, was less stark than it first appeared. The Reagan Administration was able to use force against targets of convenience in the Third World but found it difficult to go beyond this. The Reagan Doctrine, in a sense, was an indirect approach to the Third World, and was based on the assumption that the United States could use proxies as effectively as the Soviet Union had apparently used Cuba during the 1970s.

For all the rhetoric, therefore, the United States — like the Soviet Union — remained aware of the unpredictable outcome of crises in the volatile political terrain of the Third World, and this cautioned against overly vigorous attempts to fuel regional crises. As well as being aware that it was vulnerable to manipulation by regional allies who were resistant to superpower control, Washington also realised that investments in such states could be ephemeral, and the gains transient. In view of the more assertive American attitudes, however, it is not entirely surprising that in the 1980s more serious thinking about crisis avoidance seems to have been done in Moscow than in Washington.

SOVIET THINKING ON CRISIS PREVENTION IN THE 1980S

In the early 1980s the Soviet political leadership shifted the thrust of its policy towards the Third World and made new attempts to engage the United States in collaborative understandings to avoid dangerous escalation in Third World conflicts. At the Twenty-sixth Party Congress in 1981, neither the divisibility of *détente* nor Soviet revolutionary assistance to Third World states was questioned, and Brezhnev expressly committed the USSR to combat the 'export of counter-revolution'. In retrospect this appears as a last defiant gesture and, after the Congress, Soviet leaders implicitly began to acknowledge that superpower *détente* could not accommodate the degree of Soviet military activism in the Third World characteristic of the 1970s.

In April 1981 Brezhnev called for norms of conduct in the Third World, thereby signalling a shift in Soviet policy towards a more cooperative approach (see Appendix 3). In part, this attempt to revive a collaborative arrangement to govern great power conduct in relation to the Third World reflected Soviet uncertainty about the continued relevance of the Basic Principles Agreement of 1972. Brezhnev made oblique reference to this when he observed that the United States was 'always appealing to the USSR and its allies to agree to observe some sort of "code of good behaviour" with regard to the young states of Africa, Asia and Latin America'. Insofar as such a code meant 'some sort of "rules" which would perpetuate imperialists' pillage and diktat' in the developing states or 'the establishment of some sort of "spheres of influence"', then Moscow could not accept it. This did not mean that the Soviet Union was unalterably opposed to codes of conduct. Indeed, Brezhnev appealed to the United States to observe certain 'norms of international law' in the Third World, which he described as 'the code of conduct which we recognise and are always ready to observe'. These norms were drawn from the UN Charter, the Helsinki Final Act of 1975 and 'the well-known agreements of the 1970s between the USSR and the USA ... which today, unfortunately, are being trampled on by the American authorities'.

The provisions of Brezhnev's code were not novel; most of them simply reaffirmed general principles advocated by the nonaligned states. Furthermore, the public unveiling of the code during a visit by Colonel Gaddafi to Moscow implied that it was less a serious proposal for consideration by the United States than a political overture to the Third World at a time of mounting criticism over the continued Soviet presence in Afghanistan. At the same time, the provision in the declaration which explicitly rejected attempts to include nations in superpower spheres of influence was directed against unilateral attempts by the United States to define certain regions such as the Middle East or the Persian Gulf as spheres of vital interests to be defended, if necessary, by resort to arms.

Soviet leaders had denounced the Carter Doctrine (which asserted American interests in the Gulf) and sought to dissuade Washington from issuing similar proclamations for other volatile regions. At the same time, Soviet spokesmen claimed that the USSR itself necessarily had a security interest in the Persian Gulf and Middle East on the basis of geographic proximity. Brezhnev also issued a warning against American intervention in Iran on the grounds that Soviet security interests were linked to developments in that country. Iran had become a particularly serious issue between the superpowers in the autumn of 1980, when the possibility of another hostage rescue attempt by the United States combined with the outbreak of the Iran–Iraq War to create an extremely sensitive situation.[27] Tension was worsened by the fact that recent Soviet military exercises had included a simulated invasion of Iran. It was against this background that Brezhnev, in December 1980, enunciated a proposal for the neutralisation of the Persian Gulf region. Although American policy-makers, disillusioned with the efficacy of advance commitments to declaratory principles and reluctant to renounce military preponderance in the region, evinced no serious interest in Soviet proposals, the communications that occurred between Moscow and Washington underlined their tacit acceptance of Iran's status as a 'mutual no-go zone'. Formal agreement was elusive, but there was a mutual recognition that the dangers involved in intervention in Iran were prohibitive. Neither superpower felt able to intervene without provoking counter-action by the adversary. This understanding may have been one of the most positive results to emerge from a very negative period in Soviet–American relations.

The tone of the relationship improved with Gorbachev's advent to power. The new Soviet leader proclaimed a new commitment to 'mutual security', to a global security system based on political accommodation between the superpowers, and to initiatives aimed at settling regional conflicts. The Twenty-Seventh Party Congress in February 1986 advanced fundamental principles for a comprehensive system of international security, including security in the Third World. Soviet demarches also sought to reinvigorate earlier proposals for the demilitarisation of the Indian Ocean and the Mediterranean. In an important speech in Vladivostok in July 1986, Gorbachev built on previous Soviet suggestions for 'a separate conference of Pacific Basin countries to consider questions of security', and called for discussions to reduce naval activities in the Pacific and armed forces in Asia. Soviet diplomats also campaigned more vigorously for a comprehensive Middle East settlement and adopted a more conciliatory stance towards Israel. In addition, the USSR displayed greater flexibility over the Afghan and Kampuchean conflicts in calling for broader-based coalition governments of national reconciliation.

These campaigns were widely interpreted in the West as evidence of a Soviet inability to compete with the United States in the Third World. The Reagan Doctrine, it was asserted, had helped to tilt the psychological balance against Moscow. Such an interpretation was all the more persuasive as it became apparent that the Soviet leadership had made an explicit decision not to assume new, large-scale military commitments in Asia, Africa and Central America, especially where these might meet resistance from the United States or its military clients. It was given added credence by the low priority attached to the development of Soviet power projection capabilities despite the regeneration of US capabilities for rapid military intervention.

By 1987, Soviet spokesmen claimed that 'restructuring' in the USSR had extended to a reassessment of the Soviet approach to regional turbulence. The primary Soviet concerns were the danger of superpower crises arising from such conflicts and the economic costs of extended Soviet involvement in them. The prominent Soviet foreign affairs specialist, Ye. Primakov, alluded to the first of these when he explained that the new Soviet philosophy 'must include the rejection of the horizontal spread of confrontation between the USSR and the USA and between the Warsaw Treaty and NATO'. In this connection, it was 'particularly important to stop examining regional conflicts from the angle of US–Soviet rivalry, which hinders their settlement'.[28] Soviet commentators also stressed that 'under present-day conditions the growth of one armed conflict often triggers eruptions in other zones'.[29] In a similar vein a recent American study on superpower involvement in the Third World was commended by its Soviet reviewers for drawing the conclusion that 'the Soviet Union and the United States have an equal interest in preventing a direct confrontation between themselves because of the conflicts which can arise in the developing countries'.[30]

Such arguments appeared to give credence to the Reagan Administration's claims that 'negotiating from strength' had compelled a reassessment in Soviet policy. Yet this change also reflected leadership changes and the growing acceptance within the USSR of a new non-confrontational attitude to superpower relations. Furthermore, it was at least as much a response to internal needs as to external pressures. The domestic compulsions behind Soviet policy towards regional conflicts in the late 1980s were revealed by the Soviet Deputy Foreign Minister, A. L. Adamishin, in a televised discussion of 'regional conflicts in the nuclear age'. According to Adamishin, restructuring in the USSR had led to a more 'realistic' and 'active' Soviet approach to regional conflicts. He observed that the Soviet desire to settle such conflicts was based on the 'deepest internal needs'. The current priority was to implement a radical restructuring of Soviet society, and 'for this purpose we need a calm situation in the world . . . we need there to be no wars, especially wars near our border'.[31] In June 1987, Soviet Foreign Minister, Eduard Shevardnadze, placed a similar emphasis on the desire of the USSR to avoid entanglements in conflicts and crises. Addressing officials of his ministry, he emphasised the need to 'enhance the profitability' of Soviet foreign policy to achieve 'a situation in which our mutual relations with other states burden our economy to the least possible extent and create a stable psychological atmosphere in which Soviet citizens can work in peace'.[32] These needs could not be fulfilled through interventionism or brinkmanship in the Third World.

The Geneva accord on Afghanistan in April 1988 appeared to substantiate the new Soviet policy line on regional conflicts. The agreement provided for Soviet force withdrawals, although in a separate understanding with the United States the superpowers remained free to provide arms and assistance to their regional clients involved in the Afghan conflict. However, despite the decision to withdraw from Afghanistan and the novel Soviet concern about the 'profitability of foreign policy', Soviet officials have been careful not to give the impression that the USSR will readily abandon its interests in volatile regions or renounce its commitments to Third World allies embroiled in conflicts on a unilateral basis. After talking about avoiding wars near the Soviet borders, for example, Adamishin reaffirmed Soviet opposition to the export of counter-revolution and promised that, if necessary, Soviet military assistance would be provided to counteract 'a whole series of attempts to subvert legitimate governments'. Furthermore, although he acknowledged that the Soviet Union did not see regional conflicts in terms of superpower confrontation, Adamishin noted nonetheless that the Soviet capacity to intervene had a deterrent effect on the Western powers and prevented them 'crossing a certain line'.[33]

The Soviet experience in Afghanistan has led to open expressions of Soviet disenchantment over the prospects of unilateral military intervention in the Third World in support of client regimes and has reinforced Soviet opinion in favour of cooperative superpower approaches to regional conflicts. At the end of

1987 two Soviet specialists defined the new Soviet strategy of 'reasonable sufficiency' on the regional level as including 'the abstention of great powers from attempts to act as "guarantors" of regimes in developing countries which lack a broad social base and are unable to defend themselves'.[34] However, following the signing of the Geneva accord on Afghanistan the Soviet press observed that the superpowers 'for the first time, acted *jointly* as intermediaries and guarantors of the settlement of a regional problem' (our emphasis). *Pravda* claimed that this 'could become a key to unblocking such "fossilized" conflicts as, say, the Middle Eastern one', and called for a 'realistic interaction of Washington and Moscow rather than total rivalry'.[35] This emphasis may eventually be reflected in greater Soviet flexibility over a variety of regional conflicts.

Under Gorbachev, Soviet policy towards crisis zones in the Third World has, in general, been characterised by considerable caution. Although the superpowers may have tacitly accepted the dangers attendant upon intervention in Iran, the Gulf region remains one of the focal points of competition between them. The desirability of some regulatory arrangements for this volatile region in which both superpowers are involved was evident in Soviet declarations on the Gulf as tensions increased during 1987.

The occasion for this increase in tensions was the reflagging of Kuwaiti tankers. Kuwait had become a front-line state during the Gulf War largely as a result of its support for Iraq's war effort. Consequently, in September 1986, Iran began to attack tankers trading with Kuwait. In response, the Kuwaitis asked the members of the UN Security Council for reflagging of Kuwaiti tankers to ensure their protection. In December 1986 the Soviet Union agreed to a limited reflagging exercise – a move which touched off the competitive elements of Soviet–American relations. The United States, afraid that the Soviet Union would use the opportunity to increase its influence and transform the Gulf into a 'Russian lake', and more than willing to confront Iran, engaged in a more ambitious reflagging exercise.

The Soviet response to the increasing American activity was one of criticism and caution. In May 1987 a Soviet commentator asserted that the increase in American naval patrols in the Gulf was 'assuming an increasingly dangerous nature which threatens to escalate tension in the whole region, or perhaps spread the conflict outside the region'.[36] Although Soviet spokesmen noted that the USSR had interests and a naval presence in the Gulf, Moscow showed no desire for confrontation. In July, a commentator in the Soviet military press criticised a Soviet reader for suggesting that the USSR should take resolute action, including military measures, to defend vital Soviet interests and enhance Soviet prestige in various parts of the world. Although the United States was condemned for declaring vast regions of the world as spheres of vital interests in which it could assert its military presence, it was emphasised that such provocative actions should 'not serve as a model for emulation by the USSR'. What was clearly a pragmatic risk assessment was given an ideological rationale with the assertion that the Soviet Union could concentrate on political rather than military solutions since it was not driven by 'militarist forces, monopoly capital, and the military industrial complex'.[37]

In July 1987 a Soviet Government statement claimed that events in the Persian Gulf were 'approaching a danger line beyond which the regional conflict risks developing into an international crisis situation' (i.e., a superpower crisis) and proposed the withdrawal of all warships belonging to states external to the region.[38] This Soviet proposal was similar to previous ones for the demilitarisation of the Gulf and was not made in the expectation that it would be taken up.[39] At the same time the USSR was reluctant to commit itself to the enforcement measures envisaged in a broader peace plan for the Gulf proposed by the permanent members of the UN Security Council.[40] Moscow was prepared to collaborate to some extent with Washington in searching for an Iran–Iraq ceasefire, but was unwilling to impose sanctions against Iran at a time when the Soviet–Iranian relationship was improving. Although Soviet spokesmen continued to warn of the dangers of escalation on the one hand and to propose schemes for minimising these dangers on the other, the evolving situation highlighted the limited influence the superpowers have over Iran and Iraq. If the Gulf War was not readily amenable to a resolution arranged by Moscow and Washington, however, the superpowers were at least able to regulate their degree of involvement in the conflict and thereby avoid confrontation. In this sense, for the period 1986–8, the Gulf conflict acted as the focus of superpower efforts at crisis prevention in the Third World.

Although Soviet spokesmen acknowledge the need for crisis avoidance, the notion of conflict control has been regarded with suspicion as a Western stratagem. Reckless behaviour is decried as 'provocative' or 'adventuristic', but the Soviet attitude towards the concept of 'controlling' conflicts – a concept which Soviet specialists point out is closely related to that of 'managing' (*upravleniya*) crises – has been ambivalent. Soviet writers contend that both concepts signify a collection of measures designed to promote one-sided crisis outcomes. As a rule, it is argued, controlling or managing crises does not presuppose their resolution, which is the only means to a more peaceful world.[41] In this view, the attention paid by the United States to 'regulating' (*uregulirovaniyu*) conflicts in the 1970s was based primarily on self-interest. The Camp David agreement for the Middle East, for example, was seen by the Soviets as a means of extending American influence. Furthermore, these attempts to extend influence through conflict control are seen as contributing to long-term instability. One Soviet study concluded that 'the whole complex of measures for "controlling" or "regulating" conflict situations leads in the final analysis to an expansion of military tensions, contributes to conflicts going beyond regional bounds and conceals within it a threat to international security'.[42]

If such views are widespread within the Soviet elite, then it would appear that Moscow places little trust in the idea of conflict regulation or management by the superpowers, seeing in such an approach the opportunity for the United States to expand its influence at Soviet expense. It would also appear that the Soviet Union does not favour the Western notion of crisis management. Since the decision to withdraw from Afghanistan, however, a different emphasis has begun to appear in Soviet publications. This is expressed in an appeal for joint action for 'averting, localising and regulating crises'. Crises, it is argued, should be regarded 'as a dangerous anomaly of international life'.[43] On the twenty-fifth anniversary of the Cuban Missile Crisis the Soviet press praised the 'common sense, flexibility and prudence' shown by both superpowers in making 'reciprocal concessions' during that crisis.[44]

It is clear that the Soviet leadership retains an interest in avoiding superpower crises and is not averse to tacit understandings or even regimes for crisis avoidance in the Third World. Part of the reason for this is that superpower crisis-prevention understandings and agreements have both broad and narrow objectives. The broad goal is to transform the Soviet–American relationship into one of collaborative – rather than confrontational – competition. The more specific objective is to reduce the likelihood and intensity of dangerous confrontations between the superpowers. The experience of the 1970s suggests that it is possible to avert direct confrontations yet still be far removed from the degree of collaboration that seems to have been envisaged in the euphoria of the Moscow Summit of 1972. It also reveals that there are no simple solutions in the management of a mixed, complex and often highly ambivalent relationship between the superpowers.

In the chapters which follow, an attempt is made to explore both the impulses for superpower competition and the opportunities for collaboration in different regions. One of the implications of the first part of the book is that Soviet–American competition in the Third World is inescapable. The chapters by Robert Litwak and Derek Leebaert (2 and 3 respectively), outlining Soviet and American objectives and instruments in the Third World, highlight the incompatibilities between the two states and show very clearly how their policies have been formulated and implemented predominantly in terms of the central rivalry between them rather than in terms of indigenous problems in the Third

World. Both authors examine the historical background to Soviet–American competition, and identify Soviet and American objectives and instruments of policy. Litwak and Leebaert also assess the prospects for greater collaboration between the superpowers. Their conclusions are sober and hard-headed. They suggest that competition is likely to continue, although neither excludes the possibility of limited collaborative measures.

A similar appraisal is evident in chapter 4, by Roger Barnett, which explores the maritime dimension of superpower rivalry and offers a critical appraisal of the intervention capabilities of the Soviet Union and the United States. In this chapter, Barnett also focuses upon the prospects for further initiatives in maritime arms control, although he remains unconvinced that major progress can be made in this area. As well as resorting to direct use of military force, the two superpowers have made extensive use of arms transfers as a means of winning friends and influencing governments. The use of this instrument, as well as the restraints that are imposed upon it, are explored in chapter 5 by Joanna Spear and Stuart Croft. This chapter brings out very clearly the way in which the competitive dynamic of US–Soviet relations is held in check by a series of informal or tacit regulations, while also highlighting the difficulties in any attempt to formalise these restraints.

All four of the chapters in the first section of the book reflect the pervasiveness of superpower rivalry and the pressure for collaboration. The second section of the book has a similar tension while adding to this an appreciation of the security issues evident in particular regions. The purpose of the second part is to examine potential flash-points and to assess the prospects for superpower collaboration in ensuring that turbulence and instability do not lead to Soviet–American confrontations. The analytical framework for the regional analyses is set by Alexander George (chapter 6), who differentiates regional security problems in terms of the level and symmetry of superpower interests. The subsequent chapters use the frame of reference offered by George while also exploring the relationship between patrons and clients and the prospects for greater collaboration in managing or defusing regional tensions. Each of the chapters deals with the historical background of superpower involvement, assesses Soviet and American interests and involvements with clients in the particular region, and considers ways in which crisis prevention might be enhanced.

Robert Freedman's analysis of the superpower competition for influence in the Middle East (chapter 7) offers an important historical perspective on the protracted conflict between Israel and the Arab states and shows how this has intermeshed with the Soviet–American struggle for influence in the region. It also identifies some changes in the middle and late 1980s which suggest further scope for the mitigation of Soviet–American rivalry. The chapters on the Gulf by

Shahram Chubin, and on Southwest Asia by Roy Allison (chapters 8 and 9 respectively), analyse regions which have had a high profile in superpower calculations during the 1980s. Both chapters lay considerable stress on the intersection of Soviet and American interests and offer careful appraisals of the potential for superpower conflict as well as the possibilities for collaboration in crisis prevention. Peter Shearman (chapter 10) examines Soviet–American rivalry in Central America, placing particular emphasis on the asymmetry of superpower interests and on the indigenous nature of much of the instability in the region. Similarly, in chapter 11, on Southern Africa, Geoff Berridge gives considerable attention to the peculiar problems of the region while also highlighting the interactions between regional problems and superpower activities. In chapter 12, on Southeast Asia, Paikiasothy Saravanamuttu not only considers Soviet and American interests but also demonstrates how the complicating factor of China sets the region apart from the others that have been examined. The concluding chapter offers an overall appraisal of the prospects for superpower conflict and collaboration in the Third World and, in light of the earlier chapters, suggests ways in which the Soviet and American capacity for crisis prevention could be enhanced.

NOTES

1 K. Waltz, *Theory of International Politics* (London: Addison-Wesley, 1979), p. 171.
2 For a fuller analysis of this tendency in the United States see Robert Johnson, 'Exaggerating America's Stakes in Third World Conflicts' *International Security* 10, 3 (Winter 1985–6), pp. 32–68.
3 For a Soviet analysis of the Cuban Missile Crisis see A. A. Gromyko, 'Karibskii krizis', *Voprosy istorii*, 7 and 8 (1971).
4 *Pravda*, 21 May 1964.
5 V. V. Zhurkin and Ye. M. Primakov, eds., *Mezhdunarodnye konflikty* (Moscow: mezhdunarod-nye otnosheniya, 1972), pp. 65–6.
6 The term was coined by Alexander George.
7 H. Trofimenko, 'The Third World and the US–Soviet Competition: A Soviet View' *Foreign Affairs* 59 (Summer 1981), p. 1039.
8 S. Hoffmann, *Dead Ends* (Cambridge, MA: Ballinger, 1983), p. 90.
9 See A. L. George, ed., *Managing US–Soviet Rivalry*: (Boulder, CO: Westview Press, 1983) for a fuller analysis.
10 See M. Katz, *The Third World in Soviet Military Thought* (London: Croom Helm, 1982), pp. 97–8.
11 The terms are used by George Breslauer in 'Why Detente Failed: An Interpretation', in George, ed., *Managing US–Soviet Rivalry*, pp. 319–40.
12 H. Kissinger, *Press Conference* in Kiev, 29 May 1972 (USIS Official Text), p. 3.
13 These agreements are discussed more fully in George, ed., *Managing US–Soviet Rivalry*.
14 *Ibid*. p. 110.
15 R. Garthoff, *Confrontation and Detente* (Washington, DC: Brookings, 1985), p. 338.
16 O. Johnson, 'US Move in Angola Seen as Spur to Russia' *International Herald Tribune* 29 Nov. 1975.
17 Trofimenko, 'The Third World and US–Soviet Competition', p. 1028.
18 R. O. Keohane, *After Hegemony* (Princeton, NJ: Princeton University Press, 1984), p. 99.

19 For a fuller analysis see M. Bowker and P. Williams, *Superpower Detente: A Reappraisal* (London: Sage for RIIA, 1988).

20 V. V. Zhurkin, *SShA i mezhdunarodno-politicheskie krizisy* (Moscow: nauka, 1975), pp. 254, 293–4.

21 See H. Adomeit, 'Soviet Crisis Prevention and Management: Why and When do Soviet Leaders Take Risks?', *Orbis*, 30, 1 (Spring 1986).

22 See G. Golan, 'The Soviet Union in the Middle East After Thirty Years', in A. Korbonski and F. Fukuyama, eds., *The Soviet Union and the Third World: The Last Three Decades* (New York: Cornell University Press, 1987), pp. 189–91, 204–5.

23 Trofimenko, 'The Third World and US–Soviet Competition', p. 1040.

24 Yu. Ya. Kirshin, V. M. Popov, R. A. Savushkin, *Politicheskoe soderzhanie sovremennykh voin* (Moscow: Voenizdat, 1987), pp. 144–6, 222–35. S. Shenfield is to be thanked for this reference.

25 See Z. Brzezinski, *Power and Principle* (New York: Farrar, Straus, Giroux, 1983), p. 189.

26 See Ye. Primakov, 'Osvobodivshiesya strany v mezhdunarodnykh otnosheniyakh', *Mirovaya ekonomika i mezhdunarodnye otnosheniya*, 5 (1982), 23.

27 See J. Anderson and D. Van Atta, 'Carter's Foiled "October Surprise"' *Washington Post* 24 June 1987, for an intriguing, although brief, account.

28 'The New Philosophy of Foreign Policy', *Pravda*, 9 July 1987.

29 See, for example, V. Kazakov 'Regional Conflicts and World Security', *International Affairs* (Moscow), 2 (1986), pp. 46–7.

30 G. Starushenko and G. Kozhevnikov, 'How American Political Scientists View Regional Conflicts', in *International Affairs* (Moscow), 11 (1987), p. 143. This reviews M. D. Shulman, *East–West Tensions in the Third World* (New York and London: W. W. Norton and Co., 1986).

31 Soviet television, 19 August 1987, in BBC *Summary of World Broadcasts. Soviet Union* (henceforth SU) 8656/A1/8. K. M. Tsagolov, faculty head at the Frunze Military Academy and author of 'a number of studies on crises' was among those contributing to the discussion.

32 *Vestnik Ministerstva inostrannykh del SSSR*, 2 (1987), 31. Cited in V. Yasmann, 'The New Soviet Thinking in Regional Conflicts: Ideology and Politics', *Radio Liberty Research*, RL 493/87, 3 December 1987, p. 2.

33 Soviet television, 19 August 1987, in SU/8656/A1/8–9. For a similar hard-line assessment by a Soviet military specialist see V. Serebryannikov, 'Sootnoshenie politicheskikh i voennykh sredstv v zashchite sotsializma', *Kommunist vooruzhennykh sil*, 19, 1987, 12.

34 V. V. Zhurkin, S. A. Karaganov and A. V. Kortunov, "O razumnoy dostatochnosti "*SShA: Ekonomika, Politika, Ideologiia*, 12 (1987), 20.

35 *Pravda*, 17 April 1988.

36 Radio Peace and Progress, in Arabic on 20 May 1987, in SU/8576/A4/3.

37 See *Krasnaya Zvezda*, 10 July 1987.

38 Soviet Government statement in Tass in English, 3 July 1987, in SU/8612/A4/1.

39 For a broad Soviet survey of the Gulf crisis see R. Makaryan, 'K Krizisy v zone Persidskogo Zaliva', *Mirovaya ekonomika i mezhdunarodnye othosheniya*, 12 (1987).

40 See *The Times*, 25 June 1987.

41 See I. Evyagel'skaya, 'Evolyutsiya podkhodov SShA k konfliktnym situatsiyam v Azii', *Mirovaya ekonomika i mezhdunarodnye otnosheniya*, 2 (1987), 64.

42 *Ibid.*, pp. 64, 68, 72.

43 A. Kolosovskiy, 'Regional'nye konflikty i global'naya bezopasnost'', *Mirovaya ekonomika i mezhdunarodnye otnosheniya*, 6, 1988, 38–9.

44 *Izvestiya*, 23 October 1987.

Part One: Superpower competition: objectives and instruments

2   Soviet policies in the Third World: objectives, instruments, constraints

Robert S. Litwak

During the post-war period, the Third World has emerged as the major arena of active East–West competition. This transformation has stemmed, in large part, from two developments: first, the evolution of Soviet military power, which by the early 1970s provided the Soviet Union with a global reach comparable to that of the United States; and, second, the political and military stabilisation of inter-bloc relations in Europe, which provided further impetus to diverting Soviet–American rivalry to the Third World. This ongoing competition is one of the primary determinants of the superpower relationship. During the 1970s, Soviet political and military involvement in key areas of the Third World contributed to the demise of *détente* and the consequent deterioration in Soviet–American relations. Although the evolution of Soviet military capabilities provided the requisite means for intervention, the basis of the heightened activism resulted largely from political developments within these regions themselves – for example, rapid decolonisation in Portuguese Africa following the April 1974 *coup* in Lisbon. The culmination of this decade of activism came in December 1979 with the Soviet invasion of Afghanistan.

In contrast to the 1970s, the first half of the 1980s witnessed far less dramatic Soviet behaviour in the Third World. One possible explanation is that the relative decline in Soviet adventurism is a product of renewed Soviet respect for American power under the Reagan administration. In this interpretation, the Soviet leadership is being deterred from the type of 'meddling' witnessed in the 1970s by a more probable American counter-response. Alternatively, decreased Soviet activism in the Third World could reflect fewer available and attractive opportunities in the developing world. Finally, Soviet quiescence may be the result of internal preoccupations associated with the drawn-out succession crisis following Leonid Brezhnev's death in November 1982, as well as possible financial constraints stemming from the USSR's unsatisfactory economic performance.

Robert S. Litwak

General Secretary Mikhail Gorbachev's accession to power in March 1985 came at the end of a thirty-year cycle of Soviet activism in the Third World which began under Khrushchev. While the past provides no ready guide to the future, Soviet policy in the Third World under Gorbachev will be powerfully conditioned by the legacy of the last three decades. This inheritance, and its bearing on future Soviet behaviour, underscore the need for a timely reappraisal of Soviet policy – particularly in light of Gorbachev's political report to the Twenty-seventh Party Congress in February–March 1986.[1]

The starting point of this inquiry will be an examination of the fundamental objectives of Soviet policy in both historical and prospective terms. Attention will next shift to the policy instruments available to the Soviet leadership, as well as constraints on the effective implementation of Soviet policies. The following section will explore the extent to which the Soviet calculus of risk-taking may have changed during the post-Brezhnev period. Finally, the focus of analysis will return to the dynamics of the superpower relationship – specifically, the potential for moderating East–West competition in the Third World through such political mechanisms as spheres of influence, tacit rules of engagement, or an explicit 'code of conduct'.

HISTORICAL BACKGROUND

In the late 1970s, Soviet direct and indirect intervention across the geographical zone spanning Southern Africa and Southeast Asia (Zbigniew Brzezinski's 'arc of crisis') presented a pattern which greatly concerned Western policy-makers. Given the rise of radical leftist regimes (such as Angola, Ethiopia and Afghanistan) with close economic, diplomatic and military links to the USSR, many Western scholars perceived the USSR gaining momentum in the Third World.[2] Not surprisingly, these developments featured prominently in the optimistic report presented by Brezhnev at the CPSU's Twenty-sixth Congress in February 1981.[3] From the Soviet perspective, the balance sheet after thirty years of activism in the developing world was clearly positive. Yet the gains accrued by the USSR are not as unambiguous as Western observers declared them to be – or as Soviet policy-makers perhaps noted. Moreover, Soviet gains have often proved transient and carried considerable politico-economic costs – thus raising the question of just how much success the USSR can actually afford.

In assessing the Soviet record in the Third World, one need recall the relative international position of the USSR when Nikita Khrushchev and his colleagues took power in 1953.[4] Diplomatically, the Soviet Union had no substantial ties with South Asian and Middle Eastern states, and was completely shut out of sub-Saharan Africa and Latin America. In military terms, the USSR was a Eurasian land power lacking the conventional capabilities to provide it a truly global reach. These limitations prompted one observer to quip that the designation of the Soviet Union as a superpower in the early post-war period was more an 'ascriptive courtesy' than a reflection of reality.[5]

The initial burst of Soviet political activity in the developing world came in 1955 with the conclusion of a secret arms sale agreement with Egypt (using Czechoslovakia as the conduit for the transfer) and the highly publicised visit of Soviet party leader Khrushchev to India.[6] Prior to 1955, the USSR's Third World policy reflected the rigidities of the Stalinist system. During the final years of Joseph Stalin's rule, the USSR's scope for diplomatic manoeuvre in the Third World was severely limited because of Moscow's castigation of such nationalist leaders as Indian Prime Minister Jawaharlal Nehru and Indonesian President Ahmed Sukarno for their supposed collaboration with the Western colonial powers.

The death of Stalin in March 1953 paved the way for the dramatic shift in Soviet policy towards the Third World. This change in attitude was manifested in Khrushchev's enthusiastic response to the meeting of Asian and African leaders at the 1955 Bandung Conference. In contrast to Stalin's exclusive emphasis on local communist parties, Khrushchev pursued a policy of courting national bourgeoisie as a means of weakening Western influence in these states. Increased Soviet political flexibility, as well as the dramatic development of its nuclear and conventional forces during the 1960s and 1970s, permitted the USSR to compete actively with the United States for influence in the Third World.

In specific arenas, the Soviet Union took advantage of the 1959 Cuban revolution to undermine the American monopoly of military power in the Western hemisphere. The USSR's 1955 breakthrough in relations with Egypt, and its support of the 1958 Iraqi revolution, allowed the Soviet Union to outflank and then effectively neutralise the Baghdad Pact/CENTO alliance system. Continued Soviet support of the Arab states in their conflict with Israel has prevented any subsequent construction of anti-Soviet alliances in the Middle East. Sustained military assistance to North Vietnam brought the collapse of SEATO and the replacement of American with Soviet military power in Indochina. The Soviet-backed victory of the MPLA in the 1975–6 Angolan Civil War considerably enhanced the USSR's capacity to destabilise Southern Africa and take advantage of that process. The Soviet Union's intervention on behalf of Ethiopia in the 1977–8 Ogaden War with Somalia enabled the USSR to secure a position on both sides of the Straits of Bab-al-Mandeb and, hence, the capacity to interdict the shortest sea route from Europe to the Persian Gulf. Finally, the USSR's December 1979 invasion of Afghanistan to prop up an ailing client

31

regime marked the first direct involvement of Soviet military forces on a mass scale in a Third World conflict.

In contrast to this successful record of Soviet activism, the 1960s and 1970s witnessed a relatively rapid decline in the Western position in the Third World. Decolonisation removed much of the Western military presence in Africa, the Middle East, and Southeast Asia. New Third World governments – many of which strongly objected to purported exploitation at the hand of the 'metropolitan' countries and the United States – were committed to distancing themselves from the Western alliance system. As reflected in the rise of the Non-Aligned Movement, these former colonial states actively sought ties with the USSR to balance their unequal relationship with the West.

Generalised American opposition to radical social change and to movements advocating such ideas alienated large sections of Third World opinion, thereby leaving the way open to Soviet penetration in Latin America and Southern Africa in particular. Western support for Israel from 1948 to the present has been a political liability for its relations in the Islamic world and triggered the Arab oil boycott during the October 1973 War. The American entanglement in Vietnam and the subsequent collapse of the US-backed government in Saigon further damaged the US position in the Third World. In conjunction with Watergate, the Vietnam War fostered a domestic political climate in which the use of force to defend Western interests in the Third World was no longer credible. The reduced will of the American polity to deploy force was reflected in defence cutbacks which in turn rapidly eroded US capabilities. On the one hand, weakened US resolve was understood by America's allies, who then sought other means to preserve their security. On the other hand, it was perceived by America's rivals as an invitation to adventurism.

The degree to which many of the USSR's relative gains in the developing world can be attributed to Soviet policy itself is another matter. In the aftermath of the Second World War, the moral and physical exhaustion of the principal colonial powers, as well as the rising nationalist consciousness of Third World elites, made decolonisation inevitable. Given that the anti-colonial movement was widely perceived to be a struggle against the West and the international capitalist system, the foreign policies of many of the newly independent states were, not surprisingly, hostile towards the West. The USSR often found itself well-placed to take advantage of regional trends and events whose origins were primarily indigenous.

Moreover, many of the major setbacks of the West in the Third World were the product of errors in policy and judgement on the part of the Western powers themselves. The 1956 Suez Crisis, for example, considerably enhanced the Soviet position in the Third World. This Soviet gain, however, was in large part due to the intransigence of British and French policy towards Egypt. Although the communist victory in Vietnam was made possible by Soviet military assistance, American political leaders now acknowledged that US objectives were ill-conceived, its forces were ill-suited to jungle conditions, and its population was ill-prepared for a protracted, limited war. In Africa, Western economic and, to some extent, military support of Portugal's colonial wars prolonged the struggles in Angola, Mozambique and Guinea-Bissau, and heightened the prospect that the liberation movements would emerge from battle closely linked to and dependent upon the Soviet bloc. US refusal to recognise the MPLA regime in Luanda and its apparent diffidence concerning South Africa's destabilisation of neighbouring states (notably Angola and Mozambique) preserve and strengthen these ties.

In Central America, where the Sandinista leadership's socialist leanings and its ties with Cuba and the USSR are clear and of long standing, US hostility to the Sandinista movement and sustained pressure on Nicaragua since the 1979 revolution have strengthened Nicaraguan–Soviet bloc relations. In the military sphere, the continuing American-backed challenge to Sandinista rule (i.e., the 'Contras') has fostered substantial dependence on Soviet material support. Such pressure has facilitated the Sandinista hold on power within the country at the expense of more moderate forces. In short Soviet success in the Third World has proved largely to be the outcome of events that neither the USSR nor the United States controls. More significantly, in the foreign-policy context, much of it has been the product of the Western powers' own acts and omissions, rather than the result of Soviet shrewdness or of some inexorable flow of history.

In surveying the USSR's record in the Third World during the 1955–85 period, one must examine the debit side of the ledger to assess the costs of Soviet activism. In a number of cases, Soviet success has proven to be temporary and reversible. The close ties of the USSR with Ghana, Indonesia, Mali and Algeria, cultivated at considerable expense in the early 1960s, fell prey to military *coups* in the middle of the decade. In the early 1970s, the Soviet Union lost its two most important installations in the Middle East – those in Egypt and Somalia. When these clients re-defined their interests in a manner inconsistent with the prevailing relationship with the USSR, the Soviet Union was ordered out, and left. The recent history of Soviet foreign policy in the developing world suggests that the USSR has been as much a victim of the self-interested particularism of Third World nations as the United States. Indeed, the experience of both superpowers demonstrates the intractability of the target environment, its resistance to external manipulation and control of any type and, consequently, the great difficulty – short of military occupation (e.g., Afghanistan) – of establishing long-term, advantageous relations with Third World actors.

Robert S. Litwak

OBJECTIVES

Among Western analysts, the motivations underlying Soviet policy in the Third World remain a subject of perennial dispute. Many see Soviet projection into these regions as part of a broad offensive challenge to Western interests – the result of a profoundly expansionistic Great Russian nationalism or the imperatives of an empire in decline.[7] Others consider Soviet behaviour in the Third World, as elsewhere, externally determined and largely defensive in nature – the product of an obsessive concern with national security which in turn is fostered by an historical experience of repeated invasion.[8] Analysing the sources of Soviet policy under Gorbachev is a particularly complicated task, as they may be internal and external, permanent and temporary, general to the Third World as a whole or specific to certain regions and states. It seems clear though that Soviet behaviour in the developing world since 1955 has stemmed from three permanent factors: the international system, Soviet political culture, and the USSR's political structure.

In evaluating the first of these sources – the changing nature of the international system – the most salient point is the emergence of the Soviet Union since the late 1960s as a global military power. With this altered status has come a broadened conception of Soviet interests and prerogatives. At the Twenty-fourth Party Congress in April 1971, Soviet Foreign Minister Andrei A. Gromyko baldly stated: 'There is not a single significant question which today can be decided without or in defiance of the Soviet Union. And if anybody were to try to show that one could manage without the Soviet Union in the resolution of these issues, people would consider him odd.'[9] The Soviet claim to political co-equality with the United States has been expressed with particular vehemence in the Middle East, where they have maintained that no settlement is possible without Soviet participation.

Apart from the United States, the other major power which, in historical terms, has been a primary determinant of Soviet policy in the Third World is the People's Republic of China (PRC). While the present quiescence of Sino–Soviet rivalry within the 'world revolutionary movement' mitigates the importance of this factor, the salience of this competition in Soviet policy calculations has varied considerably over time. The manipulation of Third World issues as part of the struggle between Moscow and Beijing for leadership of the international communist movement was particularly significant in the 1960s (with a brief hiatus during the Cultural Revolution) and the first half of the 1970s when Chinese questioning of the USSR's revolutionary credentials pressured the Soviet leadership into more substantial support of Third World radical regimes

34

than it might otherwise have chosen. Colin Legum, for example, has argued persuasively that 'Sino–Soviet rivalry was a major feature of Moscow's approach to the [1975–6] Angolan conflict'.[10] The last decade, however, has witnessed a profound change in the Chinese regime's policy orientation. The emphasis in Beijing has been on the 'four modernisations' campaign and the further improvement of relations with the Western powers. With this reduction in Chinese revolutionary fervour, the importance of Sino–Soviet rivalry as a determinant of Soviet activism in the Third World has been greatly diminished. Indeed, the rise of a more pragmatic leadership in Beijing is viewed with anticipation in Moscow as creating the possibility of improved Sino–Soviet relations.

Gorbachev's devoted courting of the PRC and Japan is clearly intended to weaken those countries' presently close ties to the United States. At Vladivostok in late July 1986, the Soviet leader resurrected the USSR's long-dormant proposal for an Asian collective security conference. Originally mooted by Brezhnev in March 1969 with the clear intent of containing China, the purpose of the proposal in its latest incarnation is to exclude the United States from Asian affairs. Despite this Soviet diplomatic offensive, the broad range of the USSR's political and territorial differences mitigates against any dramatic breakthrough in Moscow's relations with the PRC and Japan.

While the Soviet Union has become more assertive in pressing its interests, the international system is increasingly pluralistic and less hierarchical. This fragmentation of the world order has generated greater local opportunities for Soviet foreign policy. Opportunities, however, are tempered by constraints: most notably, Soviet risk-taking in the Third World is conditioned by the USSR's perception of American willingness and capacity to define and defend US vital interests.

A second source of the USSR's policy in the Third World is Soviet political culture, several aspects of which intensify the competitive aspect of Soviet behaviour in the Third World. Although the direct relevance of Marxism-Leninism to Soviet foreign-policy decision-making is questionable, as an intellectual construct, ideology deeply influences leadership perceptions. According to the Marxist-Leninist view of international relations, a permanent, ineradicable contradiction between the capitalist and socialist world systems renders global competition inevitable. Where accommodation with capitalism occurs, it is a tactical adjustment designed to consolidate gains, to facilitate Soviet access to skills and goods which are necessary to sustain the competition, or to reduce the risks associated with the competition. This assumption of permanent conflict enhances the USSR's concern with security and encourages a zero–sum approach to world politics.

Another aspect of Soviet political culture is Russian and Soviet history. While much of the obsessive preoccupation with the Second World War in the Soviet literature is a form of legitimising propaganda, the experiences in this century of two catastrophic foreign incursions have had a profound impact on the population's and the leadership's perception of external threat. In short, the Soviet historical experience reinforces its concern for survival and security. The combination of systemic, ideological, and historical factors described above has produced a conception of national security which is extreme. It dictates a quest for military superiority and a continual struggle to control the Soviet periphery or to deny American access to that periphery. Buttressed by the force of nationalism, this preoccupation with border security was a major factor governing Soviet decision-making over Afghanistan. Thus, in a characteristic justification of Soviet policy, Brezhnev maintained that events in Afghanistan prior to the intervention constituted a serious threat to the security of the USSR's southern border.

A third and final factor affecting the conduct of the USSR's policy in the Third World is the Soviet political process. Foreign-policy successes play an important role in building and preserving authority within the ruling oligarchy. Likewise, as demonstrated in the aftermath of the 1962 Cuban Missile Crisis, a policy failure is both a source of discontent and a powerful weapon in the hands of a leader's opponents. In periods of domestic difficulty, those in power may attempt to extend the external influence of socialism in order to stabilise or strengthen their internal positions. This explanation may in part account for the erratic character of Khrushchev's foreign policy in the 1960s. Conversely, Soviet leaders are reluctant to abandon previous commitments and established positions and anxious to prevent any erosion of power. Soviet military assistance to Egypt during the October 1973 Middle East War and the December 1979 Soviet invasion of Afghanistan reflect this latter tendency.

In assessing Soviet objectives in the Third World, a key consideration is that of time-frame. This is of particular significance in light of the distinctive approach adopted by Gorbachev. Under his leadership, the overall importance of the Third World within Soviet strategy has clearly been downgraded relative to other foreign-policy objectives (e.g., arms control) and his domestic programme of economic reform. As discussed below, this development has stemmed, in large part, from the perceived economic and political costs of the kind which typified the late Brezhnev period. While Gorbachev attempts to court important capitalist-oriented Third World states such as Mexico, Nigeria and Indonesia, the Soviet leadership has not abandoned its prior emphasis on socialist-oriented states (e.g., Angola, Ethiopia, South Yemen) with Marxist–Leninist vanguard parties. Indeed, the magnitude of Soviet involvement in these latter countries – as measured in direct *matériel* support – remains impressive with no visible signs of retrenchment. The likely prognosis is a continuation of this strategy into the foreseeable future: Gorbachev will vigorously maintain the existing structure of Soviet commitments in the Third World, while exercising caution in assuming major additional ones. This approach reflects a desire to channel all available financial resources into CPSU's ambitious domestic economic programme, as well as a recognition that Third World adventurism could, as in the late 1970s, derail arms-control negotiations and generally complicate relations with the West.

INSTRUMENTS AND CONSTRAINTS

This section surveys the various policy instruments available to the Soviet leadership, as well as the constraints on their effective employment. An attempt will be made to assess the changes in Soviet policy during the post-Brezhnev period and the new strategy, as it has emerged, under Gorbachev.

As discussed above, the Soviet Union, like the United States, has confronted the problem of building durable influence relationships in the developing world. In addition, Soviet activism in the Third World has entailed mounting economic costs. The expansion of force projection capabilities was part of a comprehensive military buildup which, in the 1970s and 1980s, commanded resources from other sectors of the Soviet economy, in all likelihood complicating the problem of economic growth. Client states such as Ethiopia, South Yemen and Angola pose a significant drain on limited Soviet resources. A conservative estimate of the combined assistance to Cuba and Vietnam, the USSR's two largest aid recipients, is $11–18 million per day or $4–6 billion per year.[11]

The use of economic instruments to affect policy outcomes has been hampered obviously by the poor performance of the Soviet economy. The Soviet Union's minor role in the international economy provides little market power or leverage. Where close economic links have been promoted (e.g., India, Nigeria), the USSR has experienced considerable difficulties in interfacing command and mixed economies. The inconvertibility of the rouble and subsequent emphasis on barter trade have diminished the availability of Soviet financial assistance to developing countries. Moreover, the recent declining level of Soviet foreign economic assistance as a percentage of GNP reflects continued scepticism about the efficacy of such aid. As early as 1962, Soviet development economists criticised Soviet assistance programmes as misdirected and wasteful, given the limited absorptive capacities of recipient economies.[12] The value of such assistance became questionable on political grounds as well in the mid-1970s when, despite massive Soviet assistance on the Aswan Dam and the Helwan steel complex, Egypt rather unceremoniously severed its ties with the USSR. As a consequence of these developments, the Soviet leadership considers trade with Third World countries more in terms of potential economic benefit to the USSR than as a source of influence.[13]

As had been made plain by Gorbachev, the CPSU's strategy of economic 'acceleration' will leave few resources to expend on new Third World commitments. This situation prevails at a time when Soviet access to financial and technological assistance from the West is constrained, and the Soviet Union's precarious economic position is exacerbated by the need for the USSR to assist its troubled East European allies. In a formulation indicative of the Gorbachev leadership's attitude towards economic assistance to the Third World, the new edition of the Party Programme states that the Soviet Union will assist socialist-oriented states 'to the extent of its abilities'.[14] Gorbachev has gone so far as to argue that the USSR can best assist the international communist movement and developing countries in general by serving as a model of socialist development: 'the CPSU see as its main international duty the successful progress of our country along the path opened up and laid down [by the Twenty-Seventh Party Congress]'.[15] Under present economic conditions, the prognosis is that Soviet assistance to existing recipients (especially the two largest – Cuba and Vietnam) will level off, while the leadership resists any new large-scale commitments.

The utility of ideology as an instrument of foreign policy has been diminished by the loss of much of Soviet Marxism's earlier revolutionary appeal. The degree to which ideological affinity operates as a conduit of Soviet influence in the Third World is limited.[16] Despite an impressive expansion since 1955 of diplomatic links with Third World regimes, the USSR remains at a significant disadvantage to Western states which, by contrast, enjoy deep historical and cultural ties to ruling elites in the developing world.

The sole sphere in which the Soviet Union and its socialist allies have developed a comparative advantage is military power. The absence of other available instruments of policy to affect events in the Third World confirms the USSR's status as a one-dimensional superpower. In the post-Khrushchev period, the Soviet Union has relied heavily on arms transfers, military training and assistance, and the use of force either in conjunction with allied states, such as Cuba, or directly, as in the case of Afghanistan.

Arms transfers have historically been the principal form of Soviet military involvement in the Third World. Given the nature of the Soviet arms procurement system, large stocks of transferable weapons are usually available. Moreover, the USSR's secret decision-making process is subject to few domestic constraints of the type which have bedevilled American arms transfers to Latin

America and moderate Arab regimes. The net result is that the USSR can deliver large quantities of weapons at short notice with little embarrassing publicity. The value of Soviet arms transfers, totalling an estimated $70 billion during the 1955–81 period, has been growing steadily since the initial sale to Egypt in 1955. In 1979, the value of Soviet arms transfers to the non-Communist Third World ($6.6 billion) exceeded that of the United States for the first time.[17]

Although arms transfers have been a significant component of Soviet bilateral relationships in the Third World (e.g., India, Vietnam, Iraq, Egypt, etc.), the degree to which they have been an effective and reliable instrument in the pursuit of influence may be questioned. The Middle Eastern cases underscore, moreover, that dependence is often a two-way street. Arms transfer relationships with uncontrollable allies may lead to situations in which the USSR is faced with the choice of escalating its involvement in regional conflicts or losing its investment. Given these limitations, Soviet policy-makers apparently now regard arms transfers less as a source of influence and more as a means of obtaining hard currency (e.g., Libya), or as a barter item for needed commodities (as was possibly the case with Soviet offers of arms assistance to Argentina during the 1982 Falklands War). Soviet arms transfers have thus taken on an increasingly commercial rather than political character. Grant aid or concessionary long-term credits to finance arms are now reserved primarily for states considered ideologically reliable (i.e., vanguard party regimes) and those recognised by the Soviet Union as socialist (e.g., Vietnam and Cuba).

With the notable exception of Afghanistan, Soviet military deployments and rhetorical posturing about the use of force in the Third World during the 1955–85 period stand in contrast to the relative infrequency with which the Soviet Union has actually exercised its military option. In general, the USSR's intervention in Third World combat situations has been of a 'cooperative' nature in that emphasis has been on the use of non-Soviet forces (principally Cuban).[18] The Soviet role has been confined largely to logistical support, as in Angola, and/or command and control, as in Ethiopia.[19] This prudence suggests continued Soviet concern regarding the possibility of confrontation and escalation with the United States – a concern which has regained strength in the 1980s.[20] When the USSR has deployed its forces in regional conflicts, its actions have been in defence of important established commitments and positions which are in jeopardy.[21]

Soviet activism in the Third World in the 1970s contributed to the demise of *détente* and NATO's subsequent commitment to upgrade the alliance's conventional and nuclear capabilities. The USSR's actions along the Afro-Asian periphery provided substance to the previously ethereal spectre of the 'Soviet threat'. While Soviet commentaries during the period of *détente* denied the existence of any linkage between its actions in the Third World and the development of East–West relations, more recent writings suggest some recognition that, whether or not in theory such a linkage should exist, in fact it does. Thus, one may account for the post-Brezhnev debate about Third World issues in the Soviet literature and for the relative quiescence of Soviet policy during the 1980s not only in terms of domestic preoccupations, the reassertion of American military power, or a dearth of promising opportunities to exploit in the Third World, but also in terms of a growing Soviet awareness of the direct and indirect costs associated with previous activism.

In terms of the international context of Soviet policy, an additional (arguably the most important) determinant is the nature of the target environment in the Third World itself. For the Soviet Union, as with the United States, the quest for durable influence in the Third World has been elusive. As a consequence, Soviet commentaries in the late 1970s, when contrasted with those of the Khrushchev and early Brezhnev eras, reflected a lower expectation of the USSR's ability to preserve 'the gains of socialism' in the developing world. For example, Karen Brutents, currently a Deputy Chief in the Central Committee's International Department, concluded in a 1977 study, *National Liberation Revolutions Today*, that 'zigzags are both possible and likely; that the choice of a socialist orientation does not necessarily ensure the victory of socialism and does not exclude the possibility of backward movement, of a "return" to the capitalist path'. This more sober assessment of Soviet influence-building in the Third World was accompanied by the emergence during the late Brezhnev period of a new approach embodying two complementary strands.

The first element has been the move towards more open-ended policy pronouncements reflecting a broader definition as to what constitutes a 'progressive' regime. This tactical adjustment has provided the Soviet leadership greater flexibility in exercising its options in the Third World. Moscow thus has been able to court a wide variety of regimes. The second strand has been increased emphasis on the development of vanguard parties in those states where local circumstances permit. Renewed focus on the role of vanguard parties is a direct response to the periodic reversals of the last two decades which have underscored the problem of regime maintenance. The creation of vanguard parties in the states of 'socialist orientation' is viewed as the most effective means of institutionalising power in the hands of client regimes and thereby providing the basis for a long-term relationship with the Soviet Union.

While safeguarding Soviet interests in the Third World, this approach serves the additional function of ostensibly legitimising or validating the global mission implicit in Marxist–Leninist doctrine. Recent scholarship on Soviet policy *vis-à-vis* socialist-oriented regimes suggests that the Kremlin leadership draws a sharp distinction between states in which a Leninist vanguard party has emerged and those in which one is not presently manifest. Soviet emphasis on organisational issues has been coupled with continued attention to the tactics pursued by socialist-oriented regimes in the implementation of their political and economic programmes. The major impetus is the desire to maintain 'progressive' regimes in power and thereby safeguard the 'gains of socialism' in the Third World.

The pursuit of this objective has led to numerous instances in which the Soviet Union has counselled moderation to its Third World clients in order to minimise the risk of 'reversal' (e.g., internal counterrevolution, as in Chile). In the economic sphere, Soviet commentators have spoken of the need for a gradual transition toward socialism and cited Lenin's New Economic Policy as a doctrinal precedent for such an approach. Soviet criticism has been directed at client regimes whose draconian social programmes ('infantile' leftism in Leninist political parlance) has contributed to popular disaffection. In the case of Afghanistan, the Kabul regime was urged to broaden the People's Democratic Party of Afghanistan's (PDPA) political base by expanding its links with the business and religious communities.[22] Similar Soviet sensitivity has been exhibited in the foreign-policy realm of the socialist-oriented states. The March 1984 Nkomati Accord between Mozambique and South Africa, for example, was sympathetically depicted in the Soviet press as a pragmatic adjustment by the Frelimo government to precarious internal and external circumstances that threatened the stability of the regime.

Since Brezhnev's death in October 1982, the socialist-oriented states and the concept of the Marxist–Leninist vanguard party have come under some criticism. In his address to the Central Committee Plenum in June 1983, Yuri Andropov expressed Soviet irritation with client regimes whose commitment to socialism is more rhetorical than real: 'It is one thing to proclaim socialism as one's aim and quite another to build it.'[23] Such statements have been accompanied by heightened emphasis under Gorbachev on the major capitalist-oriented states in the Third World, such as Brazil and Mexico. This shift to a more Khrushchev-type approach reflects certain misgivings about the Brezhnev legacy of the 1970s. Prominent Soviet specialists on the developing world, such as Karen Brutents, have observed that while the USSR forged close links with a number of radical Third World regimes during that period (e.g., Angola, Ethiopia and the PDRY), it paid scant attention to the more successful capitalist-oriented countries. Gorbachev's moves to extend the USSR's political and commercial links in the Persian Gulf (e.g., the establishment of diplomatic relations with Oman and the United Arab Emirates in 1985) and with the member-states of ASEAN (Association of South-East Asian Nations) are consistent with this shift in emphasis.

The courting of capitalist-oriented states, however, is not an alternative, but rather a supplement to Moscow's vanguard party approach in the Third World. In the socialist-oriented countries, the creation of a vanguard party and other Leninist institutions remains the USSR's best means of preventing a reversal (or 'zigzag') and thereby ensuring long-term Soviet influence.[24]

OPPORTUNISM AND RISK-TAKING

Since assuming the office of CPSU General Secretary in March 1985, Gorbachev's attention has centred on the consolidation of his political leadership and the continuing poor performance of the USSR's economy. The role of foreign policy in authority-building within the Soviet leadership is of particular relevance in the present, post-Brezhnev succession. Foreign-policy successes can help to build and preserve authority within the ruling oligarchy while failure can generate considerable political opposition.[25]

Given both the historical importance of foreign policy in authority-building within the Soviet leadership and the USSR's present domestic circumstances, is Gorbachev likely to be more or less assertive in the Third World than his predecessors? This question is difficult to answer in terms of the personal proclivities of Gorbachev and his colleagues, since the nature of their foreign policy (*vis-à-vis* specific regions and functional issues) is continuing to unfold. One might argue that, as this generation of leaders is a product of established and stable Soviet power, its ideological attachment to the cause of world revolution is liable to be less intense. The apparently shrinking commitment to Marxism–Leninism within the Soviet population and elite might also favour a reduction in expansionist behaviour designed to secure popular compliance. Such an argument is strengthened by the disappearance of more orthodox elements within the leadership.

Some aspects of the Gorbachev succession suggest future circumspection by the USSR in the Third World. The succession was seemingly well-prepared and the new CPSU General Secretary is experiencing little difficulty in consolidating his political position. One indicator of Gorbachev's success in expanding his power-base within the Soviet oligarchy is the current composition of the Central Committee (CC). At the Twenty-seventh Party Congress, the turnover in Central Committee membership was over 40 per cent – a figure only comparable in magnitude to the wholesale changes in personnel made by Khrushchev at the Twentieth Party Congress in 1956 and the Twenty-first in 1961. By contrast, the turnover, at Brezhnev's final party congresses of 1976 and 1981 was 11 and 13 per cent, respectively.[26]

Gorbachev's bid as CPSU General Secretary to reassert tighter party control over Soviet foreign policy was reflected in the replacement of Gromyko by Shevardnadze at the Foreign Ministry and the appointment of Anatoly Dobrynin, the USSR's long-serving ambassador to the United States, and Alexandr Yakovlev, Director of the Institute of World Economy and International Relations (IMEMO), to head key departments in the Central Committee's Secretariat. With Gromyko's elevation to full Politburo membership in 1973, the decision-making importance of the Foreign Ministry appreciably increased during the late Brezhnev period. This role was further enhanced by the deaths of Brezhnev and Defence Minister Marshall Dmitri Ustinov in November 1982 and December 1984, respectively. Gorbachev's 'promotion' to the chairmanship of the Supreme Soviet Presidium, as well as the placement of his protégés at the Deputy Foreign Minister-level, will permit Gorbachev and his senior colleagues in the CC Secretariat to exert more direct control over the formulation and execution of Soviet foreign policy. The shift in institutional power from the Foreign Ministry to the CC Secretariat was symbolised in an unprecedented speech delivered by Gorbachev on 23 May 1986 to a conference of senior Soviet diplomats summoned from their posts around the world. In calling for the adoption of (what TASS termed) a 'more dynamic diplomacy', Gorbachev left little doubt that he meant a change from the methods and procedures of the Gromyko era.

With the continuing extension of his control over the party and government apparatus, Gorbachev may have little need, at least in the short term, for conspicuous success in the foreign-policy realm to stabilise his position. Indeed, the record thus far indicates that Gorbachev intends to rely on domestic-policy initiatives to enhance his authority. The centrepiece of his address to the Party Congress in February 1986 was the strategy for the 'acceleration' (*uskorenie*) of the USSR's socio-economic development. The speech was noteworthy for its blunt assessment of the country's economic situation. Gorbachev spoke of 'signs of stagnation' and the rise of a 'peculiar psychology – how to improve things without changing anything'.[27] Despite this rhetoric, the basic issue remains whether the Soviet Union is capable of systemic change that goes beyond marginal reform. The failure of past reform efforts (e.g., the economic measures advocated by Soviet Premier Alexei Kosygin in the mid-1960s) does not augur well for the future. Gorbachev, for example, has been openly critical of the Chinese and Yugoslav experiments with market socialism. Like its predecessors, the new Soviet leadership is unlikely to countenance any major changes which would appreciably reduce party control within the society.

In charting his programme, Gorbachev thus confronts the traditional bind of those who would seek to reform the Soviet system: namely, how to remove the structural rigidities plaguing Soviet economic performance without de-Leninising (i.e., delegitimising) the political system. Gorbachev's current focus is on mechanisms to improve economic productivity, as well as the continuation of the anti-corruption and anti-alcoholism campaigns initiated under Andropov. Foreign-policy considerations have been subordinated to the demands of the Soviet Union's domestic agenda. Gorbachev has baldly stated that 'the fundamental tasks of the country's economic and social development . . . determine the CPSU's international strategy'.[28] To the extent that foreign-policy issues occupy the attention of the Soviet leadership, the emphasis – as indicated by Gorbachev's Twenty-seventh Congress Party address – is on relations with the United States and arms control rather than the development of dramatic initiatives in the Third World.

While acknowledging the primacy of domestic considerations, Soviet behaviour in the Third World will also be shaped by the type of international environment in which the USSR operates. In this realm, the dominant factor is the United States and the emergence after 1980 of an American administration which was both militantly anti-Soviet and pursuing a policy of rapid rearmament. This change in the external environment forced the Soviet leadership to concentrate available resources on maintaining parity with the United States in the central military competition, and increased the perceived risks associated with the projection of Soviet military power in the Third World. The fact that this shift in American posture is partly a result of prior Soviet activity encourages the USSR's foreign-policy establishment to reassess the realities of linkage between Soviet–American competition in the Third World and other aspects of the superpower relationship. Following a decade of American retrenchment in the developing world, the return to a more assertive, activist approach was manifested in the Reagan Administration's covert or explicit support for several insurgency movements against pro-Soviet regimes (e.g., the Afghan Mujahidin, the Contras in Nicaragua, and UNITA in Angola).[29] The sustained Soviet verbal assault against this policy of 'neo-globalism' suggested heightened concern about the USSR's ability to defend the 'gains of socialism' in the Third World in the face of this new American strategy.

An important question generated by this analysis is the extent to which these developments will affect the Soviet propensity for risk-taking. The likely prognosis is a continuation of the trend identified in the review of the historical balance sheet: namely, a greater tendency by the Soviet leadership to assume risks albeit only in defence of important established commitments and positions which are in jeopardy.

At the same time, there are limits to Soviet support even in instances where an explicit commitment exists. In the case of Nicaragua, for example, the Sandinista regime has been pointedly reminded by Pravda that 'the revolution must defend itself'. Similarly, the qualified nature of the Soviet commitment to Libya was manifested in its purely rhetorical response to US naval manoeuvres in the Gulf of Sirte and the American air raid against Tripoli and Benghazi in April 1986.

IMPLICATIONS FOR CRISIS MANAGEMENT AND PREVENTION

The preceding discussion has focused on the principal elements of Soviet policy in the Third World as they have emerged under Gorbachev. An important related question – particularly as one addresses the prospects for conflict management and prevention – is Soviet perceptions of American policies in the developing world. Soviet commentaries on the sources of Third World conflicts and instability offer a striking contrast to the Western debate. They assert that the West, primarily the United States, seeks to generate regional crises as pretexts for military intrusions in order to prop up reactionary regimes, thereby preserving or obtaining strategic and economic benefits. The latter principally take the form of access to raw materials, especially oil. A complementary view is that such activity is intended to close off these regions to Soviet influence, and in certain instances to use them to threaten the Soviet Union. From the Soviet perspective, there would be no 'hotbeds' if the imperialists, through their attempt to suppress national liberation and re-establish hegemony, did not create them. These themes particularly characterise Soviet depictions of American policies in the Persian Gulf and Southwest Asia – a Third World region of primary importance to Soviet policy-makers because of its geographical proximity. US support for the Afghan Mujahidin, for example, was depicted as an attempt to transform that country into a hostile base against the Soviet Union. Likewise, the United States, according to Soviet commentaries, has used the Iran–Iraq war as a pretext for increasing its military presence in the region. The Soviet Union has sought to counter American policies in Southwest Asia with a policy which is striking because of its quintessentially regional character. Although the Asian 'collective security' proposal, first advanced by Brezhnev in 1969, has failed to win any international backing, the scheme does suggest the broader context within which Persian Gulf and Southwest Asian affairs are viewed. While the tendency in the West is to dismiss such Soviet proposals, the Soviet leadership rarely drops diplomatic initiatives *per se*. Rather, it allows them to remain dormant until the proper political circumstances for their revival arise. The 1975 Helsinki Conference was thus used by Moscow as an occasion to refloat the Asian collective security scheme; the clear message was that the Helsinki experience should be replicated in Asia using the Brezhnev proposal as its basis. The treaties of friendship negotiated by the USSR with various Asian states (e.g., India, Iraq) are depicted not as strictly bilateral arrangements of limited scope; rather, they are characterised as elements of a continental security edifice that has not yet fully taken shape. While comprehensive, the Asian collective security scheme affords the Soviet Union considerable diplomatic flexibility. The ability of Soviet proposals to be recast as tactical circumstances warrant was evident in the December 1980 proposal of Brezhnev, which called for a specific linking of an Afghan settlement with a Persian Gulf security scheme. In creating such a security framework, the Soviet objective is to become the security manager for the region – that is, the power that must be consulted on all issues affecting Asia. The exclusion from regional affairs of all non-Asian states (namely, the United States) is, of course, the obverse of this policy. Within this context, the Soviet-chaired Tashkent Conference (ending the 1965 Indo–Pakistan War) is viewed as a precedent that the Soviet Union would like to see transformed into a norm. In keeping with this policy, the Kremlin made repeated offers to serve as a mediator between Iran and Iraq in their attritional conflict.

Despite the unsatisfactory experience with *détente* in the 1970s, the Soviet and American leaderships continue to acknowledge their shared interest in resolving regional conflicts and minimising the dangers of superpower entanglement and inadvertent escalation. In September 1984, Secretary of State George P. Shultz and former Soviet Foreign Minister Andrei Gromyko agreed to a series of informal discussions on regional problems with the potential for widening into major conflicts. Since that time, bilateral meetings at the Assistant Secretary/ Deputy Foreign Minister-level have focused on the Middle East, Afghanistan, Southern Africa and the Far East.[30] In addition to these recent publicised meetings, there have been persistent unconfirmed reports of information exchanges between the two sides *vis-à-vis* the Iran–Iraq War. More prominently, regional questions were a major agenda item at the Reagan–Gorbachev Summits from 1985 onwards. Such periodic consultations, while unlikely on their own to yield solutions to regional issues, provide a channel for communication and thereby reduce the risk of unstructured superpower competition in the Third World.

The Soviet leadership has welcomed this dialogue with the United States on the Third World. From a Soviet perspective, these discussions, if accomplishing nothing else, have served to underscore the USSR's political status as a superpower with global interests. The Kremlin leadership's main fear is political exclusion – hence its strong opposition to the Camp David negotiations and persistent calls for an international conference on the Middle East co-chaired by the superpowers.

As is evident from the preceding analysis, contending Soviet and American conceptions of regional stability militate against a formalised 'code of conduct' governing superpower competition in the Third World. The prognosis is the continued pursuit of unilateral advantage by both sides in Third World regions to the extent that their resources and local circumstances permit. If a formal comprehensive accord on superpower behaviour is not politically feasible, however, agreement might be possible on specific questions that are related to concrete Soviet and American interests. The superpowers might, for example, discuss measures to stabilise further the situation on the Korean peninsula. While some regions – notably the Middle East – will be far less susceptible to such an approach, the superpowers have a mutual interest in building upon the already existing incentives for joint restraint. How they might do this is one of the themes addressed in subsequent chapters.

NOTES

1 Political Report of Mikhail Gorbachev, General Secretary of the Central Committee, to the XXVII CPSU Congress, 25 February 1986 in FBIS, *Soviet Union* (Supplement), 26 February 1986, pp. 1–42; hereafter cited as *XXVII CPSU Congress Report* (1986). The author gratefully acknowledges his debt to S. Neil MacFarlane at this and other places in this paper.

2 See, for example, Donald S. Zagoria, 'Into the Breach: New Soviet Alliances in the Third World', *Foreign Affairs* (Spring 1979), pp. 733–4, 739–41.

3 Report of Leonid Brezhnev, General Secretary of the Central Committee, to the XXVI CPSU Congress, 23 February 1981 in *Current Digest of the Soviet Press* 33, 8 (25 March 1981), p. 3. Brezhnev observed that the 1976–81 period 'were years of further growth for the might, activity and prestige of the Soviet Union and the other countries of the socialist commonwealth'.

4 For a discussion of Soviet policy prior to Stalin's death see Roger E. Kanet, 'The Soviet Union and the Colonial Question, 1917–1953' in Roger E. Kanet, ed., *The Soviet Union and the Developing Nations* (Baltimore, MD: Johns Hopkins University Press, 1974), pp.1–26.

5 Philip Windsor, 'The Soviet Union in the International System of the 1980s', 'Prospects of Soviet Power in the 1980s', part II, *Aldephi Papers*, no 152 (London: IISS, 1979), p. 2.

6 For an authoritative account of the negotiations leading to the Egyptian arms agreement see Mohammed Heikal, *Sphinx and Commissar: The Rise and Fall of Soviet Influence in the Middle East* (London: Collins, 1978), pp. 56–63.

7 Cf, for example, Harry Gelman, *The Brezhnev Politburo and the Decline of Detente* (Ithaca: Cornell University Press, 1984), pp. 22, 25, 32–5, and *passim*; Zbigniew Brzezinski, 'The Soviet Union: Her Aims, Problems and Challenges to the West' in 'The Conduct of East–West Relations in the 1980s', part I, *Adelphi Papers*, 189 (London: IISS, 1984), pp. 3, 5; Edward Luttwak, *The Grand Strategy of the Soviet Union* (New York: St Martin's Press, 1983), pp. 32–41.

8 See W. W. Rostow as cited in Samuel Sharp, 'National Interest: the Key to Soviet Politics' in Erik P. Hoffman and Frederic J. Fleron, eds., *The Conduct of Soviet Foreign Policy* (New York: Aldine, 1980), p. 113. The impact of repeated invasions on Soviet perceptions of external threats is discussed by William T. Shinn, Jun., in 'On Russians and Their Ways', *Washington Quarterly* 8, 1 (Winter 1985), pp. 3–18.

9 *Pravda*, 4 April 1971, p. 8.

10 Colin Legum, 'Angola and the Horn of Africa' in Stephen Kaplan, ed., *Diplomacy of Power: Soviet Armed Force as a Political Instrument* (Washington, DC: Brookings Institution, 1981), p. 578.

11 Soviet assistance to Vietnam has been estimated at $3 to $6 million per day; see US House Committee on Foreign Affairs, p. 119. Merritt Robins put the Cuban figure at $8 million per day in 'The Soviet–Cuban Relationship' in Roger E. Kanet, ed. *Soviet Foreign Policy in the 1980s* (New York: Praeger, 1982). Raymond Duncan estimated Soviet assistance to Cuba at $13 million per day in 'Soviet Interests in Latin America' in *Journal of Interamerican Studies and World Affairs* 26, 2 (May 1984), p. 167. Soviet aid to Ethiopia has been estimated at $3 million per day or

$1 billion per year in Paul Dibb, 'The Interests of the Soviet Union in the Region' in T. B. Millar, ed. *International Security in Southeast Asian and Southwest Pacific Region* (St Lucia: University of Queensland Press, 1983), pp. 65, 67.

12 See Elizabeth K. Valkenier, 'Soviet Economic Relations with the Third World' in Roger E. Kanet, ed. *The Soviet Union and the Developing Nations* pp. 225–7.

13 *Ibid*, pp. 219–21.

14 New edition of CPSU Programme in FBIS, *Soviet Union*, 10 March 1986, p. 03.

15 *XVII CPSU Congress Report* (1986), p. 033.

16 See S. Neil MacFarlane, *Superpower Rivalry and Third World Radicalism* (Baltimore, MD: Johns Hopkins University Press, 1985), pp. 210–15 and *passim*.

17 Central Intelligence Agency, *Communist Aid Activities in Non-Communist Less Developed Countries, 1979 and 1954–1979*, ER-80-10318U (October 1980). If one includes Soviet arms transfers to Cuba, Vietnam, Laos, Vietnam and North Korea, the USSR presumably unseated the United States somewhat earlier.

18 'Cooperative intervention' is a term coined by Stephen Hosmer and Thomas Wolfe in *Soviet Policy and Practice Toward Third World Conflicts* (Lexington, MA: D.C. Heath, 1983), pp. 79–108.

19 Although the USSR mounted limited air-support missions in North Yemen (1967), Sudan (1970–1) and Iraq (1973–4), Soviet regular forces have experienced little direct combat. The deployment of some 12,000–15,000 missile crewmen and 200 pilots to Egypt during the 1970 War of Attrition was apparently an act of desperation in the face of Egyptian threats to cut their ties with the USSR, and again entailed very limited involvement in combat. In Syria, the 6,000–8,000 Soviet air defence personnel (augmented since the 1982 Israeli intervention in Lebanon) are probably there just as much to ensure the non-use of long-range surface-to-air missiles as they are to symbolise the seriousness of the Soviet commitment to the Assad regime.

20 See S. Neil MacFarlane, 'The Soviet Conception of Regional Security', *World Politics* 37, 3 (April 1985), pp. 309–10.

21 This argument is advanced by Dennis Ross in 'Risk Aversion in Soviet Decision-making' in Jiri Valenta and William Potter, eds., *Soviet Decisionmaking for National Security* (London: George Allen & Unwin, 1984), pp. 242–3, 249.

22 See, for example, 'Za rasshirenie sotsialnoi bazy afganskoi revolyutsii' ['For the expansion of the Afghan revolution's social base'], *Pravda* (unsigned), 21 December 1985.

23 The significance of the Andropov speech is analysed in Francis Fukuyama, *Moscow's Post-Brezhnev Reassessment of the Third World*, no. R–3073/1–NA (Santa Monica, CA: Rand Corporation, September 1983), p. 18.

24 Rostislav Ul'ianovskii, a prominent academic and Deputy Chief of the CC Secretariat's International Department, offers a spirited defence of the vanguard party approach in *Pobedy i trudnosti Natsionalno-Osvoboditelnoi borby* ['Victories and Difficulties of the National Liberation Struggle'] (Moscow: Izdatelstvo politicheskoi literatury, 1985), pp. 89–90.

25 The concept of authority building as a central preoccupation of Soviet leaders is developed by George Breslauer in *Khrushchev and Brezhnev as Leaders* (London: George Allen & Unwin, 1982); see, in particular, pp. 3–23.

26 Thane Gustafson and Dawn Mann, 'Gorbachev's First Year: Building Power and Authority', *Problems of Communism* (May–June 1986), pp. 3–4.

27 *XXXVII CPSU Congress Report* (1986), p. 01.

28 *Ibid*, p. 028.

29 See Mark Katz, 'Anti-Soviet Insurgencies: Growing Trend or Passing Phase?', *Occasional Paper*, No. 210 (Washington, DC: Kennan Institute for Advanced Russian Studies, 1986).

30 Michael A. Armacost, Under Secretary of State for Political Affairs, has stated that '[t]he purpose of these talks is not to negotiate solutions to regional conflicts behind the backs of the parties concerned. Rather, they provide a forum for airing concerns in order to lessen the risks of misperception or miscalculation.' See 'US–Soviet Relations: Coping with Conflicts in the Third World' in US Department of State, Bureau of Public Affairs, *Current Policy* 879 (October 1986), p. 4.

3   US policies in the Third World: objectives, instruments and constraints

Derek Leebaert

Concern over US–Soviet competition in what, since the 1950s, has been called the Third World has framed both US academic and strategic analyses for more than a generation. Americans have debated from the earliest cold-war years the extent of their interests and capabilities in what policy-makers initially deemed the 'exposed' or 'far-flung' regions of the globe. Washington's conclusion throughout the first decade after the Second World War was that US power was dangerously 'spread around the world from hell to breakfast'.[1] This sense of attenuation – of dubious allies, inflationary defence budgets, and 'imperial overstretch' – has once again come to characterise both American foreign policy and America's sense of the future.

There is a telling difference between the original Reagan penchant for rhetorically confronting rather than rationalising Soviet military initiatives (a sense of confidence reminiscent in its unilateralism of the 1950s) and the more bewildered views of US commitments which surfaced during the administration's last year. These arise not only from Vietnam but from the US failure to catalyse Third World development, and from the absence of vigorous allied assistance in nearly every non-European area of engagement with Soviet pressures. In the last decade of the century, however, the United States is less likely to rethink its position as a great power than it is to unburden itself of $15 billion a year of foreign aid. Similarly, it is unlikely casually to despatch military assistance groups to foreign jungles and deserts, and to welcome indiscriminately to Fort Bragg any uniformed foreigner who might call himself an anti-communist – practices which had become routinised by the mid-sixties. Furthermore, the United States has not only radically qualified its view of development, but has recognised that Third World countries have authority, objectives, and intense wills of their own.

The underdeveloped world nonetheless remains a theatre of political action permeated by subversion, and by intense economic and social pressures. Radios,

49

rapid communications and automatic weapons have ensured that the sounds of the most developed parts of the world are combined portentously with the aspirations of the most impoverished. The small elite parties which can rapidly overturn the order of events force such regions to endure a kaleidoscope of political rules. The personalism of politics and the dominance of cliques not only add to instabilities but have the potential for making a communist party a very important factor in national events. Although these regions have been in a perpetual state of struggle, the US has pursued the goal of establishing within them stable governments and market economies resembling those of highly industrialised states.

US–Soviet antagonism in these regions, amazingly, has been at one remove. The vision of twenty-five years ago, of hand-to-hand combat in jungles, deserts and mountains, has greatly receded. Nor has a shot been fired between formal US and Soviet military units. There has even been a steady loss of excitement in both superpowers over the underdeveloped regions. The US has been disappointed too often over its aspirations for Third World development, and over the extent of political baggage carried by many of the poorer members of the 'Free World'. Moscow, in turn, no longer seems to perceive vulnerable expanses in the Third World which require only a push to revolution, although its vision of opportunity remains.

It is against this backdrop of ceaseless manoeuvring, recurrent crisis, frequent disappointment, fractured domestic politics and alliance relations, and immense expense, that the US approach to security in the Third World has to be examined. First, the early rationale for US behaviour is considered. This is particularly important since the dynamism of the superpower competition in the Third World is full of resurfacing influences and ironies, as well as of changing assumptions. Second, America's perspectives of the superpower competition are assessed. Such an examination is pivotal since US policies are shaped by shifting beliefs about Soviet capabilities and motivations. Third, examples of US policy instruments (and obstacles to their use) are clarified by discussing the military and political priorities of the late 1980s: the cases of US interventionary capabilities, as demonstrated in the Persian Gulf by CENTCOM, and of the beleaguered foreign-aid budget, highlight chronic problems. The final section offers thoughts on what may lie ahead.

PRECEDENTS, PATTERNS AND OBJECTIVES

In the last months of the Reagan Administration, a group of prominent Americans and Soviets released a three-year joint study calling for far-reaching steps to demilitarise US–Soviet competition, especially in the Third World. An array of former senior US officials from the State and Defence Departments and the CIA joined with Soviet participants, such as Georgi Arbatov, from semi-official institutes, to recommend that the Soviets end their traditional military support for national liberation movements and that the US end military activity under the 'Reagan Doctrine' to overthrow communist governments. The study group recommended that the two major powers should formally agree not to use their military forces in Third World regional conflicts, not to send proxy, volunteer or covert paramilitary forces into such conflicts, and not to send more than 'a specific small number' of military advisers or trainers, probably around 200, to developing countries. The study also proposed developing a list of sophisticated weapons that the two powers would not transfer to Third World nations.[2] Does Gorbachev's 'new thinking' make such agreement possible after forty years of cold war? And what of US objectives?

The broad goals of US foreign policy are today simply stated as protecting national security, promoting domestic prosperity, fostering democratic values, advancing humanitarian ideals, combating narcotics' trafficking and thwarting terrorism.[3] These are the aims of a satisfied constitutional power, although the last two are reflections of twentieth-century anarchy. Switzerland could have the same aspirations. Problems arise, however, because the US has a way of debating foreign policy on the basis of first principles which can be regarded either as adolescent or invigorating.

The sweeping objectives identified above are essentially the foundation of the major points of bipartisanship which characterised US foreign policy during the first twenty years after the Second World War: America would not return to isolationism, the country would accept the importance of power in international affairs, Congress would play a formative role in most aspects of foreign policy, there would be an economic as well as a political commitment to promoting international stability and, most of all, there would be a recognition that the struggle for international peace was the struggle for agreed standards of international conduct.

The pursuit of overly ambitious objectives in the Third World, however, ended the brief life of bipartisanship. Similarly, the attempt to achieve US goals in the Third World during the 1980s led to scandal at home and to a widening gap between overseas commitments and the willingness, rather than simply the capabilities, to meet them. This lack of willingness is apparent in the declining percentage of GNP to be devoted to military spending. Nonetheless, the original objectives which have been pursued since 1947 in an effort to 'contain' Soviet power, and to arrest the social, economic and political instabilities which accompany such power, remain central to US foreign policy.

Pursuing US objectives in general, and specifically implementing them through containment in the Third World, led to confusion and imprecision. It is necessary, therefore, to search for the underlying patterns of forces and circumstances which made it extremely difficult for Washington to compete successfully over time with the Soviet Union in the Third World. Moreover, it is helpful to identify both the origins of US commitments and the extent to which they are the price of world power rather than the results of simple economic or ideological ambition.

Recent US and Soviet disappointments are ironic to the extent that the superpowers' initial involvement in much of the undeveloped world was propelled by disappointments in Europe during the early inter-war years. American hopes in the vision of Versailles collapsed at the same time that the Bolsheviks realised that there would be no revolution in Germany. Each insular power directed its energies elsewhere. The US continued the Roosevelt-Taft hegemonic approach to the Caribbean Basin and moved awkwardly to contain Japan in the Far East – at least assuring that today's allies in these two regions rarely echo Western Europe's fear of US isolationism. The Soviet Union, in turn, penetrated Mongolia and, in characteristic support of the local power elites, backed Chiang Kai-shek in China. If revolutionary outcomes in Europe required patience, however, Moscow, in other regions, was eager to support potentially Marxist industrial classes against a rural lumpen proletariat. In China, the despatch of experts by both the United States and the Soviet Union and the inclination to confront each other through proxies rather than directly, presaged one of the features of the cold war.

Any more ambitious Soviet ventures were limited by poverty and by the land-locked geographic position of the state beyond which Moscow could barely reach until the 1960s. The convulsions of the Second World War, however, coincided with two key influences. First, the speed of colonial retreat was further increased by the fact that the European empires had to be rescued by the noisily anti-colonial Americans, and by the fact that the war had just been fought, at least in Europe, against doctrines of racial superiority which were now also being contested by subject races in the colonies. Second, the war ensured the international respectability of the Soviet state. Above all, however, the war meant that what Britain acknowledged in 1945 as the 'gigantic system of bluff' by which it had defended its empire was finally being called.[4]

The British in 1945 were far more exhausted from their life or death struggle than they realised, or than Washington was able to understand until NSC 75 ('Britain's Retreat from Military Commitments') followed Britain's financial crisis of 1949. Neither Britain alone, nor even Britain in partnership with America, could uphold its three traditional defence principles of preventing hegemony in Europe, assuring freedom of trade routes, and protecting territories in the Near and Far East. In the aftermath of earlier wars, Britain had been able to marshal its resources to bolster foreign governments by means of credit, loans and trade agreements. This was no longer the case and Washington felt increasingly alone as it faced the perceived expansion of a vast new form of national socialism. America initially began to respond not through military containment, but rather as Britain had once done – by a balance of power that required aid, credits and a preeminent navy.

The analogy between the US and Britain is deeply interesting. The function of an island power had now migrated west – and island powers have special relationships with the unformed regions of the world. Once Germany was off the board and a Eurasian power was in the game, Britain's strength began to appear increasingly modest, and Americans learned, albeit rather slowly, that the Western hemisphere could no longer be defined as the basic geographical foundation of national security.

Much as Britain had explained its empire since the nineteenth century, Americans came to believe, as George Marshall stated, that they could 'no longer count upon others to carry the burden of safeguarding our civilisation'.[5] Becoming increasingly sceptical of the prospect of permanent peace, Washington was loathe to renounce precipitously the 434 military bases of various dimensions it had acquired around the world. It knew by 1945 that it had national interests in its own latitude as well as longitude; no responsible American was prepared to relinquish Europe or Japan to communism. The question was, when would the US begin to recognise vital global positions beyond the Americas, below the latitude of New York and San Francisco – in the Middle East, in Africa, in the sub-continent and in Southeast Asia? The Truman Doctrine alone did not commit America to anything, even in Europe.

The interregnum between British withdrawal, which could only briefly be rationalised as retrenchment, and American achievement of 'world military power' following the Korean War was dominated by a preoccupation with 'power vacuums'.[6] This anxiety was a result of pre-Second World War experiences and would become a staple of strategic analyses involving the Third World. The term was an antonym to 'balance of power', which had reassuring connotations of stability and which Americans hoped would enable them to stay an ocean apart from Soviet power. The vacuums were, in fact, much larger and more severe than anyone thought.

Towards the end of the Second World War, and increasingly thereafter, Washington and Whitehall detected such lacunae almost everywhere. Presidential Advisor Clark Clifford warned in 1946 that revived Russian ambitions in the Middle East threatened to 'create a power vacuum into which Soviet political and military influence may move'.[7] Well before Western Europe, the Middle East became the first region which US planners labelled as 'vital' – rather than the lesser 'critical' – to US interests.[8] 'We couldn't just withdraw and leave a vacuum', Prime Minister Attlee subsequently explained in relation to British planning in the Eastern Mediterranean and elsewhere.[9] Every facet of British political life wanted above all to 'avoid creating by our withdrawal vacuums into which the other Great Powers might surge'.[10]

As if the 'vacuums left by the collapse of the German, Italian and Japanese powers' were not worrying enough for US planners, the unexpected 'gaps' and 'vacuums' created by Britain's sudden and deliberate 'shock tactic' withdrawals assured that this geophysical term became part of the US idiom.[11] The term was an easy means to avoid addressing the complexity of events when explaining the destinies of distant and unfamiliar peoples and places.

Prudent Americans such as Walter Lippmann understood that 'it was impossible to fill every vacuum of power' around the world.[12] It was remarkable, therefore, how many vacuums the US quickly began to fill. The immediate US-sponsored rebuilding of Europe and particularly of Japan, which had been knocked back into the Third World, revealed Lippmann's lack of awareness of the immense opportunities available to the United States. By the time that Peace Corps volunteers were offered to Japan in the sixties, they could be politely declined.

Some caution was nevertheless appropriate in the light of the spiritual 'vacuum in Britain' resulting in a large part from the effects of two world wars. Britain had been labelled one of the three 'superpowers' in 1944.[13] This status certainly did not disappear with a splash in the winter of 1947. But Britain could only maintain the appearance of a superpower – global power combined with mobility – if it succeeded in deploying American strength behind its three principles of defence. Britain therefore worked deliberately to ensure US involvement in contested regions (which included Europe), as did France and the Netherlands.

The first step was in the Middle East through the Pentagon Talks of 1947, then in Europe through Britain's spearheading of the Western Union initiative and the Atlantic Treaty, and then in East and Southeast Asia. 'When discussions with the Americans on the Far East and the Middle East have been completed and when similar talks take place on Western Europe', the British chiefs of staff noted in 1948, 'we shall have covered the whole world with the exception of the American continent'. Foreign Secretary Bevin, in turn, spoke of 'casting the net' to draw American power into areas beyond Europe.[14] Britain had no intention of leaving US commitments in the Middle East and Asia to time, and therefore to chance. The degree of British influence upon Washington in the critical years between the Second World War and the Korean War is debatable. What is clear, however, is that Bevin's band of like-thinking states, cemented by treaties and stretching from Western Europe through Southeast Asia into the Western Pacific, was in place by the mid-50s. American power was the foundation of all of these conveniently pronounceable treaties: SEATO, CENTO, NATO, ANZUS, etc.

Retarding the spread of Soviet power, simplified as global communism, increasingly became the guiding principle of post-war US foreign policy. But despite the hyperbole of 'the American Century', Americans themselves did not believe that there was 'a bottomless cornucopia' to underwrite foreign policy. They insisted that potential allies recognise that 'the US and its citizens do not have unlimited wealth'.[15] There were vociferous domestic debates both in and out of government over the extent of defence spending, and whether the US would appear to the Europeans to be risking inflation reminiscent of Weimar by assuming a federal deficit. Washington had no intention of filling 'power vacuums' alone.

Throughout the US foreign-policy archives of the post-Second World War decade it is possible to discern the dual fear of making meaningless declarations in the style of the Kellogg–Briand Pact, or becoming militarily over-extended beyond Europe. Washington took no comfort from the fact that Britain's 'old instinct for imperialism and defense of British rights' had become a shadow of what it once was.[16] While Britain had no enthusiasm for involving itself with the French and the Dutch in reassertions of colonialism, neither was it as predisposed toward Third World nationalism as were the Americans. Tension also arose from the US need to placate new NATO allies, such as the Dutch, who foresaw Soviet victories on the other side of the globe 'if the Indonesian extremists are allowed to fill the vacuum which will be left'.[17] Yet US sympathies wavered as Americans who once identified with every nationalist increasingly saw a communist behind every nationalist bush.

Some Americans took Ralph Waldo Emerson's dictum literally, that it was America's office to liberate, and others simply feared the consequences for America in having Europeans reimpose themselves in Asia. The Europeans, in turn, discounted US views on regional politics, believing that most Americans sadly shared one of Palmerston's few delusions, that all nationalists are democrats. The US dilemma became painful once Washington faced the prospect of colonial administrations supplanted by apparently Russian-controlled regimes.

Britain was frustrated by 'the American sensitiveness about having burnt their fingers in China, and the consequent reluctance to become involved in further commitments, either there or in South East Asia'.[18] Despite British scepticism about China's susceptibility to Soviet dictates, there was a conviction in

Whitehall that something had to be done to prevent communist inroads in Southeast Asia, which would jeopardise Malaya and India. The British had no intention of letting anyone else rule Malaya.

Consistent with the national security postulate that developments halfway around the world impact directly on core interests, the British insisted that 'the grave situation in China makes it all the more important to close our ranks in the Middle East'.[19] Although Washington resisted further joint military planning in the Middle East, American policy makers, along with many of their British counterparts, began to see a Molotov/Mao Tse-tung strategy pressing down on the borders of India and Indochina. Since the Foreign Office concluded both that Malaya's loss would be crippling and that its first line of defence lay in Indochina, an increasingly convincing case of dominoes began to be made to Washington.[20]

It is difficult to gauge the influence which British importuning had on Washington. But the arguments for some sort of US commitment in Southeast Asia – made in Washington by Ambassador Oliver Franks and from Malaya and even Saigon by British Commissioner Malcolm McDonald – resonated increasingly with US inclinations and carried more weight than similar arguments from the French and Dutch. And the notion of a Sino-Soviet axis was not as naive as it may now appear. Washington was susceptible to worst-case reasoning. The country had come a long way since 1940 when Senator Robert Taft could state that a German army invading America was as inconceivable as an American army invading Germany.

As Soviet ambitons in Europe were interpreted in the shade of Munich, so Peking's efforts came to be seen in Washington as an attempt to recreate a variation of the Greater East Asia Co-Prosperity Sphere. In Asia, as in Europe, the sprat for assuring US commitments was the prospect of effective regional groupings which would need to be supported only indirectly. Americans expected these groupings to be more than military alliances, which was one reason that the Commonwealth gave Britain such inflated stature in Washington until Americans in the 1950s finally saw for themselves the centrifugal forces of nationalism at work.

Third World development from above became a central part of the cold war – a term which itself meant that war in the normal sense was unlikely and that peace in the normal sense was improbable. There would be 'neither war nor peace' in Lenin's classic formulation of the ideological state. The cold war involved primarily a struggle for the minds of men, for spiritual allegiance. The definition of cold war did not exclude actual warlike acts, and covered localised wars as in Korea. But the concept of a cold war really involved the whole question of how America would maintain its new global position, especially beyond Europe, and how this position could be equated in the long run with general US foreign policy.

The period from summer 1945 through the Korean War presented the issues which, with varying intensity and shifts in focus, have been central to the US reaction to Soviet power in the Third World for more than a generation. After Korea, it was no longer a question of mobilising other democracies to fulfil generalised legal obligations, but rather one of making specific strategic arrangements with whatever states were prepared to oppose the Kremlin. At the same time, this realism brought Americans to measure their allies in terms of actual and potential contributions rather than against a yardstick of desirable international and internal behaviour. The contradiction in US policy, however, was that Americans were reluctant to abandon their hopes for agreed standards of conduct (meaning liberal democracy) in the Third World. Disappointment and indecision became inevitable.

In the year after the outbreak of the Korean War, George Kennan published a seminal work of foreign-policy analysis, *American Diplomacy 1900–1950*. His argument was designed to move US views about the aims and methods of foreign relations out of the conventional grooves of simplistic anti-communism in which they had tended to run. He explained the enduring priorities of US security in his classic formulation: 'Our interest has lain . . . in the maintenance of some sort of stable balance among the powers of the interior, in order that none of them should effect the subjugation of the others.' US diplomacy must therefore support the powers around the ocean rim and, particularly, the powers of the West. He argued, moreover, that American diplomacy should concern itself with the realities of political and economic power instead of pursuing high-sounding moral themes. Kennan regarded the legalistic and moralistic approach to international problems as potentially disastrous, preferring what the Germans called 'realpolitik'. The expression means maintaining equilibrium, searching for compromise, not trying to change nations by imposing democracy on them, and understanding that the power of even the greatest state is limited in its dealings with other countries. He was opposed to America riding around like Don Quixote trying to rescue damsels like Poland and Hungary (or, later, South Vietnam and Afghanistan) from the reach of Soviet power and often making matters worse than before. He tried to represent a turning away from moralistic intervention for its own sake.

Kennan's fears about the limits of US power were quickly refuted. He was wrong in expecting a collapse of Western Europe and Japan or, at best, a Europe in the process of recovery dominated entirely by Germany. His view was also an entirely military one, and he was silent about the prospects and consequences of economic dynamism in international politics. Americans, moreover, proved unable to sustain a starkly strategic world view. In fact, much of the strength and inspiration of US policy has lain precisely in the presentation of new slogans and moralistic statements to the world: The Open Door, self-determination, crusade in Europe, and human rights. The so-called Reagan Doctrine of undermining Soviet military-backed clients in the Third World is only the latest example of security policies being cloaked in moralistic themes. Defining policy in this way, as Presidents Eisenhower, Kennedy, Johnson, Carter and Reagan have all done, despite their often different world views, has been a tactical necessity. Irrespective of sound strategy, such moralising proved convenient to encourage the fractious US electorate to respond to a hostile power which was only the latest to be based on the concept that the individual must be in service to the state.

Kennan feared, however, that the American penchant for a world renewed would lead to new crusades, as in Vietnam (an unwinnable crusade given the demands of President Johnson's social crusade at home). His lectures and writings preached a diplomatic technique of realism and of calm, of old-fashioned diplomacy and even of Christian charity. And he tried to bring this realism and calm into harmony with the more restrained foreign-policy traditions of the founding fathers and the Middle West. So he insisted less on the need for containment on the more distant borders of the Soviet Union than on the need for US moderation to avoid a direct war which Moscow was equally unwilling to face. But if agreement was impossible and war was nevertheless avoided while Washington focused on traditional interests in Europe, the prospects in the rest of the world would be all the more troubling for East–West relations and for America's new role as a global power.

Kennan argued that the Soviets were in part ideological and in part imperialistic but also highly realistic in adjusting themselves to facts. The uncertainty about what these 'facts' might be emphasised the weakness in his argument. Thus, arrangements reached with Moscow would be useful when they registered an existing situation (which was dangerous in assuming things would stay the way they were) but useless when they were merely agreements about desirable futures. Tacit or explicit understandings about permissible behaviour were, therefore, possible in Europe, but clearly not in Southeast Asia, in the Middle East, and in Africa where there were 'situations of weakness' or 'vacuums', and where clear lines of demarcation had yet to be drawn.

It was controversial to conclude that situations had to be built which extended the area of possible agreement – that is, to create strength in otherwise vulnerable regions. Assumptions had to be made about which 'situations' were temporary (such as a weakened Europe and Japan) and which might be permanent. Moreover, there were at least two dilemmas in creating strength beyond Europe: the extent to which the US would commit itself to buttress artificially such 'situations of weakness', especially once it became evident that it would do so without the previously enthusiastic European powers, and the extent to which the US object of stability clashed with its enduring faith in liberal democracy.

MANAGING THE SUPERPOWER COMPETITION

Soviet consolidation of Eastern Europe in the Warsaw Pact and communist control of China bracketed the ideological and strategic no man's land of the Middle East, Southeast Asia, and Africa – while Latin America eventually yielded its anomalous position as a non-belligerent in the cold war. The construction of an intricate network of alliances and guarantees beyond the traditional ocean rim meant that Soviet initiatives would be met in a variety of different ways: by regional war (Korea and Vietnam), by the threat of a wider war (the 1973 Defcon 2 alert in the Middle East and the Carter Doctrine for Southwest Asia), and by US covert action (Latin America and Africa). The two front-door confrontations over Berlin in 1961 and over Cuba in 1962 were the key isolated intrusions by the Soviet Union into clearly existing positions of US strength.

The nature of cold war, however, emphasised the limited utility of military confrontation at whatever level of violence. Two additional tactics were essential. The US and the West in general needed to ensure their own prosperity. Sound economies both ensured resources for distant involvements and could exert some attraction for developing states. Second, the US needed to exploit the contradictions between communism as an international creed on the one hand, and Soviet national aggrandisement on the other. US diplomacy could try to show the Third World that accepting the creed of the socialist model of development did not have to be synonymous with accepting the Kremlin as the sole repository of faith. Yet drawing such subtle distinctions in international diplomacy did not play to America's strong suit.

Rarely have US policies in the Third World echoed the appropriate cynicism of Robert Cutler, Eisenhower's national security advisor. Amid high-sounding talk of US motives in defending Seoul, Cutler sardonically asked, 'Just what do you mean, Mr President, by the *survival* of democracy in South Korea?'[21] Playing the Great Game meant highly flexible definitions of 'Free World', as well as a reluctance to acknowledge the sordidness of the competition.

Whereas Americans all along expected rapid examples of democratic virtue in their protégés, the Soviets have a Russian patience and a Hegelian notion of dialectic progress: if history is following one certain path, what difference does it make whether or not a right-wing dictatorship is supported by Moscow? Ideological detachment is one of the benefits of a Marxist education. If there is a true faith, the differences between the unbelievers along the way are insignificant. In contrast Washington has been consistently shocked when a right-wing dictatorship has established good relations with a communist government. Whereas Moscow has been able to 'do business' with a military dictatorship very well, the realpolitik which Kennan prescribed does not appeal to the United States. This is most evident in dealing with the Third World. Journalist Henry Fairlie, for example, still remembers his amazement when he moved to the US from Britain in 1965 and discovered that Americans actually did believe that they were in Vietnam to fight for democracy.[22]

For the United States any setback, even in the most distant regions, was assumed to upset a delicately poised balance of power – one which, at least since NSC–68 in 1950, has defined US security interests in terms of Soviet threats. Although America's energy and articulated ideals were a source of its strength, they limited the US room for manoeuvre and encouraged the involvement in Vietnam. Consequently, in the 1970s the US became especially vulnerable to rapid disillusion and ensuing media and Congressional strictures. There was an undeniable tendency among Americans in the 1970s to use any item of good news as a pretext for relaxing efforts abroad. *Détente* was later explained by its architects as an attempt to shore up the fading consensus for containment and to avoid ever repeating the devastating unanticipated sacrifices of what in the fifties would have been called a 'fringe war'. In fact, *détente* was a highly personalised effort by US initiators who sought to be present at the creation of new (and ultimately myopic) arrangements with Moscow.

Alternatives to military power were found for encouraging Soviet cooperation in the developing world, and the Nixon administration launched an ambitious effort to achieve this in the early seventies. The accords concluded at the May 1972 and June 1973 summit meetings were characterised by Secretary of State Kissinger as 'a code of conduct'. These principles were to be upheld by a system of incentives and penalties to induce moderate Soviet behaviour in the Third World – regions which had become far more important players in 1973 than in 1963. But Nixon and Kissinger disdained economic policy. They grossly underestimated Moscow's economic needs and motivations. And they ignored the fact that the Soviet Union could thereafter move as it pleased in the Third World with few economic consequences.

The costs of creating 'situations of strength' had proved unbearable, and the disposal of Diem retrospectively confirmed for US critics the distance which America had strayed from its ideals. Instead, the US tried to build bridges to the East with cheap credit, advanced technology, and military restraint. Moscow continued a military build-up and simultaneously backed Hanoi's conquests in Southeast Asia, supplied or led Cuban surrogates in Angola and Ethiopia, and used Cuban 'volunteers' or Soviet advisers in Mozambique and Yemen. In practice, the adroit 'linkage' of functional (e.g., trade, arms control) and regional (e.g., Vietnam, the Middle East) issues by the Nixon and Ford administrations was unrealistic. The mutuality of superpower interests in arms control and especially in economic relations allowed Moscow to compartmentalise successfully its relationship with the US. Regional turmoil meanwhile confirmed for Americans that *détente* was not a structure of superpower relations but rather an inherently fluid condition.

One school of American Sovietologists concludes that there was a perception within the Politburo by the early 1970s that assertive behaviour even further afield would produce increasing international gains.[23] Moscow perceived the United States was losing its role and capacity as a great power, which thereby opened up new opportunities for the USSR. As Moscow understood, it held an advantage because *détente* exposed the many asymmetrical vulnerabilities of special interests and popular pressures within US society. The disappointments and ferocious pluralism of the mid-seventies made it impossible for Washington to concert its foreign policies or to sustain its defence budgets, let alone to consider additional Third World military commitments, as in Angola. If the Soviets were incredulous about the extent to which the United States was not in command of its resources after Vietnam, they were quick to detect practical advantages for themselves in the kaleidoscopic US policy process. They saw a paralysing US absence of consensus by the mid-seventies.

Moreover, applying the linkage approach raised problems both with Washington's NATO allies and at home. Few Europeans welcomed an American political strategy towards the Soviet Union that held the tangible benefits of *détente* on the continent hostage to Third World instability. Viewed from a European perspective, *détente* was an inherently 'divisible' concept. The American domestic reaction to the Nixon–Kissinger strategy was vividly apparent during the acrimonious 1976 presidential primaries and election. To conservative critics, conferring incentives on Moscow was tantamount to appeasement. To their liberal counterparts, the occasional necessity of implementing penalties against the Kremlin marked not the continuation of administration policy but its failure. In addressing these criticisms, Kissinger subsequently maintained that linkage was not conceptually flawed but that domestic and alliance constraints had undermined its implementation.

The rapidly worsening international climate of the late seventies hastened US abandonment of the optimism which had been most obviously reflected in President Carter's warning against 'inordinate fear of communism', a sanguine view of a satiated Soviet Union which was similar to the arguments of Kennan. The spur was the renewal of the Great Game in Afghanistan. A century ago Lord Curzon coined the phrase 'power of menace' to describe Russian actions in Central Asia. A keen student of the Brezhnev era, British diplomat Robin Edmonds, revived the phrase to note the numerous foreign and military initiatives taken under Brezhnev of which Afghanistan was merely the spotlight.[24] Menace was particularly evident in the correlation between Moscow's new strategic nuclear programmes and the more extended Soviet role in world affairs – a pattern which Americans had traced since the first Soviet atomic detonation in September 1949.

The Reagan administration took office believing that US policy-makers had erred critically by ignoring the assumptions of implacable Soviet ambitions which had guided early US post-war policy, and by letting the Kremlin exploit US retrenchment. The Soviet foreign minister denounced the 'neo-globalism' of administration aid for anti-Soviet insurgencies while at the same time US scholars criticised 'Cold War II' and the medley of programmes which composed the Reagan Doctrine as redolent of NSC–68's indiscriminate delineation of US interests.[25] The 'doctrine' itself held that the US should bypass nervous and sometimes unreliable foreign friends in order to harass and, if possible, overthrow Moscow's clients in the Third World.[26] In backing ostensibly democratic forces against Soviet-imposed regimes, however, the Reagan doctrine fundamentally replicated the liberal outlook of the late 1940s. What was different was the determination to use American military power against enemies anywhere in the world, regardless of whether the US had the support of its allies.

The apparent Soviet foreign-policy successes of the 1970s, however, became the costly Third World clients of the 1980s. Leninist parties were no antidote for festering insurgencies in proto-communist states such as Afghanistan, Angola, South Yemen, Ethiopia, or in Southeast Asia. In view of the demanding arguments of power projection, Moscow has felt the financial cost of supporting 'states of socialist orientation'. Threatening as these apparent gains appeared to America by the late seventies, they have proved not to be the beginning of an ascending curve of Soviet intervention.

INSTRUMENTS AND OBSTACLES

US successes in the Third World were measured in the 1980s not just by the absence of defeat but, tellingly, by the gains of democracy. This was especially true following controversies over contras in Central America and convoys in the Gulf. Washington explained its successes by the fact that in 1979 only one of the six Central American states could remotely be considered a democracy. Eight years later, the argument went, the situation was reversed with Sandinista Nicaragua being regarded as the only non-democratic government. Moreover, Washington emphasised that it had supported the overthrow of the Somoza regime, in concert with other OAS nations, based on Sandinista promises to bring democracy to Nicaragua. Democracy itself was not the sole and simple objective, according to the US formula. Equally important, and presumably inseparable, was the evolution of a market economy which could be equated with stability. Somoza's downfall was not just attributed to oppression, which was modest by Third World standards, but to the fact that corruption and family monopolies ensured the disaffection of what passed for the middle classes.

The attempt to ensure democracy and liberal capitalism in Central America while simultaneously searching for stability in the Persian Gulf has underscored the continuing US quarrel over the proper powers of the president and Congress in conducting foreign policy. The president reigned supreme after the Second World War, managing the cold war with a firm and single hand. But the notion of a president's free hand has really been an economic concept. An expansive 'imperial presidency' was more acceptable during prosperous times. In fact, the United States has been acutely sensitive to real costs, as shown not just by Vietnam but by the mounting public frustration which surrounded the Korean War.

Congress's eventual insistence on the War Powers Act and its demand for a veto over US arms sales ensured the widest and most public consultation about all efforts to project US power abroad. The Iran–Contra Hearings were only the most dramatic manifestation of the problems of previous Congressional over-reaction, as in the 1976 blanket ban on US aid to Angolan rebels or as in the Boland amendment's vaguely worded legislation restricting US aid to Central America. The problem has been that Congressional review often shades into Congressional direction – or 'micro-management' – which then moves America as far as possible from any semblance of realpolitik in dealing with the Third World.

There are chronic difficulties for such an open democracy in pursuing covert action, as Gregory Treverton has explained.[27] But the US activities in the Gulf which became entangled in the Central American controversy reflected more traditional great power problems of matching commitments and willingness. Although the word domino was notable by its absence from the national debate, the second Reagan administration clearly detected dominoes wobbling in Central America and the Middle East.

The Administration, however, was constrained because Americans in the 1980s still carefully reckoned the costs in a manner they had not done in the early 1960s. Upon entering office on the highest tides of 1980 and 1984 Ronald Reagan could never have pledged in his inaugural address to 'bear any burden and pay any price'. Americans suspected that such talk would lead them into multi-billion dollar quagmires or, at best, into muddled shoot-outs, as in Grenada where officers would have to call in fire support through their telephone credit cards.

Intervention through aid and advisors in Central America has been nothing new to US foreign policy in this century. Yet Americans quickly saw limits beyond which they would not go – such as placing only fifty advisors in El Salvador. The limits to US development spending in the Caribbean Basin and elsewhere, even after Grenada, re-emphasised that America could no longer act as a cornucopia.

Similarly the US attitude towards the Gulf had much more in common with the caution of the initial years after the Pentagon Talks than it had with the exuberance which followed. Nevertheless, planning for 'rapid response force options' was underway in the summer of 1977, well before either Iran or Afghanistan had reached their later prominence in the public consciousness. Achieving the status of a separate unified command as an instrument of US policy – the Rapid Deployment Force which evolved into US Central Command (USCENTCOM) – was not an end in itself. The US has always had such a force in the Navy–Marine Corps team, in fact if not in name. Moreover, the Army and the Air Force had jointly prepared to act in such a capacity since the early sixties, first in Strike Command and then under the auspices of Readiness Command (REDCOM).[28] Indeed, the successful US intervention in Lebanon in 1958 attests to the prior existence of some capacity to respond rapidly to some of the types of contingencies the Rapid Deployment Joint Task Force was supposedly created to meet. But CENTCOM has now become representative of US interventionary abilities and inclinations in the 1990s.

What was unique to the creation of CENTCOM was that it explicitly contemplated a direct engagement with Soviet forces, rather than Soviet proxies or Third World militias as had previously been the most likely case. There was a belief by 1980 that it was important to oppose the momentum of Soviet power in the region, thus providing a strategic counterweight to regional instability which Moscow either stimulated or was prepared to use to its own advantage.

There were two key assumptions behind the creation of CENTCOM. One was that Americans would once again agree to uphold 'situations of weakness' without seeing in every US intervention the prospect of disastrous limited war. The second assumption was that in contrast to the experience in Vietnam, America's allies in Europe would be politically supportive and possibly militarily cooperative. In the words of US Army War College Professor Alan Sabrosky it would be operational burden-sharing writ large – a development facilitated by the obvious dependence of so many of those countries on the oil lifeline whose defence would most likely prompt the engagement of US CENTCOM forces in the first place.[29]

There is much irony surrounding the US military position in the Gulf, as there is elsewhere beyond Europe. Tensions have existed from the first within

NATO over what is called the members' 'out-of-area' responsibilities. However, it was the Europeans who originally insisted that the common defence also required joint efforts in the Middle East and Asia. They urged Washington to help counter what they saw as Soviet flanking efforts which, coincidently, often overlapped with areas of colonial disaffection. The Americans at first shunned such cooperation. By the sixties, however, Washington concluded that the Europeans themselves had withdrawn intellectually as well as operationally from world responsibility.

The role of the European allies now has to be weighed in any US Third World venture. Either their assistance can be publicly legitimising, as in Lebanon after the Israeli invasion or in the Gulf during 1987, or their criticism can erode both core interests within NATO and domestic support in the US. Current disagreements about commitments beyond Europe result from long-standing differences in both perceptions and style. While neither Washington nor the Europeans have a better sense of the future, the latter tend to believe that the US pushes forward with ill-considered haste and impatience whereas the uncertain future renders them cautious and eager to proceed on the assumption that conflict can be avoided. The tepid entry of Britain and the Netherlands into the Gulf in 1987 is only a recent example. The European allies believe in particular that the US underestimates the importance of strictly regional influences which only helps Moscow further its own ends, as in the Middle East and Central America. Moreover, the allies note, with some justification, Washington usually avoids asking the single question which should be posed before injecting troops into any foreign conflict: how do you know when you have won?

The US habit of giving public notice of its national security interests is not favoured by the European allies, the difference being due largely to the formalism of their own procedures. Such differences of style in decision-making affect impressions of any willingness to undertake distant commitments. The allies are disinclined to commit themselves in advance or to answer hypothetical questions. They see the course of history as too complex and too full of the contingent for any other practice to be wise. While Washington wants its opponents to be clear about its interests to avoid misunderstandings or misadventure, the European preference is to finesse distant challenges in a fashion that Americans tend to regard as accommodationist.

Immediate European interests are nonetheless specifically affected by the US creation of CENTCOM: first, there is a 50 per cent shortfall in sealift capacity to deal with a simultaneous deployment to Europe and Southwest Asia; second, authoritative US critics, such as former National Security Adviser Brzezinski, insist that such a Third World interventionary force must be supplemented by withdrawing a third of US troops from Europe.[30] In this connection, the Reagan administration's effort to improve strategic lift was the most ambitious and sustained programme in twenty years, and it reflected the perennial great power determination to bring commitments into line with capabilities.

Multilateral ventures, as envisioned originally in the early cold war years, have become an imperative for US military involvement abroad – even if the allies are simply expected to take up the slack in Europe after US forces are despatched elsewhere. Whereas the US was prepared and willing to act unilaterally in 1958, Beirut twenty-five years later could only be endured because the flags of France, Italy and Britain flew alongside the stars and stripes in the Multinational Force. Even in Grenada, the presence of token forces from a half-dozen Caribbean states added an essential measure of legitimacy to the US intervention. Yet the fact that most US allies are reluctant to tie themselves to US Third World ventures, especially with respect to probable USCENTCOM contingencies, does not augur well for USCENTCOM's successful employment.

A cottage industry developed in the 1980s around criticism of new and expensive US interventionary capabilities. Important strategic and doctrinal reservations have been made about the use of these capabilities irrespective of problems of insufficient allied or even domestic political support. The prospect of withdrawing 100,000 US troops from Europe for Third World interventions, for example, would be exceedingly risky. These troops are not the mobile light infantry divisions which are popularly envisioned. The US Army's new 'light' divisions are in fact regular infantry with less heavy equipment but with training and tactics still more suited to flat European terrain than to mountain, jungle or tundra warfare. They are cumbersome to deploy and to support, and they would also be unable to meet the Soviet doctrine, as practised in Afghanistan, of achieving sudden *coups de main* before invasion. Once the Soviets seize airfields and deploy fighters and reinforcements elsewhere in Southwest Asia, these would-be interventionary forces will have lost their mission.

The US force structure – despite the attention surrounding both CENT-COM, the frustrated slogan of a 600-ship US Navy, and allied fears of US preoccupation with the Pacific – remains highly Eurocentric. Time and distance do not always favour the Soviet Union, of course, nor can the Soviets hope to prevail in all respects in every given part of the world. In general, however, while the US can project larger forces over greater distances than the Soviet Union, the Soviets can get more resources faster to the Persian Gulf. The emphasis in CENTCOM's charter of directly confronting Soviet power places demands upon the force which widely exceed its current and attainable capabilities.

If the US focuses instead on meeting non-Soviet contingencies in Southwest Asia or elsewhere in the Third World, however, many of the military obstacles which surround CENTCOM can be avoided. Force ratios at the point of contact are no longer inherently unfavourable, and troops assigned to Europe are no longer certain to be drawn off. Time and distance still remain important influences, but the lift requirements are more likely to be satisfied. Undertaking a Grenada-style operation in the Emirates, for example, is of a different order of magnitude than attempting to counter a Soviet armoured thrust into Iran. In short, expectations for US military performance in the Third World may have again to be lowered to conform with strategic reality; being lower and more realistic, they are likely to be met more successfully.

Historical precedent shows that once the US goes beyond a force commitment of around 20,000–30,000 men, as in Lebanon in 1958 or in the Dominican Republic, the next threshold seems to be involvement at the level of the Korean and Vietnamese wars – one third to one half million men on the ground. Certainly this does not eliminate the possibility of some intermediate level of involvement. But it does suggest that probable operational requirements in the Third World are likely to be at the lower end of that range. It also suggests a primary requirement for light forces, with selected heavy forces in reserve, rather than the reverse or even some mix of the two.

If a direct US–Soviet Third World confrontation remains improbable (and often untenable), it would seem to follow that Washington would continue to rely all the more on the development assistance which has shaped its Third World security efforts since the early 1950s. The US potential for foreign assistance, like the fact of independent allies which underlies the US concept of collective security, is one of the few clear-cut Western advantages in opposing the combination of Soviet military power and client states. A critical and often overlooked US asset is the extent to which the European allies, despite popular American complaints of timidity and parochialism, pursue similar objectives of Third World development and stability. Britain, for example, has retained a discrete security relationship with the lower Gulf states while France has an impressive record of aid and intervention on behalf of its own associated regimes in Africa.

It is inevitable, however, that Washington will continue to shoulder the bulk of Western development aid even if it is on a lesser per-capita basis than thirteen other Western industrial countries. Instability rooted in poverty, rather than just Soviet subversion alone, influences a range of US security problems in the Third World. Such instability caused the US a quarter century ago to pour 25,000 combat troops into Santo Domingo to thwart a popular uprising which President Johnson believed was coming under the influence of Cuban-controlled communists. More recently, Secretary of State George Shultz repeatedly cited the Dominican Republic as exemplifying 'our principal foreign policy problem' – the Reagan administration's failure to dissuade Congress from making deep cuts in the US foreign-aid programme. Shultz's view was that the Dominican Republic is just one of the many time bombs ticking away unnoticed in odd corners of the Third World that could some day explode against American interests.[31]

Foreign aid, however, has become one of the most unpopular spending items before Congress, and an especially ripe target as the federal deficit forces a reordering of spending priorities. Shultz insisted, soon after joining the conservative administration in 1982, that foreign aid could no longer be dismissed as little more than a socialistic raid on the US Treasury. Instead, foreign aid would hasten Third World efforts to decentralise, deregulate and denationalise. Entrepreneurial initiative in a market environment was intended to prevent an ominous cycle of economic instability leading to political upheaval.

The myriad examples of rusting or rotting foundations of development projects abandoned when foreign-aid projects failed because of thievery, bureaucratic mismanagement of showy but unsuccessful hardware projects such as hydroelectric plants, or sudden shifts in development policy, have instead fuelled American cynicism towards approximately $15 billion a year for foreign aid (the ratio of expenditures normally being about two-thirds economic aid and one-third military assistance). Recurrent examples of US money being used to shore up grossly inefficient nationalised industry and agriculture – such as subsidising Mexico's state steel sector or contributing to Africa's agricultural decline by buttressing state marketing boards – diminishes any popular interest in foreign aid.[32]

Shultz instead spoke of a self-inflicted US 'strategy of retreat'. He argued that apparent progress toward the stability of privatisation, as evident in the commitment to more open markets by the African nations at the 1986 UN Special Session on Africa, was undercut by the US penchant for quick-fixes. Cuts in the foreign-affairs budget of between 20 and 50 per cent were seen as threatening vital US interests not just in one or two regions but around the globe. Shultz warned Congress that such cuts 'threaten the stability of our allies. They threaten our war on terrorists. They threaten our attempt to promote democratic values and reforms . . . And they threaten our ability both to understand and influence developments in a dynamic international environment.'[33] Among the national security interests being jeopardised, Shultz insisted, were aid to Pakistan and its costly support of the Afghan refugees, security assistance to countries providing the US with base rights, counterbalancing Soviet inroads in the South Pacific, and general efforts towards stability in Latin America and the Middle East.

What Americans had forgotten over forty years, according to the Shultz prescription, was the fundamental lesson that it takes financial resources –

modest but sustained, applied credibly over time – to advance US interests. 'While we are cutting ourselves to ribbons', Shultz's deputy John Whitehead echoed, 'our adversaries are pursuing a well-organised and well-financed effort to gain global influence and strategic advantage.'[34] The State Department insisted that the Soviets spent over $100 billion worldwide in bilateral economic and military assistance while the US spent $52 billion during the same period.

What the State Department calls the foreign-affairs budget crisis continually spotlights the dilution of US potential by the realities of domestic politics. Congress has been disinclined to vote more money for dubious foreign recipients when thousands of American farmers faced bankruptcy and foreclosure and the inner-city poor suffered the progressive whittling away of federal benefits. An increasing popular wariness arose in the late eighties among Americans who were tired of being exploited abroad, first directly by Third World kleptocrats and then, indirectly, through major US bank write-offs in the Third World. Americans and their representatives who would have been happy to contribute to victims of Bangladesh floods despaired over aid programmes which they suspected kept Mexican mistresses in Mercedes.[35]

CONCLUSIONS AND PROGNOSES

There are more destabilising situations in the Third World today than forty years ago because there are more resources to cause destabilisation on an international scale. Moreover, crises which may be characteristically Third World in their inception are traditionally strategic in their solution. They are likely to be defined by familiar concepts such as geography in Grenada or by tremendously dispersed national vitality as in Vietnam, rather than by the fact of under-development itself. The location of a Third World superpower dispute is a primary influence on its outcome, but so are the traditions and resources of the Third World country or region involved. An installed government, for example, can eventually be accepted by one state whereas it would be inconceivable in another. Mindful of the likely fate of North Vietnam if China, in 1967, had held its current view of Hanoi, Third World confrontations will be shaped by the number and extent of other powers involved.

There are at least three sets of Third World conflicts which affect the US–Soviet competition. First, there are specific strategic challenges as in Cuba in 1962, as in the threatened Soviet Middle East intervention in 1973, or as in the US worst case planning over possible Soviet bases in Nicaragua. Second, there are those tensions arising from the adventures of Soviet-backed allies, such as Vietnam versus China, India's rivalry with Pakistan, or Cuba's troops in Africa. A third set includes *ad hoc* Soviet opportunism encompassing everything from terrorism to fomenting major conflict: festering events play to the advantage of the state which will not work in the international division of labour, and to the advantage of the state with a zero-sum vision. Each type of conflict suggests different intensities of superpower response and whether an intervention is likely to grow septic, as in Vietnam or 1983 Lebanon, or whether it can be settled overnight as in the rare case of Grenada.

The potential which underdeveloped states have to do harm to each other increases steadily. India was able to reduce Pakistan from the world's largest Muslim country to merely the third largest Muslim state on the sub-continent. Yet future stakes could be even larger given emerging nuclear capabilities and the simple chemical-biological weapon capabilities which have long been called 'the Third World deterrent'.[36] Meanwhile, the likelihood of a major international dimension to a southern Africa convulsion rises; it is highly unlikely that this generation has seen the last Middle East war; the killing fields of the North Gulf deserts guarantee years of instability even if no Iraqi or Iranian territory changes hands; fighting continues in Southeast Asia; the dream of Mapilindo may not be concluded in the Western Pacific; the demographics of Latin America grow increasingly desperate; and seemingly momentary crises keep piling up, such as Libyan incursions in Chad or Algerian dealings with the Polisario.

It is difficult to see issues for sustained Soviet–American cooperation rather than competition in the Third World. Presumably health interests are shared. But the hope that Moscow might respond to other topics has proved elusive. Even Third World nuclear proliferation, which in the 1970s seemed an obvious problem for collaboration, has been futile. The next Third World state which goes nuclear is simply going to be a regional rather than a global nuclear power. It will therefore threaten primarily only one superpower. Moscow, therefore, has no motivation to pressure a highly nationalistic Argentina or Brazil on these matters, and the United States, in turn, is unlikely to threaten Pakistan. In East Asia, only a nuclear South Korea might be unsettling for Moscow; but it would be worse for the US given the devastating impact on Japan and the fact that a Soviet umbrella would immediately cover North Korea.

The prognosis is a continued and even accelerating search for unilateral advantage by both sides to the extent that resources and circumstances permit. The rules of engagement are likely to remain tacit at best. US policy, as Robert Litwak explains, can nonetheless contribute to the stability of the overall competition in at least five ways.[37]

First, a sustainable US role in international politics requires a non-universalistic conception of US interests abroad. Rational debate cannot flow from abstract and emotional slogans such as George McGovern's 'Come Home America'. Domestic consensus is more likely when a finite set of US security interests is delineated. Policymakers can calculate their cost in light of the degree of existing or likely Soviet involvement.

Second, clear communication of US commitments and interests can avoid miscalculation irrespective of allied reservations. The seeming US indifference to events in Afghanistan following the April 1978 pro-Soviet *coup* encouraged Moscow to believe that it could intervene overtly with minimal consequences. The Soviets are naturally likely to assume greater risks where they are defending established positions in the Third World. The US is therefore obliged to prevent Soviet *faits accomplis* in areas of vital Western interest. Regular bilateral meetings, such as those held since the Shultz–Gromyko agreement of September 1984, provide a potentially useful channel for discussing regional questions.

Third, there is little harm in the US continuing to seek limited agreement on specific questions which are related to concrete US and Soviet interests or which build on existing incentives for restraint. Conceivably, even arms sales limitations could be discussed again some time in the future. Similarly, measures concerning the stability of the Korean peninsula might warrant consideration.

Fourth, US support for security initiatives originating within a particular region may insulate those areas from superpower competition. Such efforts are likely to be most successful in areas such as Chad, the Western Sahara or Namibia, where the superpowers are not yet engaged. In this context, one may wonder what the outcome of the Angolan conflict would have been if the US had strongly supported the OAU initiatives in mid-1975 to ensure an orderly transition to independence.

Fifth, and finally, the US cannot avoid maintaining key regional military balances in the Third World. Whether through its own forces or underwriting those of an ally, military power is a prerequisite for any diplomatic initiatives in areas such as the Gulf and Central America. Some sort of judicious and effective economic assistance is also unavoidable. The Soviet Union is otherwise likely to benefit frequently from the shadow effect of having the adjacent geographic advantages of a massive land power.

What, then, is the future of America's policies, not just in the Third World but as a global power? As the century's last decade approached, America had nearly convinced itself that its burden was too great – that far more responsibility had to be shared in order to avoid the 'imperial overstretch' that took down the profligate Spanish, Dutch, French and British world-realms.[38] Indeed, America gave up in Vietnam; stepped out from under the dollar-dominated price of gold which drove the world economy for a quarter of a century; behaved not once but twice like a lamb toward OPEC; and publicly considered dropping the Korean commitment and others. Such moves, however, reveal neither a power in love with imperial status nor that rigidity of behaviour which crucifies aging realms upon their past supremacies. America is not an overstretched empire but a genial coasting bourgeois republic and one with a continual role in upholding world order.

In this complicated world there exists only one world power. In the global economy there exists only one really unmercantilist nation. Everywhere the United States still makes up the missing margin of resources – for China's sovereignty and for GATT, for a Europe secure without being armed to the teeth, for turbo-charging Japanese development. Although the original impulses that created the American order are mostly spent, the necessity for American resilience and strength is in fact subtly augmented. The US has been the guardian not of property but of possibility. America is not being bled by an imperial posture, but rather is profiting from the cooperative world which it created out of separated isolationist continents. America sees all its external arrangements as temporary. But it must still buy time for a world order which is visibly emerging but not yet achieved.

NOTES

1 Robert Lovett, as Deputy Secretary of State. Oral History, Harry S. Truman Library.
2 Report by the American Committee on US–Soviet Relations, 'Superpower Proxies in Third World Deplored', *The New York Times*, 6 May 1988.
3 US Department of State, Memorandum to the Secretary, SP (Policy Planning Staff), 10 March 1987.
4 Ernest Bevin, 7 November 1945, *Hansard*; H. V. Hodson, *Twentieth Century Empire* (London: Faber & Faber, 1948), p. 49.
5 17 March 1948. Testimony of Secretary of State George Marshall to the US Senate Armed Services Committee, 80th Congress, 2nd Session.
6 See Francis Williams, *A Prime Minister Remembers* (London: Heinemann, 1961), p. 175; also 6 November 1947 PPS 13 (Policy Planning Staff), Resume of the World Situation, State Department Files, US National Archives.
7 David Aaron Miller, Search for Security: *Saudi Arabian Oil and American Foreign Policy 1939–1949* (Chapel Hill, NC.: University of North Carolina Press, 1980), p. 166.
8 Pentagon Talks, 24 November 1947, *Foreign Relations of the United States (FRUS)*, 5, p. 575.
9 Williams, *A Prime Minister Remembers*, p. 175.
10 Labour Party document, 'Cards on the Table', included in US National Archives, RG 84, London Post Files, PI 1947.
11 19 August 1947, 'Tactics with the United States Administration', as cited by Henniker to Sargent, Public Record Office, FO 371/61003; see also Francis Williams, *Ernest Bevin* (London: Hutchinson, 1952), pp. 264–8; and 9 September 1947, 'Monthly Political Report: Sentiment Towards Britain', PRO, FO 371/61050.
12 Walter Lippmann, *The Washington Post*, 8 March 1947.
13 W. T. R. Fox, *The Super-Powers* (New York: Harcourt Brace, 1944).
14 6 January 1948, PRO, JP(48)4, D4/10.
15 May 1947 *Fortune*; also see FRUS 1948, 1, p. 595, 20 July 1948.
16 23 April 1948, US National Archives, RG 84 US Naval Attache to CNO, London Post File.
17 6 October 1949, US National Archives, State Department Files, FE 889, 880 and 7 October 1949, 901 from The Hague.
18 23 March 1949, PRO, FO 371/101267, FZ 1195/G.
19 22 December 1948, PRO, Bevin to Franks, FO 371/74183, AN308/1053/445G.
20 5 February 1952, PRO, FO 371/101267, FZ 1195/G.

21 Henry Fairlie, *The Kennedy Promise* (Garden City, NJ: Doubleday), 1973, p. 132.
22 Personal discussion with Henry Fairlie.
23 The best expression of this view is Harry Gelman, *The Brezhnev Politburo and the Decline of Detente* (Ithaca, NY: Cornell University Press, 1984).
24 Robin Edmonds, *Soviet Foreign Policy: The Brezhnev Years* (New York: Oxford University Press, 1983), p. 5.
25 For cold war comparisons, especially with NSC 68, see Samuel F. Wells, jun. 'Sounding the Tocsin: NSC 68 and the Soviet Threat', *International Security* (Spring 1978).
26 See Strobe Talbott's essay, 'Going It Alone', *Time*, 28 April 1986, which includes the quote by Eduard Shevardnadze.
27 See Gregory F. Treverton, *Covert Action: The Limits of Intervention in the Postwar World* (New York: Basic Books, 1987).
28 These predecessors of the RDJTF are summarised in Robert J. Haffa, jun., *The Half War: Planning US Rapid Deployment Forces to Meet A Limited Contingency, 1960–1983* (Boulder, CO: Westview Press, 1984), chapter 5.
29 See Sabrosky's unpublished manuscript, 'USCENTCOM Reconsidered: A Case for Reform', with William J. Olson, US Army War College, Carlisle, PA.
30 Zbigniew Brzezinski, *The Game Plan* (Boston, MA: Atlantic Monthly Press, 1986).
31 4 September 1987, George Shultz in the *Washington Post*.
32 See 'World Bank Sows Bad Advice in Africa', Melanie S. Tammen, the *Wall Street Journal*, 13 April 1988.
33 US Department of State, Information Memorandum S/S 10 March 1987, Testimony Before the House Foreign Operations Subcommittee.
34 US Department of State, Information Memorandum S/S, 27 May 1987, to Deputy Secretary of State John Whitehead from Policy Planning.
35 The best and most policy-relevant book concerning corruption in Third World countries is Robert Klitgaard, *Controlling Corruption* (Berkeley, CA:, University of California Press, 1988).
36 Tariq Osman Hyder, 'Inchoate Aspirations for World Order Change', *International Security* (Spring 1978).
37 See the complete text of Robert S. Litwak's conference paper, 'Soviet Policies in the Third World', prepared for the Ford Foundation Project Symposium on Superpower Relations, Guernsey, UK, March 1987.
38 The phrase has been popularised by Paul Kennedy, *The Rise and Fall of the Great Powers* (New York: Random House, 1987). Interest in the political consequences of America's relative economic decline has also been fuelled by Peter G. Peterson, 'The Morning After', *The Atlantic*, October 1987, and by essays such as Louis Uchitelle, 'When the World Lacks A Leader', the *New York Times*, 31 January 1988.

4   US and Soviet maritime rivalry in the Third World

Roger W. Barnett

For the United States and its allies the main competition with the Soviet Union and its allies takes place along three fronts: the Western, or European, the Eastern, or Asiatic and the Southwestern, or Arabian. The rest are strategic sideshows, and should be thought of as such.[1] This taxonomy does not split the world into geopolitical areas of First, Second and Third Worlds, but along a different fault line, serving as a reminder that, except perhaps in the Persian Gulf, competition between the superpowers in the Third World does not broach the core security interests of either. It should be absolutely clear, however, that for the United States and the Soviet Union it is the competition between them which is paramount, not the transient animosity between the United States and Libya or Cuba, or between the Soviet Union and Afghanistan, to select some obvious examples.

A geostrategic *tour d'horizon* setting forth rival US and Soviet interests in various countries of the world would exceed the scope of this chapter and encroach on the efforts of other contributors to this volume. It is important, however, to make some general observations on how the two superpowers might become embroiled in conflict. A fairly large, and growing, menu of possibilities can be constructed. One expert offers these, for example:[2]

1 Demonstrations of right: rights of passage, freedom of navigation, fisheries, and territorial claims;
2 Demonstrations of resolve: passage of shipping against opposition, bombardment of the shore, denial of passage, and denial of sea areas;
3 Amphibious landings by invitation or against opposition;
4 Evacuation of nationals;
5 Counter-terrorist operations;
6 Control of illegal immigration;
7 Counter-piracy operations;
8 Protection of offshore installations.

These contingencies appear to include the various ways in which the Soviet Union and the United States might become directly involved in a Third World

74

conflict, which in turn might lead to a confrontation between them. As a geographic postscript, one should note that states supported by the United States and the Soviet Union more or less alternate all along the littoral of the Third World. This physical relationship provides a setting for direct interaction between US and Soviet military forces, either on the ground in support of a friendly state, or – in the more likely case – at sea.

If, in a very abbreviated way, these set forth the possibilities and the structural seeds of conflict, what are the declaratory policies of the superpowers in this regard? Secretary of Defense Weinberger has been quite outspoken on the subject of US intervention in the Third World. In his Fiscal Year 1988 *Defense Report*, or 'Annual Posture Statement', one can find statements of US threat perception and intervention policy:

In a sense, we face a dual threat. First, there are the political, social, and economic instabilities endemic to many Third World nations that make them ripe for exploitation by radical or disenfranchised internal elements . . . Secondly, the Soviet Union is eager to exploit this instability directly or through its proxies, to promote terrorism, subversion (as in Grenada, Ethiopia, Afghanistan in 1978, and South Yemen) and insurgency, thereby undermining US security interests through this 'indirect approach'.[3]

Policy statements from the Soviet side follow lines much like the following excerpt from the *Seapower of the State*:

The Soviet Navy is also being utilized in the foreign policy measures of our state. But the aims of this utilization differ radically from the aims of the imperialist powers. The Soviet Navy is an instrument of a peace-loving policy and of friendship of peoples, a policy of suppressing the aggressive aspirations of imperialism, of deterring military adventures, and of decisively countering threats to the security of peoples on the part of the imperialist powers.[4]

Both sides profess to their support for the independence of developing countries, and both indicate their intentions to resist inroads by the other. As the list derived from Admiral Hill's book indicates, moreover, there appears to be no paucity of opportunities for the United States and the Soviet Union to become embroiled in a conflict in the Third World, perhaps directly. The next section of this chapter, however, indicates that the capabilities of the two superpowers to conduct military operations in the Third World are very different.

SOVIET AND US MILITARY CAPABILITIES IN THIRD WORLD: BASES AND FORCES

Soviet capability

Soviet activity in the Third World has demonstrated a large upswing over the past twenty years or so. About 24,000 Soviet military advisors are posted to about thirty countries today, which is fully four times the number of advisors so stationed in 1965. Soviet ships today call on ports in twenty different countries. In 1965 the number was zero. Overall naval out-of-area activity mushroomed from in the neighbourhood of 6,000 ship-days in 1965 to about 45,000 ship-days in 1983.[5] Today the Soviet Navy enjoys naval access in Vietnam, the Seychelles, South Yemen, Ethiopia, Angola, Guinea, Libya, Syria and Cuba. Cam Ranh Bay, Vietnam represents the Soviet Union's first true overseas base. In fact, it is now the 'largest forward deployment base and staging facility outside the Soviet Union'. Squadrons of both Bear- and Badger-type aircraft operate from Vietnamese airfields. These deployments of strike aircraft extend Soviet operational reach by 2,000 miles beyond the Japanese island choke points. They threaten the PRC, all of ASEAN's capitals, the Indonesian straits, US bases in the Philippines, northern Australia, and all important sea lanes. And, as an additional complication, amphibious exercises conducted in the Gulf of Tonkin in the spring of 1984 were the first demonstrations of Soviet power-projection capabilities in that part of the world.[6] With the exception of Cam Ranh Bay, these are not true naval bases with a full range of logistic replenishment, repair, communications and training support. They do offer at a minimum, however, protected berthing and access to tenders and supply ships.

The US Secretary of Defense claims, moreover, that 'Soviet naval activity recently has been to acquire assets that could help them project their power at great distances. Their first two heavy aircraft carriers are already well advanced.'[7] Also, Soviet air forces enjoy access at each of the places listed above for naval access with the exception of Guinea. This extension of the reach of Soviet tactical air power has been noteworthy, and brings a very necessary capability to whatever military activity might be contemplated in the Third World. In fact, the 1983 deployment of *Badger* strike aircraft to Cam Ranh Bay in Vietnam was the first Soviet deployment of strike aircraft outside the Warsaw Pact since 1970.[8]

Ships that would be especially useful in interventionary action in the Third World include:

1   Four *Kiev*-class small aircraft carriers, each of which carry approximately thirty-five aircraft in a mixture of *Forger* vertical take off and landing aircraft.
2   Two *Ivan Rogov* amphibious assault ships, each of which can lift a reinforced (thirty armoured personnel carriers, ten tanks) battalion of Soviet naval infantry troops and three air-cushion landing craft. The Soviet total inventory of seventy hovercraft for amphibious operations stands as the world's largest.
3   On the order of twenty-five amphibious vehicle landing ships, and an additional fifty amphibious assault landing ships, which are much smaller

than the *Ivan Rogov* class. The latter classes would be of marginal utility for out-of-area operations unless they were forward-based. Transfers of amphibious ships to South Yemen, Algeria, Indonesia, India, Iraq and Somalia bear witness to the fact that the Kremlin is sensitive to this fact as well.

4   Reconfigured roll-on/roll-off (RO/RO) ships have been used to experiment with vertical take off and landing aircraft, much in the same way the British used some of their merchant ships in the Falklands war of 1982. Moreover, '. . . the current Soviet inventory of roll-on/roll-off and roll-on/float-off ships comprises over 100 units . . . The average RO/RO in the Soviet merchant marine can carry 125 medium tanks. The RO/RO ships alone can move up to five Soviet Motorised Rifle Divisions in a one-time lift'.[9]

5   The Soviet merchant fleet is administratively controlled by the Navy. It contains over 500 ships that might be useful to out-of-area operations, and increases the Soviet sealift capability to five divisions.

6   Two hospital ships which, while their appearance in the Soviet naval order of battle seems non-threatening, are the best indicator of the Soviets' intention to be prepared to treat battle casualties in remote areas of the world.

The Soviet 'marine corps' which they call 'Naval Infantry' has fewer than 20,000 fighting men split across the four Soviet fleet areas. This is a modest force, especially compared to the US Marine Corps, but it is in keeping with the amount of assault lift the Soviet Navy can provide. In airborne troops, in contrast, the seven divisions of the Soviet Airborne Forces (VDV), each of which has about 8,000 men, is fully three times the US strength in this area. Interestingly, the VDV is not under the regular command structure of the Soviet Armed Forces, but has its operational lines through a special directorate, an indicator that the leadership in the Kremlin wishes to exert a special degree of control over this capability.

The logistic support the Soviet military provides for its forces stands as one of its most prominent weaknesses. Typically, Soviet forces require reinforcement and re-supply within four to five days. In contrast, US forces arrive in a posture that is self-sustaining for up to sixty days. Soviet Transport Aviation (VTA) has concentrated its capability on the ability to move forces and material on internal lines within the Soviet Union. In comparison to the US strategic airlift force, the VTA exhibits shorter range and smaller lift capacity. The trends point towards greater size and capability for the VTA, however. It has more than doubled in the past decade, and the Soviet commercial carrier, *Aeroflot* could add about 25 per cent to the VTA's cargo-carrying capability and increase its passenger capability by a factor of about three. In operational terms, a good approximation would be that at ranges less than 2,000 miles from the Soviet Union, VTA can deploy about 30,000 troops in a single sortie of existing VTA aircraft, and close the force in less than twelve hours.

Airlift has utility in bringing small amounts of material and people quickly to the scene, but the bulk of re-supply must be transported by sea. In either case – airlift or sealift – there must be suitable secure locations for off-loading, and in-theatre transportation to distribute the materials once they arrive.

The ships and aircraft that might be brought to the locus of a crisis in the Third World need frequent replenishment. While ships carry large amounts of fuel with them, they also use fuel at a fairly high rate. Most of today's ships, moreover, unlike their predecessors of the First and Second World Wars, require distillate or refined fuel. The importance of this requirement resides in the fact that even a nearby, friendly, oil-producing nation might be incapable of keeping a ship that burns refined fuel from running dry.

For other than nuclear-powered ships, the first limiting logistic factor in the absence of open hostilities is fuel. Next comes food. Of course, should weapons be used, they might well be expended faster than fuel. The weapons of naval warfare tend towards the large calibre variety, and ship magazines cannot accommodate very many of them. Fuel, food and ordnance – all require at-sea replenishment or nearby shore points of re-supply if ships are to be sustained in an area geographically remote from their home bases.

The normal mode of operations for the Soviet Navy, is 'at home'. In general, only 15 per cent of Soviet ships are regularly deployed away from local waters, whereas the US Navy maintains at least twice that percentage of ships away from home port. It has been estimated that the daily petroleum product requirement for the deployed Soviet naval units is about 5,000 tons. Naval replenishment ships with major ocean-going capability – which number eleven in the Soviet Pacific fleet, and seven each in the Baltic and North Fleets – provide about two-thirds of the Soviet Navy's needs, while their merchant ships cover the remainder.[10]

Support capability that is not mobile must be provided from the homeland, from friends and allies, or with the consent of others from advance bases. As was mentioned previously, the Soviets enjoy access to a variety of countries in the Third World, and logistic and administrative support would probably be available to their ships in time of crisis. On the other hand, it is unlikely in the absence of major deployments of tactical aircraft from the Soviet Union to such bases that they would be able to offer direct combat support to Soviet forces.

US capability

The United States maintains large contingents of army troops only in central Europe and in South Korea. Nevertheless, a group of air bases and navy marine corps bases around the world has great utility for power-projection operations in the Third World. Principal among the former, one can list:

Lajes Field, Azores;
Howard Air Force Base, Panama;
Clark Air Base, Philippines;
Andersen Air Force Base, Guam;
Kadena Air Base, Okinawa;
Izmir and Ankara Air Stations, and Incirlik Air Base, Turkey;
Iraklion Air Station, Crete;
Hellenikon Air Base, Greece;
Comiso Air Station, Sicily.

The latter include:

Guantanamo Bay Naval Station and Naval Air Station, Cuba;
Agana, Guam Naval Air Station and Naval Ship Repair Facility;
Camp Smedley D. Butler, Kawasaki Marine Corps Base, Okinawa;
Naval Station Subic Bay, Philippines;
Navy Support Facility, Diego Garcia;
Naval Air Station, Sigonella, Sicily.

The capability represented by these various bases differs greatly, and their availability for supporting military operations in the Third World is subject to the particular arrangements that have been made with the host country and the political climate prevailing at the time. In addition to bases, however, the United States maintains 'host nation' agreements and facilities to support the possible deployment of military forces to remote locations. These are not bases, but facilities constructed in such places as Egypt, Kenya, Oman, Somalia and elsewhere.

Periodically base-rights agreements must be updated with host countries, most recently highlighted by US negotiations with Greece, Spain and Portugal. Of greatest prominence, however, has been the raging debate over the most important US bases for contingencies in the Third World – those in the Philippine Islands. It is readily evident that the functions performed by these bases, Subic Bay and Clark, could not fully be duplicated anywhere else in the Pacific – that much is admitted by proponents and opponents alike. The current prospectus continues to be that the new Philippine government will fulfil the agreement for US use of the bases until they are due for renegotiation in 1991. Renewal of the agreement will depend in large measure on what transpires between now and then.

The capability of United States military forces for power projection in the Third World in direct comparison to their Soviet counterparts can be generally assessed as superior, with but a few minor exceptions. In tactical air capability, the US aircraft carrier is clearly unsurpassed. At present, the United States maintains a fleet of fourteen deployable large aircraft carriers, and it's building toward a force of fifteen. In addition to the normal complement of fighting ships that would accompany the aircraft carrier – cruisers, destroyers, frigates and nuclear-powered submarines in direct support – the United States maintains the following forces that might be useful in a contingency operation in the Third World:

1   Three active US Marine Corps Divisions, about one division of which can be transported in Navy assault shipping. A Marine Assault Division with its own reinforcing air wing – called a Marine Amphibious Force, or MAF – numbers over 30,000 troops, 70 tanks, 280 fixed-wing aircraft and 340 helicopters.

2   The Marine Corps is further organised into Marine Amphibious Brigades (MABs), which approximate the size of a regiment. MABs are also very heavy in organic air power, counting over 200 aircraft, both fixed wing and helicopters in their numbers. Three MABs are supported by the three squadrons of Maritime Prepositioning Ships that are now operational – one each in the Atlantic, Pacific and Indian Ocean areas.[11]

3   Amphibious lift ships, numbering over 150 in the late 1960s, but the inventory of which has declined to less than half that today. Several new classes of major amphibious ships are under construction, and the navy is purchasing air-cushion landing craft leading toward a force goal of about ninety.

4   Two hospital ships, recently converted from surplus 90,000 ton tankers. Each has a 1,000-bed capacity.

5   In addition to one air assault division and one airborne division the US Army can now point to three light infantry divisions in its force structure. According to the Commanding General of those forces: 'Light infantry divisions . . . can deploy with speed and agility in a pre-crisis or low-intensity setting and can be augmented to be employed in a mid- to high-intensity situation. The light infantry divisions increase flexibility, rapidity, and sustainability of response.'[12]

6   A very substantial strategic, or inter-theatre, airlift capability that now stands at about nearly 40 million ton-miles per day, and is building toward a goal of 66 million ton-miles per day.

7   A sealift capability that has atrophied over time, but is enjoying a new injection of vitality as a result of the efforts of former Secretary of the Navy, John Lehman. According to the Secretary of Defense, the various portions of

the sealift fleet are capable of carrying '85 per cent of our 1,000,000 ton goal of unit equipment in a single voyage'.[13]

8 By far, the world's foremost capability for at-sea replenishment. Eleven fast combat-support ships sail with carrier battle groups, and the plan is to purchase three more of them. A group of fleet oilers shuttle fuel from shore sites to the support ships organic to the battle group, and ammunition, tender (repair) and stores ships round out the inventory.

From the foregoing, it is evident that both superpowers maintain a variety of instruments that might be used for expeditionary purposes in the Third World. A great amount of variation exists also in their striking power, their sustainability and their readiness. Given this backdrop of the ways forces might be employed, and the forces available to the United States and the Soviet Union, what are the prospects for direct conflict between the superpowers, and how might such conflict be limited?

PROSPECTS FOR DIRECT CONFLICT AND ITS LIMITATION

In general, the perception among analysts centres on what has been called 'the fundamental rule of prudence for avoiding nuclear war'. This rule holds that 'neither should initiate use of any kind of force against the military forces of the other super-power'.[14] Another expert holds that:

It is conceivable that two lesser powers, or one lesser power and a Super Power could engage in a maritime conflict that would be decided by the balance of aggregate resources. But, once that conflict reaches the stage of *folie à deux*, it is no longer reasonable to suppose that it could remain primarily maritime, that it could continue to be limited or that it could have any meaningfully decisive outcome.[15]

The basis for this line of reasoning stems from the conviction that direct conflict between the United States and the Soviet Union must necessarily follow a rapid and uncontrollable powder trail to a widespread war between them that would soon lead to the use of nuclear weapons.

This must be classified either as a most pessimistic view of the leadership existing in the two countries, or as a vote of no confidence in their ability to control their military forces, or as a belief that the escalatory process is so mechanical that it would thwart human intervention. Of course, it might also be seen as an attempt by analysts to sensitise the superpowers to the possibility of conflict between them in order to preclude such conflict. Yet, although the Carter Doctrine promises US military involvement in the Persian Gulf in response to specified actions by others in that area, there is reason to believe that if US and Soviet forces should be drawn directly into conflict with one another, policymakers would realise in the first instance that the situation did not touch on their core security values, and therefore must be limited in scope and intensity. Indeed, there are grounds for suggesting that if the military forces of the two sides began shooting at one another in the Third World, forces in other geographic areas would be putting as much distance as possible between themselves and the forces of the other side precisely so that the conflict would not spread. It is difficult to imagine that either side would prefer that a confrontation in the Third World should ignite additional conflicts elsewhere.

Consequently, if Soviet and US forces were shooting at one another in the Indian Ocean, South China Sea or Gulf of Mexico, the reasonable expectation should be *not* that a nuclear war would be the result, but that the US Sixth Fleet and the Soviet Fifth Escadra in the Mediterranean and all forces elsewhere would sail in opposite directions so that they could not be put in the awkward position of saluting one another while their cohorts were killing each other in a different part of the world. Very powerful pressures would come to play to keep the conflict encapsulated, because neither side would assess the risks to be worth the limited gains that might be made: that is to say, the stakes would not be high enough, and neither would seek to raise the ante.

The very tone of the oft-repeated 'tests to be applied when the United States is considering committing US forces to combat' emphasised by former US Secretary of Defense Caspar Weinberger strikingly underscores these assertions. They provide such powerful evidence of the careful consideration of these important questions, at least by officials of the US government, that they bear extended quotation here:

1 The United States should not commit forces to combat unless our vital interests are at stake . . .
2 If we are unwilling to commit the forces or resources necessary to achieve our objectives, or if the objective is not important enough, we should not commit our forces at all.
3 The relationship between our objectives and the forces we have committed – their size, composition, and disposition – must be continually reassessed and adjusted as necessary . . . We must continuously keep as a beacon light before us the basic question: Is a vital US interest at stake?
4 Before the United States commits combat forces abroad, the US government should have some reasonable assurance of the support of the American people and their elected representatives in the Congress . . .
5 Finally, the commitment of US forces to combat should be a last resort – only after diplomatic, political, economic and other efforts have been made to protect our vital interests.[16]

While not all of this should be accepted uncritically, it was a rather clear declaratory statement of intentions from a leading government official of the Reagan Administration. And, whether or not one believes that the 'rules' are unduly and unreasonably restrictive, their existence will almost certainly have an effect on the thinking of decision-makers in time of crisis.

Nothing comparable exists on the Soviet side. Moreover, the genuine concern that a direct US–Soviet conflict might spread in both geographic scope and perhaps involve the use or the threat of use of nuclear weapons cannot be dismissed out of hand. There is a real possibility that a conflict could erupt suddenly and spread quickly and uncontrollably. Nevertheless, there are reasons to be optimistic. The statement of Secretary Weinberger cited above demonstrates a mind set that is very cautious, not trigger-happy. Furthermore, it is very likely that in any situation in which US and Soviet forces might become directly embroiled with one another then the rules of engagement will be very restrictive; and the Soviet Navy and the US Navy have a twenty-five year legacy of their 'Incidents at Sea' agreement that will undoubtedly act as a damper on rash behaviour. That agreement will be examined later in this chapter.

Soviet thinking on the subject also supports a belief that the superpowers will recognise that their vital interests lie elsewhere, and that they will seek to encapsulate and to defuse any open conflict between them in the Third World. According to Benjamin Lambeth:

Since the Soviets are risk-averse by disposition and constantly fear the prospect of losing control of events, any confrontation in which the forces of the opposing superpowers are directly engaged must be viewed with the utmost concern and managed with appropriate dispatch . . . For them, war of any sort is to be avoided with every effort unless circumstances rule out less uncompromising alternatives.[17]

It is possible to suggest situations in which the United States and the Soviet Union might become caught up in a Third World conflict, especially at sea. It might happen if, for example, two adjacent Third World countries, one supported by the United States and the other by the Soviet Union went to war. It is not difficult to visualise a time when a beleaguered client would request support from the nearby maritime forces of its superpower benefactor. An easy extension leads directly to a scenario where military forces supporting friends or allies become engaged with one another. Indeed, the situation might become one of a test of fidelity – a superpower feeling obliged to support its client to demonstrate its commitment to the integrity of its other alliances. Another entirely plausible possibility is that one of the belligerents might establish a maritime exclusion zone (such as the 200-mile zone the British declared around the Falkland Islands in 1982) underwritten by its superpower friend. The other superpower might feel obliged to offer a challenge in order to protect its right to use the seas.

THE 'INCIDENTS AT SEA' AGREEMENT, RULES OF ENGAGEMENT, AND PROSPECTS FOR MARITIME ARMS CONTROL

To help dampen the propensity for small encounters to blossom into more inflammatory events, the United States and the Soviet Union concluded in 1972 an agreement 'On the Prevention of Incidents on and over the High Seas'.[18] Following some potentially dangerous occurrences between units of their Navies, the two sides concluded that setting forth some 'rules of the game', along with a mechanism to review and update them would be helpful. The agreement 'has reduced the number of dangerous incidents and cases of harassment at sea'.[19]

In addition to underscoring the 'good manners' clauses of the maritime rules of the road – the 'INCSEA' agreement, as it is known, proscribes certain practices that contribute to tension or that might be dangerous in their ambiguity. Specifically, these are the most important provisions:

1   Military formations – most importantly those in which ships are launching or landing aircraft, or engaged in underway replenishment – are explicitly recognised and accorded special privileges;
2   surveillance, while permitted, must be undertaken so as not to embarrass or endanger the platform under surveillance;
3   simulated attacks are prohibited, as are launching of 'any objects' in the direction of or illuminating the navigation bridge of 'passing ships'; and,
4   performance by aircraft of acrobatics over ships, or dropping objects near ships in such a way as to be hazardous.

A 1973 protocol extended some of the provisions, most notably the prohibition on simulated attacks, to the non-military ships of each party.[20]

INCSEA stands as an excellent example of an arms control regime, or confidence-building measure, that has helped to ease tensions and reduce the possibility of inadvertent conflict. If tensions were high, however, while its long-term conditioning of the parties might have a beneficial effect, the agreement could not be relied upon to maintain the peace, for some of the measures it prohibits might well fall under what one or the other of the competitors believed was necessary to the accomplishment of its mission, or to its survival. In such a case one enters the realm of rules of engagement.

Rules of engagement (ROE) should be thought of as the instructions provided to military forces by policy-makers defining the situations and prerequisites under which they are permitted to use force prior to an actual outbreak of hostilities. Traditionally and typically, it has been the general understanding that rules of engagement for Western countries have hinged on the policy that one does not initiate hostile action. Returning fire is sanctioned, but provoking hostile acts is not. The fact of the matter is different, however. According to a legal expert: 'It is a common misconception that under the peacetime ROE a commander must "take the first hit" and cannot act in self-defence until the opposing force has missiles away. That is not the law and is not required by our general peacetime ROE . . . Whether or not a force is declared hostile, where the hostile intent amounts to a threat of imminent attack, the right exists to use proportional force in self-defence by all authorised means available.'[21] Premised on the fact that anti-ship missiles launched from close range can be fatal to a ship, US naval units might be expected to act if unambiguous 'hostile intent' were detected.

Permitting the use of force under rules of engagement based on indicators of hostile intent – all such indicators of which, by the way, would be contrary to the Incidents at Sea agreement – is one method to gain control of the rules of engagement. The Maritime Exclusion Zone around the Falklands also attempted to capture control of the rules, and one might expect in time of increased tension or crisis such zones, or cordons sanitaire, would be created. Whether the announcement of such a zone would serve to offer a more rapid path to open conflict or would serve as a powerful, clear signal of intent that would tend to dampen the enthusiasm for adventure cannot be assessed in the absence of a real context. Persuasive argument might be made for either outcome, depending on the specifics of the encounter.

As the May 1987 Iraqi attack on the USS *Stark* in the Persian Gulf demonstrates, however, hostile intent is not particularly easy to identify, and there are usually inhibitions at work to forestall precipitate action. Finally, it should be made very clear that the rules of engagement are fully under the control of each country for its own military forces. While, according to the discussion above, normal US peacetime ROE permit acting in self-defence to prevent attack, the rules can be made more restrictive should a situation warrant.

The Incidents at Sea agreement does not exhaust the possibilities for arms control in the maritime arena. Soviet policy-makers have been particularly active in this regard. For example, in a letter to the Secretary General of the United Nations, then Soviet Foreign Minister Gromyko issued a comprehensive call for:

1   not expanding naval activities of states in areas of conflicts or tensions;
2   eliminating situations where naval fleets of major powers cruise for a long time far away from their shores;

3 withdrawal of ships carrying nuclear weapons from certain ocean and sea
   areas and the fixing of limits on the presence of ships of different types there;
4 a limit on number of principal types of naval ships;
5 future reductions, on a balanced basis, of the number of ships making up the
   regular navies of major powers. Special attention 'then' to warships such as
   aircraft carriers, 'which are of an especially destabilising nature';
6 imposition of limitations on anti-submarine forces and systems;
7 measures with regard to naval bases in foreign territories; and,
8 coordinating the enforcing of Confidence Building Measures to help prevent
   conflict situations.[22]

Most of these were echoed in Secretary Gorbachev's speech in Vladivostok in
July 1986.[23] He has also announced that: 'If the United States, which is situated
thousands on thousands of miles from the Mediterranean, pulled its fleet out of
there, the Soviet Union would simultaneously do the same.'[24]

No examples of a US maritime arms-control agenda seem to be in the offing,
nor does the US appear interested in negotiating on the Soviet agenda. It would
seem self-evident that the world's greatest landpower would seek ways to hobble
the world's greatest seapower, and to reduce the effectiveness of the maritime
alliance it faces to the West through arms control.

CONCLUSIONS

This analysis yields several major conclusions. First, competition in the Third
World between the superpowers should be thought of as a peacetime
phenomenon. One might expect that if Soviet forces were left adrift in the Third
World in time of war they would be mere sacrificial forces with little save
nuisance value.

Second, both the United States and the Soviet Union have expressed their
interest in – and intention of – conducting affairs of state in the Third World.
Both have political and economic interests there, of varying degrees. The two are
represented by military forces in widespread areas of the world. Although it
appears unlikely that US and Soviet land or air forces would become directly
engaged – and even if they did the numbers of combatants would probably be
small – such a possibility cannot be ruled out completely. More likely, though,
would be a situation in which naval forces might come into direct conflict.

Third, the Soviet Union maintains large military forces optimised for
operations on the immediate Soviet periphery. Geostrategic circumstances
endow the Soviet Union with a particular ability to exert influence and pose a
direct threat to its neighbours. At distances removed from its borders, however,

86

the strength of the Soviet Union, primarily a land power, atrophies sharply. The lack of high-quality organic tactical air power is a critical limitation upon Soviet power-projection capability. This means that power-projection operations cannot be seriously considered if opposition, particularly by air forces, is anticipated. This in turn means that large operations cannot be mounted beyond the range of strong support from land-based aircraft.

The fourth conclusion is that the United States has a much weaker homeland defence capability than the Soviet Union, and relatively much stronger ability to project power overseas. With its powerful and growing force of large aircraft carriers, its unequalled amphibious assault capability, and its ability to sustain its forces in areas far removed from the US homeland, the United States maintains by far the world's largest, most highly skilled and well-equipped arsenal of interventionary and expeditionary forces.

Fifth, while direct conflict between US and Soviet military forces in the Third World is conceivable, especially in maritime environments, the possibility of uncontrolled escalation or the geographic spreading of such a conflict is low. Even so, the Incidents at Sea agreement has been useful in establishing and regulating norms of behaviour between ships and aircraft of the United States and the Soviet Union operating in close proximity to one another. It has helped, therefore to defuse potential crisis-sparking situations. Its value is clearly restricted to peacetime, however, and to disciplining at-sea commanders in time of crisis, since they would always be aware of exceeding the bounds of the agreement. In potential situations of direct conflict both sides will have a stake in maintaining control through their selection of rules of engagement. While there are certainly dangers of misinterpretation and inadvertent attack, there is also a wealth of evidence that decision-makers on both sides are amply aware of the problem, and unless a major war between them was desired for some reason, would take strong actions so that a local confrontation in the Third World between the superpowers would not spread.

NOTES

1 This theme is pursued, along with the warning that Central America might become a new strategic front, in Zbigniew Brzezinski, *Game Plan: A Geostrategic Framework for the Conduct of the US – Soviet Contest* (Boston, MA: The Atlantic Monthly Press, 1986).

2 Rear-Admiral J. R. Hill, *Maritime Strategy for Medium Powers* (Annapolis, MD: Naval Institute Press, 1986), pp. 117 ff.

3 Secretary of Defense Caspar W. Weinberger, *Annual Report to the Congress, Fiscal Year 1988* (Washington: US Government Printing Office, 1987), p. 57.

4 Admiral Sergei G. Gorshkov, *The Seapower of the State*, 2nd edn., p. 365.

5 See Commander Bruce W. Watson, USN, 'The Soviet Navy in the Third World' in James L. George ed., *The Soviet and Other Communist Navies: The View from the Mid-1980s* (Annapolis, MD: Naval Institute Press, 1986), pp. 251–72.

6 See 'Statement of Rear-Admiral John L. Butts, US Navy, Director of Naval Intelligence before the Seapower and Force Projection Subcommittee of the Senate Armed Services Committee on the Naval Threat', 26 February 1985.
7 Weinberger, *Defense Report FY 1988*, p. 66.
8 Butts, 'Statement'.
9 Weinberger, *Defense Report FY 1988*, p. 37.
10 G. Jacobs, 'Soviet Navy: Logistic Limitations', *Navy International*, October 1986, pp. 602–3.
11 The Maritime Prepositioning Ships permit administrative landings only, they cannot be used in the face of opposition. They feature 'balanced spread loading', which means that no one ship carries the full inventory of any critical item, and all carry water, fuel, etc. The MPS can be off-loaded in three days at a pier, or in five days in a stream or roadstead. With favourable geography, they can close with the airlifted marine brigade in ten days.
12 General Joseph T. Palestra, US Army, 'FORSCOM: Ongoing Search for Excellence', *Army* (October 1986), p. 51.
13 Weinberger, *Defense Report FY 1988*, p. 231.
14 Alexander L. George, 'Crisis Management: The Interaction of Political and Military Considerations', *Survival* (September/October 1984), p. 232.
15 Sir James Cable, *Diplomacy at Sea* (Annapolis, MD: Naval Institute Press, 1985), p. 50.
16 These were first set forth in a speech to the US National Press Club, which was delivered on 28 November 1984, and reported in the *Washington Post*, 29 November 1984, p. A1, *passim*. This list is extracted from Weinberger, *Defense Report FY 1987*, pp. 78–9.
17 *On Thresholds in Soviet Military Thought* RAND P 6860 (Santa Monica, CA: Rand Corporation, March 1983), p. 5.
18 US Department of State, *Prevention of Incidents On and Over the High Seas*, Treaties and Other International Acts Series (TIAS) 7279.
19 For an extended discussion, see Sean M. Lynn-Jones, 'A Quiet Success for Arms Control: Preventing Incidents at Sea', *International Security*, 9, 4 (Spring 1985), pp. 154–84.
20 In July 1986, the United Kingdom and the Soviet Union concluded a bilateral Incidents at Sea agreement, which in all important respects is the same as the US–Soviet agreement. Text in *Naval Forces*, 8, 1 (1987), pp. 14–15.
21 Captain J. Ashley Roach, JAGC, US Navy, 'Rules of Engagement', *Naval War College Review* (January–February 1983), pp. 47–8.
22 This letter was reprinted in *Defense Science 2002* (October 1984).
23 There the General Secretary called for agreement to 'reduce the activity of military fleets in the Pacific and above all, nuclear-armed ships', and for 'restriction of rivalry in anti-submarine weapons – specifically, an arrangement to refrain from anti-submarine activity in certain zones of the Pacific would help strengthen stability'. Mikhail Gorbachev's speech at the ceremony to present the Order of Lenin to Vladivostok, *Pravda*, 29 July 1986.
24 Mikhail Gorbachev's speech at a dinner for President Chadli Benjedid of Algeria, 26 March 1986, reported in the *Washington Post*, 27 March 1986, p. A–9.

5　Superpower arms transfers to the Third World

Joanna Spear and Stuart Croft

The transfer of arms to Third World states through sales, credits and aid has long been a foreign-policy tool of the superpowers. The tool has been used both to gain allies and to protect existing allies from the adversary superpower and its clients. If arms transfers are one of the most useful foreign-policy instruments available to Moscow and Washington, however, they are also an instrument which engages the competitive urges of both superpowers. In many regions, arms transfers by one superpower elicit a response from the other. To regulate this competition and manage their relationship, the superpowers have accepted constraints on, and exhibited restraint in, the use of arms transfers. The difficulty, however, is that the Third World recipients have not always appreciated the constraints and have actively opposed the restraint. This has given arms transfers an important North–South dimension which both overlays and complicates the East–West dimension.

In order to disentangle the complexities of the arms-transfer process, this chapter is divided into four parts. The first assesses the utility of arms transfers as an instrument of superpower foreign policies. The second examines the kind of restraints in the use of that tool that are accepted because of the dangers attendant on superpower competition. The third section looks at the attempts to formalise such restraints in order to develop greater predictability and stability. The final section examines the role of Third World recipients of arms transfers and considers the strategies they adopt to ameliorate their dependence on Moscow and Washington – strategies that, in some cases at least, may seriously complicate superpower efforts to impose stability.

THE UTILITY OF ARMS TRANSFERS

The nature of Soviet–American political competition has led both nations to acquire and maintain friends and allies throughout the Third World. Important geopolitical regions outside the military blocs in Europe have been vigorously contested as the superpowers have struggled to obtain the allegiance and support of Third World states, and to impose their dominance in particular regions. Third World states themselves have encouraged this process, sometimes deliberately, sometimes unwittingly, by seeking superpower commitments to their security. In response the superpowers have initiated actions or adopted policies designed to demonstrate their commitment and support. These include naval visits, the deployment of forces and use of bases on the territory of the Third World state and the provision of arms.

Arms transfers have been seen as a useful foreign-policy tool for military, political and economic reasons. The superpowers differ from medium-sized suppliers such as France and Britain in that the latter tend to be motivated primarily by economic factors. For Moscow and Washington, in contrast, political and military considerations are dominant.

The traditional rationale for supplying arms to the Third World is the military requirement to fulfil the security needs of allies. As one study put it, 'Security assistance, and in particular arms sales, are an increasingly important dimension of US policy, which seeks to ensure the security of friends and allies and thereby enhance its own.'[1] A variant on this theme occurred in the early 1970s with the declaration of the Nixon Doctrine, through which the United States increased the supply of arms to allies in order to lessen the likelihood of direct American intervention in various regions. While this impulse remains, albeit in diluted form, transfers also make superpower intervention easier should it become necessary. Arms supplies ensure that allies have equipment in their inventories compatible with that of the superpower patron. This is an important logistical consideration for both superpowers, as it enhances their ability to project power by facilitating joint military action with allies in times of crisis. In addition, transfers provide opportunities for military equipment to be tested in a variety of climatic and geographic conditions and in a range of battlefield contingencies.

Arms transfers are politically valuable to the superpowers because they provide access to and influence over Third World elites. Michael Klare has concluded that 'Major arms transfers – particularly those involving high-technology equipment – can provide the supplier with considerable influence over the political behaviour of the recipient.'[2] Former Secretary of Defense James Schlesinger concurs in this judgement and has argued that 'The degree of influence of the supplier is potentially substantial and, typically, those relationships are long enduring.'[3] Once the equipment is in the inventory of Third World states they become dependent on superpower support and expertise for training, maintenance and spare parts. The ability to cut off this support can be a source of considerable influence for Washington and Moscow, not least because arms transfers may be used by Third World governments to retain power and suppress internal dissent or opposition. Indeed, knowledge of this potential sanction may be enough in itself to moderate the behaviour of recipient states. If this does not work then the superpower may still be able to achieve its goals through more overt threats to halt the supply of spare parts or to withdraw support.

In short, arms transfers are important to the superpowers as a means of acquiring influence over Third World states and influencing both their internal politics and their external orientation. Arms transfers also help to demarcate or reinforce spheres of influence and can be particularly important in underlining superpower commitments to particular states. Arms transfers can be regarded, therefore, as a major tool in the superpower competition for power and influence. In this connection, Third World allies are not valued in terms of the resources they bring to that competition, but more as constituents or objects of superpower rivalry. Such an approach reflects a strong tendency in both Washington and Moscow to indulge in zero-sum assessments of geopolitical competition. It also increases the desire of both superpowers to attempt to make pre-emptive transfers in order to prevent the adversary from obtaining a foothold or expanding its influence in a certain state or region. Indeed, arms transfers are one of the major tools available to the superpowers to send a signal of support for a particular state both to other states in the area and, more significantly, to the rival superpower. In this matter, however, there is a major asymmetry between the superpowers. Whereas the United States has other means of obtaining influence (such as economic aid and the supply of highly valued manufactured goods) arms transfers are a particularly important tool for a Soviet Union which has been conspicuously unsuccessful in penetrating international economic markets.[4]

RESTRAINT IN THE USE OF ARMS TRANSFERS

Despite these motivations for superpower arms transfers, there seem to be several mutually acknowledged and accepted limits on the use of this foreign-policy tool. These result from the need to manage and constrain the superpower competition and can be understood as a mixture of prescription and proscription. They pertain to four different though not mutually exclusive areas: the enticement of Third World states to change blocs, regional stability, regional arms racing, and Third World conflicts. The limits are not absolute or immutable, of course. Nevertheless, it is possible to discern patterns of restraint. Furthermore, not only do these patterns seem to be consciously recognised by both superpowers but also there appears to be a degree of reciprocity in the way in which the superpowers observe the limits – something which makes it possible to talk about 'norms of competition'.

The first area where the superpowers mutually accept the need for restraint is on cross-bloc transfers and the enticement of Third World states to realign. There is a strong element of expediency in this. Attempting to entice Third World states to change allegiance is, under most circumstances, a high risk political strategy that is unlikely to yield a high reward. Cross-bloc arms transfers add to the political risks involved in enticement since they are unlikely to endow a superpower with additional influence unless the recipient state is already in the process of leaving the orbit of its present patron. Additionally, such transfers run the risk of granting the adversary superpower access to one's own advanced technology – a risk which is more salient for the United States than for the Soviet Union which has few technological leads to guard.

Notwithstanding such considerations, enticement has taken place under certain circumstances. It has occurred, for example, when there has been a radical change in the domestic politics of the Third World state, making its orientation incompatible with the ideology of its erstwhile patron. Alternatively, it has occurred either when the patron state has ceased to demonstrate a strong commitment to its arms recipient in the Third World, or the client has adopted an independent stance in which its desire to realign is manifest. The growing restiveness of the client and the weakening of the patron's commitment tend to go hand in hand with the result that the strains in the relationship very obviously offer opportunities to the adversary superpower. This was the case with the Egyptian defection from the Soviet to the American camp in the early and mid-1970s. Sadat's dissatisfaction with the level of Soviet support and Moscow's reluctance to give Sadat all the arms he desired coincided with Kissinger's desire to exclude the Soviet Union from the Middle East. In circumstances such as these, the transfer of arms by the other superpower has been accepted as a legitimate and useful instrument in the attempts to attract the Third World state from the adversary's tutelage. Another way in which this could occur was illustrated in the late 1970s by the move of Ethiopia from the American camp into that of the Soviet Union and the corresponding reversal of Somalia's political allegiance (although only Ethiopia's shift in loyalties was accompanied by a change in internal regime). Both nations received substantial supplies of arms from their new superpower patron.

What is perhaps most interesting about these examples is that they are unusual. It would be going too far to suggest that they are the exceptions which prove the rule. Yet, merely because there are exceptions does not mean that the rule has no meaning or effect. When a state obviously has a very close allegiance to the adversary superpower, that allegiance is not seriously challenged either through the use of arms transfers or any other instrument. Yet, as the examples show, the fluidity of Third World politics offers opportunities and poses problems for the superpowers. Domestic political change or the dynamics of regional politics mean that the traditional patterns of involvement by Moscow and Washington no longer prevail. In these circumstances the application of the rules is much more difficult.

The second area of mutual restraint in the use of the arms-transfer instrument relates to concerns over regional stability. Each superpower has attempted to maintain broad stability in the relationships between its own allies and those of the other superpower. Indeed, both Washington and Moscow have tacitly recognised that the transfer either of large quantities of weaponry which exceed those held by other regional adversaries, or the transfer of weaponry with a higher level of sophistication, might tempt the recipient to attack other states in any area in which there are strong local rivalries. Conversely, it might encourage regional enemies to launch preventive strikes before the weaponry is in place. Both situations have been recognised as undesirable by the superpowers since they fear loss of control over the ensuing conflict, with the result that it could lead to direct superpower confrontation or humiliating retreat. To prevent this, the superpowers have tried to retain the maximum possible control over transferred weaponry through the deployment of civilian and military personnel to provide support and assistance, through careful spare-parts management and through the maintenance of control over essential logistical support. The Soviet Union has for a number of years kept a large number of its advisors in Syria for this reason, and deployed its own personnel in Syrian SAM batteries in the Beka'a Valley.[5] The United States followed a similar line through careful management of its arms transfer relations with Iran until the early 1970s. Large numbers of American personnel were employed to support and maintain weaponry acquired by Iran in an effort to ensure that the country could not go to war without active American backing. This policy of control over transferred weaponry has also been employed by the United States more recently in its relations with Saudi Arabia. Some critics contend, however, that even with these safeguards the supplier cannot obtain the degree of control desired and remains vulnerable to reverse leverage.

A further strategy of the superpowers for maintaining stability has been to avoid transferring high-profile weapons to low-priority areas. This helps to ensure that the political stakes are not raised beyond the strategic value of the area and that the superpowers do not become embroiled in futile competition requiring an unwarranted expenditure of resources. Another reason for restraint in relation to such areas is that major arms-transfer initiatives may be interpreted as a signal by the adversary that the area concerned is becoming a new arena for competition. The Reagan administration's decision to sell F-16 aircraft to Venezuela, for example, was seen by the Soviet Union as such a signal for the north of Latin America. Furthermore, Venezuela's neighbours felt the need to acquire weapons to counter those supplied by the United States – a need which provided the Soviet Union with an entrée to the region. At the same time Soviet influence in a region so close to the United States must be fairly tenuous. If certain areas can be maintained either as competition-free or low-level competition zones, therefore, it may have advantage to all concerned.

There has also been a degree of mutual restraint in the transfer of weaponry by the superpowers to areas deemed to be unstable. Arms suppliers generally are reluctant to become too heavily entangled in regional conflicts in which their allies are in direct opposition. Consequently, they have tended to avoid providing weapons to combatants or to states on the verge of war unless there is already a very strong link between supplier and recipient. This has been true even in the Middle East where both superpowers have considerable interests at stake and the alignments are long-standing. Although the concern with stability has not translated into a prohibition on the supply of arms to the regional combatants, there has been a desire to impose restrictions on the kinds of weapons that are transferred.

The Soviet reluctance to meet Sadat's demands for particular kinds of weapons was a major factor in the expulsion of Soviet advisors from Egypt in 1972. During the Middle East War of 1973 both Moscow and Washington supplied massive amounts of arms to the belligerents – but even then they did so in an effort to ensure that the other side did not obtain decisive advantage. Furthermore, in one sense their arms transfers can be understood as a substitute for more direct intervention. Elsewhere the superpowers have been even more cautious and have recognised that attempts to disengage when conflict is imminent may be too late if a commitment has already been made. Consequently, both superpowers have been anxious not to become too directly or too heavily involved in situations such as the Gulf War, although they have clearly sought to use arms covertly in order to gain influence in the region, particularly in Iran.

The third area of mutual restraint relates to regional arms races between Soviet and American clients. Arms races may prove particularly inimical to superpower interests and can disrupt superpower efforts at cooperation or mediation in regional conflicts. Part of the problem is that Soviet and American political stakes in a region are increased with each shipment of arms. The superpowers have therefore attempted to avoid generating or encouraging arms races. Furthermore, once an arms race has begun, they have often attempted to constrain it by controlling both quantitative and qualitative transfers of arms. In the Middle East, where the stakes are already so high, this restraint has been less evident, but it is clearly very important in other areas of the world, such as Latin America. When an arms race has occurred, the superpowers have attempted to slow it down by carefully grading the increases in the sophistication of the weaponry they supply. There has also been a recognition that superpower understandings are especially necessary in circumstances such as these. Regardless of the origins of the contest, the value of each superpower's commitment to its ally or allies is inevitably called into question and the attempts of Moscow and Washington to uphold, reinforce or re-establish their commitments can all too easily increase the potential for direct Soviet–American conflict. If such dangers are to be avoided or managed successfully by the superpowers, the signals they provide each other through the types of weaponry supplied and the timing of the delays between request and supply are particularly significant.

The fourth area of mutual restraint on the use of arms transfers relates to regional conflicts. The restraint here, however, has not been absolute. When war has broken out between superpower allies, arms have been transferred to support clients, partly to uphold commitments and partly because defeat of a client will be seen as a victory for the adversary superpower. The cessation of arms transfers as a means of indicating displeasure over a client's actions in a conflict or a potential conflict, therefore, has only been acceptable when the other superpower is unlikely to gain from such a measure. Considerations of this kind can be discerned in American arms-transfer policy towards India and Pakistan. The ban on transfers to both parties in the 1965 Indo–Pakistan War has not been repeated since, because of the Soviet Union's relationship with India and the Soviet invasion of Afghanistan, both of which led to increased American support for Pakistan. Similarly, in wars between their allies each superpower has usually matched the supplies of the adversary in order to prevent the defeat of its ally. At the same time, both superpowers have sought to keep the conflict within certain limits. Above all, each superpower has attempted to avoid directly challenging the other. This has required that each refrain from transferring weaponry into an area where nationals of the other superpower are based, thereby minimising the possibility that the adversary's forces will come under attack. The classic example of such restraint took place over Vietnam. Blechman, Nolan and Platt have argued that

Throughout the Vietnam war ... the United States and the Soviet Union avoided a direct superpower confrontation. The United States chose not to interdict the flow of military supplies to North Vietnam, avoiding targets that ran the risk of harming Soviet nationals until near the end of U.S. involvement. Meanwhile the U.S.S.R. decided not to supply certain weapons to North Vietnam that might have threatened U.S. naval vessels operating in the Gulf of Tonkin. For example, the Soviet Union did not send North Vietnam either land-based surface-to-surface missiles or fast patrol boats equipped with anti-ship missiles until 1975. Yet, these types of weapons were transferred to Soviet Middle East clients throughout this period.[6]

Although restraints of this kind have normally been accepted, on occasion one or both superpowers have chosen not to observe them. Can the restraints still be viewed as mutual and effective if they are not always observed? In this connection, it is important to distinguish between two kinds of deviations – those which are occasional and departures which are more fundamental. This is not necessarily a rigid distinction, of course, since occasional violations may develop into a more far-reaching abandonment of the restraints. Nevertheless, it is a helpful distinction which offers valuable insight into the nature of superpower competition in arms transfers.

Occasional deviations from the 'norms of competition' generally involve localised and limited departures from the restraints that are usually observed. Both the initial breach and the response of the adversary must be isolated. Although the adversary obviously reacts to the regional challenge, elsewhere that superpower continues to behave within the normal pattern of restraint. This, of course, assumes that the challenge is not of such magnitude that it is deemed to represent a direct threat requiring a vigorous and extensive response. Deviations of this kind are relatively easy to cope with and do not undermine the general principles of mutual restraint in the field of arms transfers. These principles, therefore, help to compartmentalise superpower competition, enabling Moscow and Washington to manage relations in other regions despite instability or uncertainty in one area.

If occasional deviations from the reciprocal patterns of restraint in arms transfers are manageable, serious and persistent non-compliance challenges not simply regional understandings but the very principle of mutual restraint. Such challenges come in several forms, but generally involve attempts to obtain unilateral advantage or to impose asymmetrical sacrifice. One side may simply ignore previously observed restraints by extensively transferring high-technology weaponry to various regions and by refusing to recognise the adversary's right to act similarly.

During President Reagan's first administration, the United States came close to this position before reverting to a more restrained approach. What the Reagan Administration hoped to achieve *vis-à-vis* the Soviet Union by departing from previously accepted, if still tacit, forms of restraint is open to question. It could be that in line with its aims in other key areas, the administration sought to send a message to Moscow that the United States was now prepared to compete vigorously with the Soviet Union at all levels. In this connection, the Reagan Administration's emphasis on the global nature of the Soviet threat suggests that it was reluctant to compartmentalise issues – a reluctance that was also evident in the administration's emphasis on 'horizontal escalation' of regional conflicts. An alternate explanation is that the Reagan Administration had no clear knowledge of the principles of mutual restraint or that it considered them to be less important than had previous administrations.

If the Reagan Administration's motives were open to conjecture, the effects of departing from previously observed restraints were very clear. The sale of highly sophisticated F-16s to Venezuela sharply raised the stakes in that part of Latin America, and had a destabilising effect on the region. Similarly, the administration's decision to sell F-16s to Pakistan, despite the divergent threat perceptions of patron and would-be recipient, showed a certain scepticism about or disregard for superpower restraints aimed at regional stability and especially at the prevention of arms races and regional conflicts between Soviet and American allies in the Third World. Since that time, however, the American challenge both to the Soviet Union and to the 'norms of competition' has diminished as the United States has once again appeared to accept the need for restraint in its use of arms transfers as a tool of foreign policy.

The Reagan Administration's willingness to accept mutual restraints in arms transfers, grudging and belated though it was, was partly an acknowledgement of the strength and durability of the Soviet challenge to United States interests in the Third World. It was also an acknowledgement of the limits within which American power in this area of competition had to operate. Partly because of these limits, there was a recognition in Washington that some form of tacit regulation would not only make the competition safer and more predictable, but by demanding Soviet restraint, it could be used to the advantage of the United States. These factors seem to have been recognised even more by the Congress which increasingly sought to impose restrictions on the executive in the area of arms transfers. Although these efforts are explicable partly in terms of the dynamics of congressional–executive relations, they also reflect congressional sensitivity over the impact of arms transfers on regional stability – a sensitivity that was very evident in the opposition of both House and Senate to the administration's plans to sell AWACS to Pakistan.

FORMALISING THE RESTRAINTS

The one recent attempt by the superpowers to reach a formal agreement on controlling the supply of arms to the Third World was the Conventional Arms Transfer (CAT) Talks held in four rounds in 1977–8. The CAT Talks eventually broke down largely as a result of bureaucratic disputes within the Carter Administration which led to the American rejection of the two regions suggested by the Soviet Union as candidates for restraint. One of these areas was termed 'East Asia' and, in effect, referred to China. This selection fell foul of the United States' effort to improve Sino–American relations, a policy which was being pursued at the same time as CAT control, even though the two were not entirely compatible. The Soviet Union, in fact, may have chosen the region deliberately to complicate the burgeoning Sino–American relationship. In the event, it was the arms-transfer negotiations which suffered as the Sino–American dialogue culminated in the December 1978 announcement that United States–Chinese relations were to be 'normalized'.

It is also worth emphasising that both superpowers were using similar tactics in the CAT Talks when identifying candidates for regional restraint. Each superpower's selection of regions contained one area which was defensive in nature (that is, it attempted to maintain a regional status quo in which the adversary had minimum influence), and one which was offensive in nature (that is, it involved an attempt to weaken the adversary's influence). The defensive choices were East Asia for the USSR, and Latin America for the USA. The offensive choices were 'West Asia' for the USSR (which included the close American allies of Iran and Saudi Arabia), and Sub-Saharan Africa for the United States. The latter choice reflected American concern at Soviet activities in Africa in general and in Angola and Ethiopia in particular. Indeed, at the preliminary meeting of the CAT Talks in Washington in December 1977, the Head of the American Delegation, Leslie Gelb, had been instructed by his superiors to use the occasion to protest to the Soviet delegation about the high level of Soviet involvement in Ethiopia.

If each superpower sought unilateral advantage from the CAT Talks, the negotiations were also complicated by the decline of superpower détente. Although the discussions centred around limiting arms transfers to the Third World and the basis on which this might be done, officials within the United States National Security Council and State Department viewed the talks as an opportunity to discuss the limits of permissible behaviour in the Third World – and what were regarded as the Soviet violations of these limits. This was related to the wider Soviet–American competition which was also evident in the Helsinki round held in May 1978, when the concluding joint communique made a direct link between the CAT Talks and the Basic Principles Agreement of 1972.

The problems of formalising superpower restraint were clearly demonstrated by the CAT Talks. It is obviously difficult to separate discussions on arms transfers from the wider debate concerning permissible superpower activity in the Third World. Indeed, it could be argued that one reason for entering into discussions on formalising restraint on the use of arms transfers as a foreign-policy tool is that this may help to clarify the wider 'norms of competition'. If tacit but mutually accepted restraints are sufficient to regulate superpower competition in arms transfers then, arguably, there is little need for more formal measures. On the other hand, both tacit and formal restraints may be challenged or weakened by the actions of Third World states, who may be oblivious of, or even hostile to the 'norms of competition'. This re-focuses attention on relations between the superpowers and the Third World.

THE RESTRAINTS AND THE THIRD WORLD

The reactions of Third World states to superpower competition and the use of arms transfers may vary considerably, and this variation has implications for the maintenance of restraint by Moscow and Washington. Although the range of Third World reactions is very large, it is possible to identify three broad strategies used by Third World states in response to the dominance expressed by the superpowers' arms transfers: acquiescence, exploitation and subversion. Some states follow all three tactics in different situations, although most fall largely into one of these categories.

Third World states which acquiesce in superpower dominance operated at least in part through arms transfers have usually been in a position of extreme political weakness *vis-à-vis* their patron either strategically, as with Cuba and Honduras, or in terms of the domestic regime's dependence on external support to maintain power, as with Chile. For the superpowers, such states, in some senses at least, represent 'ideal' allies. They are usually sufficiently subservient not to complicate the Soviet–American relationship.

Third World states which attempt to exploit the existence of the superpower competition in the use of arms transfers for their own benefit include Pakistan and Iran under the Shah. Pakistan has been able to extract weaponry from the United States for its own regional ends, whilst cloaking these in the rationale of the East–West competition. For the United States, Pakistan's receipt of F-16s was necessary primarily to protect the country from Soviet activity in Afghanistan, while for Pakistan it was viewed essentially in terms of defence against India. The Shah of Iran used a different tactic. He often threatened to make major purchases from the Soviet Union in order to force the United States to provide Iran with its most sophisticated weaponry. Indeed, on occasion Iran did purchase arms from the Soviet Union as well as from other, European, suppliers. By playing on American fears of losing influence to the USSR in a vital country, the Shah was able to promote his own foreign-policy objectives. A similar strategy was successfully employed by Jordan to persuade the United States to supply it with 500 Hawk surface-to-air missiles.[7]

It has to be acknowledged that the total or near total dependence of a state upon Moscow or Washington may have costs as well as benefits for the superpower concerned. Chief among the costs is 'reverse leverage', a phenomenon first identified in a 1968 staff study for the United States Senate Foreign

Relations Committee.[8] Reverse leverage is a term used to describe a situation in which a superpower is not only able to exert influence over a recipient of arms transfers, but is also subject to the exertion of influence by its client. A state may be so tied to a superpower that it can influence certain types of policy and extract concessions from its patron. One of the major fears expressed in the 1968 report was that reverse leverage would result in a superpower becoming embroiled in a regional conflict (owing to the number of key personnel it had in the country) from which it would be unable to extricate itself. This fear was first raised in relations between the United States and Iran, but it seems applicable to many other states which have significant numbers of superpower nationals in their country. It is not immediately obvious that a state might be wholly dependent upon a superpower yet still be able to manipulate the relationship to its own advantage, but this might happen if the state in question is of great strategic importance to the United States or the Soviet Union. The relationship between the United States and Israel, for example, highlights the way in which influence can be exercised by a client over its patron. Several factors have increased Israel's bargaining position *vis-à-vis* Washington. Not least among these is the strong domestic support for Israel in the United States, as manifested most dramatically in the activities of the American Israeli Public Affairs Committee. The special position of Israel with the United States gives it considerable discretion, since it need fear consequences no more serious than a stiff rebuke. Furthermore, on several occasions the Israelis have used their significant lobby power to pressure an administration either into providing extra arms transfers to Israel or to refrain from arms transfers to Arab states. The 1978 'planes package' deal initiated by the Carter administration to provide advanced fighter aircraft to Israel, Egypt and Saudi Arabia in an attempt to assist the Camp David peace process was subject to this Israeli lobbying power. Pro-Israeli lobbies, inside as well as outside Congress, agitated so successfully about the sales to the two Arab states that Israel's allocation of F-16s was significantly increased.

The third strategy followed by Third World states has been to subvert the superpowers' use of the arms-transfer tool. Some Third World states have sought to extract themselves from superpower disputes either by acting through the non-aligned movement or by other means. In terms of arms transfers, this has led some countries to diversify their sources of supply, thereby loosening the hold of one or other of the superpowers. Third World countries can lower their dependence and reduce superpower leverage even by buying from West European states which are closely allied to the United States. Some have even attempted to take this further and purchase from other Third World states as well (as the Saudi Arabians and Zimbabweans attempt to do), or to become practically self-sufficient in arms, as in the case of the Brazilians. In such circumstances, superpower arms transfers have little or no role as a foreign-policy tool.

Those states which acquiesce in, and even those which attempt to exploit the existence of superpower competition in arms transfers for their own purposes, have effectively been perpetuating superpower dominance. The challenge of those states who have attempted to subvert the system, however, makes predicting and controlling the competition increasingly difficult in many regions. It is somewhat ironic that the attempts of certain Third World states to increase their own security by diversifying suppliers could result in a destabilisation of the superpower relationship, which in turn could have serious repercussions for the Third World. Yet there may be something inevitable about this: the existence of a growing number of alternative suppliers means that the superpowers will face an increasingly difficult task in imposing bilateral arrangements of mutual restraints on an increasingly multipolar situation.

CONCLUSION

The success of tacit restraints in making the use of arms transfers a safe instrument for continuing the superpower competition depends on mutual understanding and reciprocity. As long as both superpowers continue to understand the need for restraint in their behaviour, accept these restraints as in their interests and act accordingly, then there seems to be little utility in formalising the situation. Indeed, as the CAT Talks of 1977–8 illustrated, attempts to formalise tacit understandings can be damaging to the wider process of superpower accommodation, since the negotiations also present opportunities for airing disagreements and for attempts to obtain unilateral advantage. Furthermore, a formalising of the restraints could have a profoundly negative impact on superpower relations, by making each side far more sensitive to the actions of the other. The more formal the regulations the more carefully each side's behaviour will be scrutinised and the more likely that violations will be found – thereby adding additional strains and tensions. Tacit 'norms of competition' mean that if a superpower sees advantage in abrogating restraint in a particular situation (that is, it engages in an occasional break), this need not have serious implications beyond the region concerned. If the same situation arose with a formal regime in place, the situation would undoubtedly be much worse. An occasional break would be quickly turned into a fundamental one by the response of the adversary to what would be seen as an arms-control violation and possibly a major challenge. As suggested above, in practice, the dividing line between observing and not observing restraint is a fine one, and often depends on interpretation. This remains problematic since it requires effective communication and continuous signalling by the superpowers. In a formal regime characterised by a higher political profile, such problems could be even more formidable. It is not difficult to envisage a situation in which problems over the maintenance or implementation of a formal regime may go beyond the agreement itself and damage the wider superpower arms-control process by raising questions over verification and, above all, the trustworthiness of one or other power. If there are doubts about the desirability of such a regime, there are also doubts about its feasibility. It is uncertain that a formal agreement is possible in view of the unwillingness of both superpowers to resist the advantages derived from occasional breaches of the restraints, as well as their inability to impose similar restrictions on third parties.

The formalising of restraints could also harm relations with those Third World countries that fear superpower dominance. To focus on the superpowers alone, therefore, can be misleading. The superpowers not only have to interact with each other, but also with other nations as multipolarity becomes increasingly evident in the arms-transfer field. Indigenous production has provided one method whereby Third World states can overcome dependence on the superpowers, although, as the Egyptians have discovered, this is not an easy route. The proliferation of arms producers means that superpower dominance in this field is diminishing – and will continue to do so. The implications of this for stability are uncertain. As multipolarity in the arms field increases and certain Third World states reduce dependence on the superpowers, so tacit patterns of restraint in arms transfers may become more difficult to impose. Although these restraints are incomplete and imperfect, they help to ensure that Soviet–American competition in arms transfers remains manageable. As far as the Third World is concerned, however, manageability is little more than a euphemism for superpower dominance. The implication of this chapter is that such dominance is far from complete.

NOTES

1 Roger P. Labrie, John G. Hutchins, Edwin W. A. Peura & Diana H. Richman *U.S. Arms Sales Policy Background and Issues* (Washington, DC: American Enterprise Institute for Public Policy Research, 1982) p. 61.
2 Michael T. Klare, *American Arms Supermarket* (Austin TX: University of Texas Press, 1984), p. 30.
3 Appearance of Defense Secretary Schlesinger before the Foreign Affairs Committee, 1974. *FY 1975 Foreign Assistance Request, Hearings* 93rd Congress, 2nd Session, 1974, p. 80.
4 See Peter Shearman, 'Soviet Foreign Policy in Africa and Latin America: A Comparative Case Study' In *Millennium Journal of International Studies* 15, 3 (Winter 1986), pp. 347–8.
5 See J. G. Whelan and M. J. Dixon, *The Soviet Union in the Third World: Threat to World Peace?* (Pergamon-Brasseys, USA, 1986), pp. 180–1.
6 Barry M. Blechman, Janne E. Nolan and Alan Platt, 'Pushing Arms' in *Foreign Policy* 46 (Spring 1982) p. 140.

7 Andrew J. Pierre, *The Global Politics of Arms Sales* (Princeton, NJ: Princeton University Press, 1982), p. 15.
8 Chris Carr, 'Reverse Influence, Interdependence and the Relationship between Supplier and Recipient in Arms Transfers', referenced in J. Simpson ed., *The Control of Arms Transfers* report of a FCO/BISA Seminar, 23 September 1977.

Part Two: Superpower competition and regional conflict

6   Superpower interests in Third Areas

Alexander L. George

This chapter describes a general framework for analysing superpower involvement in regional conflicts that the authors of the following chapters draw upon in analysing specific regions.[1] The origins of this framework may be of interest. For a number of years several groups of Soviet and American specialists have met periodically to discuss various approaches for managing and regulating superpower competition in Third Areas.[2] Their discussions have focused upon the task of avoiding involvements in regional conflicts that might draw the United States and the Soviet Union into warfare or lesser crises that damage overall US–Soviet relations. These discussions, it should be noted, have a pragmatic policy-orientation; they have been conducted on the basis of available analyses and impressions regarding relevant historical experience. The participants in these discussions have not attempted to prepare detailed scholarly analyses of how and why the two superpowers have or have not become involved in regional conflicts and under what conditions their involvement did or did not lead to US–Soviet confrontations in a particular region. Considerable historical research of this kind has been undertaken, of course, by other scholars but it would be going too far to assert that a broad scholarly consensus exists as regards the central questions of interest here. Moreover, while Soviet academicians also analyse relevant historical experience, there is reason to believe that their explanations and interpretations of past regional crises diverge in important respects from those offered by many Western analyses.

Despite the unsatisfactory experience with the Basic Principles Agreement of 1972 and the Agreement on the Prevention of Nuclear War of 1973, the Soviet–American groups began their discussions by investigating the possibility of formulating better general principles, guidelines, or 'rules of conduct' for regulating superpower involvement in Third Areas. Progress was made in clarifying the difficulties this approach encounters. In the early 1980s, at one of the first meetings of the Dartmouth Conference Task Force on Regional

Conflicts, the Soviet and American delegations each formulated a set of general principles, but the two drafts had little in common. It was then agreed that the US and Soviet participants in these meetings should jointly examine actual or potential crisis situations in a number of regions to see how various general principles might apply in concrete cases. Not surprisingly, the discussion of specific situations led the participants to try to identify the respective interests of each superpower in each area and to consider how the assessment of its interests would be affected by hypothetical developments and by the behavior of the other superpower (and its allies and proxies).

Members of these discussion groups, Soviet as well as American, share the belief that the shift in focus of their discussions from general principles to specific situations and to the interests engaged and pursued in those situations has been worthwhile from an analytical standpoint. In other words, the experience of the discussion groups has led them to seriously question, without rejecting altogether, the search for a single set of general principles regulating superpower involvement that would apply to all regional conflicts and all circumstances surrounding them. Most members of these discussion groups favour the alternative of an *ad hoc*, case-by-case approach that considers how and why superpowers become involved in particular regional issues, and how they might limit, if not avoid, competition and involvement in each case.

To facilitate a case-by-case approach the author outlined several years ago a general conceptual framework that focuses upon the relative interests of the United States and the Soviet Union in different parts of the world. Embedded in the 'meta-game' global rivalry between the two superpowers there are, in fact, a variety of competitive 'games' in different parts of the globe. By taking into account the *magnitude/strength* of each superpower's interests in a particular area and whether their interests in that area are *symmetrical* or *asymmetrical*, a conceptual framework can be mapped out that identifies six 'games' of a distinctive kind that are embedded in the overall global competition. This six-fold typology will first be succinctly characterised with reference to the strength and symmetry of US–Soviet interests, and then its applicability and limitations will be discussed.

1 *High-interest symmetry*: locales such as Central Europe in which both superpowers have very strong, vital interests.
2 *Low-interest symmetry*: locales such as in parts of Africa and Asia in which both superpowers have quite modest interests.
3 *High-interest asymmetry favouring the Soviet Union*: locales such as Eastern Europe in which Soviet interests are clearly and substantially more important than those of the United States.

4 *High-interest asymmetry favouring the United States*: locales such as the Caribbean in which US interests are clearly and substantially more important than those of the Soviet Union.

Each of the preceding types of competitive 'games' rests upon the important assumption that the two sides agree on that particular characterisation of the balance of their interests. This, of course, is not always the case, and so we must add to our typology two other 'game' structures:

5 *Disputed interest symmetry*: locales in which the two superpowers do not agree on what the balance of interests between them is.
6 *Uncertain interest symmetry*: locales of an ambiguous or fluid nature in which one or both superpowers are not certain of their own or the other's interests and find it difficult to assess how and to what extent their interests will become engaged in a developing, unstable situation.

An analytical typology of this kind is useful, but only as a starting point, in several respects. It suggests the need for a *differentiated* approach for understanding the dynamics of superpower involvement and interaction, and the escalation and/or the resolution of US–Soviet competition in particular areas. It also suggests the need for a differentiated approach to conflict control, and for developing norms of competition or 'rules of the game'. Norms or rules considered appropriate for areas in which both superpowers have strong interests are not likely to be acceptable for locales in which only one superpower has a dominant interest. Similarly, norms or rules considered appropriate for locales in which both superpowers have very modest interests are not likely to be acceptable for areas of disputed interest symmetry.

This is not to imply, however, that each type of game has a simple, clear-cut logic as to the norms or rules that should govern competition in those locales and that can be easily recognised and agreed to by the two superpowers. The task of developing and applying such understandings is complicated by a variety of other factors – for example, the variation in *resources* and *strategies* available to each superpower for competing in different locales; the variation in *domestic* and *international constraints* on a superpower's efforts to *define* its interests; the *ideologies, images* and *perceptions* that enter into the interactions between the two superpowers and influence their conception of their own and the other's intentions.

If space permitted we could consider what the 'logic' of relative interests implies for assessing the conflict potential and the norms or rules of competition for each type of game, and how this simple 'logic' is likely to be affected by the other factors we have identified. Since a comprehensive treatment of all types of games is not possible here we shall limit discussion to the competition of the superpowers in regions of 'low-interest,' 'disputed', and 'uncertain-interest' symmetry since these probably characterise most of the regions discussed in the following chapters.

AREAS OF DISPUTED OR UNCERTAIN SYMMETRY OF INTERESTS

The Middle East may be regarded as a locale of disputed symmetry of interests and, therefore, one for which the superpowers find it particularly difficult to agree upon norms or 'rules' by means of which to regulate their competition. While both superpowers acknowledge that each has important interests in the Middle East, the Soviet Union, claiming superpower equality with the United States, has tried unsuccessfully for a number of years to get Washington to regard this area as one of high-interest symmetry that requires a joint Soviet–American approach to peacemaking in the Arab–Israeli conflict.

For the two superpowers to sort out and delimit their respective interests in the Middle East is a particularly difficult task for several reasons. Unlike the situation in Europe, there is no clear geographical line dividing East and West in the Middle East that serves to separate each superpower's area of predominant interests and provides it with a reasonably stable, quasi-sphere of influence. Instead, proclaimed US and Soviet interests in the Middle East overlap and intermingle geographically. Aggravating efforts to define and delimit their interests is the pronounced instability within the region which makes it difficult for either superpower to be content with the measure of influence it has managed to achieve for the time being with one or another Middle East country.

The volatility and geographically open-ended characteristics of superpower competition in the Middle East serve, in turn, to exacerbate the already existing tendency for global, geopolitical considerations to magnify each superpower's conception of its purely regional interests. The tendency to assess one's interests in the Middle East from a global standpoint as well as in purely regional terms is not confined to the United States; the Soviet Union, too, finds itself obliged to view some of its interests in the Middle East from a global perspective.[3]

In brief, the circumstances under which the superpowers interact in the Middle East exacerbate the 'basic security dilemma' that is deeply embedded in the nature of the international system. That is, what one side does to enhance its security is often perceived by the other side as a threat to its own security which requires it, in turn, to undertake additional actions to buttress its security that can have a similar effect on the adversary. Thus is set into motion a vicious action–reaction cycle of heightened distrust and tension. In this situation neither side is disposed to take at face value the assurances of the other that it acts solely for defensive purposes or to ensure deterrence. Since an adversary's intentions, particularly the relationship of its current actions to its longer-term aims, are difficult to ascertain reliably, one is inclined to judge those intentions not by what the opponent says but rather on the basis of one's perception of the possible implications and long-run *consequences* of its current actions. Given the ambiguity of an adversary's intentions, policy-makers feel obliged to attach greater significance to the possibly threatening consequences of the adversary's behaviour. This is the source of much difficulty in superpower relations generally and this is certainly the case in the Middle East. Thus, the American effort early in the cold war to implement containment in the Middle East in response to what were perceived as Soviet expansionist aims was perceived in Moscow as hostile encirclement motivated by offensive aims. And, similarly, assurances such as those offered by Ye. Primakov, currently director of the Moscow Institute of World Economy and International Relations and a member of the USSR Academy of Sciences, that the Soviet Union seeks to increase friendly relations and influence with Middle East countries in order to counter American efforts 'to involve the countries of the region in anti-Soviet plans and actions', and that 'all this does not represent any attempt on the part of the Soviet Union to force the United States from the Middle East', cannot allay concern over the adverse consequences (whether intended or not) of Soviet actions for the Western position and suspicions regarding longer-term Soviet aspirations and intentions.[4]

Much of the superpowers' competition for influence in the Middle East seems to lack self-imposed restraints of a clear or consistent character derived from delimitation of one's interests rather than constraints imposed by other considerations. As a result US–Soviet competition in that region tends to take on some of the characteristics of a zero-sum game. Thus, each superpower tends to view any increase in influence in the area by the other superpower as a set-back for itself and fears that it will further destabilise the region and contribute to a further weakening of its own overall position.

Nonetheless, as Robert Freedman emphasises in the following chapter, the two superpowers do have important common interests in the Middle East. Only one of these common interests, certainly the most important one, is discussed here. Both Moscow and Washington genuinely fear that a war in the Middle East between their regional allies might drag them into war with each other. But while both superpowers have firmly and successfully attempted on occasion to restrain their regional ally from initiating a local war, on other occasions they have supported a regional ally's resort to military action, acquiesced in it, or failed to exert strong pressure to prevent it. These latter instances arise when the need to support a regional ally has taken precedence over a reluctance to see war break out.

Although the superpowers have not succeeded in preventing wars among their regional allies, they have at least managed to develop a pattern of behaviour (perhaps accompanied by the emergence of a tacit norm) for regulating and limiting their own involvement in Arab–Israeli wars. This norm has emerged from experience gained in dealing with an acute policy dilemma that arises for both superpowers when war breaks out among their regional allies. In this situation both superpowers must back their local allies but, at the same time, they must avoid being dragged into a war with each other.

The United States and the Soviet Union managed to cope with this policy dilemma successfully in the Six Days War in 1967, the War of Attrition in 1970, and the October 1973 War. Their behaviour during the course of these three wars evinces a pattern of restraint or, perhaps, even a tacit understanding with regard to what a superpower is and is not entitled to do (hence, suggesting the relevance of a principle of 'legitimacy') in support of its regional ally and what restraints it must observe in this respect. Thus, each superpower has learned that it must reckon with the likelihood that the other superpower will intervene militarily in some way to prevent its regional ally from suffering a catastrophic defeat at the hands of other regional actors. To avoid such an intervention, the superpower backing the winning local actor must recognise the necessity to pressure its ally to stop short of inflicting an overwhelming defeat on its opponent.[5] Consistent with this tacit ground rule is Primakov's observation that in the war crises of 1967, 1973 and 1983 the USSR made it clear that it could not agree to allowing Israel to threaten the existence of Arab regimes allied to the Soviet Union.[6]

Variations of this tacit ground rule can be seen in all three Arab–Israeli wars. Towards the end of the Six Day War Premier Kosygin threatened Soviet intervention if the Israeli army marched against Damascus; he was assured by President Johnson over the Hotline that this would not happen. In early 1970, at a critical juncture of the War of Attrition, when the Israeli air force's deep penetration raids against Egypt were threatening to topple Nasser, Kosygin sent a note to Nixon indirectly warning that the Soviet Union would have to act if the Israelis continued their attacks. Kosygin's warning was not correctly interpreted; Washington did not see the need to exercise its influence with Israel, and the Soviet Union gradually introduced substantial air defence forces into Egypt which brought about a curtailment of Israeli air operations against Egypt. The United States was taken by surprise and did not attempt to deter the Soviet Union from intervening militarily; after the fact it implicitly accepted the legitimacy of the Soviet move to save its Egyptian ally from suffering a catastrophic defeat. Subsequently, it is true, Washington did give the Israelis advanced electronic countermeasures equipment and Shrike missiles by way of 'countering' the air defences the Soviets had introduced into Egypt.

Similarly, in the October 1973 War when Israel violated the cease-fire worked out by Brezhnev and Kissinger in Moscow and Israeli forces threatened the destruction of the Egyptian Third Army, Brezhnev sent a note to Nixon suggesting joint Soviet–American military intervention to end the war and backed it with a threat of unilateral Soviet intervention. The Brezhnev note was a stern reminder to the United States of its obligation to control its ally. And while Washington responded to the Soviet threat of intervention with an alert of US military forces, it also immediately pressured Israel to stop its efforts to capture the Egyptian Third Army.

The United States, too, on one occasion has invoked this tacit norm. Thus, when Syrian tanks rolled into Jordan in the autumn of 1970, threatening to topple King Hussein, Washington held the Soviet Union responsible for securing a withdrawal of Syrian forces from Jordan and backed this demand with a threat of military intervention by Israeli or US air forces on Jordan's behalf.

As these four historical cases demonstrate, the tacit norm comes into play only when the regional ally of a superpower is threatened with imminent defeat. Under these circumstances the balance of interest – i.e., what is at stake – clearly shifts in favour of the superpower backing the regional actor that is in serious difficulty, making it both 'legitimate' and credible that the superpower would intervene, if necessary, to save its local ally from a shattering defeat. At the same time, it should be noted that the tacit norm that enjoins the other superpower to restrain its victorious regional ally does not come into play automatically; rather, it must be activated by a credible threat of intervention by the defending superpower. For various reasons, therefore, this tacit ground rule cannot be regarded as a stable, reliable basis for enabling superpowers to back their regional client states without being drawn into war with each other.

AREAS OF LOW-INTEREST SYMMETRY

At first glance it would appear that geographical areas in which both superpowers have only modest interests should facilitate non-involvement or limited involvement, and help them to avoid escalation of involvement to dangerous confrontations. One would also expect areas of low-interest symmetry to lend themselves to norms and rule-making in the interest of crisis prevention. Underlying this 'logic' is the presumption that since what is at stake for the two superpowers in such areas falls well short of engaging vital interests it would be highly rational and hence relatively simple to agree on ground rules that would strictly limit both the levels of investment in their competition and the risk that such competition would escalate to mutually undesired levels of conflict.

As experience demonstrates, however, such a presumption is not always justified. In the first place, it has often been noted, great powers that have global interests tend to gradually expand the concept of their security requirements. The defence of critical outposts or lines of communication tends to lead to an inflated conception of security requirements. Robert Jervis cites Balfour's complaint to illustrate the tendency of security requirements to snowball and to take on an open-ended character: 'Every time I come to a discussion – at intervals of, say, five years – I find there is a new sphere which we have got to guard, which is supposed to protect the gateways of India. Those gateways are getting further and further away from India, and I do not know how far west they are going to be brought by the General Staff.'[7]

In the second place, the simple logical premise that the superpowers should find it relatively easy to limit competition in areas of low-interest symmetry overlooks incentives and complications that can and do emerge. In fact, the superpowers may find a contrary 'logic' more appealing: it is precisely in areas in which one's opponent has quite modest interests that policies to increase one's influence, even at the expense of the opponent's interests, can be safely pursued. In other words, areas of low-interest symmetry may be perceived as offering *opportunities* – not dangers – for *marginal gains*, particularly when such policies are judged not to carry with them any appreciable risk of uncontrollable escalation to a war-threatening confrontation with the superpower adversary.

Competing with the rival in areas of low-interest symmetry may also be viewed as offering tempting opportunities for pursuing a longer-range strategy for gradually weakening the other superpower's regional and global influence. Thus, one superpower may attempt over time to gain a series of marginal gains in a number of areas each of which is admittedly of limited value but which cumulatively would substantially weaken the other superpower. This strategy may be regarded as an attractive, low-cost and low-risk way of enhancing one's own global security position: thus any weakening of the opponent's influence and control, even in peripheral areas, puts him on the defensive, distracts him and reduces his capabilities for threatening and damaging your own interests. In other words, an 'offence' of this kind is really a good indirect 'defence'.

The mere possibility that the adversary is pursuing a long-range 'offence–defensive' strategy of this kind creates the basis for distrust and misperception of intentions underlying some of the specific, more limited actions it undertakes in Third Areas. Since an adversary's intentions, particularly its longer-range aims, are often difficult to ascertain, one is inclined to judge those intentions not by what the opponent says but rather, as noted earlier, on the basis of one's perception of the possible long-run *consequences* of the adversary's behaviour. The ambiguity of the adversary's 'intentions' and the greater significance in many instances of the 'perceived consequences' of its behaviour is the source of much difficulty generally in superpower relations.

We have noted the tendency for the abstract 'logic' of restrained competition in areas of low-interest symmetry to be displaced by the quite different 'meta-logic' of global superpower competition. What ought to remain a low-stakes 'game' in areas in which Moscow and Washington have only modest interests assumes inflated importance from time to time because such contests *cannot be easily or reliably de-coupled* from the higher-stake 'games' in which they are engaged in other geographical areas. As is well known from the experience of the cold war, 'grey areas' of little importance in and of themselves are often perceived by one and/or the other superpower to have considerable actual or potential strategic or cold war significance. In addition, the loss of influence in these areas is sometimes expected to have adverse political consequences in the domestic arena or on the international scene.

As a result, superpower competition in Third Areas is ridden with numerous complexities and uncertainties of a kind that cannot be easily anticipated. This increases the likelihood of misperceptions and actions that contribute to escalation of the stakes and additional superpower involvement. In addition, one or both superpowers may experience the dilemma of 'sunk costs' in an area in which its efforts to compete have not gone well. When an initially low-level, low-risk involvement on behalf of quite limited objectives unexpectedly fails, it is difficult to avoid the temptation to increase one's involvement somewhat in order to avoid a setback and in the hope of securing a better outcome. Thus, the mere expenditure of resources by a superpower in a Third Area competition increases its stakes in that competition and in this sense, 'sacrifice creates value'.

Not merely the expenditure of resources but the commitment of prestige can also increase the stakes and encourage escalation. Prestige is often put on the line in the course of public statements and military manoeuvres that are intended to convey resolution in order to impress the opponent. But the rhetorical inflation of the importance of what is at stake that often accompanies efforts to signal strong and credible resolution is not without its own kind of costs and risks since, if it does not have the desired impact, it leaves the dissatisfied superpower in the unsatisfactory position of having either to back down, to make concessions to secure a compromise solution, or to escalate its involvement.

In principle, to be sure, if the superpowers do not agree beforehand upon the ceiling to place on their involvement in the Third Area they can presumably cooperate to establish *ad hoc* 'ground rules' to limit the danger of escalation after they begin to compete. Acceptance of ground rules, however, implies a mutual willingness to accept whatever outcome, however disadvantageous, of the competition conducted within those ground rules. Otherwise the only alternative to further escalation by the disadvantaged side as the competition evolves is the willingness of its adversary to offer it an acceptable compromise settlement. But the side that holds the advantage in a local contest – as the Soviets did in Angola in late 1975 – may be unwilling to forego the full measure of its prospective success for various reasons. It may feel that its objectives are 'legitimate' whereas those of its opponent are not, that it has earned its success, that the opponent must be taught a lesson, that there would be a serious domestic backlash if it granted its opponent a generous compromise settlement, etc.

We have discussed a variety of factors that constrain and complicate the ability or willingness of the superpowers to limit involvement in regional issues and to cooperate in developing ground rules or norms for keeping their competition in areas of mutual low-interest at safe levels. One should not conclude from this that superpower cooperation for this purpose is wholly infeasible but, rather, that further efforts to arrive at such norms and 'rules' must take better account of complexities that are better known now than in the early 1970s when Nixon and Brezhnev took the first steps toward developing such understandings. It is clear from their abortive effort, as events later in the decade were to make plain, that Moscow and Washington had not really agreed on whether, to what extent, and how to de-couple their competition in Third Areas from their global competition. The 'lessons' of this experience need to be clearly understood if the superpowers are to be more successful in preventing competition in Third Areas from undermining any new efforts they may make to improve and stabilise their overall political and strategic relationship.

Underlying much of the preceding discussion of the various 'logics' for regulating US–Soviet competition that might be implicit in the particular configuration of their relative interests in different parts of the globe is *the assumption that each superpower is capable of determining what those interests are and of successfully communicating this to its adversary.* We need to examine this important assumption more closely now.

DIFFICULTIES OF DETERMINING AND COMMUNICATING INTERESTS

It is often said, with considerable justification, that the United States and the Soviet Union can reduce the risk of confrontation by timely clarification and communication of their interests in particular areas and situations. If we were to systematically examine the history of US–Soviet relations from this standpoint, however, we would find many episodes in which they failed to do so. Some of these failures might be attributed to oversight, human error or technical communication difficulties of a kind that could be avoided in the future.

Other failures to define and communicate one's interest effectively and successfully cannot be so easily explained and are rooted in causes that cannot be so readily eliminated. One root cause has to do with *difficulties of diplomatic signalling and communication* – e.g., a failure to convey what one's interests and intentions are in a timely, clear manner that is comprehensible and credible to the opponent; or a failure of the recipient to attend properly to serious communications directed towards him and to interpret them correctly. There are various constraints on the ability of the superpowers to communicate effectively with each other that deserve the most careful study. Indeed, this is a common problem that could greatly benefit from joint US–Soviet analysis of past failures. It is passed over quickly here to turn to another root cause of failures to convey one's interests on a timely basis – namely, *the difficulty superpowers often experience in deciding what their interests are in a timely and reliable way.*

It is relatively easy for a state to recognise that it has interests in a particular area that are as yet not achieved or are being threatened by another state. It is a far more difficult, and yet a necessary task for political decision makers to assess the *value* they should place on the achievement or protection of those interests. Judgements of the value of one's interests are often difficult to make in the abstract and in advance of actual decisions to expend resources to protect or enhance those interests. Thus, *the real value of one's interests often can be determined only by deciding what price one is prepared to pay in order to realise or protect those interests.* But the price one is willing to pay may be difficult to anticipate in advance of circumstances which require expenditure of resources for that purpose. As a result, *prior* evaluations of the value one will place upon protecting one's interests may prove to be grossly unreliable. The advance valuation of interests may turn out to be either a substantial *overestimate* or *underestimate* of the level of costs and risks one is willing to accept when action is required.

Miscalculations by policymakers of the value of state interests arise from a number of different sources. Fundamental is the fact that the concept of 'national interest' has the characteristics of what decision-making theorists refer to as a 'nonoperational goal' – i.e., one that does not provide a measuring rod for comparing and choosing among alternative policies.[8] National interest is similar in this respect to concepts such as 'the general welfare' and 'the public interest'. Such concepts cannot be employed as a utility function in rigorous policy analysis; they can be related to specific choices of action only through various subgoals which they presumably encompass. In an area such as the Middle East the national interest of the United States includes a variety of subgoals that usually *compete* with each other for influence in the conduct of foreign policy. An operational common denominator for weighing the relative importance of these subgoals is lacking. Hence, the relative weight to be given to various subgoals and the trade-off among them are matters left to the authoritative (but subjective) judgement of one or more top-level officials. Their judgement, in turn, is subject to the play of political forces and the requirement for some degree of consensus as to the level of costs and risks to accept in pursuing the national interests in the particular situation at hand and as that situation evolves.

The task of differentiating one's interests in various parts of the globe or, indeed, in any one country such as Iran (as Chubin shows in his chapter) and the additional task of determining the value to be accorded them do not account for all the difficulties foreign policymakers experience in deciding what their state's interests are and conveying this reliably to others. In addition, we must recognise that a superpower's interests in some Third Areas are often *complex, contingent* and *context-dependent* in ways that neither the superpower itself nor its opponent can foresee. A superpower may have diverse, competing interests in a particular area that are not easily sorted out and balanced in order to decide what actions to undertake on their behalf. To this complexity of interests is often added the fact that the value of some of these interests may be highly contingent upon the circumstances under which it becomes necessary to decide by what means and how far to go in support of those interests. Thus, for example, in 1949 US policymakers placed modest value on the strategic importance of South Korea in the event of a general war with the Soviet Union, but then in late June 1950 Washington suddenly placed much higher value on the cold war importance of South Korea's defence when it was attacked by North Korea. As this example illustrates, the definition and valuation of interests is often highly context-dependent and the context in which such judgements have to be made often changes unexpectedly and dramatically in ways that even sophisticated contingency planning cannot easily anticipate or accurately predict.

Similarly, the value a superpower places on its interests in a particular area may escalate simply in consequence of the momentum and dynamics of competitive interaction with the other superpower or its clients. And domestic and allied constraints, as is well known, are often unpredictable factors complicating a superpower's ability to make reliable determination of its interests in a particular area or to pursue those interests in ways policymakers, freed from such constraints, would think appropriate. It should be recognised that constraints of domestic or allied opinion may work in either direction, either to magnify or to reduce the level of resource expenditures policymakers believe to be consistent with the true value of the interests at stake.

The willingness and ability of the superpowers to clarify their interests and intentions is, perhaps paradoxically, sometimes more problematic in their competition in areas of relatively modest or low interest. One reason why Soviet and US leaders seem reluctant in many situations to define and delimit their interests is that by doing so they might appear to 'give away' such areas or encourage the other side to proceed to enhance its influence.[9] Additionally, US policymakers are sometimes constrained from delimiting their interests in certain Third Areas by domestic politics or by sensitive allies. There is the ever-present likelihood that someone in the foreign-policy bureaucracy, Congress, or vocal interest groups will be quick to charge the administration with being insufficiently attentive to the need to protect American interests abroad.

Sometimes responsible policymakers simply are not able to judge the full weight of US interests in an area until competition with the Soviet Union or its proxies has escalated and approached a crisis stage. Often only when a situation has deteriorated to a certain point do its broader ramifications for US interests become evident in Washington, forcing consideration of a strong response. Such dilemmas cannot be avoided merely by enjoining American policymakers to define their interests in advance and to 'draw a line', for in many situations what is at stake for the United States does increase substantially and somewhat unpredictably as a result of actions by the Soviet Union or its proxies, or through internal developments in the area in question.

Thus far we have emphasised and tried to explain why superpowers often find it difficult to decide what their interests are in certain areas and, in particular, the value to be accorded those interests. The other side of the coin, of course, is that each superpower also often finds it difficult to ascertain its opponent's interests and, even more so, the costs and risks the opponent is likely to be willing to incur on behalf of those interests under different circumstances.

In conclusion, while this chapter has noted the difficulties that stand in the way of moderating superpower involvement in regional security issues, we should not end on too pessimistic a note. As the following chapters will indicate, there are many reasons why superpower involvement in regional matters is not likely to result in a direct military conflict between the Soviet Union and the United States. In addition, the possibility cannot be excluded that the superpowers may gradually redefine and delimit their global aspirations.[10] Both the United States (despite the 'Reagan Doctrine' for aiding 'Freedom Fighters' in various regional conflicts) and the Soviet Union are drawing, and may be expected to continue to draw sober lessons from their experiences in the Third World. Both superpowers have ample cause to come to a better understanding of the limits of military power and economic resources for maintaining and extending their global positions. This process of learning is not confined to the United States, where the earlier impact of the Vietnam experience on public and policy views on foreign policy has by no means dissipated. For a variety of reasons (as Litwak has discussed) the Soviet elite, too, has had ample cause to reassess its policies and aspirations in the Third World. The analyst of US–Soviet relations might well venture the prediction that the issue of what global 'equality' of the two superpowers means will be displaced in the future by the necessity both Moscow and Washington will experience to redefine and shrink their conception of what kind of a global role remains a viable goal. Not only will the task be difficult and painful; it could accentuate the competitiveness and instability of superpower global rivalry, especially if either superpower attempts to exacerbate, and gain advantages for itself from the difficulties the other is experiencing in maintaining or withdrawing from positions of influence in the Third World. Hopefully, however, it might also enhance superpower incentives for mutual restraint and tacit cooperation in reducing involvements abroad.

NOTES

1 This essay draws directly from the author's previous publications, in particular chapter 15 of *Managing US–Soviet Rivalry: Problems of Crisis Prevention* (Boulder, CO: Westview Press, 1983), and on a more recent paper 'US–Soviet Global Rivalry: Norms of Competition' presented at the Thirteenth World Congress, International Political Science Association, Paris, July 15–20 1985. Additional documentation for materials presented in this paper will be found in these two earlier publications.

   The author is pleased to acknowledge support for the research on which these papers are based provided by the Carnegie Corporation of New York and the Center for International Security and Arms Control, Stanford University. The ideas presented in this paper benefited from the opportunity to participate in several dialogues of American groups with Soviet academicians: the meeting in Moscow, November 24–December 3, 1983 of the Dartmouth Conference Task Force on Regional Conflicts and three meetings of the Harvard–Soviet group on Prevention of International Political Crises, beginning in May 1984, sponsored by the International Research & Exchange Board (IREX).

2 See preceding footnote.

3 See, for example, Yevgeny Primakov, 'The Soviet Union's Interests: Myths and Realities' in Harold H. Saunders, ed., *The Superpowers in the Middle East*, a special issue of the *AEI Foreign Policy and Defense Review*, 6, 1 (1986) pp. 26–34.

4 *Ibid.* p. 30.

5 A number of other analysts of the Middle East conflicts have also noted this tacit norm. See, for example, Bradford Dismukes and James M. McConnell, eds., *Soviet Naval Diplomacy* (New York: Pergamon Press, 1979), pp. 276–8; Christer Jonsson, *Superpowers: Comparing American and Soviet Foreign Policy* (London: Frances Pinter, 1984); chapter 5, 'Crisis Management in the Middle East', Yair Evron, 'Great Powers' Military Intervention in the Middle East', in Milton Leitenberg and Gabriel Sheffer, eds., *Great Power Intervention in the Middle East* (New York: Pergamon Press, 1979), pp. 17–45.

6 Primakov, 'The Soviet Union's Interests,' p. 30.

7 Cited by Robert Jervis, 'Cooperation Under the Security Dilemma', *World Politics* (January 1978), p. 169.

8 See the discussion in A. L. George, *Presidential Decision-making in Foreign Policy* (Boulder, CO: Westview Press, 1980), pp. 217–37.

9 This point, rarely acknowledged in Soviet writings, was sharply stated by Primakov ('The Soviet Union's Interests', p. 30). Commenting on the limited utility of 'rules of conduct, however thoroughly thought over, agreed upon in detail, and linked to specific situations', Primakov noted that 'the formulation of such rules is fraught with some danger, because they may be taken for the "limits of the permissible". Thus interpreted, which is inevitable, they may even stimulate activity, which in itself would lead to a dangerous aggravation of the situation.'

10 This paragraph draws from the author's chapter on 'Problems of Crisis Management and Crisis Avoidance in US–Soviet Relations' in Oyvind Osterud, ed., *Studies of War and Peace* (Oslo: Norwegian University Press, 1986), pp. 225–6.

7   The superpowers and the Middle East

Robert O. Freedman

In the period since the Second World War, the Middle East has emerged as perhaps the world's most serious zone of conflict, with the potential of precipitating confrontation between the superpowers. Wars between Israel and her Arab neighbours have occurred in 1948, 1956, 1967, 1969–70, 1973 and 1982; war was waged between Iran and Iraq from 1980 to 1988; the wars between Egypt and Libya in 1977 and between Ethiopia and Somalia in the 1977–8 period have been followed by continued border conflicts; Morocco has been battling the Algerian and occasionally Libyan-backed Polisario in the former Spanish Sahara since 1976; North and South Yemen have alternated between war and talks of unity; and major internal conflicts have raged in Lebanon, the Southern Sudan and Kurdish areas of Iraq. Of all these conflicts, the Arab–Israeli conflict has been the most serious in terms of threatening a superpower confrontation.

Given the nature of the war-torn Middle East, it would appear desirable that some form of superpower crisis prevention, or, at the minimum, crisis management arrangement, should be operative, if only to prevent regional turbulence from escalating into a superpower clash. Yet, for reasons to be discussed below, except for the Basic Principles Agreement of 1972 – a pledge which lost any significance due to Soviet behaviour during the 1973 war – no superpower crisis-prevention system of any kind has been operative. As far as crisis management is concerned, this has basically been limited to hotline messages (1967), a Soviet warning to the US prior to sending air defence troops to Egypt (1969–70 war), a trip by Kissinger to Moscow and a subsequent Soviet warning of unilateral intervention (1973 war) and much milder Soviet hotline and public warnings to the US to control Israel (1982 war). Underlying this superpower behaviour has been a mistrust of each other's goals and policies in the region which, particularly in recent years, may have been perceived by each superpower as an effort by the other to oust it from the Arab world.

Robert O. Freedman

INTERESTS AND OBJECTIVES

When one compares the basic interests of each side, however, they are not all mutually exclusive. First among the compatible interests is a desire to avoid a confrontation leading to nuclear war. In addition, both superpowers want freedom of navigation through Middle East waterways for themselves and for their allies. Freedom of navigation is more important for the USSR, which uses the Black Sea–Mediterranean–Suez Canal–Indian Ocean route for goods and material sent from the European section of the USSR to Siberia, than it is for the US. Conversely, freedom of navigation, particularly for oil tankers, is more important for US allies than for Soviet allies. A third area of common interest lies in the free flow of energy from the Middle East. While Moscow itself imports oil and natural gas from the region and the USSR's Eastern European allies are also consumers of Middle Eastern energy, it is America's NATO allies and Japan whose energy interests are greatest. The US can ill-afford to allow these energy supplies to be disrupted lest the NATO alliance and US–Japanese relations be severely damaged.

A fourth area of common interest is the preservation of the State of Israel. While America's commitment to the existence of the State of Israel (if not to its continued occupation of the West Bank and Gaza) has long been well known, the USSR, despite breaking diplomatic relations with Israel during the 1967 war, has also proclaimed itself committed to Israel's existence. It has done this not only in communication with Israeli and American leaders, but also in the various peace plans it has proposed since the 1973 war, peace plans for which it has sought to gain Arab support.[1]

If there are areas of common interest in the Middle East policies of the superpowers there is one overriding clashing interest – the superpower competition for influence. Western specialists disagree about what Mosocw wants in this influence competition. Their divergent views lead to very different policy prescriptions especially over the desirability of the USSR participating in such crisis-prevention arrangements as a settlement for the Arab–Israeli and Iran–Iraq conflicts.

The first Western school of thought as to Moscow's Middle Eastern policy may be characterised as the 'offensive-successful' school. This school, looking primarily at Soviet military power in the region, argues not only that Moscow is offensively inclined and seeks to oust the West from the oil resources and strategic communication routes of the Middle East, but also that it has been quite successful in exercising influence, primarily by intimidating the states of the region. According to this school of thought, the USSR should not only be excluded from peace-making efforts in the region, but it must be confronted wherever possible to prevent the Middle East from falling into Soviet hands.[2] On the opposite end of the spectrum of Western analysts of Soviet goals and behaviour is what may be termed the 'defensive-unsuccessful school'. This school of thought contends that Moscow is basically defensively oriented in the Middle East, given both higher priorities elsewhere in the world and the intractability of the region.[3] Given this situation, it is argued, Moscow can be invited to participate in peace-making efforts because it wants stability along its southern periphery. The final school of thought, to which this author belongs, may be termed the 'offensive-unsuccessful school'. This school argues that while Moscow is essentially offensively oriented in the Middle East and will seize upon virtually any opportunity to weaken American influence there, the USSR has been basically unsuccessful in extending its influence in the region because of the independence of the local actors and their resistance to Soviet control.[4] This school of thought, looking at the offensive orientation of the USSR in the Middle East is wary of inviting Moscow to participate in any peace-making efforts, arguing that while there might well be tactical compromises by the USSR in specific situations, the USSR cannot be trusted to fulfil its part of any agreement in the long term. Past Soviet behaviour in crisis situations, and the Soviet peace plan for settling the Arab–Israeli conflict support this argument.

For its part the Soviet conception of US policy in the Middle East is considerably more simplistic. Viewing American policy in the Middle East essentially in ideological terms, as 'imperialistic', Moscow has repeatedly called for the Arab states to put aside their internecine conflicts and join together, along with the communist parties of the region (which are usually distrusted by the one-party Arab regimes) in a large anti-imperialist front directed at 'the linchpin' of Western imperialism in the region – Israel.[5] It appears to be Moscow's expectation that if the Arab regimes cement their efforts against Israel in a controlled conflict situation, pressure would be brought to bear not only against Israel but also against the United States. Soviet commentators fondly recall the situation at the time of the 1973 Arab–Israeli War when an Arab coalition was forged against Israel, and an oil embargo imposed on the United States and Western Europe, causing severe dislocations. It should be pointed out, however, that it was Egypt and not the USSR who put together the Arab alignment of 1973; when Sadat changed his policy and turned to the US, the Arab coalition fell apart, and the USSR has been seeking to revive it ever since. Interestingly, in his first trip to the Middle East as US Secretary of State in 1981, Alexander Haig called upon Israel and the Arab states to put aside their differences and join together in a common front to fight Soviet imperialism – a virtual mirror image of Soviet policy efforts, but one which met with even less success.[6]

With this background of common and conflicting interests of the super-powers, a brief historical overview of Soviet–US relations in the Middle East can be presented. Particular emphasis is placed on areas of cooperation and conflict, and on the differing superpower plans for a peace settlement. The analysis focuses on the post-1973 war period, when the US became actively involved in the peace process, and pays particular attention to the patron–client relationships (particularly US–Israel and Soviet–Syria) in the post-1980 period when the two superpowers became increasingly tied to their regional clients, a situation which often complicated each superpower's general policy in the region.

HISTORICAL OVERVIEW: THE BREZHNEV ERA

It is only in the last twenty years that the Arab–Israeli conflict has threatened a superpower conflict. In 1948, the Soviet Union strongly and the United States somewhat less so, supported Israel in the first Arab–Israeli war, and in 1956 both superpowers opposed the tripartite Franco–British–Israeli attack on Egypt. Between 1956 and 1967, the Middle East remained relatively dormant as far as the superpowers were concerned, although the US deployment of troops to Lebanon (and British troops to Jordan) after the 1958 Iraqi Revolution did cause a minor superpower contretemps. In 1967, for the first time, there was the possibility of a major superpower confrontation, and the hotline was used on four different occasions. When the war erupted, Moscow used the hotline to make clear that it would work for a ceasefire and called on the US to exert influence on Israel. Similarly, the US used it to tell Moscow it had not aided Israel's attack on Egypt, Syria and Jordan. In addition, when the USS Liberty was attacked and the US launched some carrier aircraft to come to its aid, it informed the USSR that it was not thereby entering the conflict. A fourth use of the hotline came at the end of the war when the USSR called on the US to stop Israel before it destroyed the Syrian army, with Moscow threatening 'necessary actions, including military'. The US movement of its fleet toward Syria, however, and the agreement of Syria and Israel to a ceasefire, defused the crisis.[7]

In the aftermath of the 1967 war, the Arab–Israeli conflict rose to the top of Middle Eastern concerns and, as a result, became a key issue in Soviet–American relations. Diplomatically, both superpowers (as well as Egypt, Israel and Jordan) accepted the rather vague UN Security Council Resolution 242, as the guideline for a peace settlement, but neither this document nor subsequent Soviet–American bilateral talks succeeded in achieving a settlement. Military develop-ments, by contrast, were far more dramatic. The Soviet Union, in rebuilding the Egyptian military forces after the war, obtained important naval facilities in Egypt. Following the escalation of the Egyptian–Israeli war of attrition in 1969–

70, the USSR also obtained control of a number of Egyptian airports while deploying 15,000 air defence personnel and pilots in Egyptian territory.[8] Before this deployment, however, the USSR sent a message to Washington that unless the US stopped Israel's deep-penetration bombing of Egypt (this was Israel's response to Nasser's War of Attrition), the USSR would have to take action. For its part, the United States, by selling Phantom Jets in 1968, had moved to replace France as Israel's primary arms supplier. Nevertheless, its failure either to challenge the Soviet deployment of forces to Egypt – a deployment that led to combat between Israeli and Soviet forces – or, initially, even to send Israel new aircraft to counter the Soviet presence, dismayed many Israelis and may have sent the wrong signal to the USSR.[9] The US seized the initiative in August 1970, however, by working out a 90-day ceasefire between Israel and Egypt (to which Jordan adhered). When the ceasefire was violated, as Egypt, with Soviet help, consolidated its missile emplacements along the Canal, the US reacted angrily, especially when Soviet duplicity in this operation was followed by perceived Soviet help to Syrian forces which invaded Jordan during King Hussein's crackdown on the PLO in September 1970.[10] Clear signals of US–Israeli military activism served, at least in part, to deter Syrian Defence Minister (and later President) Hafiz Assad from committing the Syrian airforce to the fighting. Similarly, the Soviet Union, already involved in a move toward *détente* with the United States (and concerned about a possible Sino–American *rapprochement*), appeared to be taken aback by the American–Israeli move. During a visit by then Soviet President, Nikolai Podgorny in January 1971, the new Egyptian President, Anwar Sadat, was cautioned against going to war against Israel.[11]

The no-war no-peace situation, by giving the Soviet Union access to air bases in Egypt at a time when the USSR possessed no aircraft carriers to counter those of the Sixth Fleet, suited Soviet strategic interests. Unfortunately for Moscow it did not meet the needs of Anwar Sadat. Although the new Egyptian leader proved willing to extend the ceasefire, as Moscow consummated its *détente* relationship with the United States, Sadat grew increasingly disillusioned. Following the first Nixon–Brezhnev summit in 1972, in which the two superpowers signed the Basic Principles Agreement,[12] Sadat, fearing the USSR would not support him in war against Israel, ended Soviet control of Egyptian air and naval bases (although the USSR was still permitted to use them) and expelled most of the Soviet troops in Egypt. When this ploy did not elicit the requisite American pressure on Israel to meet Egypt's demands, Sadat built an Arab coalition and went to war against Israel in October 1973.[13] For its part, Moscow, stung by its losses in Egypt in 1972, decided to supply the weaponry needed by Egypt to cross the Canal (although not to attack Israel proper), in an effort to rebuild its position in the Arab world's most important country. Once the war was underway, Moscow engaged in a major air and sea lift of weaponry to Egypt and Syria, urged other Arab states to aid the Egyptian and Syrian war effort, supported the Arab position at the UN, and encouraged the Arab oil embargo against the US – actions which were in clear violation of the Basic Principles Agreement in that they exacerbated an ongoing conflict and sought unilateral advantage against the US. At the close of the war, Brezhnev threatened unilateral intervention if the US did not join Moscow in a joint military force or did not compel Israel – which by then had crossed the Suez Canal and was threatening Cairo – to accede to a superpower-agreed ceasefire. The Brezhnev note led President Nixon to call a nuclear alert, and a major confrontation appeared imminent. Following the US countermove, however, the crisis was defused as Israel agreed to another ceasefire after further improving its military position.[14]

Soviet political gains in the 1973 war proved ephemeral. Sadat, noting the rapid US airlift of weaponry to Israel during the war, realising that only the United States could bring the requisite pressure on Israel, and skilfully utilising the Arab oil embargo to ensure the issue was high on US priorities, turned to Secretary of State Henry Kissinger who negotiated the Sinai I agreement (January 1974) and the Sinai II agreement (August 1975). These accords secured Israeli withdrawals in the Sinai in return for increased Egyptian commitments to peace with Israel. During this period Kissinger also secured an Israeli–Syrian agreement on the Golan Heights (May 1974) which ended the War of Attrition there, and secured both an Israeli troop withdrawal and a Syrian pledge (often forgotten today) that this was 'a step toward a just and durable peace on the basis of Security Council Resolution 338' (the resolution, incorporating UN Resolution 242, which ended the 1973 war).[15]

Against this background in which the United States controlled the peace process, and in which there was increasing conflict among the Soviet Union's Arab allies, the Soviet Union in April 1976 unveiled a peace plan of its own. The peace plan which has been repeated, with minor variations, in 1982, 1984 and 1986, is worth examining in some detail to see whether it contains genuine elements of a conflict-prevention scheme. Essentially the plan has three major components: Israeli withdrawal from all territory captured in the 1967 war; the establishment of a Palestinian state on the West Bank and Gaza; and the acknowledgement of the right of all states in the region, including Israel, to exist. From time to time, Soviet leaders have added – and dropped – other components of their peace plan: Security Council or superpower guarantees for a peace settlement; compensation for Palestinians who choose not to return; negotiation of final borders between the parties themselves; and a phased Israeli withdrawal from the West Bank and Gaza before a Palestinian state emerged. The vehicle for such a peace settlement, according to Soviet leaders, would be an international conference (preferably a reconvened Geneva Conference where the USSR would serve, along with the United States, as co-chairman) attended by all parties to the conflict, including the PLO.[16]

The advantages of such a peace plan to Moscow are clear. First, it would preserve the state of Israel, which, as mentioned above, has become an important part of Soviet strategy in the Middle East, albeit in a negative way (as the focus of anti-imperialist Arab unity). Second, an Israeli withdrawal to the pre-war 1967 lines would not remove the potential threat of a future Israeli attack on the Arabs (or *vice versa*) or the memories of the generations-long Arab–Israeli conflict. By supporting the concept of a limited peace, as opposed to the concept of a more extensive peace, in which Israel would have trade, cultural and diplomatic relations with its neighbours, the Soviet Union hopes to keep a certain amount of latent hostility alive in the Arab–Israeli relationship. This would compel the Arabs to retain at least a modicum of unity while reinforcing Moscow's importance as an arms supplier to the Arabs. The provision of arms has been the Soviet Union's most important means of influence in the Arab world for many years, as well as an important source of hard currency for the USSR. A third benefit of such a plan would be the termination of the US role as mediator in the Arab–Israeli peace process, a role which has been a key to US influence in the Arab world since the 1973 war. Furthermore, such a settlement would end the quarrels between the Arab states over the making of peace with Israel, quarrels that have impeded the creation of what Moscow hopes would be an anti-imperialist Arab unity.

The establishment of a Palestinian state would also benefit the Soviet Union. Moscow seems to have felt since 1976 that such a state would be an ally of Soviet policy in the Arab world and would help combat US influence. Because Syria, Libya and South Yemen, the Soviet Union's most important Arab allies, are mistrusted by their fellow Arab states, the Soviet Union would clearly gain from having another ally in the centre of the Middle East. In addition, the Soviet leadership may hope that a Palestinian state on the West Bank and in Gaza would be dependent on Soviet support because it would be sandwiched between a hostile Israel and an almost equally hostile Hussein regime in Jordan which has not forgotten PLO attempts to overthrow it in the past. Indeed, Soviet attempts to foster the creation of such a state lie at the heart of the various peace plans which Moscow has presented since the end of the 1973 Arab–Israeli War.

The Soviet peace plan of April 1976, however, seemed more of a desperation move to reverse negative Middle Eastern trends and received little support in the region. Moscow's Middle East position weakened further as the Lebanese civil war intensified during the summer and Syria was isolated because of its involvement in the war. Soviet fortunes improved, however, following the election in November 1976 of Jimmy Carter as America's President. Jettisoning Kissinger's step-by-step approach, Carter embarked on an effort to achieve a comprehensive Middle East peace settlement, and decided that Moscow could be a suitable partner in this endeavour.[17] This approach seemed to be based on two assumptions. First, the Carter administration saw Geneva as the only way to bring about an overall peace settlement. Therefore, in the words of Carter, it was better 'not to have a co-chairman who might publicly and privately oppose any peaceful solution'.[18] Second, the administration apparently believed that the USSR would use its influence to make both Syria and the PLO agree to a peace settlement. The result was the joint Soviet–US statement on the Middle East of 1 October 1977 which remains the most definitive joint superpower position on a peace settlement.

The statement emphasised that a settlement should be comprehensive, that Israeli armed forces should withdraw from the territories occupied in 1967, that the legitimate rights of the Palestinian people should be ensured, and that normal peaceful relations should be established on the basis of mutual recognition of the principle of sovereignty, territorial integrity and political independence. International guarantees were to be provided if necessary and the peace process was to be facilitated through the Geneva conference.[19]

The US administration's reasoning in bringing the USSR back into the Middle East peace process was questionable on several grounds. In the first place, it was doubtful whether Moscow had enough influence with either Syria or the PLO to 'deliver' them at Geneva. Second, the Soviet peace plan was quite different from that of the United States. The US plan called not only for an Israeli troop withdrawal, but also for positive relations between Israel and its Arab neighbours in areas such as trade, tourism, cultural and diplomatic relations. The Soviet peace plan – whose concept of normalisation was embodied in the joint Soviet–US statement – called for little more than a codified armistice, much like the one between North and South Korea, as the Soviet media, both before and after the joint statement, attacked the American concept of a peace settlement.

In the event, the joint Soviet–US statement soon became moot as Anwar Sadat's surprise visit to Jerusalem and the subsequent Camp David agreements and Egyptian–Israeli peace treaty (which embodied the US plan for a peace settlement), radically altered Middle East diplomacy. While the United States tried to expand its concept of a Middle East peace settlement to include as many Arab states in the Middle East as possible, Moscow sought to isolate Egypt in the Arab world and prevent the US-mediated peace process from expanding.

Initially, Moscow seemed to meet with success as the Arab world greeted the

Egyptian–Israeli peace treaty with almost complete antipathy. Indeed, Moscow appeared to hope that the large Arab coalition which had come together in Baghdad in November 1978 might form the anti-imperialist bloc the Soviet Union had long sought.[20]

At the same time that Moscow was taking satisfaction from the formation of the anti-Camp David bloc in the Arab world, it received another bonus – the fall of the Shah of Iran. Iran had served as the pivot-point of what might be termed a US-aligned Middle Eastern grouping of Egypt, Israel, Saudi Arabia and Iran which, by combining military and petro-dollar power, effectively limited Soviet influence in the region. When the Shah fell, and the successor Khomeini regime adopted a very hostile attitude both to Israel and Egypt, therefore, it appeared as if US policy in the Middle East was in shambles.

Although this worked to Soviet advantage in the superpower competition for influence in the Middle East, the USSR itself was subsequently to run into serious difficulties, with the invasion of Afghanistan and the outbreak of the Iran–Iraq war having a very negative effect on the Soviet position.

In response to these developments, the Soviet Union drew closer to the Syrian regime of Hafiz Assad which, surrounded by enemies (Turkey, Iraq, Jordan and Israel) and under attack from Moslem fundamentalists at home, agreed to a Treaty of Friendship and Cooperation with Moscow which it had long resisted.[21] Moscow soon found, however, that Assad used this treaty relationship to act in ways of which Moscow did not always approve. Syrian actions increased the risks of a superpower confrontation and worked against Soviet efforts to create an anti-imperialist bloc of Arab states. As Moscow was moving closer to Syria, the United States was moving closer to Israel – and was also to find that closer ties with its client often complicated its policy in the Middle East. President Reagan, who took office in January 1981, and his first Secretary of State, Alexander Haig, were by far the most pro-Israel officials ever to serve in the American government (although Reagan's Secretary of Defense Caspar Weinberger had a more negative view of Israel), and military aid to Israel was increased. Nonetheless, as in the case of Soviet–Syrian relations, friction was not absent in the US–Israeli relationship. In 1981 alone, Israel mounted an unsuccessful campaign against the sale of the US AWACS to Saudi Arabia, bombed the Iraqi nuclear reactor at Osirak (overflying, in the process, Jordan and Saudi Arabia), and extended Israeli law to the Golan Heights, thereby in effect, annexing the former Syrian territory. The bombing of the reactor led to a suspension of US deliveries of F-16 aircraft to Israel, and the Golan Heights annexation on 14 December led to a suspension of the US–Israeli agreement on a memorandum of understanding establishing limited strategic cooperation between the US and Israel. Both suspensions, however, were only temporary despite the fact that the Israeli activities undercut the efforts of the United States to promote the Camp David peace process and improve its position in the Arab world.[22] Meanwhile, just as Israel increased its strategic cooperation with the US, so too did Syria with the USSR, as Damascus, realising it was unlikely to get Arab support against Israel, sought to obtain strategic equivalence with Israel.

Despite its closer relationship with Syria, which was reinforced by shipments of Soviet arms, Middle East trends continued to move against the USSR. Having imposed an arms embargo against Iraq when the Gulf War broke out in September 1980, Moscow, in late 1981, resumed shipments to that country. This rift followed Iran's rejection of Soviet efforts to improve Soviet–Iranian relations. At the same time, tension increased between Israel and Syria. As a confrontation over the moving of Syrian missiles into Lebanon developed in the spring of 1981, Moscow behaved with considerable caution. Although it was to be US special representative Philip Habib who (temporarily) defused the crisis, Moscow displayed its unwillingness to be dragged by Syria into a crisis over Lebanon – a pattern of behaviour to be repeated in 1983.[23] In addition, things appeared to be going from bad to worse for Moscow in Egypt, where Anwar Sadat expelled the Soviet ambassador and a number of other officials in early September 1981. Three weeks later Sadat was assassinated, but any Soviet hope that Egypt would rapidly reorient its foreign policy was dashed as Sadat's successor, Hosni Mubarak, affirmed the continuity of his regime's policies with those of Sadat's, albeit with a somewhat more neutralist tone. Mubarak's Egypt remained a major recipient of American military and economic aid and regularly carried out joint military exercises with the United States.

On the eve of the Israeli invasion of Lebanon, the major Middle East trends seemed to be going against Moscow as the Iran–Iraq war continued unabated, the US improved ties with the Gulf Arabs, and the Centrist Arab states slowly moved toward a reconciliation with Egypt. The Israeli invasion (for which Moscow blamed the US, which denied approving it), at least initially, was to cause further problems for the USSR.[24] In the first place, Soviet credibility suffered a major blow because its numerous warnings to the United States and Israel during the course of the war proved to be ineffectual in protecting PLO and Syrian forces in Lebanon or in preventing the deployment of US troops there (although Soviet warnings might have helped deter an Israeli attack on Syria proper). Second, the quality of Soviet military equipment and, to a lesser degree, the quality of Soviet training, were called into question by the overwhelming victory of US-supplied Israeli weaponry over the military equipment supplied by Moscow to Syria. (This was in clear contrast to the 1973 war in which Soviet weaponry was widely praised.) Finally, the Soviet leadership had to deal with a situation where the United States, having mediated the PLO withdrawal from Beirut (and having deployed Marines to Beirut to achieve this goal despite Soviet warnings), had the clear diplomatic initiative. On 1 September 1982 – the eve of a long-delayed Arab summit conference – President Reagan announced his plan for a Middle East peace settlement.[25] In a clear effort to gain Centrist Arab support for his plan, Reagan called for a stop to Israeli settlement activity on the West Bank and announced US refusal to accept any Israeli claim to sovereignty over the West Bank. To satisfy the Israelis, Reagan emphasised US concern for Israel's security, asserted that Israel's final borders should not be the pre-1967 war boundaries, called for the unity of Jerusalem and direct Arab–Israeli negotiations, and reaffirmed US opposition to a Palestinian state on the West Bank. In his most controversial statement, and one also aimed at obtaining Centrist Arab support, Reagan called for a fully autonomous Palestinian entity linked to Jordan.

Moscow, while denouncing the Reagan plan – and denigrating Israeli Prime Minister Begin's rapid rejection of it – was concerned that it might prove attractive in the Arab world. Indeed *Izvestia* correspondent Vladimir Kudravt-zev noted that 'judging from press reports "moderate" and "pro-Western" Arab regimes find positive elements in the American initiative'.[26]

Given this situation, Moscow seemed pleased by the outcome of the Arab summit at Fez, Morocco, which not only indicated that the Arab world had regained a semblance of unity but also that it brought forth a peace plan which, except for its lack of explicit clarity as to Israel's right to exist, was quite close to the long-standing Soviet peace plan, in that it called for an Israeli withdrawal to the 1967 boundaries but no genuine normalisation of relations.[27] Moscow was also pleased that the Sudanese proposal to formally readmit Egypt to the Arab League was rejected. Nonetheless, the Fez conference did not reject the Reagan Plan, thereby leaving it, along with the Fez Plan, as one of the solutions which the Arabs would consider to resolve the post-Beirut diplomatic situation in the Middle East. With both the Reagan and Fez Plans now being considered, Moscow evidently felt that it too had to enter the diplomatic competition and, in a speech on 15 September, Brezhnev announced the Soviet Union's own peace plan.[28] While a number of its points repeated previous Soviet proposals, new elements seem to have been added to emphasise the similarity between the Fez and Soviet plans. Brezhnev also took the opportunity to repeat the long-standing Soviet call for an international conference on the Middle East, with all interested parties participating, including the PLO, which the Soviet leader again characterised as 'the sole legitimate representative of the Arab people of Palestine'.

In modelling the Soviet peace plan on Fez, Brezhnev evidently sought to prevent the Arabs from moving to embrace the Reagan Plan. Nonetheless, with the United States clearly possessing the diplomatic initiative in the Middle East and both Jordan's King Hussein and PLO leader Arafat, along with other Arab leaders, expressing interest in the Reagan Plan, Moscow was on the diplomatic defensive – despite the massacres in Sabra and Shatilla which Moscow sought to link to the United States.

It was at this point, in mid-November, that Brezhnev passed from the scene. His successor, Yuri Andropov, had the task of rebuilding the Soviet position in the Middle East which had suffered a major blow during the Israeli invasion of Lebanon.

THE POST-BREZHNEV ERA

Under Andropov, Moscow's Middle East fortunes began to rise again, not so much because of Soviet successes as because of mistakes by the United States. To be sure, Andropov moved to restore Soviet credibility. In January 1983, two months after he took power, he sent Syria SAM-5 anti-aircraft missiles, weapons which had never before been deployed outside the Soviet bloc. In March Andropov warned Israel not to attack Syria. A shipment of SS-21 ground-to-ground missiles was sent to Syria in September following the first US–Syrian confrontation in Lebanon.[29] On the diplomatic front, the Soviet Middle East position was aided by two major developments which severely weakened US diplomatic efforts in the Middle East – the weakening of Arafat's position in the PLO and the collapse of the US position in Lebanon. Pressure from within the PLO upon Arafat led to his public rejection of the Reagan Plan, while Jordan, for its part, was unwilling to enter into negotiations with Israel without the cover of a working arrangement with the PLO. At the same time the US suffered a major debacle in Lebanon as it chose, in effect, to back Amin Gemayel and the Maronites in a civil war against Lebanese Druze and Shiites who were, as a result, driven into the arms of Syria, thereby considerably strengthening the Syrian position in Lebanon. America's pro-Maronite position soon made it a target of attacks by Moslem terrorists and, by February 1984, after a brief clash with Syria itself when two US aircraft were shot down (Moscow was conspicuous by its non-activity during this crisis despite Syrian claims of Soviet support),[30] the US ignominiously pulled out of Lebanon.

While these events strengthened Moscow's position in its zero-sum competition with the US in the Middle East, it suddenly and unexpectedly found itself confronted by a new Middle East peace process. When Syria, in late December 1983, drove Arafat out of Lebanon he went to Egypt (thereby partially relegitimising Egypt in the Arab world) and began to negotiate again with King Hussein. Next came the fall of the hard-line Likud government in Israel and the announcement of new elections. In the pre-election polls, the Israeli Labour party headed by Shimon Peres, who had endorsed the Reagan Plan of September 1982, took a commanding lead, and Moscow may have foreseen the re-establishment of a peace process which it could not control. For this reason, during the spring and summer of 1984 Soviet Middle Eastern diplomacy had a special Jordanian focus. Moscow assiduously wooed King Hussein, hoping to keep Jordan from embracing the Reagan Plan in the event that the Labour party scored a major victory in the Israeli elections.[31] In addition, the Soviet leadership prepared a new variant of its Middle East peace plan, one that might prove more amenable to King Hussein than previous Soviet peace plans had been. While the Jordanian monarch had long shared the Soviet goal of an international conference to settle the Arab–Israeli conflict, he had also long desired a link between any Palestinian entity or state on the West Bank and Jordan, whose population was more than 60 per cent Palestinian. The Soviet peace plan of 29 July, which mentioned such a link, therefore can be considered a major gesture to Hussein.[32] Modelled on the Brezhnev peace plan of 15 September 1982 which had combined the basic three-point Soviet peace plan with the major components of the Arab programme announced at Fez, the new Soviet plan had one additional key element – the acknowledgement that the new Palestinian state could decide to form a confederation with a neighbouring country.

While Moscow was able to garner at least verbal support from most of the Arab world for its peace plan, the pace of Middle Eastern events once again seemed to confound Soviet strategy. In late September 1984, soon after President Reagan, from the rostrum of the United Nations, had underlined the importance of the Reagan Plan, and a Peres-led National Unity government had taken office in Israel, King Hussein, whom Moscow had been courting, suddenly reestablished full diplomatic relations with Egypt. Nonetheless, despite resuming relations at the ambassadorial level with the USSR in August, Egypt continued its close military and economic relationship with the United States, as exemplified by the joint military exercise 'Sea Wind' carried out by the two nations in early November. The low-level treatment given to the resumption of Egyptian–Jordanian diplomatic relations in the Soviet press seemed to indicate that Moscow was trying to play down the development while continuing to cultivate Jordan.

In February 1985 Hussein and Arafat signed an agreement on a joint negotiating position in the Middle East peace process. Not surprisingly, the Soviet reaction to this agreement, and its rapid endorsement by Mubarak, was a very negative one. Indeed, the Soviet leadership (which was to undergo yet another change with the death of Chernenko and the rise to power of Mikhail Gorbachev) became concerned about the formation of an Arab alignment consisting of Jordan, Arafat's wing of the PLO and Egypt.[33] Given this problem, Gorbachev evidently decided that if Moscow were not to once again be on the sidelines of the Middle East peace effort, he had to make some gestures to Israel. Although the USSR and the US had met in February for high-level talks to discuss the Middle East (the first such superpower meeting on the Middle East in seven years), President Reagan gave no indication of wanting to include the USSR in the peace process.[34] Indeed, the most a US official would concede was that the talks were 'merely an exchange of thoughts in the hope of reducing misunderstandings. Even to call them explorations would be an exaggeration.'[35] Not unexpectedly, therefore, no agreement was reached, and the US representative, Assistant Secretary of State Richard Murphy, noted that the USSR lacked credibility as a mediator because of its refusal to resume diplomatic relations with Israel and because its treatment of Soviet Jews had alienated the Israelis. He also stated that while the USSR was pressing for an international conference involving Security Council members and interested parties in the Middle East including the PLO, the US felt that such large meetings would be counterproductive and called instead for direct talks between Israel and its neighbours.[36]

Following a late May visit to Washington by King Hussein who, perhaps both as a sop to Moscow and as a means of diplomatically protecting his flank, continued to call for an international conference with Moscow's participation, State Department spokesman Edward Djerejian listed a number of specific actions which Moscow could take to show that it was ready to play a 'constructive role' in the Middle East peace process. These included resuming full diplomatic relations with Israel, ending anti-Semitic propaganda, improving the treatment of Soviet Jews, and ending arms aid to militias in Lebanon.[37] While Soviet Middle East specialist Yevgeny Primakov, then Director of the Soviet Institute of Oriental Studies, predicted that the USSR would not accept 'one side setting preconditions for the other to meet', and stated that it was premature to ask the USSR to recognise Israel as a condition for holding an international conference on the Middle East, Gorbachev was to move in just such a direction.[38]

While signals about the possibility of the resumption of diplomatic relations had been sent from Moscow to Israel almost from the time relations were broken off during the 1967 war,[39] the signals increased in intensity soon after Gorbachev took power. The Soviet gestures were made despite a series of Israeli actions that bound the Jewish state even more tightly to the United States. Indeed, the possibility should not be ruled out that the Soviet gestures to Israel were aimed not only at gaining entry into the Middle East peace process, but also at winning favour in the United States with which a summit was on the horizon. Given Moscow's tendency to overestimate the influence of American Jews on American policy-making *vis-à-vis* the USSR, gestures to Israel, which virtually all

American Jews hold dear, could have been part of Moscow's pre-summit manoeuvring.[40]

The momentum toward even a partial Soviet–Israeli *rapprochement* – if that indeed was Gorbachev's goal – was slowed, however, as the peace process fell by the wayside in the face of an escalation of Middle East terrorism. While Moscow itself was to suffer both embarrassment and physical loss as a result of the Middle East terrorism (one of its diplomats in Beirut was murdered and two others kidnapped), the end result was that the peace process, centred around negotiations between Israel and a Jordanian–Palestinian delegation, was halted, a development from which Moscow was to profit diplomatically.

In order to maintain credibility with Palestinian hard-liners, Arafat, after the agreement with King Hussein, stressed the escalation of 'armed struggle'. Peres, who was under attack for being 'soft on the PLO' responded to the increase in terrorism by authorising an attack on PLO headquarters in Tunis on 1 October 1985, perhaps signalling to Arafat that if the PLO leader wished to fight while he was negotiating, Israel could play the same game. Moscow lost little time in exploiting the Israeli attack to try to undermine the US position in the Middle East, and once again appealed for Arab unity against Israel and the United States, as it sought to link the Israeli action to the United States. In a radio broadcast in Arabic on 2 October, the day after the attack, the Soviet commentator alleged not only that the US had used its radar posts in the Mediterranean to direct Israeli planes to PLO headquarters in Tunis, but also that the Israeli bombers took off from a US aircraft carrier – a classic case of Soviet disinformation.[41]

Even before the uproar over the Israeli attack had died down, another terrorist event from which Moscow was to profit diplomatically took place. This was the hijacking of the cruise ship Achille Lauro and the murder of a Jewish passenger, Leon Klinghoffer, by a PLO faction headed by Mohammed Abbas, a hardline PLO leader who was linked to Arafat by mutual opposition to Syrian leader Hafiz Assad.[42] The hijacking had two major diplomatic benefits for Moscow. In the first place, the action of the United States in forcing down an Egyptian plane carrying the hijackers and Abbas inflamed US relations with Egypt. Secondly, it led Peres to shift the focus of his peace policy from the PLO to Jordan. Peres proposed at the UN on 21 October Israeli–Jordanian talks under 'international auspices'. (This was a clear change from Israel's former position rejecting an international conference.) Unfortunately for Peres, however, King Hussein was not to opt for the Israeli offer and moved instead to improve relations with Syria. Moscow was clearly pleased with this limited Syrian–Jordanian *rapprochement*, and as the chances for a Middle East peace settlement brokered by the United States receded, Moscow took a much harder line with Israel. This shift occurred despite the approach of the mid-November summit between Reagan and Gorbachev in Geneva and despite reported calls by Egypt and Jordan for Moscow to restore diplomatic relations with Israel as a way to advance prospects for Middle East peace talks.[43] Indeed, on the eve of the summit, a Soviet government spokesman, Albert Vlasov demanded, as the price of renewed relations, that Israel agree not only to allow the USSR to participate in the international peace conference, but also to allow the PLO to participate – clearly something that Peres was unwilling to accept.[44] Perhaps because of this condition Peres shifted his position, and now stated that the resumption of Soviet Jewish emigration (Aliya) from the USSR was a more important precondition for Soviet participation than the restoration of diplomatic ties.[45]

Moscow's harder line policy toward Israel may have had additional causes. Arab leaders, perhaps remembering the 1972 Nixon–Brezhnev summit, seemed concerned that a superpower deal might be worked out at their expense.[46] Furthermore, Reagan's pre-summit demand for linkage between an arms-control agreement and Soviet behaviour in the Third World, may have heightened Soviet determination to prove that no such deal had taken place.[47] Indeed, in a spate of articles appearing in the Soviet media at the time of the summit, including Arabic language radio broadcasts and *Novosti* statements distributed in Beirut, the USSR dismissed as 'fabrications and lies' claims that Arab interests would be compromised at Geneva.[48]

Moscow, however, was not to limit its campaign to demonstrate to the Arabs that there was no US–Soviet deal at Geneva, to mere words. Less than a month after the Geneva summit, it was revealed that the USSR had sent SAM-5 anti-aircraft missiles to Libya,[49] a clear escalation of the Soviet military commitment to that country since heretofore only Syria, of all of Moscow's Third World allies, had received such a weapon. Given the very tense relations between the United States and Libya, as well as Libya's troubled relations with virtually all of its neighbours, the decision to send SAM-5 missiles was clearly a commitment of support to the Gaddafi regime, albeit one that was ultimately to prove costly to Moscow, as it failed to aid Libya in its military confrontations with the United States in March and April 1986.

Indeed as Libyan–US tension rose, Moscow could only have become concerned at the possibility of an Israeli strike against Syria or, perhaps even worse, an Israeli-supported American strike against Syria. In the aftermath of the US bombing of Libya for its alleged terrorist activities, Moscow could not be certain the US would refrain from taking action against Syria, another sponsor of terrorism.[50] Such action would again raise serious questions of Soviet credibility if Moscow did not aid its Middle Eastern ally (especially after its failure to aid Libya). On the other hand, if Moscow went to Syria's aid, there would be a very real possibility of a superpower confrontation. Given these unpalatable alternatives, Moscow seems to have decided to move diplomatically to avert the possibility of such a clash by negotiating with Israel to arrange consular-level talks in Helsinki, and acceding to Israel's demand to make the talks public.[51] Such a diplomatic ploy, Moscow may well have felt, would deter an Israeli attack on Syria, lest this harm a possible improvement in Soviet–Israeli relations, which in turn held out the possibility of an increase in the number of Soviet Jews allowed to leave the USSR.

A second factor which may have contributed to Moscow's decision to initiate public contacts with Israel was the USSR's continuing efforts to play a role in the Middle East peace process. Following King Hussein's split with Arafat in February 1986 (a split warmly welcomed by Moscow),[52] it appeared that the American-supported Middle East peace initiative had been derailed. Moscow sought to exploit this to gain entry into the peace process by orchestrating a pre-conference preparatory committee made up of the UN Security Council's five permanent members. Nonetheless when, in late July, Israeli Prime Minister Shimon Peres and Moroccan King Hassan had their surprise meeting in Morocco, Moscow may have become concerned that it would once again be left on the diplomatic sidelines as a major peace initiative unfolded.[53] The gesture to Israel may have been designed partly to avert this possibility.

A third contributing factor behind Moscow's request for consular talks may have been the Soviet desire to improve ties with the United States. It would not appear accidental that the Soviet announcement of consular talks with Israel on 4 August coincided with the announcement of the scheduling of the 19 and 20 September meeting between US Secretary of State George Shultz and Soviet Foreign Minister Eduard Shevardnadze to prepare for a US–Soviet summit. (An earlier meeting had been postponed by Moscow because of the American bombing of Libya in April – the only action taken by the USSR against the United States at the time.) The Soviet–Israeli talks provide a useful point of departure for drawing some conclusions about superpower policies in the Middle East as well as the possibilities for a conflict-prevention or conflict-management system in the region.

CONCLUSIONS

The first major conclusion that can be drawn from this analysis of superpower interaction in the Middle East is that neither superpower is in control of events in the turmoil-filled region, and that each is basically reacting to events beyond its control, despite all the military aid it sends to the region. Sometimes events benefit one side, while harming the interests of the other. Thus the fall of the

Shah benefited Moscow while hurting the United States, while the outbreak and continuation of the Iran–Iraq war had the opposite effect on the Middle East fortunes of the superpowers. What is important to note here is that neither superpower was responsible for causing either of these events and such benefits as accrued to the superpowers because of them were not of their own creation.

A related conclusion is the very limited amount of influence either superpower has over its main client in the region, something that has been increasingly evident since 1980. In the case of the Soviet–Syrian relationship, Soviet efforts to create 'anti-imperialist' unity in the Arab world have been hampered by Syrian President Hafiz Assad's continuing conflict with PLO leader Yasser Arafat, and by Syria's aid to Iran in the Iran–Iraq war – the Arab world's most divisive struggle. In addition, Moscow could not have been pleased with Syrian attempts to extend Moscow's support for its Lebanese activities in 1983 to the point of a Soviet willingness militarily to confront the United States on Syria's behalf. Indeed, Moscow's very low profile during the escalation of the Syrian–American crisis from September to December 1983 seemed aimed at avoiding just such an eventuality, even though this raised questions about Soviet credibility in Arab eyes. Similar questions had been raised when Moscow stood by rather ineffectually while Israel invaded Lebanon in June 1982, and these questions were raised again when the USSR did not help Gaddafi in 1986 during the US punitive strikes in response to Libyan-supported terrorism. Indeed, both Syrian and Libyan support for terrorism were also counterproductive in Soviet eyes, insofar as they raised the possibility of Israeli–Syrian or US–Libyan confrontations which had the potential for escalating into superpower conflicts.

If Syria (to say nothing of Libya) has proved a difficult client for the Soviet Union, Israel has also posed serious difficulties for the United States. Its bombing of the Iraqi nuclear reactor, and annexation of the Golan Heights in 1981, its invasion of Lebanon in 1982, its balking at US urging to negotiate with Palestinians close to the PLO, its bombing of PLO headquarters in Tunis in 1985, and its opposition to US arms sales to America's Arab friends from 1981 to 1986 – all posed obstacles to American efforts to extend the Camp David process and forge an Israeli–Arab front against the USSR.

In the light of these factors – Middle East clients who show very little obedience to their superpower patrons despite receiving vast amounts of arms from them, and the flux of events in the Middle East which neither superpower has shown much ability to control – what can be said about the possibility of crisis-prevention or crisis-management arrangements to defuse the volatile region? The historical record makes it difficult to be very optimistic. Nevertheless, several possible crisis-prevention arrangements do suggest themselves. One must start with the proposition, however, that neither superpower has heretofore displayed any serious willingness to curtail its weapons shipments to the Middle East, nor is it likely to do so. For Moscow, arms shipments are a major source of hard currency, and its primary instrument of influence; for the United States, arms sales to the Arab states are also seen as a means of obtaining influence, while arms to Israel are primarily a means of demonstrating solidarity with Israel as well as rewarding it for past territorial concessions in the Sinai II agreement and the Egyptian–Israeli peace treaty. Under these circumstances, it is doubtful if either superpower can persuade the other to limit arms (except for nuclear weapons) to its clients.

If this is in fact the case, what other crisis-prevention arrangements might be considered? The first is rather simple – periodic meetings between heads of state or high-ranking individuals of foreign ministries to discuss crisis areas. Prior to both the summits of 1972 and 1985, regional powers became concerned that a superpower 'deal' was being arranged at their expense and, paradoxically, regular superpower meetings *may* have a certain deterrent effect on the actions of client states *if* they give the impression of actively accelerating the peace process or jointly restraining the adventurism of any client state. It does not appear accidental that the greatest period of client activism against the interests of its superpower patron – 1980–5 – coincided with the sharp deterioration of superpower relations as both Israel and Syria seemed to feel they could act with relative impunity because the superpowers could not afford to alienate them by withholding support. A promising start in the area of regional meetings was seen in early 1985 as the US and USSR sat down at the deputy secretary of state level to discuss regional problems, although not a great deal has yet resulted from the meetings.

In addition to periodic meetings, which might have the value of deterring client adventurism, the superpowers might also move to more closely coordinate their respective peace plans. The Soviet peace plan, which currently calls for little more than an extended armistice between Israel and her Arab neighbours, is a non-starter both for Israel and the United States. Were Moscow to agree both to restore diplomatic relations with Israel and to support the concept of a genuine peace, with trade, cultural and diplomatic relations in return for a mutually agreed upon Israeli withdrawal, it would be considerably easier to gain Israeli and American support. It may be argued, of course, that a significant portion of the Israeli public is opposed to territorial withdrawal from the West Bank and Gaza, no matter what the terms. Nonetheless, were a genuine peace to be offered, rather than merely an extended armistice, it would be easier to get Israel's support, and the Egyptian–Israeli Treaty set a useful precedent in this regard. It may also be argued that Moscow, for its own reasons, does not want a genuine Arab–Israeli settlement – indeed, that has been the argument throughout this chapter. Nonetheless, one should not rule out the possibility that the new Soviet leader, Mikhail Gorbachev, with serious domestic economic and political problems, and with higher foreign-policy priorities elsewhere in the world, might be more amenable to a genuine peace settlement than have his predecessors. In any case, it is recommended that US–Soviet contacts in this area should be explored.

If, however, none of the crisis-prevention arrangements prove successful, what can be said of crisis-management techniques? Historically, it seems that when Arab–Israeli crises have occurred, the response by the superpowers has been essentially *ad hoc*. When the crisis has been short, as in the 1967 and 1982 wars, hot-line communications have been used; when the crisis has been more extended, as in the 1973 war, a combination of UN meetings, hot-line exchanges and even a visit by the foreign minister of one superpower (Kissinger) to the capital of the other have been employed. The degree of success of these measures, however, is open to question. While the Six-Day War ended before there was a serious chance of a major superpower confrontation, the US apparently misread the Soviet signal threatening intervention during the 1969–70 War of Attrition. Similarly Brezhnev's warning to the US during the latter stages of the 1973 war led to the US calling a nuclear alert. While the Soviet move may well have been a bluff, a superpower crisis might have resulted had Israel not agreed to a second ceasefire and it would appear that this is a highly dangerous way of bringing a crisis to an end.

In lieu of the rather *ad hoc* crisis-management activities that have existed heretofore, it is suggested that the same officials (possibly at the deputy secretary or state/deputy foreign minister level) who have been meeting since the beginning of 1985 to discuss regional affairs, establish a working group (possibly at the UN) to handle any crisis which breaks out in the Middle East. Assuming that neither side wishes to exploit the crisis for its own benefit – a major assumption – such a working group would, at the very minimum, provide an institutional arrangement for defusing the crisis, as it would bring together individuals conversant with the problems of the region who have discussed them with each other in pre-crisis meetings.

Underlying any crisis-management arrangement for the Middle East is what appears to be one 'unwritten rule' of superpower behaviour during past crises. Both superpowers have proven themselves unwilling to see a client state's regime toppled, although they have acquiesced in that regime's loss of territory. Soviet action in the 1967 war seemed aimed at preserving the left-wing Ba'athist regime which seized power in Syria in 1966, the Soviet intervention in the War of Attrition seemed aimed at preserving Nasser's regime, Brezhnev's threat to Nixon in 1973 seemed aimed at preventing an Israeli march on Cairo and thus preserving the Sadat regime, and the limited Soviet efforts in 1982 seemed aimed at ensuring that Israel did not attack Syria proper, a move that could threaten the Assad regime. Throughout this prolonged period of confrontation, the United States has remained strongly committed to the existence of the State of Israel, as has the USSR, albeit for very different reasons.

Under these circumstances, therefore, it is possible to see a future conflict limited to territorial changes although not to regime changes. Given the use of poison gas by Iraq in the Iran–Iraq war, however, Syria's acquisition of accurate ground-to-ground missiles, Israel's reported possession of nuclear weapons and Syria's reported possession of poison gas, the possibility of a more widespread war erupting, one that would not be confined to border areas (and hence presumably manageable by the superpowers), but likely to cause large casualties in civilian areas, is a very serious one. Under these circumstances a more active effort at superpower crisis prevention would appear to be in order.

NOTES

1 This point is discussed in Robert O. Freedman, 'Moscow and a Middle East Peace Settlement', *Washington Quarterly* 8, 3 (Summer 1985), pp. 143–61.

2 The main representatives of this school of thought are Dennis Ross and Uri Ra'anan. See, for example, Dennis Ross, 'The Soviet Union and the Persian Gulf', *Political Science Quarterly*, 99 (Winter 1984–5), pp. 615–35.

3 The main representatives of this school are Galia Golan and George Breslauer. See Galia Golan, *Yom Kippur and After: The Soviet Union and the Middle East Crisis* (London: Cambridge University Press, 1977) and George Breslauer, 'Soviet Policy in the Middle East 1967–1972: Unalterable Antagonism or Collaborative Competition?' in Alexander L. George, ed., *Managing US–Soviet Rivalry: Problems of Crisis Prevention* (Boulder, CO: Westview Press, 1981), pp. 65–105.

4 Cf. Robert O. Freedman, *Soviet Policy Toward the Middle East Since 1970*, 3rd edn (New York: Praeger, 1982).

5 One of the USSR's more sophisticated observers is Yevgeny Primakov. See his *Anatomiia blizhnevostochnogo konflikta* (Moscow: Mysl', 1978). The need for an anti-imperialist Arab unity has long been a staple of Moscow's public statements, and is also found in the secret discussions of Soviet Foreign Minister Andrei Gromyko with Yasser Arafat. See Raphael Israeli, ed., *PLO in Lebanon: Selected Documents* (New York: St Martin's Press, 1983), p. 47.

6 For Haig's view of the visit, see Alexander M. Haig, jun, *Caveat: Realism, Reagan and Foreign Policy* (New York: Macmillan, 1984), pp. 169–74. Haig notes 'there was, in a real, rather than a theoretical sense, a strategic consensus in the region', p. 169.

7 For details of the hotline's use, see Lyndon Baines Johnson, *The Vantage Point: Perspectives of the Presidency 1963–1969* (New York: Holt Rinehart & Winston, 1971), pp. 298–303.

8 For studies of the War of Attrition, see Lawrence C. Whetten, *The Canal War: Four-Power Conflict in the Middle East* (Cambridge, MA: MIT Press, 1974); Yaacov Bar-Simon-Tov, *The Israeli–Egyptian War of Attrition* (New York: Columbia University Press, 1980); Alvin Rubinstein, *Red Star on the Nile* (Princeton, NJ: Princeton University Press, 1977); Karen Dawisha, *Soviet Foreign Policy Toward Egypt* (London: Macmillan, 1979); Mohamed Heikal, *The Road to Ramadan* (New York: Quadrangle, 1975); and Robert O. Freedman, 'Detente and US–Soviet Relations in the Middle East During the Nixon Years (1969–1974)' in *Dimensions of Detente* ed. Della W. Sheldon (New York: Praeger, 1978), pp. 84–121.

9 Freedman, 'Detente'; Breslauer, 'Soviet Policy in the Middle East 1967–1972' has a different view.

10 Freedman, 'Detente'. For Kissinger's view of these events, see Henry Kissinger, *White House Years* (Boston, MA: Little Brown & Company, 1979), pp. 558–631. For a view that a different US policy might have at least partially defused the crisis during the War of Attrition, see Alexander George, 'Missed Opportunities for Crisis Prevention: The War of Attrition and Angola', in George, ed., *Managing US–Soviet Rivalry*, pp. 187–98.

11 Heikal, *The Road to Ramadan*, p. 117.

12 For the text of the Basic Principles, and an analysis of their origin, see Alexander George, 'The Basic Principles Agreement of 1972: Origins and Impact', in George, ed., *Managing US–Soviet Rivalry*, pp. 107–17. For Kissinger's view, see *White House Years*, pp. 1132, 1150–51, 1205, 1209. Unfortunately, both *détente* and the Basic Principles were oversold by Kissinger and Nixon, leading to a great deal of cynicism later.

13 For an analysis of Sadat's strategy, see Freedman, *Soviet Policy Toward the Middle East Since 1970*, chapters 3 and 4.

14 For detailed analyses of the war, see Freedman, *Soviet Policy*; Golan, *Yom Kippur and After*; Rubinstein, *Red Star on the Nile*; William Quandt, *Soviet Policy in the October 1973 War* (Rand paper R-1864, May 1975) and Jon Glassman, *Arms for the Arabs* (Baltimore, MD: Johns Hopkins University Press, 1975). For a more benign view of Soviet activities, see George, 'The Arab–Israeli War of October 1973: Origins and Impact', in George, ed., *Managing US–Soviet Rivalry*, pp. 139–54. For Kissinger's view of Soviet policy, see Henry Kissinger, *Years of Upheaval* (Boston, MA: Little Brown, 1982), chapters 11, 12, 13.

15 These events are discussed in Freedman, *Soviet Policy*, chapters 5 and 6.

16 For a more detailed analysis of the evolution of the Soviet peace plan, see Freedman, 'Moscow and a Middle East Peace Settlement'.

17 For analyses of Carter's strategy, see Carter's memoirs, *Keeping Faith*; William Quandt, *Camp David: Peacemaking and Politics* (Washington DC: Brookings, 1986); Steven Spiegel, *The Other Arab–Israeli Conflict* (Chicago, IL: University of Chicago Press, 1985); and Freedman, *Soviet Policy, Since 1970*, chapter 8.

18 Carter interview with newspapermen, cited in *Near East Report*, 21, 44 (2 November 1977), p. 189.

19 The text of the agreement was published in *Pravda*, 2 October 1977. The translation is from the *Current Digest of the Soviet Press*, 29, 39, pp. 8–9.

20 The events at Baghdad are discussed in Freedman, *Soviet Policy*, pp. 348–9.

21 For a background analysis of Soviet–Syrian relations before the treaty, see Robert O. Freedman, 'The Soviet Union, Syria, and the Crisis in Lebanon: A Preliminary Analysis', in the *Middle East Annual 1983* (ed. David H. Partington) (Boston, MA: G. K. Hall, 1984), pp. 103–57.

22 For analyses of Israeli–American clashes over these issues, see Spiegel, *The Other Arab–Israeli Conflict*, pp. 395–411, and Haig, *Caveat: Realism, Reagan and Foreign Policy*, chapters 9 and 15.

23 Soviet policy during this crisis is discussed in Freedman, *Soviet Policy*, pp. 406–8.

24 For a detailed discussion of the Soviet reaction to the Israeli invasion, see Robert O. Freedman, 'The Soviet Union and the Middle East – 1982', in Colin Legum, Haim Shaked and Daniel Dishon eds., *Middle East Contemporary Survey 1981–82* (New York: Holmes and Meier, 1984), pp. 40–9.

25 The Reagan peace plan is discussed in Barry Rubin, 'The United States and the Middle East', in Legum, Shaked and Dishon, eds., *Middle East Contemporary Survey 1981–82*, pp. 30–3.

26 *Izvestia*, 10 September 1982.

27 For the text of the Fez Plan, see *The Middle East Journal*, 37, 1 (Winter 1983), p. 71.

28 *Pravda*, 16 September 1982.

29 The impact of Soviet military aid is discussed in Freedman, 'The Soviet Union, Syria and the Crisis in Lebanon'.

30 *Ibid*.

31 Numerous Jordanian delegations visited Moscow, and many Soviet delegations visited Jordan, and the Soviet press was full of praise for Jordan's 'independent' position.

32 For the text of this peace plan, see *Pravda*, 30 July 1984. An English translation of the plan may be found in *Current Digest of the Soviet Press*, 36, 30, 1984, pp. 9–10.

33 Cf. *Pravda*, 20 February 1985 and Tass Report, in English, 27 February 1985 (*FBIS:USSR*, 28 February 1985, p. H–1).

34 Cf. Reagan press conference, *Washington Post*, 22 February 1985.

35 Cited in an article by Henry Trewitt, *Baltimore Sun*, 20 February 1985. The talks took place between Assistant Secretary of State Richard Murphy and the head of the Soviet Foreign Ministry's Near East Division, Vladimir Polyakov.
36 Cited in report by Bernard Gwertzman, *New York Times*, 22 February 1985.
37 Cited in report by David Ottaway, *Washington Post*, 31 May 1985.
38 Cited in report by Jim Hoagland, *Washington Post*, 8 June 1985.
39 For an excellent survey of Soviet–Israeli relations, see Arthur J. Klinghoffer, *Israel and the Soviet Union: Alienation or Reconciliation* (Boulder, CO: Westview Press, 1985).
40 This is particularly true on the issue of Soviet Jewry. On this point, see Robert O. Freedman, 'Soviet Jewry and Soviet–American Relations' in Freedman, ed., *Soviet Jewry in the Decisive Decade 1971–1980* (Durham, NC: Duke University Press, 1984).
41 Moscow International Service in Arabic, 2 October 1985 (*FBIS:USSR*, 4 October 1985, p. H–3). The disinformation was at least partially successful, as Arafat was quoted as claiming that the US helped the Israelis refuel. (Cf. report by Jonathan C. Randal, *Washington Post*, 3 October 1985.) Arafat also claimed the US was out to kill him.
42 Cf. report by David Hirst, *Manchester Guardian Weekly*, 3 November 1985.
43 Cf. report by Bernard Gwertzman, *New York Times*, 31 October 1985.
44 Cited in report by Walter Ruby, *Jerusalem Post*, 17 November 1985. Vlasov was the deputy Soviet spokesman at the summit. Yevgeny Primakov made the same point at another press conference in Geneva: KUNA, 16 November 1986 (*FBIS:USSR*, 18 November 1985, p. H–7).
45 Cited in report by Asher Wallfish, *Jerusalem Post*, 19 November 1985.
46 Cf. report by Ihsan Hijazi, *New York Times*, 20 November 1985. See also the report by David Ottaway, *Washington Post*, 8 November 1985.
47 For the text of Reagan's speech on this subject, see *New York Times*, 25 October 1985.
48 Moscow Radio International Service in Arabic, 17 November 1985 (*FBIS:USSR*, 19 November 1985, *Reportage on the Reagan–Gorbachev Summit*, p. 3). Arafat was reportedly particularly suspicious. See report by Ihsan Hijazi, *New York Times*, 20 November 1985.
49 Cf. report by Bob Woodward and Lou Cannon, *Washington Post*, 21 December 1985.
50 Cf. *Pravda*, 15 May 1986 article by Yuri Glukhov and E. Korshunov, 'Dangerous Conspiracy', *New Times*, 13, 1986, p. 12.
51 For an analysis of the events leading up to the talks, see the article in the *Jerusalem Post*, 5 August 1986.
52 Moscow was less happy, however, at King Hussein's crackdown on Jordan's Communist party and his arrest of leaders of the Jordan–Soviet Friendship Society, which the USSR may have feared might be the first step to a deal with Israel (Cf. *Pravda*, 29 May 1986).
53 Cf. *Pravda*, 11 August 1986.

8 The superpowers and the Gulf

Shahram Chubin

Despite changes in significant respects, the problems associated with the international politics of the Persian Gulf and Persia/Iran have remained remarkably durable over time. Historically the competition between Great Britain and Russia, the great game, concerned the attempts by the former to limit the encroachments of the latter through Persia on British India. The difficulty was to establish the limits of legitimate Russian claims without agreeing or succumbing to demands that gave her dominant or exclusive power in Persia. Much of British/Russian competition stemmed from an attempt by Russia to expand the zone of 'legitimate' interest and by Britain to limit it. This did not preclude occasional agreement, as in 1907, on limiting this competition by recognising each other's interests, for the pressures of European politics took precedence for both states. Nor did this competition entail automatic equality in the two states' positions. Britain always experienced difficulty in matching the advantages that Russia derived from physical contiguity, as well as the 'obvious' legitimacy of her interest in the affairs of a neighbouring state as opposed to Britain's more tenuous claim to equivalent concern over what was for her a remote area.

A continuing problem for Britain and Russia, not to mention Persia, was that while the two states could agree in general terms about their respective zones of influence, there were always pressures to expand them. In this, Persia was sometimes but not always the passive victim. The Anglo–Russian Convention of 1907, an agreement on spheres of influence, was an example of great power cooperation in the reduction of friction, a means of regulating competition in a secondary zone of interest because of the needs of the primary zone. The agreement was temporary, for it reflected political necessities and the European balance of power. In its preamble it purported to respect the independence and integrity of Persia, but it was seen by Persians as a disguised partition. By 1915 Britain went a step further and admitted the principle of partition of Persian territory with Russia in the Constantinople Agreement. By 1917 Britain established what amounted to a veiled protectorate over Persia while Russia was preoccupied with her revolution. Yet by 1921 things had gone the other way with the new Soviet regime prepared to offer the new regime in Iran far more than could the British. Persia chose to accept the Soviet offer and to ditch the already negotiated but unratified British treaty of 1919. Perhaps the Soviet landing of troops in northern Iran in May 1920 when they installed a brigand, one Kutchuk Khan, as head of Gilan province, impressed Tehran of the importance they attached to northern Persia and of the need to come to terms. Perhaps it was the new republic's stated desire for a new page in relations with its neighbour. In Harold Nicholson's phrase 'Russia was contiguous, overpowering and amazingly friendly'.[1]

Elements of this Soviet–Iranian treaty that remain of enduring interest are Articles V and VI, which were designed to reassure the new Soviet republic that Iran would not harbour the enemies of the new regime on its soil or permit the use of her territory for attacks on the Bolsheviks. In practice, despite the clear reference to the activities of White Russians in the text and associated papers of this treaty, the Soviet Union has chosen to interpret this treaty as giving it a general right to dictate to Iran, and a sanction to use force to defend its interests.[2] As a club against Iran, as a legal cloak to cover its expansionist definition of its interests, and as notice to an acquiescent US, what was intended as a means of reassuring the USSR has become an instrument whereby that state claims legal authority to use force to prevent the evolution of virtually any general development which it may not like or which it fears will be harmful to it.

Historically, competition centred around Persia not the Persian Gulf where Britain enjoyed exclusive and undisputed power, recognised by Russia. Indeed the 1907 Convention did not specifically allude to the Persian Gulf, for Russia did not deny Britain's 'special interests' in those waters.[3] This did not, however, last. As Curzon had foreseen 'Russia would not for one minute abide by the self-denying ordinance embodied in the preamble.' He was correct in that surmise.[4] In the Potsdam Agreement of 1911 Russia and Germany agreed to link the Persian–Baghdad railway to Europe. In November 1940 the Russian–German talks about a projected Soviet sphere of influence in the Middle East fixed Soviet priorities squarely 'in the direction of the Persian Gulf'.[5]

Anglo–Russian competition in and around Persia stemmed from the rival but not irreconcilable demands of the Russians for security, which they interpreted as primacy on their borders, and the British need for a buffer zone around India. The difficulties arose from the practical implementation of these needs. One problem was that no definitive arrangement was possible. As Martin Wight observed:

A buffer state is a weak power between two or more stronger ones, maintained or even created with the purpose of reducing conflict between them . . . Fluctuations of power make most buffer zones unstable and ambiguous. A policy adopted by one great power to preserve the neutrality of a buffer state may be seen by its rival as reducing the buffer state to a satellite; and a buffer state may be regarded by the same statesman, in different circumstances, as either a defensive bulwark or a springboard for further expansion.[6]

The dynamics of power and competition were accentuated by differences in objectives. A. J. P. Taylor has written, 'It is not an unreasonable generalization that the Anglo-Saxons and perhaps the French believe in buffer states and the Germans and perhaps the Russians, believe in partition as the best way to peace between great powers.'[7] Be that as it may, British and Russian interests remained asymmetrical, for Britain, even had she wanted to, could never have established a complete protectorate in Persia equivalent to what was within Russian capabilities in its contiguous empire. There was thus more than empty imperial rhetoric or hyperbole in Curzon's oration:

Was it not natural that Persia, seeking to establish and stabilize her future, should turn to us? Our boundaries march with hers for hundreds of miles on the southern frontiers. For a century we have pacified and policed the Gulf. In Mesopotamia we shall presently be her neighbours on the West. It is an obvious interest to us to have a peaceful and prosperous Persia; and as regards Persia itself, if it be true . . . that external assistance of some sort is necessary for her, is it not natural that it should be to this country that she should turn?[8]

In addition to differences in capabilities especially in relation to northern Iran where Russia was much stronger, and southern Iran where due to its maritime power Britain remained unchallenged, there was the problem of establishing a legitimacy in the respective balance of interests. An historian of the early period of rivalry concluded:

Britain's greatest difficulty, in creating a buffer zone, and in limiting the expansion of Russia in the near east, was in countering her claim that as a neighbour of Turkey in Europe and Asia, and of Persia in Asia, she had a greater interest in what happened there than Britain.[9]

A related issue was the question of goals: Britain's aim was to insulate British India from Russian power not to annex new territory, while Russia's definition of its security rarely gave it any incentive to practice unilateral restraint where it was unopposed or weakly resisted. In the early nineteenth century a simple but basic distinction was made between order and stability. Ingram observes that Britain

learnt that the best way to curb Russia in the near east, while ignoring local conditions, was to seek stability. This was not to be confused with order . . . Whether the states were strong or orderly did not matter to Britain, as long as their frontiers were settled and the great powers would agree not to interfere in their internal affairs. Because Britain had no interest in the near east except to keep out others, she had to avoid interfering there herself, except as far as was necessary to restrain them.[10]

The upshot was an asymmetry that pitted a player that sought definitive gains against another that sought to avoid defeat. In Ingram's view, 'the object of the great game was not to win; but not to lose'. Nevertheless, he concludes Britain did eventually lose.[11]

Britain as a maritime power enjoyed predominance in the Persian Gulf and southern Persia, while Russia's interest in northern Persia for security reasons, was acknowledged. Neither power was unduly exercised by developments in Persia as long as its own zone of interest was unaffected and its rival did not hold sway over the capital. More ambiguous, and deliberately so, were the respective interests of the two powers in Tehran. Such agreements as were made reflected the balance of power prevailing at any particular time. The Soviet Union's attempt, in the fluidity of the postwar period, to include northern Iran in its security perimeter, if not its empire, failed because of the replacement of British by American power. In short Persia's sovereignty in the central part of the country has traditionally provided the two powers with a buffer, though often a weak one, against the expansion of the other.

This introduction sets the scene for an examination of the contemporary period not least by underlining the continuities involved in the attempt to construct and evolve systems of conflict prevention that are resistant at least to local instabilities, even if they must reflect fluctuations in the relative power of US and Soviet interests.

America's assumption of responsibilities in the Persian Gulf was neither planned nor foreseen and it was only gradual. The US involvement in the Middle East Supply Center brought the US into the Gulf, if only temporarily during the war. Britain's withdrawal from empire only reached the Gulf in 1971 when the US, preoccupied by the Vietnam War, had neither the political nor the material resources to smooth the transition by a ready substitution of American naval power. In any case the era of unchallenged paramountcy was over as a Soviet naval flotilla paid its first visit to the Gulf only a few months after Britain's announcement in January 1968 of its intended withdrawal.

Britain had remained in the Gulf's waters, managing the foreign relations of the sheikhdoms, insulating the region from great power rivalry, and stopping the implementation of various territorial disputes (e.g., in Kuwait in 1961) until 1971. On land, too, it had taken the lead in organising, on behalf of the US its apparent successor, a coalition of states on the Soviet periphery to contain its power. The US involvement in the Arabian peninsula started with its economic interests and gradually grew to encompass politics. The US assistance first in maintaining the independence of Iran in 1945, and then in its oil dispute with Britain in 1951–3, and the fact that only the US could balance Soviet nearby power, meant a steady growth in US involvement in that country. The US had come to see the preservation of Iran's independence as something of a test case for it and as an indicator of Soviet intentions in the immediate postwar period, and so it remained thereafter. As the US became the senior partner in the Western coalition, on land and then on sea, it came to define its interests in terms of access and denial, that is the assurance of continued access to the region and its material resources and the denial of the region to the exclusive or predominant influence of the USSR.

Containment of the Soviet Union in practice meant the bolstering of Iran militarily, economically and diplomatically. Once apprised of Britain's decision to withdraw from the Gulf, the US followed the simplest strategy available to it, namely the encouragement of the local powers to assume responsibility for the region. This seemed to be consistent both with the emerging realities of politics post-Vietnam as enshrined in the Nixon Doctrine, and in wishes of the regional states themselves. At the same time the US served notice in the mid-1970s that it would under extreme circumstances arising from its 'strangulation' (i.e., the interruption of oil supplies to it due either to economic embargo or physical interruption) reserve the right to intervene forcefully. The 'twin-pillar' approach which counted on Iran–Saudi cooperation collapsed with the Iranian monarchy in 1979.

As a result of this and the perceived threat that Soviet power now posed to Western interests, the US moved to substitute its own military power in the region. In so doing it designated forces for a Rapid Deployment Force (subsequently Centcom). The fact that the US was unable to obtain any significant footholds for the deployment of these forces within the Gulf itself came to be considered a serious handicap for the defence of the Gulf and most especially of northern Iran in the face of any Soviet threat. This view was reinforced by the perception that Iran, in rejecting both superpowers, had become something of a political vacuum. The reassertion of US power in the Gulf, symbolised by the enunciation of the Carter doctrine and the designation of Centcom, served not only to underline the US refusal to acquiesce in any reordering of the balance of interests as a result of the reorientation by Iran of its political system but also to underscore Washington's continued interest in the region.

What of Soviet interests in the postwar period? These continued to remain the same, namely the establishment of a viable buffer state in Iran. Continuity was maintained as well in the Soviet tendency to want to define influence in the safest possible manner, that is control. In the early post-war period this was focused on Iran. When direct military pressure proved unrewarding, a more friendly demeanour was offered, especially after Stalin, but always to one end: the cultivation of a weak and dependent Iran. This was never clearly defined but it included Soviet aversion to any substantive Iranian relationship with the

Western powers, especially involving the modernisation of the military establishment. At times this was stretched to include the improvement of the country's infrastructure on the grounds that this too could have military applications. Most of the time it meant opposition to any military relationship however tenuous with the US, on the grounds that this threatened the security of the USSR. Unable to frighten Iran into a course of passive dependence the Soviets concentrated on Tehran's allegedly provocative policy of seeking to enhance its own security at the expense of that of its neighbour. It was not that they did not credit Iran's assurance (they argued privately) but rather that they distrusted Washington's intentions, which could force Iran to be used, against the wishes of its people, in some madcap adventure.

Unable to convince Iran of the wisdom of self-abnegation, Soviet pressure only accelerated the move toward the Western camp. However, by 1962, with the advent of the ICBM and the first signs of détente between the superpowers, the USSR accepted Iran's pro-Western orientation, and assurances that it would not allow its territory to be used in any aggression against its powerful neighbour. From 1964 Iran's pragmatic, *de facto* nonalignment and realism *vis-à-vis* the USSR, combined with the latter's greater flexibility, resulted in more cordial relations between the two states. Although the USSR was not keen to see Britain replaced in the Gulf by a resurgent Iran, Soviet criticism focused on Iran's arms build-up rather than on any particular interest in the Gulf as such.

The Iranian revolution upset all the pieces without rearranging them in a dependable or satisfactory way for anyone. The Soviet Union was unable to resist attempts to strengthen the anti-Western forces in that country even at the cost this might (and did) have for its own security, in the emergence of a militantly Islamic regime. The Soviets sought to play the role of 'protector' of the revolution, warning the US against any intervention (in November 1978) and encouraging the local communist party (Tudeh) to cooperate with the clerical regime. The opportunities presented by an Iran newly adrift were too tempting and the USSR could not resist the potential geopolitical rewards they offered. Unable to convert the revolutionaries in Tehran, the Soviets took comfort from the continuing anti-Western militance of the regime's radicals, and sought a foothold in the country by capitalising on its needs deriving from the prosecution of a long, costly and indecisive war. Indeed the USSR's policy toward the Iran–Iraq conflict demonstrated an unwillingness to choose between a regime with which it had long been associated and a regime in Iran that, however distasteful, still merited close attention.

In the light of this short summary what can we say of US–USSR interests in the region? Clearly Britain's countervailing maritime power has been replaced by that of the US. In both cases its power had to offset that of a continental

Eurasian power, a proximate power, with more apparent interest in the region's affairs. The Soviet Union no less than Russia seeks secure borders and in the era of nuclear weapons and coalitions it seeks to clear its periphery of all the vestiges of its rivals' power and to enjoy the fruits of great power status. The Soviets' perception of their interests thus, now for the first time, sometimes includes reference to developments in the Persian Gulf – usually in the formulation that it is 'in close proximity to our southern borders'. Such claims are not advanced forcefully or with great conviction, but rather, it would appear, as positions from which to bargain. In any case in an era in which the Soviets claim a right to be consulted on all major international issues, they can hardly limit their claims in reference to the Persian Gulf. More assertive and plausible is the Soviet claim that developments in Iran directly affect its security and that 'it cannot remain indifferent' to them. Sometimes and more ominously in communications with Iran, Moscow makes oblique reference to the 1921 treaty as an instrument justifying preclusive action where its security is concerned.

Western claims to interests in the region suffer from being too abstract or too specific – from the right to assist states in the maintenance of their independence to a 'vital' interest in the flow of oil. Devoid of the intuitive logic buttressing the proximate power, they derive their strength from historical precedent. However, an overemphasis on the importance of oil in the past decade has led in recent years to the perfectly reasonable Soviet observation that the US dependence on the region for oil has declined sharply and that, therefore, Centcom and associated naval deployments are pretexts for the use of 'gunboat diplomacy' rather than reflections of genuine interests.

We have alluded to the differences in the positions of the two superpowers by observing that while one is a continental state the other is a distant maritime power; while the former tends to equate security with control and influence with satellites (or protectorates) the latter is content to settle for a buffer zone that precludes the exercise of dominant power by the neighbouring superpower. In reality in the Persian Gulf region there are a series of zones of varying and, at times, overlapping concern to the superpowers which correspond with a number of categories of interest established by Alexander George in chapter 6.

1 *High interest symmetry and/or disputed interest symmetry*
   These categories cover Iran – particularly the Tehran area where government authority is located and where the two sides have strong interests but do not agree on the relative balance of their interests.
2 *Interest asymmetry favouring the USSR*
   This covers the north of Iran where Soviet interests are clearly and substantially more important than those of the US.

3   *Interest asymmetry favouring the US*
    This covers the Arabian peninsula and the southern Gulf area.
4   *Uncertain interest symmetry*
    George defines this category 'as locales of ambiguous or fluid nature in which
    one or both superpowers are not certain of their own or other's interests and
    find it difficult to assess how and to what extent their interests will become
    engaged in a developing unstable situation'.[12] This closely resembled the
    situation in the Gulf War, where interests were involved but in a murky,
    overlapping way, precluding any clear-cut response, and where uncertainty
    generated caution and suspicion on the part of both superpowers. This
    category best describes the US/USSR situation during the Iranian
    revolution. It would probably be operative in the event of a major domestic
    crisis in Iran superseding category one.

How compatible are American and Soviet interests in the region particularly in
light of obvious asymmetries in power, interests, and aims? The continuity in
Russian–Soviet pressure on its neighbours in the name of security is impressive.
Recently, in line with superpower status, such claims have been expanded to
include regions beyond the contiguous zone. At the same time, while there has
been caution in challenging US interests directly, there has been a willingness to
do so indirectly, particularly where the trends in regional politics provide the
opportunities for this. At times the result of the Soviets' excessive emphasis on a
zero-sum approach to regional issues (where every Western loss is assumed
automatically to bring a Soviet gain) has been a net deterioration in the Soviets'
regional position as well, quite apart from the impact on superpower relations.

The Persian Gulf region is unusual. Interaction between the two superpowers
there has been recent, only since 1979–80 (see below) unlike the longer standing
one in Iran. The region is not polarised on the lines of the Arab–Israel conflict
with the superpowers on either side. Nor are the superpowers' interests – in
principle – difficult to disentangle: northern Iran is clearly a Soviet concern while
the Persian Gulf remains of overriding importance to the West. The region
remains volatile with enough local sources of instability to underscore the
ambiguities surrounding the relative balance of interests and commitment in this
strategic area. There is considerable evidence that the USSR is ready here as in
the Arab–Israeli zone to settle for a comprehensive international conference that
recognises the interests of others in return for formal acknowledgement of its
own interests. The problem in the Persian Gulf as elsewhere is that such an
acceptance might contribute to conflict avoidance by delineating zones of interest
and concern, but it is by no means clear that it would preclude the expansion of its
zone by the USSR when conditions favour it. In such a case the bestowal of some

international legitimacy to its claims beforehand will have been pocketed without any tangible return in the form of more moderate behaviour or more concretely limited ambitions. Until the USSR defines its security in terms that are less absolute, and sees politics in terms other than superpower competition, the compatibility of its interests with those of the US in the Persian Gulf will remain sporadic and tangential.

CLIENTS, PROXIES AND CONTROL

The tangible elements of power that a superpower wields are vastly more impressive than the actual influence they bestow in bilateral relationships. These are more equal than appearances might suggest for a host of reasons: the phenomenon of reverse influence and focused interest which gives small, determined states a resilience disproportionate to their power; their ability to procrastinate, to deflect pressure, and to raise the costs to their ally of insisting upon a certain course of action; and the interest of the superpower in keeping a client which makes it vulnerable to the threat of a realignment and which often results in the phenomenon in which merely to retain its influence the superpower must continue and even increase its investment. Time and again we have seen that the superpowers are unable to control their clients and allies or are unwilling to pay the price that such control would entail. In the Persian Gulf the story is much the same.

In the revolution in Iraq in 1958 which ended the treaty relationship called the Baghdad Pact, the USSR found its first opening to the Arab states of the Gulf. Until 1975 a close but not necessarily warm relationship followed, built upon Iraqi weakness and a common opposition to Western power in the region. Iraq, embattled domestically, often isolated in the Arab world while pursuing a militant quest for Arab leadership, found the USSR prepared to replace its arms and extend to it oil technology to reduce its dependence on the Western states. A coincidence of interests, primarily against the West, developed which embraced Soviet aid to the Arab states against Israel. Iraq's political, financial weakness and regional isolation, gave Baghdad precious few alternatives. Even so, to take but one example, even in this era, the USSR was unable to persuade Iraq to support the Rogers Plan of October 1969.

In the period after 1965 the relationship was transformed by Iraq's greater political stability and increased resources which generated a leadership more confident and pragmatic and hence more acceptable to its neighbours. In the Persian Gulf Iraq thus ended its virtual isolation, first by mending its fences with Iran and then its Arab neighbours. At the same time it began to see the virtues of a true non-alignment especially as it clashed with the USSR on their respective policies toward Ethiopia, the PDRY and, finally, over Afghanistan. Domestically, too, the Ba'athists in Iraq had begun to suspect the Soviets of interference and the sponsorship of a communist-inspired *coup*. Outraged by this gross act of political interference, Iraq was also highly critical of the Soviet invasion of Afghanistan. It proposed an 'Arab Charter' for the Gulf in 1980 that sought to exclude the superpowers from any active role, implying the equation of the two. The greater resources released by oil enabled Iraq to diversify its purchases of arms and technology and escape the dependency to which its economic weakness and militance had condemned it in the 1958–74 period.

Since 1980 the Soviet–Iraq relationship has been mixed. In the first two years of the Gulf war the USSR, apparently annoyed at Iraq's decision to launch the attack without prior consultation, and also to improve its position in Iran, tilted toward Tehran and cut off direct new arms shipments to Iraq. In response to Iraq's pleas for new arms Soviet spokesmen spoke blithely of the 1972 treaty as 'a treaty of peace not of war'.[13] Despite some harsh words, the relationship improved after 1982 when Iran threatened Iraq, and the arms relationship resumed. The USSR remained an important influence in Iraq for the duration of the war and will do so during the reconstruction of the armed forces.

Iraq and the USSR have pursued parallel but not identical policies. Their attitudes toward Israel and Iran, for example, are by no means the same. Nor is the USSR as keen as Iraq on Baghdad's quest for Arab leadership. Iraq, in turn, has no interest in strengthening the Communist party at home, nor supporting Soviet activity in the region not least in Afghanistan. Soviet leverage has been less than complete even in the period of maximum Iraqi dependence, when Iraqi options were few. The Iran–Iraq war has weakened Iraq and may revive an earlier form of dependence but it is doubtful that this will be anything other than a 'correct' relationship.

The US relationship with Iran has not been very different, in that even close ties have not translated into 'control' and certainly not into a proxy relationship. In the first two postwar decades Iran's political and economic weakness made it dependent on foreign, especially US aid, including military assistance. While too weak to have many options, Iran was also too weak to act as a useful proxy either. By 1966 Iran was in a position to pay for its purchases and now sought to broaden its room for manoeuvre and to undertake specific regional initiatives, not least by improving ties with the USSR. Generally Iran's policies paralleled those of the US, as in the ties it had with Israel, in supporting the 'moderate' Arab states like Egypt and Jordan, and in the Gulf Saudi Arabia. Iran, for her own reasons, wanted to exclude the outside powers and hence was well disposed to regional cooperation in a 'twin pillars' approach. Where Iran was involved militarily in the region, as in the Yemen in the 1960s, and Iraq and Oman in the 1970s, the motive could be accurately ascribed to Iran's own national interest not to any US pressure. Similarly any assistance that Iran might have rendered in Vietnam, or any position it took with regard to the Horn of Africa, stemmed from its own reading of its interests and not those of Washington. Specifically with regard to Soviet activities in the region, Tehran remained extremely suspicious (especially of *détente* which the Shah considered a 'hunting licence' for competition in the Third World). This did not prevent the attempt to mollify Moscow by being sensitive to its needs. But Moscow, while appreciative of this type of realism, still considered Iran a US client and insisted on depicting its arms purchases and regional activities as part of a grand plot to make Iran 'the policeman of the Gulf'. The history of arms sales to Iran since the end of the Second World War are in fact vivid testimony to the way in which Iran obtained its needs often over the opposition of its powerful ally. And Iran's role in OPEC councils, even at the height of its relationship with the US, shows how independent it was when its own interests were concerned.

Since the revolution, Iran has expressed opposition to and reduced contact with, both superpowers, to limit the risks of cultural contamination. Necessity has subsequently coaxed a degree of pragmatism from the leadership, but it is difficult to imagine that even a weakened Iran will soon become subject to strong influence from either superpower, let alone control. Of course this does not exclude bargaining with both superpowers and using the available room for manoeuvre.

The US relationship with Saudi Arabia is essentially analogous, with a degree of leverage on either side that does not entail a proxy relationship. Saudi Arabia's oil policy has been favourable to the West not as a favour but because it suits Saudi interest as well. US arms to the kingdom help the royal family, but they also bolster the American commitment to the region which the US considers important. The Saudis can no more 'deliver' the PLO or Syria on some issues, or take the leading role in trying to do so, than the US can squeeze some weapons out of Congress. The Saudis do some things the US does not like and are unable to do some of the things that they would like. The relationship has at times been close but never intimate or something to be taken for granted.

In no case is there a time when one of the states acted as a pawn or 'agent' of the superpowers. A more accurate characterisation is that their interests have often coincided with this or that superpower. This implies that these interests may also diverge depending on the issue, and over time, and that options will depend on the relative bargaining power and priority of the two sides in the relationship. Since the mid-1970s the independence of the regional states has been enhanced by oil income but this has not in all cases freed them from dependence on a superpower. Iraq has diluted its relationship with the USSR (because, in part, of suspicions about Moscow's cultivation of Tehran) but its manoeuvre room has been limited both by the war and by US unreceptiveness. Iran rejects the 'collusive influence' of the superpowers but has secretly traded and bargained with each. The Saudis depend for their ultimate security on the US but for lesser threats they are on their own. They cannot devise a policy that, in dealing with the former, exacerbates their day-to-day security.

If superpower control is weak and possibly declining, it tends to be reactive to, rather than a shaper of, regional developments as well. It is also the case that superpower and regional 'clients' local interests are rarely the same. A good illustration of this is the Gulf War in which, until 1987–8, both superpowers manoeuvred to increase their influence in Tehran rather than seeking and possibly enforcing a settlement that might diminish the chances of influence. Another way of putting it is that the superpowers' global interests dictate their regional policies. This means that conflict management can take precedence over their regional friends' interests, but superpower competition is the principal issue and it is this that drives policy. As George Breslauer has lucidly argued, the USSR's policies in the Arab–Israeli zone show a determination to remain a force in the region and it is prepared to enter into measures with the US that give its regional presence a formal legitimacy, even in a comprehensive settlement of the Palestinian issue.[14] It is prepared to pressure its allies if it is offered commensurate rewards, but not to jeopardise these ties by excessive pressure otherwise. Usually its support for its allies' needs has been grudging, hesitant and conditional in order to retain or salvage its influence.

Whereas the US has been dealt a strong regional hand in the form of Israel in an area of polarisation, in the Persian Gulf politics lack symmetry. The superpowers were in the process of seeing their regional protégés loosen the ties that bind in the 1978–80 period, and the onset of the Iran–Iraq war found the US and the USSR confronting an unclear regional picture with no strong incentives for taking sides, and some for limiting the risks of the conflict.[15]

CONFLICTS: PATTERNS AND TACIT RULES?

The Persian Gulf is often seen as an area where overlapping superpower interests and an uncertain balance of power could result in a calculated or inadvertent superpower confrontation. In practice, superpower competition has been tempered by the mutual recognition of the hazards involved. There has been a sufficient degree of interaction in the Arab–Israeli zone, direct and indirect competition in Iran and the Arabian peninsula, for certain patterns of behaviour, if not tacit rules, to have emerged. A discussion of some of these patterns does not have to claim any formality for these 'rules' or any predictive value about the automaticity of their future application.

There have been numerous crises since 1945 that provide a rough and ready base for the discovery of any recurrent patterns of superpower behaviour. In 1945 the USSR was unwilling to prolong its stay in Iran in the face of US opposition, stubborn local diplomacy and the prospect of bad publicity in the UN. Again in Iran, in 1951–3, Moscow showed itself unwilling to put the support of the local communist party (Tudeh) behind a nationalist anti-Western party, perhaps because of a distrust of the latter's aristocratic-bourgeois elements. For its part, the US, too, has been unwilling to contemplate certain acts: the revolutions in Iraq in 1958 and Iran in 1979 which were decisively to transform those states' external orientations were more or less passively watched. In the latter case the USSR went so far as to claim to have 'warned off' the US from intervention (by a statement made by Brezhnev in November 1978) to establish its credentials as the 'protector' of the revolution. In fact, the US had no such plans and responded by denying any such intent but in turn warning Moscow against any intervention as well.

If pro-Western regimes cannot be protected against their own people, what about foreign covert activities? Here the ground rules are obviously murky. The USSR was clearly aware of US/UK activity in Iran in 1951–3, but did little. The US was well aware of some Soviet activity in Iran during the revolution but judged it as hardly decisive. Since the revolution in Iran the superpowers have been in a sort of covert race outbidding each other in their attempts to ingratiate themselves with the Islamic republic. To take but two examples: the USSR may have provided Tehran with information about the impending Iraqi attack and has extended internal security assistance to the regime, while encouraging the 1979–83 repression of the secular moderate nationalists (as potential pro-Western elements) in the regime. The UK and the US have cooperated in providing Tehran with a list of Soviet diplomats working as KGB agents and planning a *coup* attempt in Iran – thus precipitating their expulsion in 1983. Both the US and the USSR have provided arms indirectly to Tehran in the hope that they will thus have some channels open to the regime; at the same time each has funded groups opposed to the regime.

In regional conflicts, too, there has been a pattern. The superpowers in some cases have permitted or facilitated the conduct of hostilities, in others they have gone along with their regional ally, but they have not offered decisive or unlimited support. The Yemen war of 1962–6 is the most unrepresentative in that it entailed large-scale Soviet involvement. But this was due primarily one suspects because the conflict was not one polarised on East–West lines, and upping the ante held no serious consequences.[16] Even in this conflict the US saw fit to provide reassurance to the Saudis by temporarily deploying a squadron of aircraft to the Kingdom. In the Iran–Iraq border dispute in 1974, which led to armed clashes and which saw US CIA and Israeli involvement in aiding the Kurds against Iraq, the USSR confined itself to the supply of arms to Iraq. Indeed, in the Iraqi retelling, it was the lack of arms from the USSR that drove Baghdad into a settlement with Iran at Algiers in March 1975.

In 1973–5 Iran, at the invitation of the Oman government and alongside British and Jordanian troops, assisted Oman in quelling the Dhofar rebellion which had assumed a Marxist and Gulf-wide dimension when it had been renamed the Popular Front for the Liberation of the Occupied Arab Gulf. The USSR was neither very visible nor very effective if indeed it gave any more help to the PDRY for the war. Again, in the brief PDRY-YAR clashes in March 1979 (which were seen in Washington in their global/East-West perspective as a probe rather than an outgrowth of tribal feuds), while the US airlifted arms without waiting for congressional authorisation, the USSR was neither very active nor adventurous. In these cases neither superpower escalated its involvement, nor was it involved in a humiliating loss or exhilarating win. The crises seemed to fizzle out in their regional dimension. This does not discount the possibility that they constituted probes to gauge reactions. This was certainly the case in the Gulf War.[17] The US cited (in June 1984) the USSR's supply of arms to both sides in the war as one of the obstacles to the convening of an international conference on the Middle East, and distrusted the Soviet's alleged aim of brokering a peace conference on the lines of Tashkent 1965. The USSR became exercised by signs (as in mid-1984 or again in 1987) that the US was using its naval presence to reassure its allies and deter any expansion of the war. It also resented the tightening of ties with the Gulf states as evidenced by arms sales. Ironically (and it is a point that we do not have space to enlarge upon here), the USSR used the war to demonstrate its conservatism and sought to convince the more traditional states of the value of establishing formal diplomatic relations with it. The superpowers' competition here stemmed not from incompatible conceptions of the best outcome of the war, but from competition for influence in the region and especially Iran. Soviet arms to both sides reflects the use of one of the few instruments available to Moscow for cultivating these regimes and increasing their dependence. It implied no particular support for the regimes, merely an acknowledgement of their existence.

What, if any, patterns can be discerned from these cases? It would appear from the regional conflicts that neither power is willing to side definitively with its regional partner. The USSR has shown an unwillingness to push its support for Iraq in 1974, the PDRY/PFLOAG in 1975, PDRY in 1979, Iraq in 1980, to escalation and possible confrontation. Especially in the case of Iraq in 1974, where US/Israeli aid to Iran was involved, the USSR practised restraint. In the

Gulf War there was a similar pattern. While the US and USSR sought with some success to limit the scope of the hostilities, and prevent its expansion into the Gulf, neither even hinted at intervention in the defence of Iraq. An informal convention conspicuous in this conflict was the differentiation between air and sea units and ground forces. The US deployment of AWACS to the Arabian peninsula, and occasional patrols in the Gulf by US and other Western navies was regarded as limited in time and commitment and hence as unprovocative and acceptable. There is no such incipient view about ground forces.

In the cases of internal instability there also seem to be some crisis conventions. Perhaps, as Gary Sick argues, there has evolved since 1945 a tacit agreement by the superpowers not to intervene in Iran militarily.[18] If so, the agreement is a fragile and vague one open to bargaining, for the USSR has not relinquished its claims under its interpretation of the 1921 treaty. Also the line between covert competition and pure coercion is not as clear as it may appear and losses in one domain may encourage escalation to another. Would the USSR accept, for example, the return of a pro-Western regime in Iran, and what price would it be prepared to pay to prevent such a regime?

In US policies an element of non-provocation of the USSR has been evident, implying a respect for reciprocal rights and obligations. For example, the US never deployed missiles in Iran even before the advent of the ICBM; nor, apparently, used Iran for U-2 reconnaissance flights, nor introduced ground troops into the country. Even in the attempt to plug the gap made in the Baghdad Pact by the defection of Iraq, Washington offered only an 'Executive agreement', a weaker commitment than a treaty, and only to the defence of the country not to a particular regime. The US use of Iran for NSA purposes and for monitoring Soviet missile tests can hardly be considered provocative under the terms of the need for monitoring embodied in SALT 1.

Soviet policy in the Gulf has not been active in seeking to damp down the sources of conflict but this may be due to limited influence as much as to deliberate policy. Generally we can say, with Philip Windsor, that the USSR has shown more of an interest in 'crisis stabilisation' than in conflict prevention.[19] This is consistent with its aim to become 'co-arbiter', i.e., to establish enough influence to make consultation with it and solicitation of its views a practical necessity in relation to all important outstanding issues in the region. The Soviet response to the Carter Doctrine, which the US formulated and announced in January 1980 (to reduce the risk of a confrontation due to misunderstanding), was to offer to participate in an international conference on the security of the Persian Gulf including assurances on safeguarding the flow of oil.

This exchange, together with the first consultations in New York at the UN in the autumn of 1980 between Muskie and Gromyko, started a fitful dialogue on the superpowers' respective interests in the Gulf in relation to the Gulf War and Iran. These discussions continued unreported in 1983.[20] Agreement was reached in January 1984 to discuss regional issues bilaterally. The following year the Soviets indicated their preference that regional talks be combined with talks on arms control. US spokesmen emphasised that the US–USSR talks on specific regions should be seen in terms of the 'management of US–Soviet relations'; another referred to them as an 'exchange of views aimed at preventing misunderstandings on regional issues' and not as substantive negotiations about the area.[21] This type of reassurance through the clarification of respective positions and the staking out of claims in the Gulf is a useful measure that may reduce the risk of misunderstanding. Soviet claims to play a role in the entire area now have to be taken more seriously than was the case before. Western interests, too, are engaged in the Gulf. The delimitation of these respective interests and the clarification of acceptable possibly tacit rules of conduct in the area remain at the mercy of several volatile factors; the general global balance of power and overall superpower relations, the dynamics of regional opportunities, and the evolution of domestic politics in the critical country, Iran.

POSSIBLE SOURCES OF SUPERPOWER CONFRONTATION

Crises in the Gulf may lack predictability because political fluidity and the cross-cutting interests of the superpowers, which implies uncertainty and conditionality in commitments, will make reactions harder to anticipate. There is thus here more than in more clear-cut zones, or in areas of low interest, a higher probability of inadvertent crises. Increasing this risk is the problem associated with the projection of power for the West at this distance and particularly in the northern Gulf. In crises which put the premium on a speedy response, and which increase the advantages of a *fait accompli* (as opposed to the difficulties and risks of reversing undesirable events) the premium for pre-emptive involvement will be high, leading to a hair-trigger response to anticipated crises.

Specifically how might current confrontation be transferred into a superpower crisis? Until the 1988 ceasefire the most obvious candidate for this was the Iran–Iraq War which remained dangerous precisely because it was uncontrollable. The superpowers agreed that they did not want an Iranian victory but were unable to agree on their respective balance of influence in that country. Each showed a willingness to compete with the other to improve its position in Tehran. Confrontation arising from the war could have come either from a widening of the war or by an imminent Iranian victory. The prospect of such a victory could have induced the USSR to intervene to protect Iraq, and also to curry favour with the Gulf states. The US could have reacted to stop this. An alternative trigger during the Gulf War could have been military reaction of the US against Iran in defence of the Gulf states, which would then have given the USSR the excuse to invade northern Iran, or simply to offer to 'defend' the revolution for the Islamic authorities. The uncertainty which remains about respective rights and obligations in Iran in particular, though somewhat clearer now than in the beginning of the decade, provides no assurance of predictability in a crisis.

Post-Khomeini Iran remains a potential triggering point for crisis. This could take the form of an invitation to the USSR by one of the factions contending for leadership, an offer that the USSR might be unable to resist – a version of the 'sucked in' model of crisis. A variant of this is decisive intervention by the USSR, probably in Iran's northern provinces, disclaiming any intentions *vis-à-vis* the Gulf's oil, and justifying it by reference to the anarchy in Iran, the need for border security, and its interpretation of the 1921 treaty. In neither case could the US afford to take the Soviets at their word, and a crisis might result.

Another catalyst might be a *coup* in Saudi Arabia. This might be seen by the US as Iranian inspired and result in an attempt to reverse it directly or through allies. This, in turn, might inspire the USSR, capitalising on the confusion, to move into northern Iran to pressure the regime for a more compliant posture.

Various other scenarios of superpower confrontation suggest themselves but, compared to the above, appear remote. A superpower confrontation arising from Soviet pressure on Iran due to the latter's support for the Afghan resistance is a possibility. But this becomes less likely as Soviet involvement with Afghanistan decreases, and US ties with Iran remain poor. Similarly Soviet activity to prevent Iraq from drifting towards the Western camp is unlikely to meet with much of a response if force is required. Finally an East–West confrontation arising, for example, from a conflict between the PDRY and the YAR or Saudi Arabia appears doubtful, if only because of Soviet unwillingness to choose the lesser states instead of Saudi Arabia, and the differences in the balance of perceived interest and power between the superpowers in the southern and northern Gulf.

MEASURES TO ENHANCE CONFLICT PREVENTION AND MANAGEMENT

There is, in theory, no automatic or inevitable incompatibility between Soviet interests in border security and regional influence commensurate to its power and those of the West in maintaining access to, and denying the USSR primacy in, the Persian Gulf. A range of measures traditionally have served precisely such situations, ranging from formal cooperative through to informal parallel measures, encompassing active cooperation or simple agreements on abstaining.[22] On the face of it there is room for some accommodation. The USSR, with some fifty million Moslems and a long border, naturally places great weight on its relations with Iran, while the US and the West are perhaps more concerned with the southern shore of the Gulf. As Secretary of State Shultz put it in relation to the Iran–Iraq war:

This is a war that deserves attention . . . that's been very deadly, where chemical weapons have been used, where there doesn't seem to be any outcome in prospect and which is not in any inherent way a product of conflict between the US and the Soviet Union.[23]

Depending on the situation, the superpowers as 'collaborative competitors' (in Breslauer's phrase) vary the precise mix of their rivalry, collaborating formally or tacitly to damp down particularly risky conflicts, while otherwise competing relentlessly for influence. The balance between the elements of the relationship depends not only on the perceived dangers presented by regional instabilities but also on the opportunities they offer. Soviet interest in a stable, moderate, unprovocative but pro-Western Iran was less than some might have imagined. The Soviets have preferred the risks of border insecurity and US intervention as long as there is a finite chance of eliminating Western influence.

Before the ceasefire over the Gulf War there were numerous suggestions that the superpowers could and should cooperate to end the bloodshed in the Gulf War. Some envisaged superpower cooperation in the UN Security Council, to boycott the combatants' oil, and then move if necessary to impose peace, that is, to enforcement action under chapter 7 of the United Nations Charter.[24] Moves in this direction were made through Security Council Resolution 598 on 26 July 1987, which called on the two belligerents to come to a speedy ceasefire or risk the imposition of mandatory sanctions, under chapter 7. While this resolution was addressed to both parties in the war, it is clear that it was directed primarily at Iran, the state unwilling to contemplate negotiations or a cessation of hostilities short of victory. That such a measure was possible suggests a degree of progress in US–Soviet relations that needs explanation.

The superpowers' interests in the Gulf War were never irreconcilable. As Raymond Aron reminded us long ago, they share a common interest and responsibility to see that local wars do not automatically escalate or threaten global conflagration simply as a result of reflexive responses by the two blocs. In the case of the Iran–Iraq war a certain overlap of interest had long been apparent; neither superpower (for its own distinct reasons) wanted an Iranian victory in the war; neither trusted the Khomeini regime, which both have reason to consider manipulative and dangerous, and each superpower has reason to want to cultivate a new strategic dialogue with the other and to test, in concrete cases, the extent to which their relationship has indeed entered a new phase after the chill during most of this decade.

So there have been incentives for the superpowers to develop at least partially cooperative policies within a still competitive relationship. The Soviet Union has been supportive of United Nations efforts. Its rationale can be summarised thus: the Gulf War came to serve as a test case in its relations with the US in which it can show that it is truly interested in a new security relationship and dialogue with the US; to show that the USSR does not automatically act as the 'spoiler' in the Third World, and no longer views events there in terms of 'zero-sum' thinking; and to demonstrate its declared interest in reviving the United Nations as a force for peace in international politics. In addition to its concerns over confrontation with the US, the USSR has local reasons for believing that such cooperation is worthwhile.

The Soviet Union has built up considerable credibility with the conservative Arab regimes of the Persian Gulf, as a potential protector and, in any case, as an actor relevant to the politics and security of the region. Moscow will not wish to jeopardise this image and will seek to reinforce it. At the same time, the Soviet Union has fostered bilateral relations with Iran, thereby placing itself into a position of importance, while remaining prepared to punish Iran in any collective decision within the UN. This approach is based on the expectation that Iran has in the last resort 'nowhere else to go' in the sense of threatening a reversal of alliances. Both considerations imply a willingness to contemplate temporary bad relations with Iran in return for real gains *vis-à-vis* the US and Gulf states.

In addition there is another possibly overriding or dominant concern, that has conduced to an active Soviet policy in regard to the war, namely the risks, which were inherent in the war, of escalation. The longer the war went on the greater was the need of the smaller Arab states for United States' protection, and the more the attendant likelihood that the US would be able to convert this need for protection into an expanded and permanent military presence in the region. It is this consideration that the threat from Iran might justify and accelerate a US military build-up – graphically demonstrated by the US decision to deploy warships (including a carrier task force) to the environs of the Gulf – that, more than any other, catalysed a cooperative Soviet policy in the United Nations.

The reasoning of the United States has been similar. The risks of an Iranian victory to the political balance of the region and the need to reassure American friends in the area, and prevent Soviet political incursions into the area, have been regarded as paramount. In addition there has been an American disposition to test the quality and extent of the Soviet insistence that it is prepared to cooperate constructively in 'conflict management'. It is also true that to some extent the practice of holding a dialogue on 'regional' issues has improved the atmosphere between the superpowers and clarified the claims and expectations of the two parties in relation to crisis areas.

How far can we talk of a 'historic turning point' in superpower relations towards the Gulf? On the basis of current experience such a conclusion is premature, for neither side is closer to accepting the claims of the other over the extent of its interests or the corresponding degree of influence it should legitimately exercise in the region. If recent cooperation continues, it may become a precedent for similar acts elsewhere in the future. It may thus provide graphic evidence that even convergent (as opposed to identical) interests can yield limited measures of cooperation, sublimating or channelling the residual competition into less dangerous channels. This does not imply agreement on a delimitation of respective interests in Iran – the truly hard case – as I have argued in this chapter.

Yet, there may also be a growing recognition that conflict avoidance can be enhanced by the superpowers clarifying their respective interests. Past activity in relation to crises is likely to weigh more than words. The US has not acknowledged the Soviet attempt to have the Gulf region recognised as an area of legitimate interest, together with the right to be involved in any management of its problems. But it may implicitly have accepted some Soviet claims over northern Iran. Although neither superpower has complete control over its regional friends, neither is its commitment to these friends so strong or polarised as to risk an East–West crisis. Here overlapping interests – of the USSR to seek friends in the conservative camp, and stabilisation of sorts on occasion, and the US to defend the regional states without provoking the USSR – make for a more stable environment than may at first be apparent.

The tacit rules governing regional conflicts appear to be in good order. Those relating to internal conflict and instability, however, need to be developed further. Change, sometimes violent, often disruptive and leading to shifts in domestic and foreign orientations, affecting the superpowers' interests, can be anticipated. In Iran and Saudi Arabia they would focus superpower anxieties. It would be convenient and elegant if the superpowers could manage a deal giving the USSR primacy in Iran and the US the equivalent in Saudi Arabia; but this is not feasible because local politics would not tolerate it. As the *Economist* asked in an analogous context: 'Could they control their local friends before and after the deal?'[25] Also it would seem preferable, as insurance against any Soviet temptation to expand its definition of 'security interests', to maintain Iran as a buffer for the region rather than yield her intact for virtual satellisation.

It would appear that the most useful course of dialogue with the USSR would be an identification and clarification of the catalysts and elements in these states and societies likely to trigger intervention, and the forms of superpower intervention that would be permissible and impermissible. I have in mind the kind of specific rules indicating types of involvement permitted under specified circumstances on the lines outlined by Alexander George.[26]

An important element in crises is uncertainty – of the risks involved, of the

Shahram Chubin

other's response, commitment and resolve, and of the political support for any action. In the Persian Gulf the risks of deliberate confrontation appear to be remote. This makes it all the more important that commitments be made unmistakably clear, in procurement decisions and deployments as well as dialogue. Even an agreed superpower formula for the avoidance or prevention of crises in regions of recognised importance to both sides will not be self-enforcing. It would require a continued military balance and vigilance against salami-tactics. Slippage would be difficult to repair and attempts to do so might pose greater risks than the current situation holds.

NOTES

1 Harold Nicholson, *Curzon: The Last Phase 1919–1925* (London: Constable), p. 145.
2 See J. C. Hurewitz, *The Middle East and North Africa in World Politics, 1919–1945* 2 (New Haven, CT: Yale University Press), pp. 240–4.
3 P. G. Lauren, 'Crisis Prevention in Nineteenth Century Diplomacy', in A. L. George, *Managing US–Soviet Rivalry* (Boulder, CO: Westview, 1983), p. 44.
4 Nicholson *Curzon: The Last Phase*, p. 127.
5 Hurewitz *The Middle East and North Africa in World Politics*, pp. 559–61.
6 Wight, *Power Politics* (Leicester: Leicester University Press, for RIIA, 1978), pp. 160–1.
7 A. J. P. Taylor, *Struggle for Mastery in Europe: 1848–1918* (Oxford: Clarendon, 1954), p. 239, n. 1, as cited in *Ibid.* p. 165.
8 Nicholson, *Curzon: The Last Phase*, pp. 139–40.
9 Edward Ingram, *The Beginning of the Great Game in Asia 1828–1834* (Oxford: Clarendon Press, 1979), p. 329.
10 *Ibid.*, pp. 331–2.
11 *Ibid.*, p. 339.
12 George, ed., *Managing US–Soviet Rivalry*, p. 382.
13 See Zamyatin, a Central Committee member, interviewed by *As Siyasah*. Broadcast by Kuwait News Agency 2 May 1981, BBC/SU/6719/A4/2-3, 9 May, 1981.
14 G. Breslauer, 'Soviet Policy in the Middle East 1967–1972', in George, ed., *Managing US–Soviet Rivalry*, pp. 65–99.
15 For additional information see S. Chubin, *Security in the Persian Gulf: The Role of the Outside Powers* (Aldershot, Hants: Gower, for the IISS, 1982); W. Quandt, *Saudi Arabia in the 1980s* (Washington, DC: Brookings, 1981); F. Fukuyama, 'The Soviet Union and Iraq since 1968' (Santa Monica, CA: Rand N–1524–AF, July 1980); M. Smolansky, 'The Kremlin and the Iraqi Ba'ath 1968–1982', *Mid-East Review* (Spring/Summer 1983), pp. 62–7; S. Page, *The Soviet Union and the Yemens* (New York: Praeger, 1985); Mark Katz, *Russia and Arabia: Soviet Foreign Policy Toward the Arabian Peninsula* (Baltimore, MD: Johns Hopkins University Press, 1986).
16 B. Porter, *The USSR in Third World Conflicts* (New York: Cambridge University Press, 1984).
17 S. Chubin, 'Soviet Arms and the Gulf War', *International Defense Review*, June 1987.
18 Personal discussions with Gary Sick, former White House official dealing with Iranian affairs.
19 Philip Windsor, 'The Soviet Union in the International System of the 1980s', in 'Prospects of Soviet Power in the 1980s', Part 2, *Adelphi Paper*, no. 152 (London: IISS, 1979), p. 10.
20 *International Herald Tribune*, 18 January 1984.
21 *International Herald Tribune*, 20 February 1985, and *International Herald Tribune*, 19 June 1985.
22 Hedley Bull, *The Anarchical Society* (London: Macmillan, 1977), pp. 205–9.
23 The *New York Times*, 17 November 1985.
24 See, for example, Seth Tillman and Charles W. Maynes, *International Herald Tribune*, 10–11 December 1983; Robert Johansen and Michael Renner, *International Herald Tribune*, 15–16 February 1986; and Drew Middleton, *International Herald Tribune*, 9 October 1986.
25 The *Economist*, 2 November 1985, pp. 15–17.
26 See George ed., *Managing US–Soviet Rivalry*, pp. 379–82, and chapter 6 of this volume.

9   The superpowers and Southwest Asia

Roy Allison

The revolution in Iran and the projection of Soviet troops into Afghanistan changed the geostrategic balance in Southwest Asia in the space of a year. These shifts in the regional constellation of power were the first since the 1940s in this part of the world which raised the possibility of confrontation between the superpowers. This paper focuses on the 1980s since the conflicts and tensions of this period raise particular challenges which demand specific solutions. For want of space a rather limited definition of Southwest Asia is adopted below, comprising Afghanistan and its immediate neighbours, Iran and Pakistan. The security of these countries separating the Indian subcontinent from the Middle East and bordering on or proximate to the southern perimeter of the Soviet Union has become more interdependent in the 1980s. The region composed by these states is only part of the 'arc of instability' identified by Zbigniew Brzezinski in the late 1970s and has more in common with the earlier concept of the Northern Tier. The security patterns and arrangements which characterise the region formed by Afghanistan, Iran and Pakistan are closely linked to those which obtain in the Persian Gulf and which are studied in chapter 8 above.

SUPERPOWER INVOLVEMENT AND INTERESTS IN SOUTHWEST ASIA

Soviet interests

Soviet strategic interests in the region have in the first place reflected the security requirements of her long Central Asian and Caucasian borders. The Soviet southern republics cut artificially across ethnic groups and this has magnified Soviet sensitivity to developments south of the Soviet borders. It has remained a Soviet priority to insulate these republics from external influences which could challenge the prevailing social and political order. The post-Stalin Soviet leadership calculated that a political accommodation with the Northern Tier states would better serve this Soviet interest in border stabilisation than a policy of confrontation and military probing. But Soviet military intervention in Afghanistan in 1979 indicated *inter alia* that Soviet leaders reserved the right to use military force to maintain a defensive buffer on their southern flank.

Another basic Soviet interest subsumed historically under the global superpower competition has been the diminution of both the American and Chinese presence and influence in Southwest Asia. The USSR sought to cultivate security relationships with Asian states but portrayed the American presence in Asia as an alien intrusion which should be excised or at least neutralised. More specifically, Soviet interests required the separation of the Northern Tier states from the nuclear strategy and military contingency planning of the United States. Moscow also sought to deny American strategists the use of the territory of these states for intelligence gathering. The optimal Soviet solution since the late 1950s has been the full neutralisation of Iran and Pakistan. This goal relates to the Soviet interest in maintaining general limitations on the military capabilities of contiguous Third World states, especially in the area of modern military technology. Soviet leaders wish to avoid the need to maintain substantial Soviet forces on the southern flank of the USSR in the event of any general conflict.

Soviet ideological interests in Iran, Afghanistan and Pakistan have tended to be subsumed under core strategic priorities. Soviet policy towards Iran under the Shah displayed remarkable pragmatism: Soviet declaratory support for the uprising against the Shah only became pronounced once it became apparent that he no longer commanded authority. The uncertainties and inherent instabilities attached to active subversion of border states have discouraged Soviet leaders since the 1940s from pursuing such a policy. Once a pro-Soviet Marxist regime came to power in Afghanistan Soviet revolutionary credibility was at stake. But even in this case the primary Soviet interests lay in a calculation of strategic losses and gains.

Revolutionary instability in Southwest Asia at the end of the 1970s, and the real likelihood of confrontation with the United States, forced Soviet leaders to reappraise Soviet priorities in this volatile region and to define more clearly where the core interests of the USSR were at stake and where the Soviet position was negotiable. This was particularly necessary since Soviet leaders had interpreted *détente* in the 1970s and the superpower status which accompanied it as legitimising Soviet intervention in pursuit of its perceived interests in distant Third World regions.

The revolution in Iran failed to enhance stability on the Soviet southern borders and was succeeded by a dangerously destabilising conflict in the Gulf. This qualified the benefits Moscow initially derived from the overthrow of the

Shah, especially Iran's withdrawal from the CENTO Pact, the expulsion of United States' electronic intelligence facilities from Iran and the removal of American military advisers from the Iranian armed forces.[1] The new independent Iranian policy was based on neutrality and non-alignment. Faced with this strategic windfall, the primary Soviet interest has lain in reinforcing the insulation of Iran from the United States. Longer term Soviet interests would be served by the emergence of a form of neutralism in Iranian foreign policy which would favour the USSR and permit the coordination of some aspects of Soviet and Iranian policy. In the political realm Soviet interests require the cultivation of correct, preferably cordial, state to state relations with the Islamic regime despite the eventual suppression of the Tudeh Party. This requires restraint, as during the Shah's rule, in supporting ethnic particularism in Iran. At the same time Moscow wishes to contain Iranian appeals to Soviet Muslims for an Islamic revival, thereby upholding domestic stability within the USSR.[2]

The primary Soviet interest used to justify intervention in Afghanistan has been in the realm of state to state relations rather than the field of ideological commitments. A Soviet specialist maintained that the Afghan government's appeal for assistance from the USSR reflected its 'understanding and calculation . . . of the interests of the Soviet Union: since there arose a real threat of the transformation of Afghanistan into an imperialist military bridge-head' on the southern border of the USSR.[3] However, Soviet leaders themselves established no more than a permanently endangered political outpost in Afghanistan. In the 1980s Soviet policy-makers have had to consider the failure of Soviet troops to eliminate the Afghan resistance alongside the deleterious effect of this endeavour on Soviet interests elsewhere in Asia.

It remains in the Soviet interest to normalise relations with China, to wean Pakistan and a number of Gulf and Indian Ocean states from military dependence on the United States (formed bilaterally or through participation in CENTCOM), and to induce Asian states to endorse Soviet-sponsored security arrangements. A longer term Soviet interest may be to institute benign non-alignment of the Indian variety in Pakistan. All these goals were frustrated in lesser or greater measure by the continued Soviet military presence in Afghanistan.

One of the priorities of the Soviet leadership under Gorbachev became the identification of means to close the 'bleeding wound' on its southern flank and, in 1988, the decision to withdraw Soviet troops was finally announced. This decision was formalised in a United Nations mediated agreement in April of that year which provided for the withdrawal of Soviet forces from Afghanistan. This included a bilateral Soviet–American agreement which permitted each power to continue to provide military assistance to its regional ally (which Soviet leaders interpreted as Pakistan in the case of the United States). Soviet leaders hoped that a separate bilateral Afghan–Pakistani treaty, which was signed alongside the superpower agreement, would scal the Afghan Pakistani border and thereby isolate the insurgents within Afghanistan. Even following this treaty, however, American military supplies found their way to the *mujahidin* via Pakistan, so the superpower competition over Afghanistan through the provision of arms to the opposed forces in that country continued unabated.

Soviet statements indicate that under the rubric of a 'government of national reconciliation' the USSR does not necessarily require the retention of the Marxist People's Democratic Party of Afghanistan (PDPA) as the dominant political force in a future ruling coalition in Afghanistan. However, it remains uncertain whether Soviet leaders will eventually be ready to withdraw Soviet military advisers and technicians from Afghanistan alongside their forces in the field. Nor is it clear how far Moscow is prepared to renounce its influence over Afghan foreign and defence policy while that country remains in turmoil. Soviet interests remain tightly bound up with the political composition and foreign-policy orientation of Afghanistan.

American interests

For most of the postwar period American interests in Iran and Pakistan have been couched in terms of broader, global strategic priorities, in terms of the maintenance of a particular world order. The American commitment to the defence of the region was directly formulated in bilateral agreements of 1959 with Iran and Pakistan. Afghanistan, in contrast, was regarded by American officials as of minor strategic significance. In 1959 the State Department concluded that 'vital United States objectives are best served if Afghanistan remains neutral, independent and not over-committed to the Soviet bloc'.[4] As the USSR became the primary arms exporter to Afghanistan, however, the United States effectively relegated this state to a *de facto* Soviet sphere of influence. This was reflected in 1978 in the muted American response to the *coup* by the PDPA in Kabul.

A more direct American concern has been the threat which the Soviet military buildup in Transcaucasia and Central Asia has posed for Iran and the prospect of Pakistani isolation between two states, India and Afghanistan, armed primarily by the Soviet Union. The United States sought to sustain a bilateral military association with Pakistan and Iran even as the interest of these countries in CENTO dwindled in the 1960s and 1970s. Pakistan and Iran were perceived as barriers against the potential projection of Soviet power into the Middle East and the Indian Ocean. More specifically, they constituted the natural buffer to any political or military moves by the USSR towards Persian Gulf oil or against the economically vital Indian Ocean sealanes.

The fall of the Shah compelled the United States to reassess its interests in Southwest Asia. The strategic value of Iran as a buffer against Soviet encroachments southward remained, but the American ability to coordinate jointly with this crucial state was lost. The preeminent American interest lay in deterring Soviet political or military intervention in Iran in the wake of current or unforeseeable future instabilities. A more difficult tendency to preempt, but in the long term equally challenging to American interests, would be a predisposition in Iran to defer to Soviet views on regional security matters. The Soviet intervention in Afghanistan helped frustrate this possibility.

A normalisation of American–Iranian relations, with the intention of restoring certain security links in the medium term would clearly correspond with American interests and the roots of the Irangate scandal derive from such a perception. The establishment of a firm *modus vivendi* between Iraq and Iran could promote such an outcome. The protracted Gulf War showed how the disruption of Western oil supplies is more directly threatened by regional conflict than Soviet designs. However, an increase in American naval deployments in the Indian Ocean has been presented partly as a compensatory requirement in light of the land-based capabilities the Soviet Union developed in Afghanistan. In the 1980s the United States has also transformed the Indian Ocean state of Pakistan into the primary buttress against further Soviet encroachments in Asia.

American security interests ultimately are not dependent on the reconstitution of a strictly non-aligned Afghanistan. Some observers identified the main United States interest in this conflict in ensuring that Moscow remained militarily enmeshed in Afghanistan as a lesson against future adventures, as a means of fostering hostility to the Soviet Union in many Third World countries and as a bargaining chip in potential superpower negotiations on regional issues. More conservative American politicians accepted that Afghanistan itself is not important to the United States, but they promoted aid to the Afghan resistance as part of the broader ideological agenda formed by the Reagan Doctrine. Nevertheless, the agreement on Afghanistan in April 1988, which provided a face-saving means for a Soviet military withdrawal from that country, is likely in the medium term to reduce Soviet pressure on the vulnerable states of Iran and Pakistan where American interests are more pronounced. Another benefit Washington derives from this agreement is that for the foreseeable future it significantly raises the stakes and thereby discourages any Soviet attempt to create significant strategic facilities on Afghan soil.

SYMMETRY AND ASYMMETRY OF INTERESTS

By the early 1980s an axis had developed in Southwest Asia whereby Western interests were focused most directly on the Persian Gulf, Soviet interests were concentrated on Afghanistan, and both superpowers equally proclaimed a strong interest in the independence and territorial integrity of the pivotal state of Iran. American interests in Pakistan tended to be secondary, an adjunct to policy towards the Gulf and Afghanistan rather than essential in their own right. While the United States built up rapid deployment forces for the Gulf and expanded military ties with Pakistan, the Soviet Union effectively annexed the most sensitive region of Afghanistan bordering on China, the Wakhan Corridor. Soviet interests have been strongest in directly contiguous territories and have reflected land rather than sea communications. American interests have focused rather on particular strategic necessities and have been enforced more by naval instruments.

Both Moscow and Washington have regarded their superpower status as entitling their involvement to a greater or lesser extent in the regions of predominant interest to their adversary to the extent of challenging the legitimacy of incumbent, if unpopular, regimes. But both powers have recognised the need for mutual restraint in the pursuit of unilateral interests in Iran. In contrast a more active competition of interest over Pakistan may emerge if Afghanistan is not restored as a buffer distancing the Soviet presence. The strategic involvement of the USSR in the Indian Ocean is rising but it remains unclear how far Washington accepts the legitimacy of Soviet interests in this vast area. The general parameters of Soviet interests may become more identifiable as the Gorbachev leadership elaborates its proposals on 'mutual security' and as the situation around Afghanistan clarifies.

CLIENTS AND PROXIES

The Asian states territorially closest to the Soviet Union, with the exception of Mongolia and, more recently, Afghanistan, have escaped the need to enter close relations of political and military dependence on their superpower neighbour. Soviet 'client' relationships have been formed with more distant states in Asia, Africa and Latin America. Turkey, Iran and Pakistan have all ultimately been militarily reliant on the United States in any conflict involving the USSR but they have diversified their political and economic links and, at times, have consciously manoeuvred between the superpowers. The cases of Iran and Afghanistan in the 1980s have impressed most forcefully on both superpowers the ephemeral quality of their investment, the limits of control determined by the intractability of Third World disputes and the enduring nature of ethnic, religious and nationalist loyalties.

Even before the fall of the Shah Iran had set limits on the forms of strategic cooperation it engaged in with the United States and had sought to cultivate pragmatic relations with the USSR. Iran had pursued an ambitious regional policy which frequently but not invariably had coincided with American strategic goals. Revolutionary Iran resolved to end Iran's role of 'gendarme' in the Persian Gulf and the Indian Ocean.[5] The new Islamic state adopted a purist notion of non-alignment, which involved a rejection of commitments to both East and West, although this became compromised by the military needs of the Gulf War. Both superpowers strove to prevent their adversary from gaining a foothold in Iran. In the absence of effective levers to control Iranian policy they opted for a policy of denial. A Soviet article in 1984 recognised that the slogan of 'neither East nor West' was 'interpreted as signifying that Iran must not allow Soviet influence to take the place of its onetime dependence on the United States'. However, it warned against a tendency in the Iranian foreign-policy course towards 'the expansion of various kinds of ties with Western powers'.[6]

Pakistan has been a recalcitrant ally rather than a client of the United States. It has exploited its position in American geostrategic thinking, especially since Soviet troops entered Afghanistan, to manoeuvre for assistance.[7] Despite Pakistan's advocacy of non-alignment after leaving CENTO (a departure which left bilateral agreements with the United States intact) in 1981 it accepted a six-year 3.2 billion dollar aid package from the Reagan Administration subject to certain criteria. Islamabad was aware that it could exert reverse influence on its 'patron'. Defence cooperation with the United States developed further but this did not alter the basic principles of Pakistani policy. These included 'a reluctance to identify fully with US policy on the region such as would be represented by offering base rights, and a determination to protect Pakistan's nuclear option and its search for a negotiated settlement of the Afghan conflict under terms that would serve Pakistan's interests'.[8]

American aid to Pakistan has been linked in principle to Pakistan's commitment to nuclear non-proliferation. Pakistani obduracy on this issue resulted in a temporary suspension of aid in 1979. In July 1986 the White House warned the visiting Pakistani Prime Minister that Pakistan's acquisition of a nuclear bomb would result in the end of American aid. However, in spring 1987, just as the US Congress was considering a 4.02 billion dollar aid programme for Pakistan, President Zia stated that Pakistan had the potential for the production of nuclear weapons. It appeared by this stage that the Reagan administration had decided that it could not stop Pakistan acquiring such weapons. Washington apparently gave priority to resisting further Soviet pressure on Pakistan and to safeguarding the flow of American aid to the Afghan resistance.[9]

Soviet spokesmen interpreted the American readiness 'to forgive such a devoted ally [as Pakistan] even such a sin as a persistent desire to acquire its own nuclear weapons' as reflecting Washington's military priorities.[10] Soviet writers have claimed that Washington and Islamabad have signed a secret document granting the United States permission to use Pakistani naval and air bases. The issue of storing military supplies for American rapid-deployment forces in Pakistan was allegedly under consideration.[11] It is true that Pakistan has been angling for an airborne early-warning system for the Afghan border (see below) but reports on American use or control of Pakistani airbases are stringently denied by Pakistani officials.[12]

The Pakistani Prime Minister additionally refuted suggestions at the end of 1985 that 'our policy towards Afghanistan is formulated at the behest of American interests rather than our own'. This was a response *inter alia* to Soviet claims that American officials had been behind Pakistani intransigence at the United Nations talks on Afghanistan. He declared in Parliament that the Americans had 'never pressurised us on Afghanistan'.[13] There is room for doubt here, since American military assistance to Pakistan (which is used primarily to bolster Pakistan against India) has provided leverage on Pakistan to continue to act as the intermediary and support base for the 'covert' military assistance programme to the Afghan *mujahidin* primarily sponsored by the United States. On the other hand, an elite Pakistani military group may have used the Afghan conflict for its own purposes out of an awareness that American support for the *mujahidin* remains dependent on access through Pakistan. However, on a visit to Pakistan in April 1988 the American Defence Secretary, Frank Carlucci, told his hosts that the United States would keep its close military links with Pakistan even after a settlement on Afghanistan.

As the *mujahidin* groups became more reliant on the United States for sophisticated arms, and as they developed contacts with Western intelligence agencies, they themselves, despite their independent political objectives, assumed some of the characteristics of Western clients. Large quantities of these foreign arms have been siphoned off in Pakistan before reaching Afghanistan but Moscow has not minced its words about Pakistan's participation in the 'undeclared war against Afghanistan'. Indeed Pakistan's role in channelling arms funded by the United States (but also by China and some Islamic states) into Afghanistan was used by Moscow as the primary justification for the continued Soviet presence in this country.[14] Soviet commentators argued that this Pakistani role and its 'growing strategic cooperation with the USA' were 'increasing tension in Pakistan and weakening the position of the Pakistani authorities'. In their view this raised the question of 'whether the Pakistan military authorities are ready to work to serve the interests of their own country and not those of Washington'.[15]

From the mid-1950s Soviet leaders presented their relations with Afghanistan as a model of peaceful coexistence in Asia. Afghanistan maintained a credible non-aligned status until the late 1970s, although it became heavily dependent on the USSR for energy and arms imports. Soviet–Afghan foreign policy coordination remained largely declaratory. Even after the *coup* by the PDPA in Kabul in April 1978, dependence on Moscow was kept within limits by the nationalist sentiments of the new Afghan leaders, especially Hafizullah Amin. Soviet and Democratic Republic of Afghanistan (DRA) officials insisted unconvincingly that Afghanistan remained independent and non-aligned after the entry of Soviet troops at the end of 1979. But from its first days the Soviet-imposed regime, headed consecutively by Babrak Karmal and Najibullah, was dependent on Soviet troops for its very survival. Apart from this military dependence, it has relied almost exclusively on the Soviet Union and certain East European states to provide the economic and internal security assistance necessary to avert a total breakdown of the infrastructure in those areas of the country over which control has been maintained. A Soviet spokesman admitted in 1987 that 94.7 per cent of 'foreign aid' received by the DRA arrives from the Comecon countries.[16]

After talks which determined the terms of the Soviet troop presence in Afghanistan in March 1980, Gromyko affirmed 'the complete identity – I repeat, the complete identity – of the two sides' views on all questions discussed'.[17] This formula and professions of revolutionary solidarity between Moscow and Kabul were repeated in subsequent Soviet–DRA discussions.[18] However, owing to its beleaguered position, the DRA has been unable to act internationally as a proxy for its superpower patron, except by voicing declaratory support for Soviet stands or by imposing pressure on the Pakistani border regions. DRA officials echoed Soviet positions in the United Nations-sponsored negotiations on Afghanistan. By the summer of 1987 Soviet and DRA officials were prepared to offer the political opposition to the incumbent Afghan leadership 'a real sharing of power' in a future coalition government in Afghanistan, including 23 ministerial posts.[19] Even after the April 1988 United Nations-mediated agreement, however, it remains unclear how far Soviet leaders are prepared to countenance the restoration of full non-alignment in Afghan foreign and security policy.

LIKELIHOOD OF SUPERPOWER MILITARY CONFRONTATION

In the late 1970s and early 1980s United States' contingency plans in Southwest Asia were focused primarily on the possibility of Soviet military intervention in or invasion of the Persian Gulf or Iran. It was pointed out that Soviet defence planners could call on 25 divisions located in the north Caucasus, Transcaucasus and Turkestan military districts for such contingencies. Numerous threat scenarios for the Gulf were constructed which were based on an assumed Soviet military drive to control Persian Gulf oil. Soviet capabilities and constraints were analysed in detail, as were the counter capabilities of American rapid-deployment forces.[20] These analyses tended to assume that Soviet initiatives (perhaps under the pretext of the 1921 Soviet–Persian treaty) would be those most likely to occasion a superpower confrontation in this region. But not all writers discounted the possibility that 'US moves, even if invited by legitimate governments of the region, could trigger a hostile Soviet counter-intervention response in the same theater'.[21] Confrontation over the Gulf is outside the scope of this paper, but some consideration should be given to Iran as the catalyst of Soviet–American conflict.

The second scenario to consider concerns Afghanistan. Even before Soviet military intervention in this country some Western specialists predicted that an armed conflict between Afghanistan and Pakistan or Afghanistan and Iran or even political upheavals in these states resulting from separatist movements in Baluchistan or Pushtunistan would be likely to spill over into the Gulf.[22] As the civil war in Afghanistan intensified, and as Soviet pressure on Pakistan was stepped up, the United States Central Command extended its 19-country 'area of responsibility' to include Afghanistan and Pakistan. This increased the possibility of American intervention on the Afghanistan–Pakistan border under the terms of the 1959 American–Pakistan mutual security agreement, with the attendant danger of confrontation with the USSR. Western analysts regarded it as evident that 'the risks of a direct Soviet–American conflict are greater on the Afghan border than in Angola, Nicaragua or Cambodia, where neither of the superpowers has committed its own combat forces'.[23]

Moscow has refused to acknowledge the unilateral abrogation of the military articles of the 1921 Soviet–Persian treaty by the Iranian Revolutionary Council in January 1980. When Gromyko was asked, in April 1980, during the hostages crisis, about the possibility of Iran requesting the USSR for assistance if attacked by the United States, he refused to comment on 'such a hypothetical situation'.[24] However, since the first years of the Iranian Revolution, speculation has surfaced in the West about the possibility of Soviet moves to dismember Iran through providing military support for the creation of separatist pro-Soviet regimes in Iran's ethnically disparate northern provinces. An alternative Soviet strategy could be directed at the creation of a Soviet client regime in Iran as a whole through backing certain groups in their bid for power in the struggle following the death of Ayatollah Khomeini. Either of these scenarios could be construed by American statesmen as threatening vital United States' interests, although Soviet leaders could hope to avoid a confrontation with the United States through a policy of incremental gains. However, thus far Soviet leaders have given priority to fostering state relations with a federal Iran and have been unable effectively to cultivate any politically influential forces in this country.

Soviet military intervention in Afghanistan set in motion speculation among Western strategists about possible further Soviet military moves aimed at detaching the Baluchistan province from Pakistan and eventually dismembering this multi-ethnic state.[25] Any Soviet attempt to seize Baluchistan, apart from its logistical difficulties, could well have led to a direct confrontation with the United States. A Soviet/DRA punitive invasion of Pakistan's Northwest Frontier Province (NWFP), or an attempt to capture salients of Pakistani territory, would have engaged American interests less directly, but would have threatened the same outcome. In fact, Pakistani officials did not consider a major Soviet military invasion of their country likely and they remain more concerned about a possible confrontation with India.[26] Already, in June 1981, the Pakistani Foreign Minister, Agha Shahi, indicated that he accepted Brezhnev's assurances that Pakistan need not fear an attack from the USSR, since such 'an attack by a superpower on another country in the region will not remain confined to the aggressor and the victim'.[27] There may be an element of wishful thinking here since Pakistan had sought and failed to obtain a direct security guarantee from the United States in 1980. Islamabad would have preferred a NATO-type security commitment, which Washington did not consider possible or realistic. The American unwillingness to turn the 1959 Agreement into a treaty prompted the claim by Agha Shahi (after leaving office) that it was 'effectively dead'. He declared that the United States would only intervene on Pakistan's behalf if Washington considered that its vital interests were in danger.[28]

By the mid-1980s Soviet leaders appeared to change the policy they pursued in the early 1980s of discouraging DRA leaders from pressing their long-standing claims over Baluchistan and Pashtunistan. In February 1986 Moscow backed a meeting of the border tribes which apparently declared that they 'would not permit the transformation of Baluchistan into a bridgehead of aggression against neighbouring states'. Claims were made that Baluchistan was being turned into a staging post for American rapid-deployment forces.[29] Any Soviet attempt to fund a Baluch guerrilla movement would, however, be undercut by the deeply conservative and Islamic loyalties of most of the Baluch (and Pashtuns) which pit them against the DRA regime. Pakistan could contain Soviet attempts at low-intensity operations in Baluchistan.

The Pakistani army has already clashed with dissident tribesmen in the North West Frontier Province armed by the DRA regime. Soviet statements supported the Pashtuns in this conflict.[30] Soviet spokesmen have claimed that 'by embarking on a policy of direct confrontation with the Soviet Union' the Zia administration was 'acting contrary to the interests of its own people'.[31]

However, Soviet pressure against the arms-supply routes into Afghanistan and guerrilla sanctuaries in the Pakistani borderlands may be misguided. Agha Shahi has argued that Pakistan has little control over the tribal areas and that, given the choice between an internal insurrection and suffering the consequences of 'hot pursuit', Pakistan would opt for the latter. Shahi still did not expect a superpower confrontation to develop on this tense border.[32]

There have been frequent cases of cross-border Soviet/DRA violations of Pakistan airspace and incidents of cross-border artillery fire at Pakistani targets. There is also some evidence of Soviet/DRA 'hot pursuit' operations into Pakistani territory. Moscow, in turn, has accused Pakistan of 'systematically shelling borderland Afghan localities' and of using Pakistani troops to take part personally 'in the combat operations of bands on the territory of Afghanistan'.[33] These border incidents became more serious in spring 1987. Several hundred deaths resulted from Soviet/DRA bombing raids on settlements harbouring Afghans just within Pakistani territory. The Pakistani airforce shot down a couple of marauding planes and, on 1 May, lost one of their own F-16 planes. Soviet reports claimed that Pakistani planes flying over their own territory were 'striking airborne targets over the territory of Afghanistan with missiles'.[34]

Such clashes coincided with a Pakistani request to Washington to lease Advanced Warning Planes (AWP). Since the advanced onboard surveillance equipment would need to be operated by American military personnel, press speculation centred on the consequences of Afghan jets flown by Soviet pilots attempting to shoot down an AWP with Americans on board. Soviet commentators accused Washington strategists of planning to use such surveillance information to provide early warning to resistance groups against Afghan air attack.[35] The prospect of such proxy American involvement in the Afghan conflict is unsettling but strong Soviet retaliation against Pakistan remains unlikely. Managing the conflict in Afghanistan has been a continuing drain on Soviet resources and a lesson against risking new military ventures. Current American military links with Pakistan will continue to discourage strong Soviet pressure on this state even if political turbulence intensifies within it.

There is some possibility that Pakistani nuclear ambitions, and the Indo-Pakistani nuclear confrontation that this may lead to, could spark off a major crisis between the superpower patrons of these states. A Soviet statement in March 1987 observed that 'the Islamabad authorities and the US administration patronising them should ponder on the catastrophic consequences to which nuclear ambitions can lead, on mortal danger with which they threaten peoples of the entire Asian region'.[36] Another statement noted that the USSR had repeatedly expressed its concern over the military aspects of the Pakistani nuclear programme but strongly refuted reports in the Asian press that the Soviet Union was planning to bomb the Pakistani enrichment plant at Kahuta.[37] Such Soviet action is most unlikely, although the acquisition of nuclear capabilities will certainly increase the sensitivity of Pakistan as a 'frontline' state.

RULES OF THE GAME AND CRISIS PREVENTION

It may be unrealistic to expect the leaders of either the United States or the Soviet Union to draw up formal 'codes of conduct' specifying what they will and will not do in a crisis in Southwest Asia. Neither superpower would wish to renounce in advance its right to intervene in a crisis zone even if the other, probably because of a more limited definition of its interests in the area, were prepared to do so. But it remains particularly important for Washington and Moscow to regulate the competitive pursuit of their interests in a region contiguous to Soviet borders and to impart some stability and predictability to their actions in this sensitive area through developing certain 'rules of the game'. Each power should specify the standards of behaviour expected of the other in the event of a regional conflict. With this in mind this section concentrates on recent superpower conduct, since the restraints apparent to some degree in their earlier behaviour towards the Indo-Pakistan conflicts and Iran developed in a very different strategic environment to that existing in Southwest Asia in the late 1980s.

In November 1978 Moscow sought to signal to Washington the limits of Soviet tolerance over the turmoil in Iran. Brezhnev warned that 'any, particularly military, interference in the affairs of Iran, a state directly bordering on the Soviet Union, would be regarded by the Soviet Union as affecting its security interests'.[38] Soviet countermeasures in the event of American military intervention in Iran have never been spelled out. But Moscow took credit for averting such military intervention since, *Izvestiya* claimed in October 1980, Washington could not 'fail to take into account the Soviet Union's possible reaction'. This consideration was presented also as a restraint on American action in the Iran–Iraq conflict.[39] Shortly after this claim an adviser to the Iranian President referred to an American–Soviet agreement to divide the region 'to control the area and secure their interests'.[40] This was too conspiratorial, and there has been no evidence of such agreements or of plans for a superpower condominium over Iran.

It appears, however, that a tacit understanding that Iran should remain militarily a 'no-go zone' for the superpowers has held thus far. Until a new, more assertive policy was formulated in May–June 1987, the United States exercised care in deploying naval groups in the Persian Gulf area. In turn, Soviet leaders refrained from massing troops on the Iranian border. Only some of the Soviet divisions in the Caucasus region are maintained in combat readiness. Restraint towards Iran has been assisted by the Khomeini regime's unwillingness to accept American or Soviet military advisers in any capacity. Both powers have sold arms or spare parts to Iran, generally through third parties, but an open competition has been avoided by their mutual unhappiness over the prospect of an Iranian military victory over Iraq and by their reluctance to antagonise Iraq and other Arab states.

The action taken by Soviet leaders in sending troops in their tens of thousands into Afghanistan at the end of 1979 exceeded all limits the USSR had previously observed in relation to military involvement in Third World states. Western observers were prone to compare it with Soviet military intervention in Eastern Europe. However, as in the cases of Soviet intervention in Angola and Ethiopia, Soviet intervention in Afghanistan took place in a country and at a time when no other great power patron was likely to intervene directly and militarily to oppose this action. Soviet leaders correctly calculated the low probability of great power diplomatic outrage being translated into a direct Soviet–American or Soviet–Chinese military confrontation over Afghanistan.

Both Moscow and Washington have accepted certain restraints on their own involvement and that of their proxies in the conflict around Afghanistan. These have not necessarily been similar and they have remained unstated. The superpowers have sought in general to prevent the civil war in Afghanistan from spilling over into military engagements with neighbouring states. Examples of what Alexander George has described as '*ad hoc* ground rules for escalation control'[41] can be identified. The formation of such rules was encouraged by what may be described as a 'limited war school' of thinking in the American government. This school regarded the American military assistance programme to the Afghan resistance as conditional rather than an end in itself. This has been reflected *inter alia* in the American unwillingness to offer diplomatic recognition to the resistance.

In the early 1980s the United States worked by proxy through Pakistan and maintained the formally 'covert' nature of its assistance programme. Until 1984 Washington closely restricted the quantity and technological level of the armaments made available to the *mujahidin*. Soviet model rather than American weaponry was supplied until 1986. In the first half of the 1980s this aid averaged no more than 100 million dollars per year and additional aid was provided by proxy from Saudi Arabia (in return for the 1981 AWACS deal). The 'limited war school' also overturned the idea of conducting airdrops in Afghanistan using unmarked American aircraft and acted to dissuade the United States from attempting to apply a 'liberated zone' strategy to the conflict in Afghanistan.[42]

There are no grounds to suppose that American advisers have operated in

Afghanistan. In response to Soviet claims in December 1987 that an American adviser had been killed in Afghanistan, the United States administration strenuously denied that there were any such advisers in the country.[43] Nor have American military advisers or personnel openly been associated with the administering of the assistance programme to the *mujahidin* in Pakistan. In the Soviet view such an association could lead to escalation. A Soviet commentary in August 1985 warned that a recent American insistence that 'US organisations should be allowed to provide directly – and not through the Pakistan Armed Forces – materials and supplies to Afghan mercenaries living on Pakistan's territory and to guide them in their criminal activities' would 'ultimately end the Pakistan authorities' control over Pakistan's border areas and over events along the Pakistan–Afghanistan border'.[44] The removal of this 'buffer' by implication would raise the likelihood of a direct Soviet–American clash. Nevertheless, Washington still refrains from pressing Pakistan to permit the establishment of formal American supply and intelligence bases on the Afghan borders. This forestalls Soviet claims of direct American 'provocations' from Pakistan of the U2 variety, although the arrival of American early-warning planes on the Afghan border in the late 1980s could act as the catalyst for such Soviet claims.

By 1986 it appeared that certain of the unstated 'ground rules' hitherto observed by the United States over the Afghan conflict had weakened. In March 1986 the American administration decided to provide American weaponry in the form of the sophisticated Stinger missile to the *mujahidin*. American trainers linked to this programme began operating on a small scale in Pakistan. When these missiles began to arrive into the hands of the *mujahidin* in October, a Soviet Ministry of Defence spokesman regarded it as marking 'a qualitatively new stage in Washington's interference in the internal affairs of the DRA'.[45] As the USSR had just announced the withdrawal of six regiments from Afghanistan it appeared that Washington did not accept any *quid pro quo* between Soviet troop numbers and aid to the resistance. Nor were American leaders prepared to link this aid to the truce announced by the DRA in Afghanistan in January 1987.[46] Indeed, Congress appropriated 630 million dollars for such military assistance for 1987 and Washington undertook to provide 600 Stinger missiles. Large numbers of British-manufactured Blowpipe missiles also found their way into the hands of the *mujahidin*. By July 1987 Soviet spokesmen admitted that the delivery of such weapons had 'naturally led to additional losses of the Afghan and Soviet air forces', but warned that 'appropriate measures to neutralise this situation are being taken'.[47] These arms deliveries were complemented by American funds for civil-action schemes within regions in Afghanistan which were now described as 'liberated zones'. Moscow criticised 'Washington's far-reaching intrigue aimed at setting up so-called liberated zones and parallel bodies of political power on Afghan territory'.[48] These developments indicated the difficulties of achieving a functional Soviet–American understanding to restrict or cease military or other assistance to Afghanistan. A decision announced by Washington to cease the supply of Stinger missiles to the Afghan resistance in April 1987 did not, therefore, form part of a mutual restraint agreement with Moscow. It reflected the concern of the State Department that large numbers of such missiles could escape American or even Afghan control following a settlement on Afghanistan.[49]

Pakistan has ultimately determined the 'effectiveness' of the resistance, and Pakistan has been reluctant to allow guerrilla warfare in Afghanistan to escalate beyond a moderate threshold for fear of Soviet retaliation. Pakistan has had the difficult task of gauging the level of Soviet tolerance on this question. Soviet tolerance was more severely taxed in March and April 1987 when *mujahidin* groups penetrated Soviet territory, attacked the settlement of Pyandzh and killed Soviet border troops.[50] It is most unlikely that the United States has encouraged such operations over Afghan borders in Soviet Central Asia, but Soviet spokesmen linked such bold conduct with the thrust of American policy on Afghanistan. At this time Yevgeniy Primakov even claimed that 'on orders from the White House the counter-revolutionaries recently fired American-made missiles at Soviet territory, at a border area of Tajikistan'.[51]

Soviet leaders did not set restraints on their application of military force or on the use of modern military technology within Afghanistan, although they refrained from substantially increasing the number of Soviet troops deployed in this country in the first year of occupation. Indeed, this war-ravaged country has been used to some extent as a testing ground for Soviet arms and tactics for low-intensity conflict in the Third World.[52] This reflected a realisation that American leaders have no ultimate commitment to or control over the Afghan *mujahidin* groups and that a superpower crisis could originate from actions on the Afghan borders but not from action within Afghanistan. Border incidents mounted but Soviet/DRA ground forces attacked neither Pakistani military posts nor refugee tent villages across the border. Pakistani intelligence accuses Soviet/DRA sponsors of instigating a bombing and assassination campaign in the North West Frontier Province.[53] But such low-intensity operations as exist beyond the Afghan borders have remained small-scale in relation to the degree of cross-border infiltration into the DRA from Pakistan and Iran. They have probably been intended as a tactical means, initially to influence Pakistan's stand on a negotiated Afghan settlement and, more recently, to persuade Pakistan to abide by the Afghan–Pakistani agreement of spring 1988, which requires Pakistan to stem the cross-border flow of arms to the *mujahidin*. Under the terms of the agreement Afghanistan also undertook not to engage in subversive action across its border on Pakistani territory.

Soviet leaders may think in terms of much broader trade-offs to moderate their rivalry with the United States and help avert crises around Afghanistan. It is important, therefore, that Moscow so far has refrained from developing the airfields and bases it gained control over in Afghanistan into strategic bases threatening neighbouring states or Western interests in the Gulf. Despite Western concern over the Shindand base in western Afghanistan, Soviet bases in Afghanistan were developed for use in the war against the resistance rather than for broader goals. In November 1986, on a state visit to India, Gorbachev gave his word that 'we are not going to have any bases in Afghanistan'.[54] If this commitment remains true it has important implications for the strategic planning of both superpowers. It could be related to the Soviet readiness, since 1981, to discuss the 'international aspects of the Afghan problem' together with the 'questions of Persian Gulf security'.[55]

MEASURES TO ENHANCE CRISIS-PREVENTION ARRANGEMENTS

The political fluidity and instability of Southwest Asia creates pressing demands both to narrow the area in which the superpowers are inclined to take unilateral military action to protect their perceived interests and to broaden the area of regulated competition. Sufficient time has elapsed since the downfall of the Shah and Hafizullah Amin for the gradual *ad hoc* formation of certain unstated ground rules for escalation control in the conflict around Afghanistan, but these fall short of rules of engagement and no formal understandings have developed over the role of the superpowers in a potential future conflict over the key state of Iran.

Since 1979 a process of diplomatic signalling between Moscow and Washington has helped to clarify respectively the core and subsidiary interests of the superpowers in Southwest Asia, but both powers remain unwilling to forego options in grey areas (such as in relation to the 'permissible' character of future regimes in Iran and Afghanistan), which could encourage the other power to press for greater influence. However, the return of superpower summitry and consultations on regional issues since 1985, and the new Soviet commitment to the pursuit of 'mutual security', augur well. They not only encourage the search for superpower patterns of restraint but revive the possibility of some broader regional accord or of sub-regional understandings which would dampen down worst case planning and preemptive strategies.

The primary obstacle to developing more formalised crisis-prevention arrangements in Southwest Asia is the ambiguity which still surrounds Soviet political and strategic intentions towards Afghanistan. Before the qualified United Nations' mediated agreement in April 1988 this uncertainty prompted suggestions for a regional accord encompassing a settlement of the Afghan conflict. One optimistic proposal envisaged a Soviet-tilted brand of neutralism in

Afghanistan accompanied by parallel understandings between the USSR, the United States and China, designed to neutralise Pakistan and Iran as arenas of great power conflict which would rule out military alliances and special military relationships.[56] In a similar vein, Agha Shahi, the former Pakistani foreign minister, called for Iran and Pakistan to adopt 'genuine non-alignment'. In his view, an effective solution to the Afghanistan problem could lead to the proclamation of Pakistan, Iran and Afghanistan as a 'zone of peace and neutrality' free of superpower military presence. This would require a superpower agreement to respect this status for the region.[57]

In a more limited scheme, the EEC formally proposed the neutralisation of Afghanistan in 1981, the transformation of this state effectively into a 'no-go zone' outside superpower competition. This idea was flatly rejected by the DRA and the USSR.[58] Soviet interests were too deeply entrenched in Afghanistan in the early 1980s to permit such a unilateral concession. Another proposal sought mutual restraint understandings in Iran and Pakistan according to which Moscow and Washington would make 'appropriate diplomatic efforts to reassure each other that neither will introduce combat forces or mutually threatening bases or facilities'. This idea was supported by former Secretary of State Cyrus Vance following Soviet intervention in Afghanistan in 1979, but it was blocked by then national security adviser Zbigniew Brzezinski. Another suggestion by Indian and American analysts in 1986 was a withdrawal of the permanent deployment of the American carrier battle group from the Arabian Sea as a possible *quid pro quo* for a withdrawal of Soviet forces and bases in Afghanistan. This plan required an informal phasedown of military commitments on both sides.[59] The decision taken by the Soviet Union in 1988 to carry out a staged withdrawal of the troops from Afghanistan has rendered unnecessary further consideration of such *quid pro quo* arrangements to extract Soviet forces from that country. However, superpower understandings on the future political composition of Afghanistan, and on the character of bilateral military links with the regime or political groups in that country, may still be worth exploring.

The 1988 United Nations-sponsored accord on Afghanistan failed to achieve an effective agreement to stem the flow of arms from the superpowers to that country. This reduces the effectiveness of international guarantees intended to act as a tripwire to preempt the escalation of incidents around Afghanistan. Military tension will continue around Afghanistan in the absence of a clearer mutual superpower prohibition on military supplies to that country. Nor has the readiness of each superpower to pledge to recognise Afghan non-alignment and neutrality been reflected in any agreement over the composition of the government in Afghanistan. No agreement has been reached on the degree of involvement of the *mujahidin* in Afghan political life and it remains necessary to spell out the functions and role of any residual Soviet military advisers or personnel in Afghanistan following the withdrawal of Soviet combat forces. The pledges between Afghanistan and Pakistan on non-interference in their bilateral treaty so far have proven ineffective against cross-border infiltration and have failed to end the bombing campaign in North Pakistan. Therefore, ethnically based tensions between the two countries remain potent. It would appear that the April 1988 agreement leaves many unresolved issues which need to be addressed to enhance the prospects of crisis prevention in Southwest Asia.

The object of crisis prevention in this region would also be served by a clarification on the part of the United States of the conditions under which the 1959 military agreement with Pakistan could become operable and by a clearer statement of American interests in Pakistan. More information on the American presence in Pakistani Baluchistan and on any residual Soviet military presence or involvement in Afghanistan would help remove some of the ambiguity surrounding the intentions of Moscow and Washington in this region. Washington might consider it worth exploring some trade-off in information on military dispositions between the Soviet–Iranian border region and Pakistan or the Persian Gulf. Currently, many of the Soviet divisions in the Caucasus region are not combat-ready or fully manned. Bringing them to full strength would alert the Americans. Recent Soviet concessions in Europe on confidence-building measures could perhaps be adapted for application to the Soviet southern borders. Gorbachev has already proposed negotiations with the United States and interested Asian countries on confidence-building measures in the military field applicable to Asia.[60]

On a more general plane, it would conduce to stability in Southwest as well as South Asia if the superpowers could encourage India and Pakistan to agree to a non-aggression pact, perhaps through the agency of the South Asian Association for Regional Cooperation. This could combine elements of the Pakistani proposal in 1981 for a no-war pact and the Indian proposal in 1982 for a friendship and cooperation treaty between the two states. An informal superpower understanding to support such a pact could eventually be reflected in mutual restraint in arms sales to India and Pakistan (the Indians had related this issue of arms imports to their treaty proposal). Pakistan's nuclear programme is potentially more destabilising than conventional arms imports into South Asia and Washington should seek means to apply leverage on this issue in the post-Zia period. Although the talks in the United Nations on the demilitarisation and denuclearisation of the Indian Ocean remain stalled, it may be worthwhile to explore the possibility of developing the *de facto* absence of American and Soviet tactical nuclear weapons on the Southwest Asian mainland into a tacit understanding to avoid their introduction in future contingencies.

As new crises engaging the superpowers are likely to occur at short notice in the volatile political terrain of Southwest Asia, Soviet and American officials would also be well advised to maintain the practice of regular official and specialist discussions on security issues in this region. Soviet–American bilateral consultations of this kind have specifically dealt with Afghanistan and Southwest Asia on several occasions since early 1985. At the Washington superpower summit in December 1987, Afghanistan was discussed in greater depth than any other issue except for arms control, and these talks were continued at the Moscow summit in May–June 1988.[61] These meetings remain important to identify in advance possible forms of accommodation in those areas and on those issues where the interests of the superpowers appear to heavily overlap. Although not a sufficient condition for successful crisis prevention, they may be a necessary condition.

NOTES

1 For Iran's assessment of these changes, see interview of Iranian Minister of Information and Propaganda for *Pravda*; Tass in Russian for abroad, 28 March 1979, in BBC Summary of World Broadcasts. Soviet Union (henceforth SU) 6080/A4/3–4.

2 On this question see A. Bennigsen, 'Mullahs, Mujahidin and Soviet Muslims', *Problems of Communism*, 33 6 (November–December 1984); Y. Ro'i, ed., *The USSR and the Muslim World* (London: George Allen and Unwin, 1984); K. Dawisha and H. C. d'Encausse, 'Islam in the Foreign Policy of the Soviet Union: A Double-Edged Sword', in A. Dawisha, ed., *Islam in Foreign Policy* (Cambridge: Cambridge University Press, 1983), pp. 170–6; T. Kuzio, 'Opposition in the USSR to the Occupation of Afghanistan', *Central Asian Survey*, 6, 1 (1987).

3 L. B. Teplinskiy, *SSSR i Afganistan 1919–1981* (Moscow: Nauka, 1982), pp. 231, 233.

4 This reference from United States declassified documents is cited in H. S. Bradsher, *Afghanistan and the Soviet Union* (Durham, NC: Duke University Press, 1983), p. 29.

5 See S. Tahir-Kheli, 'Proxies and Allies: The Case of Iran and Pakistan', *Orbis*, 24, 2 (Summer 1980).

6 *New Times* (Moscow), 2 (1984), p. 19.

7 See T. P. Thornton, 'Between the Stools?: U.S. Policy Towards Pakistan During the Carter Administration', *Asian Survey* (October 1982), pp. 959–77.

8 T. L. Eliot, jun. and R. L. Pfaltzgraff, jun., eds, *The Red Army on Pakistan's Border: Policy Implications for the United States*, Special Report of the Centre for Asian Pacific Affairs, the Asia Foundation Institute for Foreign Policy Analysis, Inc. (Washington, DC: Pergamon, 1986), pp. 27–9.

9 See The *Guardian*, 5 November 1986, 9 March 1987.

10 Moscow World Service in English, 29 November 1986, in SU/8435/A3/1.

11 For example, A. V. Krutskikh, *Politika SShA v Indiyskom okeane* (Moscow: nauka, 1984), p. 142.

12 See President Zia's speech to the Pakistani National Assembly and Senate, in *The Muslim*, 24 December 1985.

13 Speech by Sahabzada Yaqub Khan in Parliament, in The *Pakistan Times*, 25 December 1985.

14 For an example of a Soviet map which ostensibly shows 'the wide network of training camps and bases for Afghan counter-revolutionaries and saboteurs in Pakistan' see *New Times* (Moscow), 9 (1981), p. 13.

15 Radio Moscow in Urdu, 17 August 1985, in SU/8044/A3/2.

16 Cited in SU/8530/C/7.

17 *Pravda*, 15 March 1980.

18 See, for example, Soviet–Afghan talks on 16 October 1980 during visit by Babrak Karmal to Moscow, in *Pravda*, 17 October 1980.

19 See report of talks in Moscow between Gorbachev and Najib, Moscow World Service in English, 21 July 1987, in SU/8626/A3/2.
20 See D. Ross, 'Considering Soviet Threats to the Persian Gulf' and J. M. Epstein, 'Soviet Vulnerabilities in Iran and the RDF Deterrent', *International Security*, 6, 2 (Fall 1981); R. W. Jones, 'Regional Conflict and Strategic Challenge in Southwest Asia' in W. J. Taylor and S. A. Maaranen, *The Future of Conflict in the 1980s* (Lexington: Lexington Books, 1982), pp. 267–72; K. A. Dunn, 'Soviet Strategy, Opportunities and Constraints in Southwestern Asia', *Soviet Union*, 11, pt 2 (1984), pp. 189 ff.
21 Jones, 'Regional Conflict', p. 268.
22 R. K. Ramazani, 'Security in the Persian Gulf', *Foreign Affairs*, 57, 4 (Spring 1979), p. 827.
23 *International Herald Tribune*, 3 April 1986.
24 Answer at a press conference in Paris on 25 April 1980, cited in A. Y. Yodfat, *The Soviet Union and Revolutionary Iran* (London: Croom Helm, 1984), pp. 78–9.
25 For a sober appraisal see S. Harrison, *In Afghanistan's Shadow: Baluch Nationalism and Soviet Temptations* (New York: Carnegie Endowment for International Peace, 1981).
26 For Pakistani threat perceptions see Eliot and Pfaltzgraff, eds., *The Red Army on Pakistan's Border*, pp. 20 ff.
27 Cited in *ibid.*, p. 29.
28 See H. Malik, 'Soviet Intervention in Afghanistan and its Impact on Pakistan's Foreign Policy', in H. Malik, ed., *Soviet–American Relations with Pakistan, Iran and Afghanistan* (London: Macmillan, 1987), pp. 131–3; for Shahi's comments, pp. 399–400.
29 Reports in *Krasnaya Zvezda*, 28 January 1986; Moscow World Service in English, 18 February 1986, in SU/8190/A3/1 and 2.
30 See The *Guardian*, 1 November 1985; Tass in Russian for abroad, 13 January 1986, in SU/8164/A3/4.
31 For example *Krasnaya Zvezda* article reported in Tass in Russian and English, 16 June 1987, in SU/8599/A3/1.
32 Cited in Malik, ed., *Soviet–American Relations with Pakistan, Iran and Afghanistan*, p. 400; for various scenarios of Soviet–Pakistani confrontation including the exploitation of internal Pakistani tensions see 'Soviet Intervention in Afghanistan and its Impact on Pakistan's Foreign Policy', pp. 140–3.
33 V. Semyonov, 'The creeping aggression against Afghanistan', *International Affairs* (Moscow), 10 (1986), 68.
34 See Tass in Russian for abroad, 28 April 1987, in SU/8556/A1/6; Soviet television on 6 May 1987, in SU/8567/A3/5.
35 See The *Independent*, 4 May 1987; The *Guardian*, 15 May 1987; Moscow home service, 13 May 1987, in SU/8571/A3/7; Tass in English 19 May 1987, in SU/8574/A3/5.
36 Tass commentary in English, 10 March 1987, in SU/8515/A3/2.
37 Tass in English, 28 February 1987, in SU/8505/A3/1.
38 *Pravda*, 19 November 1978.
39 See *Izvestiya*, 3 October 1980; cited in Yodfat, *The Soviet Union and Revolutionary Iran*, p. 113.
40 Yodfat, *The Soviet Union and Revolutionary Iran*, p. 94.
41 A. L. George, *Managing U.S.–Soviet Rivalry: Problems of Crisis Prevention* (Boulder, CO: Westview Press), pp. 389–91.
42 This term, and an analysis of its characteristics, were provided by Selig Harrison in a paper on 'United States Policy Towards Afghanistan' at a symposium on Afghanistan in Oxford on 1 April 1987.
43 See The *Guardian*, 29 December 1987.
44 Radio Moscow in Urdu, 17 August 1985, in SU/8044/A3/1.
45 Tass in English, 4 November 1986; in SU/8411/A3/2.
46 For the suggestions of a Soviet television commentator that the truce should be followed by a six-month cessation of American military aid to the *mujahidin* see SU/8461/A3/1.
47 See Tass in Russian for abroad, 16 July 1987, in SU/8624/A1/2.
48 See The *Guardian*, 18 June 1987; Radio Peace and Progress in English for Asia, 20 June 1987, in SU/8602/A3/2.
49 See *The Times*, 2 April 1988.
50 These attacks are described in Tass in Russian for abroad, 18 April 1987, in SU/8546/A3/1–2; *Izvestiya*, 22 April 1987, and SU/8555/A3/3–5.

51 This was claimed during an exchange of views between delegations of the US Congress and the USSR Supreme Soviet on 16 April 1987. Tass in Russian and English for abroad 16 April 1987, in SU/8547/A1/5.
52 See D. M. Hart, 'Low-Intensity Conflict in Afghanistan: The Soviet View', *Survival*, March/April 1982.
53 See, for example, *The Sunday Times*, 4 November 1985; *The Muslim*, 23 December 1985.
54 *Stability and Security – A Common Concern. Visit of General Secretary of the CPSU Central Committee Mikhail Gorbachev to India November 25–28, 1986. Documents and materials* (Moscow: Novosti, 1986), p. 14.
55 Speech by L. I. Brezhnev at the Twenty-sixth Party Congress, February 1981, in *New Times* (Moscow), 9 (1981), 28.
56 S. Harrison, 'Dateline Afghanistan: Exit Through Finland', *Foreign Policy*, 41 (Winter 1980–1), 183–6. For an Indian diplomat's view of the need to create an outer belt of neutrality as a precondition for the 'finlandization' of Afghanistan see J. S. Mehta, 'A Neutral Solution', *Foreign Policy*, 47 (Summer 1982).
57 A. Shahi, 'Pakistan's Relations with the United States', in H. Malik, *Soviet–American Relations with Pakistan, Iran and Afghanistan*, pp. 180–1.
58 For the Soviet response see *Tass*, 4 July 1981, in SU/6767/A3/1; 6 July 1981, in SU/6769/A3/1; and *Pravda*, 16 July 1981.
59 This is suggested by the Indo-American Task Force on the Indian Ocean co-sponsored by the Carnegie Endowment for International Peace in Washington and the Institute for Defence Studies and Analyses in New Delhi. See *International Herald Tribune*, 3 April 1986; and S. Harrison, 'Cut a Regional Deal', *Foreign Policy*, no. 62 (Spring 1986), 140–7.
60 See *Stability and Security*, p. 29.
61 See The *Guardian*, 12 January 1988.

10 The superpowers and Central America and the Caribbean

Peter Shearman

In considering the relative importance of Central America and the Caribbean to the superpowers, the first and most important thing to note is the asymmetry in political, economic and strategic interests between them. The Soviet Union has no long tradition of relations with the Central American republics, it has minimal economic contacts in the region, some 6,000 kilometres separate European Russia from the Caribbean and, in a hierarchy of Soviet global strategic interests, the area ranks very low indeed. For the United States, on the other hand, Central America has traditionally been seen as vital to national security interests. As early as 1823, long before American economic penetration of Central and Southern America, President Monroe announced to the European powers (including Russia) that the United States would 'consider any attempt on their part to extend their system to any portion of this hemisphere as dangerous to our peace and safety'.[1] The Monroe Doctrine, proclaimed ninety years before the Russian Revolution, reflected the important place Latin America held in American perceptions of its own security interests. In this context Central America and the Caribbean have been seen as crucial, and have witnessed a number of direct American military interventions since the late nineteenth century. Between 1898 and 1920 US marines intervened in the Caribbean twenty times, the US occupied Cuba from 1917 until 1923, the Dominican Republic from 1916 to 1924, Haiti from 1914 to 1934 and Nicaragua from 1912 to 1925.[2] American marines intervened four times during this period in the internal affairs of Honduras (in 1907, 1911, 1919 and 1925).[3]

This American inclination to intervene declined in the 1930s, with Roosevelt promising a 'new deal' for South and Central America under the rubric of his 'good neighbour policy'. Roosevelt revoked the Platt Amendment to Cuba's constitution which had given the United States legal justification for intervention, and withdrew American marines from Nicaragua (following another intervention in 1926); the US Congress ratified principles of non-intervention;

and Latin American states agreed to consult with each other and the United States in the event of any external threat to hemispheric security. As Robert Wesson puts it, 'The Monroe Doctrine seemed thereby converted into a collective security agreement, and the US sphere of influence entered a new era in which the use of force by the hegemonic power was no longer permissible – and was no longer undertaken except when Washington perceived a threat to the political integrity of the hemisphere.'[4]

SOVIET AND AMERICAN INTERESTS

The outcome of the Second World War, however, produced a situation characterised by bipolarity and ideological antipathy. Rivalry between the United States and the Soviet Union was made all the more difficult to manage by competing world views and differing political and social organisations, which undermined any prospects for crisis management and conflict resolution through the methods of classical balance of power politics of nineteenth-century Europe. The United States, seeing the Soviet Union and the spread of communism as the major threat to American global interests, began forming alliance structures to contain Soviet power. In Latin America this was manifested in the Rio Treaty, the Inter-American Treaty of Reciprocal Assistance, and the establishment of the Organisation of American States in 1948. The OAS was an instrument the United States hoped to use to ensure American hegemony in the Western hemisphere and, in 1954, the organisation ratified the Caracas Declaration which extended the Monroe Doctrine to Latin America. The Declaration stated that 'The domination or control of the political institutions of any American state by the international communist movement, extending to this Hemisphere the political system of an extracontinental power, would constitute a threat to the sovereignty and political independence of the American states . . .'[5]

The first perceived communist threat to American interests was in Guatemala in 1954 when the Arbenz government instituted land reform and nationalised American corporations. The United States was not successful in getting full backing from the OAS to undertake action to remove Arbenz from power, so Eisenhower left it to the CIA to organise his ouster.[6] The successful overthrow of Arbenz was seen by Eisenhower as one of his major foreign policy achievements, and he defended the action with constant references to the Soviet threat in Guatemala, which was leading to a beachhead of international communism. In reality the Soviet Union had very little interest in Guatemala and had not made close contact with the Arbenz government – although there was one small arms-transfer agreement made through Czechoslovak intermediaries.[7]

Of far more significance for the United States was the challenge Castro posed to perceived American interests in the Caribbean following the Cuban Revolution in 1959. This revolution also had a profound impact on Soviet perceptions. In an action–reaction cycle, Cuba and the United States engaged in a number of hostile acts undermining the interests of the other in ways which, in retrospect, were destined to bring about Cuban dependency on the Soviet Union. But, although this was the final result, neither Cuba nor the United States actually wanted it. The major beneficiary was the post-Stalin Soviet leadership which had embarked upon a deliberate strategy of gaining allies in the Third World by offering economic inducements to anti-American governments. It is remarkable that this strategy succeeded in, of all places, the Caribbean – an area the Soviet Union has always considered to be the strategic preserve of the United States.

The significance of the Cuban Revolution for the Soviet Union was that it demonstrated the bankruptcy of 'geographical fatalism' and the Monroe Doctrine. The United States tried using similar tactics to those used in Guatemala to overthrow Castro, with a CIA financed, organised and led invasion of Cuban exiles at the Bay of Pigs in 1961. The failure of this operation and the success of the Cuban Revolution in breaking out of the American hegemonic grip in the Caribbean was a major blow to the United States and a handsome gain for the Soviet Union as Castro ultimately developed a Marxist–Leninist political system and acted in concert with Moscow in regional conflicts. Henceforth, American strategy in the region was to prevent any more Cubas, whilst ensuring that the Soviet Union did not instal offensive weapons on the island. Although Cuba represented a challenge to US interests and prestige, the United States has been successful in ensuring that its primary geostrategic concern in the Caribbean was not totally undermined: the Soviet Union has not established offensive military bases in Cuba while the United States has retained its large naval base on the strategically important end of the island at Guantanamo overlooking the Windward Passage.

By the 1960s, then, Soviet perceptions had undergone a profound change following Castro's triumph. The United States, however, still perceived the region as vital to its own national security, for the Caribbean Basin is one of the principal supply routes between America and Europe in the event of conflict in the European theatre, while the Panama Canal links the US East and West coasts. Consequently any military bases of foreign powers in the area would be a direct challenge to American power on its own doorstep. There was also a strong psychological factor, in that if the United States could not even control the small states in its own 'backyard', this would erode its prestige and have a demonstration effect on other states. It could also undermine global perceptions of US resolve and willingness to defend its own self-expressed security interests.

In the hierarchy of Soviet global interests, Central America and the Caribbean in the 1960s still ranked low, but now Soviet prestige was tied up with the fate of Cuba as the only socialist state in the Western hemisphere.

Events in the region during the 1970s and 1980s reinforced American fears about the threat of communism and the expansion of Soviet influence. Revolutions in Grenada and Nicaragua, and civil war in El Salvador, put the Caribbean Basin at the top of American foreign-policy concerns during the presidency of Ronald Reagan. These events were seen in a positive light in Moscow, for they provided the Soviet Union with an opportunity to help tie the United States down in a region of little concern to itself and with little risk of a direct superpower confrontation. The Soviet Union has given relatively small amounts of aid to these revolutionary forces (in comparison to its commitment to Cuba in the 1960s), but it provides the Sandinistas with sufficient military hardware to defend Nicaragua in its war against the contras who, in turn, have received support from the Reagan Administration. In the 1980s Reagan's overriding policy objective was to ensure the overthrow of the Sandinista government and to ensure defeat of the rebels in El Salvador. Reagan's perceptions of a threat of Soviet global expansionist ambitions was the driving logic behind American policy in the region. Holding a simple bipolar view of the world, American policy-makers failed to consider the real dynamics undermining stability in the polycentric areas of regional conflicts. American objectives remained the same as they have always been: to ensure perceived American national-security interests. But the basic analysis of the challenge to these interests was profoundly mistaken, based as it was on a misperception of the role the Soviet Union plays, can play, or indeed wishes to play. This, in turn, led to a strategy and tactics which were less likely to attain American goals than to exacerbate the problems.

There are three underlying themes of American policy: Moscow has expansionist ambitions in the region; if one state falls under Soviet influence, then the others fall too (i.e., the domino theory); and Cuba acts as a surrogate for Moscow. In large part, these assumptions developed out of the perception in the United States at the beginning of the 1980s that the *détente* process of the 1970s had benefited the Soviet Union, allowing Moscow to make unilateral gains in the Third World at America's expense. Nixon and Kissinger's 'linkage' strategy and Carter's initial focus on North–South issues were considered to have been responsible for undermining American power in global politics. Hence a return to confrontation and containment through a resurgence of American military power and resolve was deemed necessary to regain Washington's position. With the overthrow of Somoza in Nicaragua, and the threat of revolution in El Salvador, the Reagan Administration perceived the problem in simple East–

West terms, as a competition between the superpowers in a zero-sum game, the rules of which called for a strong military response (through proxies) and economic warfare against the Sandinistas.

Yet American policy in the 1980s was based on a number of misperceptions. First, the events of the 1970s which served to undermine America's global influence had little, if anything, to do with the Soviet Union. The OPEC oil embargo and price increases, the Iranian Revolution, the Tehran hostage crisis, the Iran–Iraq war, revolution and civil war in Central America, the developing internal crisis in Mexico, the international debt problem, international terrorism, anarchy in the Lebanon, the international drugs trade – the causes of these events were not to be found in Moscow. The 'gains' the Soviet Union made in the Third World in the 1970s were also exaggerated: Angola and Ethiopia, whilst strategically of value, are two of the poorest and most underdeveloped states in the world and did not compensate for the loss of Egypt and Somalia. Furthermore, the Soviet Union did not create the conditions which led to conflict and revolution, but simply took advantage of the opportunities provided, with the final Soviet–Cuban cooperative intervention in southern Africa and the Horn resulting from a complex action–reaction cycle involving a host of regional and external actors. It is not then Soviet expansionist ambitions which create regional conflict – the causes are rather to be found in the regions themselves. The major problem in the 1970s, which led to what some refer to as the Second Cold War in the 1980s, was the absence of any effective mechanisms for superpower crisis prevention – the lack of instruments for managing superpower competition in the inevitably changing Third World arena.

Although it is true that conflict and revolution in Central America and the Caribbean have indigenous roots, with the success of the Sandinista Revolution in a new period of increasing superpower tensions, the Soviet Union in the early 1980s came to accept, and to support, the long-held Cuban thesis of armed struggle. In the 1960s Castro and Brezhnev had engaged in polemics over this issue, with the Soviet Union being strongly opposed to Cuba's advocacy of violent revolution in Latin America, supporting instead a peaceful road to socialism through the traditional communist parties. The Soviet Union's basic objectives in Latin America had been to establish mutually beneficial political and economic state-to-state relations and to avoid the risk of confrontation with the United States. But following the Nicaraguan Revolution, in a series of articles in the Moscow-based Latin American Institute's journal, *Latinskaia Amerika*, Soviet specialists came to see the armed path to revolution as an appropriate model.[8]

Changing Soviet perceptions of the prospects for revolutionary change in Central America, however, did not lead to a radical or long-lasting change in

Soviet strategy and tactics in the region. Again taking advantage of opportunities wherever they arise, the Soviet Union has established close links with the Sandinista regime and supplied Nicaragua with military equipment and economic aid. Yet Soviet priorities have not changed as the USSR continues to court the large and more important Latin American countries, such as Mexico, Brazil and Argentina, through state-to-state contacts. Aid to Nicaragua is not great, and sophisticated fighter aircraft have not been supplied to the Sandinistas. For a brief spell between 1980 and 1981 Soviet commentaries on the situation in El Salvador suggested that Moscow was optimistic about a victory for the rebels. However, no conclusive evidence is available to show that the Soviet Union was supplying the revolutionaries with military equipment and, by 1982, optimism gave way to pessimism and support for a 'political solution' to the conflict. This is not surprising. The Soviet Union has, with the exception of the Cuban missiles in 1962, been consistently cautious in its probes in Central America and this caution is likely to increase now that the old guard in the Kremlin have departed the scene. Gorbachev represents not just a new Soviet generation, but a new orientation in Soviet foreign policy. It is clear that under Gorbachev the Soviet Union's basic priority is domestic, economic and political reform, and this focus on domestic issues has important consequences for external relations. Reading the speeches of the new Kremlin leadership it is evident that radical socialist-oriented regimes in the Third World will no longer be able to rely on large injections of Soviet aid, as the focus is now increasingly upon the more dynamic developing states of a capitalist orientation. The Soviet Union, as it seeks to develop closer mutual economic relations with these states, will not want to alienate the larger Latin American countries by stepping up support for the Sandinistas, to say nothing of support for the guerrillas in El Salvador.

In sum, American objectives in Central America have remained constant over time. The United States seeks to ensure stability in the region and to prevent intrusion from external powers. Stability is seen as maintenance of the status quo against the intrusive power of the Soviet Union. The exaggerated perception of a Soviet threat in the region has led to a militant policy of containment, a policy which is blind to the real dynamics of conflict and change at the local level. The Soviet Union seeks to establish mutually advantageous economic and political relations with the larger Latin American nations, but will take careful advantage of opportunities in Central America to forge closer ties with radical states which challenge American interests. Moscow recognises the indigenous causes of conflict, but does not undertake a high-risk policy of becoming actively engaged in the revolutionary process. It is only *after* a radical regime has seized power (as in Cuba, Grenada and Nicaragua) that the Soviet Union begins to play an active role in supporting the regime against internal and external counterrevolutionary threats. Even here this support is restricted, as evidenced by the Soviet reaction to the American-led invasion of Grenada in 1983. America looks upon the region as vital to its own national security. For the Soviet Union, Central America and the Caribbean are of little consequence strategically or economically. Both the United States and the Soviet Union have interests in the region tied up with their overall global image and prestige. This is far more critical for the United States, for it is important to Washington that its friends and adversaries alike perceive America as having sufficient resolve to maintain its interests in its own 'backyard'. For the Soviet Union, Cuba is important as the only socialist state in the Western hemisphere, thus its survival is important for Soviet prestige. Overall, however, there is a marked asymmetry of interests between the superpowers in the region – historically, economically, politically and geostrategically. It is perhaps more sensible to compare Central America with Eastern Europe than with other Third World regional conflicts. This has a bearing on policy prescriptions for crisis prevention and management. Before addressing this, it is necessary to examine patron–client relations and the role of proxies in the area.

PATRONS, CLIENTS AND PROXIES

In order to avoid risking a direct superpower confrontation, and to prevent hostile international reactions, both the United States and the Soviet Union have found it advantageous to rely upon client states to intervene in regional conflicts on their behalf. Such actions carry far less risk than a direct superpower military intervention. Israel, for example, is considered by many to be America's most important client state, or 'proxy', for defending American interests in the Middle East against the expansion of Soviet influence. Similarly, Cuba is seen as the Soviet Union's principal instrument for fighting proxy wars in regional conflicts, evidenced most dramatically by the decisive role Cuban combat troops played in Angola and Ethiopia in the 1970s. Non-state actors too – national liberation movements, communist parties, counterrevolutionary armies, business corporations – have also been used to further the interests of the superpowers. We should turn now to examine the role of superpower clients and proxies in the regional conflict in Central America, before going on to assess the prospects for crisis prevention.

THE UNITED STATES

Since the Sandinista Revolution the most notable American proxies in Central America have been of course the 'contras'. Viewing Nicaragua as potentially the first of the dominoes in mainland Latin America to fall under Soviet influence,

Reagan's overriding priority for the region was the removal of the Ortega regime in Managua and the re-establishment of a pro–American government. In order to attain this objective the Reagan Administration, through the CIA, helped to create, organise and finance a counter-revolutionary army made up of former National Guardsmen and other disaffected Nicaraguan groups opposed to the Sandinistas. In conducting this not-so-secret war, as revelations regarding the Iran–Contra link displayed, certain groups on the President's staff went to remarkable lengths to ensure, without Congressional approval, that the contras were adequately supplied with funds. Whilst the United States has not had total control over the actions of the contras, either on the ground in terms of battle operations or with internal faction fighting, control has been sufficient to ensure that the objectives the counter-revolutionaries are pursuing are those set by the Reagan Administration. The Americans had long had a reliable client state in Nicaragua under Somoza, and Reagan wished to re-establish American hegemony.

The other Central American states are in a difficult position regarding Nicaragua and the US-backed contra war against the Sandinistas. Whilst they share American concern about the prospects of a Marxist–Leninist government allied with the Soviet Union, they dislike Reagan's military strategy, favouring, albeit with different degrees of commitment, a regional diplomatic solution to the conflict. However, with the outbreak of the contra war there has been a radical escalation of a regional arms race as both the Sandinistas and the other Central American governments have undertaken a massive build up of their armed forces. American economic and military aid to Central America has increased dramatically since the Nicaraguan Revolution, making the states ever more dependent on Washington for their very survival. In 1979 US economic aid to Central America totalled $126.3 milliion, and military aid stood at $3.7 million. By 1982 these figures had reached $445.6 million and $109.1 million respectively.[9] Costa Rica, with one of the highest per capita foreign debts in the world, has, since the Nicaraguan Revolution, received a level of per capita economic aid from the United States second only to that awarded Israel. In 1985 Costa Rica received more aid from the United States than it had during the whole of the eighteen-year period before the overthrow of Somoza.[10] The objective of granting large amounts of economic and military aid is not to provide the means required to develop the Central American economies, but rather to pressurise the governments into supporting the war against the Sandinistas. In the cases of Honduras and Costa Rica this strategy initially paid at least limited dividends, as the contras were allowed to operate from their respective territories bordering Nicaragua (especially in the case of Honduras), and both states held reservations about the Contadora peace process. However, in 1987 the President of Costa

Rica drew up a new peace plan for the region, which was finally accepted by all Central American states in August of that year.

Israel has also played a role in Central America, some would argue as a proxy of the United States. Israel has sold a substantial amount of arms in Central America and a former member of the Knesset has stated that the sale of arms to Honduras and El Salvador was 'made in accordance with the explicit request of the United States'.[11] According to some American sources Israel supplied several million dollars of aid to the contras through a South American intermediary. Israel has also supplied military advisers to Guatemala and there are said to be Israeli mercenaries working with the contras. Israel was also used by the United States in the Iran–contra hostage fiasco, being asked to supply the first batch of arms to Iran from its own stockpile in order to conceal the role of the Americans.[12] The extent to which the United States controls these Israeli actions is not clear, but given the level of economic aid Israel receives each year, it is perhaps not unlikely that any covert action is conducted at least in cooperation with the Americans.

THE SOVIET UNION

Cuba is possibly the Soviet Union's most reliable and stable partner when it comes to cooperative intervention in the Third World – at least in those cases where the two sides share common perceptions and goals. In Central America, however, there were disagreements between Moscow and Havana concerning military intervention in local conflicts, with Castro advocating the 'export of revolution' and the Soviets seeking to restrain him. These disagreements were largely resolved by the early 1970s, and since this time there has been no direct Cuban military intervention in Central America. However, Cuba has played some role in the region, providing ideological guidance, military training, economic aid and other forms of assistance to the revolutionaries. The question here is, to what extent does Moscow control Cuban activity in Central America?

If Latin America is not an area of great concern in Soviet global interests, this is manifestly not the case for Cuba. Cuba is itself a Latin American country and, in Havana's hierarchy of interests, Central America and the Caribbean are of paramount importance. Whilst both the Soviet Union and Cuba would like to see more socialist regimes in the region, Havana's commitment to the 'revolutionary struggle' is much stronger than Moscow's. Castro does not need to be persuaded by the Kremlin to give assistance to the Sandinistas and, in the case of the New Jewel Movement in Grenada, it was the Cubans who had to persuade the Soviets to provide aid, and not the other way around. This emerged in the Grenada documents discovered by the invading US marines in 1983.[13] The New Jewel

Movement received only minimal aid from the Soviet Union, and that was largely due to Cuban lobbying on behalf of the Bishop regime. Grenada was of little relevance or interest to Moscow, but for Cuba, as a Caribbean country itself, the calculation was very different. During the internal party conflict which led to Bishop's murder and the foreign invasion, evidence suggests that the Soviet Union and Cuba were divided in their support for the different factions, with the Soviets possibly supporting Coard, and the Cubans certainly supporting Bishop. There is little evidence that Cuba was acting under orders from, or as a surrogate of, the USSR.

Both states, however, support the Sandinistas, although here again Cuba's commitment is stronger than that of the Soviet Union. Neither Havana nor Moscow was actively engaged in the civil war which overthrew Somoza, nor in the *coup* which ousted Gairy in Grenada. It was only after the revolutionary regimes gained power that the Cubans and the Soviets became actively involved. Although it does appear that Cuba had earlier contacts with the Sandinistas and had encouraged the different factions comprising the revolutionary movement to drop their differences for the sake of solidarity in the struggle against Somoza. However, it is also true that, prior to 1979, Costa Rica provided more economic and logistical support to the Sandinistas than did Cuba.

For all this, the Soviet Union, once it decided to render support to a revolutionary regime in the area, used Cuba as an intermediary link for supplying equipment, particularly military equipment. The military hardware that Moscow supplied to the New Jewel Movement was delivered in Soviet ships to Cuban ports, with the Cubans then transporting it on to Grenada. In the early 1950s, Czechoslovakia was used to tranship a small supply of military equipment to Arbenz in Guatemala. In Nicaragua, East Germans and Bulgarians are assisting the Sandinistas in the construction of internal intelligence and security services, and Cubans are serving as doctors, teachers and military advisers. The actual Soviet presence in the country is fairly limited, evidence of considerable caution and restraint in an area of close proximity to the United States. The client states of the Soviet Union do serve a useful purpose in helping to achieve Soviet foreign-policy goals.

THE DANGERS OF A SUPERPOWER CONFRONTATION

The likelihood of a direct superpower military confrontation in Central America is very slim. The Soviet Union has marginal interests in the region, certainly not sufficient to risk a major confrontation that could lead to a nuclear war. It should be remembered that Cuba, despite requests in the 1970s to join, is not a member of the Warsaw Treaty Organisation. Indeed Cuba is almost unique among Soviet

Third World clients in not having a bilateral Treaty of Friendship and Cooperation with the USSR. Such treaties often include a security clause guaranteeing mutual assistance in the event of external aggression, and it is significant that the Soviet Union has not signed such a document with Cuba. The only American action which would lead to a major East–West crisis would be an invasion of Cuba, but even then it is unlikely that the Soviet Union would risk escalation by directly intervening in an attempt to defend the island. Such an action on the part of the United States is difficult to imagine under present circumstances. The Kennedy–Khrushchev agreement of 1962 resolving the Missile Crisis has stood up well to the test of time, and neither side is likely to break it. The Soviet Union will not place offensive weapons on the island and, so long as this is the case, the United States will not launch an invasion. The prospects for a superpower confrontation over Cuba, therefore, are not very great.

With regard to Nicaragua, there is even less chance of a confrontation. The Soviet Union's commitment to the Sandinistas is nowhere near as great as the one it made to the Cuban Revolution in the 1960s, and Gorbachev has actually made it plain that Nicaragua, whilst being able to rely upon the USSR for some economic assistance, cannot expect any direct Soviet military assistance to support the revolution. This would be the case even in the event of a direct American intervention. The Soviet Union did nothing to support the Grenadians when American marines landed on the island in October 1983, and even when a Soviet ship was mined in Nicaraguan waters the response from Moscow was mild. Although there is little prospect for a superpower confrontation in Central America, however, this is not to deny that there is room for improvement in the way the superpowers manage their competition in the region.

PROSPECTS FOR CRISIS PREVENTION AND RULES OF THE GAME

With regard to Central America there are several possible techniques which could be adopted to manage superpower relations and avoid crises and confrontation, and with Gorbachev in power in the Soviet Union the prospects for superpower crisis prevention are perhaps better than ever before. Although the limited attempts at crisis prevention from the *détente* of the 1970s are generally agreed to have been a failure, Gorbachev has on a number of occasions, referred to this period as one from which the superpowers could learn lessons and build a more stable relationship for the future.[14] Perhaps one of the most important of these lessons is that any generalised principles on codes of conduct for superpower behaviour have to be made more region-specific.[15] In the case of

Central America and the Caribbean there already exist a number of 'rules' regulating superpower activities, and these rules could be developed to facilitate crisis avoidance in the region.

Raymond Cohen suggests that 'rules of the game' perform the same function for international society as norms in domestic society; they indicate 'the limits on permissible conduct, thereby permitting conflict to be contained'. Rules are 'expectations of right conduct in defined circumstances'.[16] The striking thing here, which sets the Caribbean off against other Third World regional settings, is the existence of relatively explicit rules for superpower behaviour which have been tried, tested and refined since they were first established in 1962. The Kennedy–Khrushchev agreement which resolved the Cuban Missile Crisis of October 1962 set out the 'limits of permissible conduct' of the superpowers, thereby creating the foundation of a body of rules which both sides recognise and adhere to. The Soviet Union agreed not to place offensive weapons on the island, and the United States gave an undertaking not to invade Cuba. This agreement has endured for over a quarter of a century, and during this time it has served as an effective crisis-prevention regime.

The United States, the Soviet Union and Cuba all benefit from the agreement. US security is guaranteed, the USSR maintains its close relationship with Cuba, and Cuba itself is free from the threat of direct American military intervention. The agreement, as it has evolved and been tested, contains a number of important 'rules', stemming from the Soviet acknowledgement at the end of the Missile Crisis that placing nuclear missiles or offensive weapons in Cuba was effectively prohibited. Although this agreement in its origins related only to Cuba, it very soon took on much wider applicability as President Kennedy, in November 1962, stated that 'If all offensive weapons systems are removed from Cuba and kept out of the hemisphere . . . we shall neither initiate nor permit aggression in this hemisphere.'[17] In effect, the Soviet Union, as Jorge Dominguez puts it, 'recognised US nuclear exclusivity in the Americas – a technological updating of the Monroe Doctrine'.[18] This is a unique admission on the part of the Soviet Union, effectively guaranteeing that a large geographical area (i.e., the whole of Latin America and the Caribbean) is out of bounds as far as Soviet nuclear bases are concerned. In 1970 the United States became concerned that the Soviet Union was seeking to circumvent the agreement by constructing a submarine base at Cienfuegos. However, this 'mini-crisis' was resolved by US and Soviet affirmation of the 1962 agreement, and the Soviets agreed not to construct port facilities which could be used as a base for nuclear-armed submarines. The 1970 Cienfuegos episode clarified the rules and, since that time, there has been no indication that the Soviet Union has considered breaking them and establishing nuclear bases in Cuba or elsewhere in the Americas.

With regard to 'offensive weapons', which the Soviets also agreed not to place in Cuba (and, by extension, the rest of the region), the agreement is more ambiguous. Often what one state deems to be 'defensive', another state will classify as 'offensive'. Whilst it is true that Cuba possesses the largest regional armed forces, Cuba has not been given the same level of military hardware as other favoured Soviet clients such as Syria. The MIG-23s in service with the Cuban airforce are not in such significant numbers that they could pose a threat to US security, nor are they of the type capable of carrying nuclear weapons – thus the 1962 agreement has not been breached. Soviet military supplies to the Sandinistas in Nicaragua have increased substantially during the past few years but, despite some American claims to the contrary, the Soviets have not agreed to deliver sophisticated fighter aircraft which could threaten the security of the United States. In Grenada, under the New Jewel Movement in the early 1980s, the Soviets acted with caution, supplying the revolutionary government with little more than small arms for defensive purposes. Indeed, at the Washington superpower summit in December 1987, the Soviet Union tentatively proposed an agreement to prohibit arms transfers to Central America which would exclude only the provision of arms for local policing. This offer was not developed and the United States indicated that it was unprepared to accept such restraints on its action in this region.

The Soviet Union has also been careful not to breach the 1962 agreement by ensuring that the level of Soviet troops and military advisers in the region does not represent a self-sufficient offensive combat force. This part of the agreement was tested in 1979 when the issue of the Soviet combat brigade in Cuba became a factor in US domestic politics and threatened to spill over into a superpower crisis. The whole affair was bungled by the United States, for the so-called combat brigade had been stationed on the island since the early 1960s and its functions and composition had not changed markedly since that time, having never posed a threat to the United States. This mini-crisis critically delayed Senate consideration of the SALT II Treaty, but it did at least further clarify and reaffirm the 1962 agreement, with the Soviets making a clear commitment that their military contingent in Cuba would retain its training function and would not be transformed into a coherent combat force which would be able to threaten neighbouring states.

For its part, the United States has accepted the ideological breach of the Monroe Doctrine in so far as successive US administrations have stuck by the 1962 agreement and not attempted to invade Cuba. The agreement has served the test of time and constitutes today a unique arrangement between the superpowers in moderating their behaviour in relation to Cuba. Whilst the agreement has certain limited applicability beyond Cuba, there are no clear rules of crisis prevention stemming from it which pertain to those countries in Central America that are so clearly prone to crises. The United States may have reluctantly accepted the ideological breach of the Monroe Doctrine in relation to Cuba but, since the early 1960s, successive US administrations have sought to ensure that there are no more 'Cubas' in the region, displaying a willingness to use direct military force (the Dominican Republic, Grenada) and covert action (Chile), and to support counter insurgency (Guatemala, El Salvador) and proxy forces (Nicaragua). Therefore, the agreement over Cuba should not be seen as a model that could be used to create security regimes in relation to other third countries in the Western hemisphere. Rather it should be seen as a unique arrangement, albeit one which does provide some lessons for preventing superpower crises in Central America.

One simple but important lesson is that both sides can successfully cooperate in defining, and refining, rules of conduct in order to avoid crises. Norms and tacit rules are much more likely to operate effectively if they are limited to particular regions or specific countries and if they acknowledge asymmetries of interests. In the Caribbean and Central American region there is a marked asymmetry of interests favouring the United States, and the Soviet Union has shown a tendency to accept this and to moderate its behaviour accordingly.

The importance of Central America and the Caribbean for the United States can be compared to Eastern Europe's importance to the Soviet Union. Each side has in the past accepted the other's sphere of influence. The Soviet Union recognised the Monroe Doctrine, and did nothing to counter American actions in Guatemala, Cuba, the Dominican Republic or Grenada. The United States has recognised the Brezhnev Doctrine, and did nothing to counter Soviet actions in Hungary, Czechoslovakia or Poland. Yet, the world is changing and becoming more complex and, in this changing world, spheres of influence are not only becoming more difficult to maintain, but may also become strategically less relevant. The superpowers need to recognise the internal dynamics for change in their respective peripheries, and to avoid seeing external factors as responsible for forcing changes in the status quo. In a sense both the Soviet Union and the United States need to formulate a mechanism for managing the decline of their power in their respective spheres of influence whilst ensuring that their basic security interests are guaranteed. Without such a mechanism there is a danger that misperception could provide an action–reaction cycle as a result of which the United States and the Soviet Union are drawn into a direct confrontation that neither wants but both may conclude is impossible to avoid.

Change in the Third World is inevitable, and control over client states and proxies is diminishing. Exaggerating the threat from the adversary superpower carries the danger of a self-fulfilling prophecy, as intervention in regional conflicts spawns a localised arms race and increases the importance of the military aspect of regime turbulence. This in turn leads to a distortion in American and Soviet national priorities, raises superpower tensions and undermines the credibility and prestige of both sides in global politics. Suppressing the forces for change, for social, political and economic justice in the peripheries, in order to maintain a stable sphere of influence (in Central America and Eastern Europe) is a dangerous and short-sighted policy. Thus both sides need to come to terms with these forces for change, accept their indigenous, local roots, and find a way to deal with them without risking crises and militarising what are essentially political problems. It took a dangerous and major crisis in 1962 for the superpowers to devise a regime for crisis avoidance over Cuba. In one very important sense the resolution of this crisis has ensured that a similar crisis could not occur again, for the Soviet Union has recognised US nuclear exclusivity in the Americas. However, there is a possibility, even if very slight, that the present situation in Central America could result in a superpower confrontation with all the dangers of escalation that this entails. Superpower relations will continue to be competitive. But there are several ways in which the superpowers could better manage their relationship in regard to Central America so as to avoid crises, while upholding their own security interests and those of the local actors themselves.

First, the superpowers have to accept the legitimacy of each other's interests and be willing to treat the other as a diplomatic and political equal. This does not imply simple recognition of spheres of influence and regional balances of power but, rather, recognition that the two states do have in some regions, such as Central America, an asymmetry of interests which has to be considered in any crisis-prevention regime. In the 1970s the Soviet Union was not given more than token recognition by Nixon and Kissinger as America's political equal. In any future crisis-prevention arrangements each side must treat the other as its political equal. The Soviet Union has developed fairly close ties to the Sandinistas in Nicaragua, and the United States claims that the Soviets have a great deal of influence on the internal politics of the Nicaraguan government. It would be appropriate, therefore, for the US to accept that the Soviet Union has at least a limited diplomatic role to play in the region. Given the asymmetry of interests this need not imply that Moscow be accorded equal status in terms of influence over events but, by treating the Soviets as legitimate diplomatic actors, an asymmetrical agreement favouring US interests would more likely result. This could be formulated in conjunction with a reciprocal code of conduct relating to Eastern Europe or Afghanistan, areas of high-interest asymmetry favouring the Soviet Union.

Second, each side should carefully evaluate and assess the other's intentions and actions and not fall back on ideological stereotypes which can lead to distortions and dangerous misperceptions. The Reagan administration consistently exaggerated the role the Soviet Union plays in Central America, strengthening the perception among leading politicians and the wider public that Soviet interference rather than local unrest was responsible for the conflict. What is required is careful and systematic objective intelligence gathering and analysis upon which policy should be based. The whole affair surrounding the so-called Soviet combat brigade in Cuba in 1979 was largely a result of incompetent intelligence-gathering and a lack of institutional memory. In part, the problem is exacerbated by Soviet secrecy, which makes it very difficult for the United States to assess real Soviet interests and objectives in Central America and the Caribbean. Often the Soviets, too, must find difficulty in assessing US interests and objectives, as different bureaucratic groups speak with different voices. This lack of coherence, and the dangers it can produce, is evident in the Iran–contra episode. Both sides should seek to avoid misperceptions and misunderstandings by careful and sensible information gathering, processing and analysis. This could be facilitated by diplomatic signalling in which the superpowers communicate to each other what their interests and objectives are.

Third, and following on from this, the superpowers need to communicate with one another on a regular basis, according to established procedures, as part of a regional crisis-prevention regime for Central America and the Caribbean. This does not have to imply written rules, or general principles. Tacit rules of behaviour can be formulated and understandings reached regarding acceptable actions through diplomatic and personal communication. But the communication process should be systematic and continuous. This might best be achieved through the establishment of a crisis-prevention centre which could consider regional developments as they occur. Regular exchanges by professional diplomats and experts in such a centre would enable each side to understand the other's interests and objectives, thus reducing the risk of misperception. Such a centre could also provide a forum for working out possible steps that could be considered at a higher level for resolving potential crisis situations. In addition, it would reduce the risk of domestic political pressures inhibiting rational decision-making – as was arguably the case in the brigade crisis of 1979. Henry Kissinger, in contrast, avoided crisis escalation through domestic pressures over the Cienfuegos submarine base by quiet, back-channel diplomacy with the Soviets. An institutionalised arrangement, through a crisis-prevention centre, could provide a more effective means of avoiding a superpower confrontation in Central America.

Fourth, both sides should recognise and accept the limited control the other has over so-called client or proxy states. American political leaders under different administrations have seen Cuba not as an autonomous actor in international relations, but as a puppet manipulated by the Soviet Union for Soviet state interests. It is true that Cuba is highly dependent upon its superpower benefactor for economic and military aid, and it is possible that this dependency in certain circumstances may reduce Cuban room for manoeuvre. But to equate economic dependency with a lack of foreign-policy autonomy is drastically to overstate the case. Cuba conducts an independent foreign policy in Central America and the Caribbean – one which, at times, has been at odds with Soviet policy. Yet the United States refuses to deal directly with Cuba. Washington would do well to accept the logic of the situation and negotiate on a bilateral basis with Moscow's ally. Castro's Cuba has a more activist foreign policy than the USSR in Central America, and so long as the United States refrains from dealing with Cuba, its policy in the region will be hampered.

Fifth, the best means of avoiding superpower crises in the Third World is to establish principles of behaviour and codes of conduct on a regional level, not a global one, taking into consideration the asymmetries of interests in different areas. With the creation of crisis-prevention regimes, another thing to be avoided is 'linkage' – linking the success of a regional understanding in the Third World to the successful outcome of other problem-solving endeavours such as arms control, human rights or Jewish emigration. The failure of superpower *détente* in the 1970s can be explained in part by US attempts to link arms control and trade agreements with the USSR to questions of human rights inside the Soviet Union. One reason that the Soviets took such an uncompromising stance over the Cuban combat brigade in 1979 was the attempt by some US Congressmen and leading politicians to link ratification of SALT II to the removal of the brigade. Such linkage serves only to complicate the issues and to jeopardise the prospects of problem solving and conflict resolution in two areas rather than one. Any superpower agreement over their conduct in Central America should not be held hostage by linking this to other issues in the bilateral relationship.

Sixth, and finally, both sides should encourage regional diplomatic processes, whereby the local actors themselves might reach an accommodation with one another. Not only would this deal with the ongoing crisis in Central America, but it might build effective measures for future regional crisis prevention. Since January 1983, when the leaders of Colombia, Mexico, Panama and Venezuela met on the Panamanian island of Contadora, up to August 1987, when the leaders of the five Central American states met in Guatemala, a regional initiative to solve the conflict in Central America was kept alive despite spoiling tactics from the United States. In fact, there are several reasons why the United States would do well to give its full backing to the agreement proposed by the President of Costa Rica and signed by the five Central American presidents in Guatemala, and which is supported by the Soviet Union and Cuba. The regional actors themselves share US concerns about a spill-over effect of the civil war in Nicaragua which could destabilise the other Central American countries. Latin American countries also share US fears about an increase in Soviet influence in the region. The Arias peace plan calls for, among other things, a regional cease-fire, an end to external military assistance and an amnesty for insurgents, political dialogue and political pluralism. Indeed, a collective regional approach in which the security concerns of all states are given weight is surely worth pursuing? The Sandinistas have shown, by signing the peace accord, a willingness to compromise in agreeing to institute more political freedoms in Nicaragua. The United States should give its support to the Arias plan and deal on a bilateral basis directly with Nicaragua to ensure its own security interests are maintained. At the Geneva summit Gorbachev told Reagan that the Soviet Union considers US security as important as Soviet security, for both sides need to feel secure in order to avoid crises and lessen tensions. Total security for one side would mean great insecurity for the other. Consequently, there is a need to compromise. By encouraging regional initiatives, the superpowers could support conflict resolution rather than turning local conflicts into areas of East–West confrontation. The mechanism is in place in Central America for such an outcome, but it could also be promoted where there is an asymmetry of interests favouring the Soviet Union.

Neither superpower can hope to prevent change and conflict in the Third World, but both sides, recognising this inevitable fact, could do more to alleviate the prospects of regional conflicts leading to a Soviet–American crisis. The world is changing, and the two most powerful nations must learn to change with it and in the process manage their relationship in such a way as to avoid direct confrontation.

NOTES

1 See Gearoid O'Tuathial, 'The Language and Nature of the "New Geopolitics" – The Case of US-El Salvador Relations', *Political Geography Quarterly*, 5, 1, January 1986, pp. 73–85, p. 74.
2 See Jenny Pearce, *Under the Eagle: US Interventions in Central America and the Caribbean* (London: Latin America Bureau, 1982), pp. 17–20.
3 Robert Wesson, 'Historical Overview and Comparative Analysis', in Jan F. Triska (ed), *Dominant Powers and Subordinate States: The United States in Latin America and the Soviet Union in Eastern Europe* (Durham, NC: Duke University Press, 1986), pp. 47–84, p. 54.
4 *Ibid*, p. 56.
5 Pearce, *Under the Eagle*, p. 27.
6 For US reactions to Arbenz and the subsequent American role in his overthrow see Cole Blasier, *The Hovering Giant: US Responses to Revolutionary Change in Latin America*, (Pittsburgh, PA: University of Pittsburgh Press, 1976), pp. 151–77.
7 Cole Blasier, *The Giant's Rival: The USSR and Latin America* (Pittsburgh, PA: University of Pittsburgh Press, 1983), p. 154.

8 For example, see S. A. Mikoian, 'Ob osobennostiakh revolyutsii v Nikaragua i ee urokakh s tochki zreniia teorii i praktiki osvoboditel'nogo dvizheniia', *Latinskaia Amerika*, no. 3, 1980, pp. 34–44.

9 Tom Barry, Beth Wood and Deb Preusch, *Dollars and Dictators: A Guide to Central America* (London: Zed Press, 1982), pp. 8–9.

10 Noam Chomsky, *Turning the Tide: US Intervention in Central America and the Struggle for Peace* (Boston, MA: Pluto Press, 1985), p. 38.

11 *Ibid.* p. 35.

12 *Ibid.* p. 133.

13 See *Grenada Documents: An Overview and Selection* (Washington, DC: Departments of State and Defence, 1984). For an analysis of these documents as they relate to Soviet ties to the New Jewel Movement, see Peter Shearman, 'The Soviet Union and Grenada Under the New Jewel Movement', *International Affairs*, 61, 4, Autumn, 1985, pp. 661–74.

14 See *Pravda*, February 25, 1986 for an example of Gorbachev's emphasis on compromise and dialogue.

15 For a fuller analysis of the codes of conduct of the 1970s see, Alexander L. George, 'The Basic Principles Agreement of 1972: Origins and Expectations', in his (ed.) *Managing US Soviet Rivalry: Problems of Crisis Prevention* (Boulder, CO. Westview Press, 1983).

16 Raymond Cohen, *International Politics: The Rules of the Game* (Harlow, Essex: Longman, 1981), pp. 6 and 8.

17 Quoted in Gloria Duffy, 'Crisis Prevention in Cuba', in George (ed.), *Managing US–Soviet Rivalry*, pp. 285–318, p. 286.

18 Jorge I. Dominguez, 'US, Soviet, and Cuban Policies Toward Latin America', in Marshall D. Shulman (ed.), *East–West Tensions in the Third World* (New York: W. W. Norton & Co., 1986), pp. 44–77, p. 47. .

11   The superpowers and Southern Africa

Geoff R. Berridge

The superpower *détente* of the 1970s rested on a balance of power between the Soviet Union and the United States and broke down when Moscow grasped that post-Vietnam America had temporarily lost the will to take risks in defence of less than vital positions. Perhaps nowhere was this more apparent than in Southern Africa.

Southern Africa is a region in which the United States long had only extremely limited interests. As a result, until the mid-1970s it allowed Britain, traditionally the paramount external power in the region and, to a lesser extent, its other NATO ally, Portugal, to make the running in tackling regional problems which threatened these interests. However, in the first half of the 1970s Portuguese colonial rule in Angola and Mozambique collapsed while British influence in the region continued its slow decline. Against this background, opportunities for Soviet intervention were provided by the civil wars in Rhodesia, Namibia and, especially, Angola. Indeed, in 1975 the Soviet Union and its Cuban associates entered the succession struggle in Angola with weapons and combat troops on behalf of the Marxist MPLA. However, the United States Congress, afraid of another Vietnam and embarrassed at being on the same side as the South Africans, tied the hands of the Ford Administration, with the result that Soviet and Cuban influence triumphed by default.

SUPERPOWER INTERESTS IN SOUTHERN AFRICA

Soviet interests

Following the Soviet/Cuban intervention in Angola in 1975, and the associated rise of Moscow's influence in Marxist Mozambique (where China's eclipse was assisted by the fact that it had backed the losing side in Angola), a general Soviet presence has become quite marked in Southern Africa, even if this is not as great as South African propaganda would have the West believe and has of late begun to diminish. With the exception of Malawi, Swaziland and South Africa itself, all states in the region host Soviet diplomats (a Soviet embassy has even been opened in Zimbabwe despite the fact that Moscow supported Joshua Nkomo in the Rhodesian civil war), and most also contain representatives from Eastern Europe, Cuba, Vietnam and North Korea. Treaties of Friendship and Cooperation have been signed by both the Soviet Union and East Germany with Angola and Mozambique.[1] Party-to-party agreements have been concluded not only with Marxist governing parties in these two countries but with UNIP in Zambia.[2] A limited economic aid programme has been initiated and advisers and technical operatives, such as harbour pilots at Maputo and Beira, together with a shore-based coordinator have been sent in considerable numbers.[3] Above all, the Soviet Union and its allies have poured into the region (especially into Angola) heavy armaments, military advisers and 20,000–30,000 Cuban troops; and the Soviet navy has paid well publicised flag-showing visits to Luanda, Beira and Maputo. The implication conveyed by all this in respect of Angola and Mozambique, is that the Soviet Union and its allies will not stand idly by if their regimes come under attack. What interests in Southern Africa have prompted the Soviet Union to make its presence felt in these ways – and give such hostages to fortune?

The South African government has ritualistically pronounced that Soviet policy in the region has two overriding purposes: firstly, to seize control of its mineral riches (if only to deny them to the West), and, secondly, to secure mastery of the sea lanes around the Cape of Good Hope. The Soviet Union, however, has made no attempt to use its influence to deny to the West minerals and other primary products from Angola and Mozambique, both of whom remain desperate to increase their exports to the capitalist world. Nor does it have any confidence in a change in this, since it regards Southern Africa as 'entirely at the mercy of international capital'.[4] Furthermore, if only because of Moscow's own anxiety to increase its foreign-currency earnings by entering the Western liner trades as a 'conference-minded' member,[5] it is difficult to believe that it would allow a pro-Soviet majority-ruled South Africa to interfere with Western shipping around the Cape in peacetime, while in a general war – even assuming a conventional stage – it is just as hard to understand why the Soviet Union would wish to interdict Western shipping as far away from its home ports as the Cape.[6] In short, the official South African view of Soviet policy in the region is not even plausible, any more than it was in the early 1950s, when the new National Party government's political generals occasioned unrestrained hilarity in Whitehall by insisting on the necessity of spending huge sums on a radar network for the Rand in order to give early warning of Russian bomber attacks.[7]

Less partisan observers have achieved a rough consensus on the general promptings of Soviet policy in Southern Africa which is distinctly at odds with the official South African view. This begins with the unsurprising proposition that, judging by the *relatively* low levels of economic and military aid extended to Southern Africa by the Soviet Union in comparison with its disbursements elsewhere in the Third World, Moscow has no vital interests in the region at all.[8] Of these less than vital interests, the first is probably the *spoiling interest* in undermining the non-economic interests of the West and China in the region and keeping them off balance at relatively low cost. Second, there is the *propaganda interest* in promoting leftist change and supporting regimes of 'socialist orientation', for this appears to confirm the claim of the Soviet Union that history is on its side and thus bolsters its prestige. Third, there is the *status interest* in reinforcing the Soviet claim to equality with the United States, that is to say, to the status not only of a 'superpower' (i.e., a great power) but of a 'world power', with a right to a seat at all conferences aimed at settling major international disputes. (This interest is promoted by the establishment of the Soviet presence in Southern Africa, partly because of the dramatic geographical reach of Soviet power of which it provides evidence, and partly because it gives Moscow an 'interest' in the settlement of problems in the region; were the Russians able to gain a seat at conclusive negotiations on Namibia, for example, it would greatly strengthen their claim to a seat in other regional negotiations of much greater interest to them, most obviously, of course, in the Middle East.) Fourth, there are *strategic interests* – one in air and naval facilities (especially in Angola), which provide Moscow with some ability to 'counter US strategic forces, monitor US military activity, and transport assistance to friendly regimes in the region',[9] and another in preventing South Africa from contributing to an increase in nuclear-weapons proliferation.

Fifth, there are some *economic interests*. These include fishing concessions off the coasts of Angola and Mozambique, arms sales and sailings for Soviet bloc vessels in the presently West European-dominated liner trades serving the region.[10] Soviet bloc lines are already members of the Europe–East Africa shipping conference (headquartered in London[11]) and are treated as 'tolerated outsiders' by the Europe–South Africa shipping conference (embracing Beira and Maputo as well as South African ports, and also headquartered in London) but, because of the wars in Angola and Mozambique, are able to lift hardly any of the valuable cargoes originating in Central Africa, most of which leave via ports in the Republic. However, if the railways in Angola and Mozambique were to be made to work again, Soviet vessels could well secure a bigger share of this trade. At the moment they are confined to shipping in arms and other military material and returning more or less empty.[12] The Soviet Union also has an interest in collaborating with Anglo–American firms in the marketing of diamond (and possibly platinum and gold) production. And its East European allies have interests in the region's raw materials.

Finally, there is the *diplomatic interest* in winning the support of Southern African states for Soviet attitudes in international forums by increasing Moscow's visibility in the 'struggle' against South Africa. Altogether, then, it seems fair to say that, while none of the Soviet Union's interests in Southern Africa is in any sense vital, collectively they make up a moderate stake. Were it to be ousted from the region altogether, this would be a considerable blow to its prestige but it would be no more than a minor material and strategic irritant: it would not compare in seriousness to the loss of Soviet influence in Egypt in 1972.

American interests

Any discussion of American interests in Southern Africa – and many other regions, for that matter – is bedevilled by two problems: firstly, the obvious lack of consensus on the question within recent administrations; and secondly, the common confusion in secondary analysis between historical accounts of what those interests are and prescriptive statements concerning what they should be. Bearing this in mind it is perhaps fair to say that the present Republican administration has more tangible interests in Southern Africa, and especially in South Africa, than does the Soviet Union and appears to attach more importance to all of its interests, collectively, than Moscow does to its own. Furthermore, it seems to believe that they are all vulnerable. Shortly before assuming a prominent role in the Reagan administration's policy-making towards Southern Africa, Chester A. Crocker described these interests as 'important' and 'exposed'.[13] However, the margin between the importance attached to their respective interests by the United States and the Soviet Union is probably not great and the only American interests which are regarded as very important – if not 'vital' – by conservative opinion in Washington are – in marked contrast to all Soviet interests in the region – in fact relatively invulnerable.

The United States and its allies appear to believe – probably rightly – that they have vital strategic and economic interests in the uninterrupted flow of merchant shipping (especially oil tankers) along the 'Cape Route'. And it is certainly true that, following the growth of Soviet naval strength in the Indian Ocean and the rise of Soviet bloc influence in Southern Africa in the first half of the 1970s, anxieties on this score were expressed by the US Joint Chiefs of Staff and the Defence Planning Committee of NATO.[14] However, for reasons already mentioned, it is extremely difficult to visualise circumstances in which NATO shipping would be threatened at the Cape, and it is probably as much for this reason as for fear of the diplomatic consequences of closer association with South Africa that no major steps – unless development of the Indian Ocean island base of Diego Garcia is included – have been taken by the United States to protect the Cape Route. Nor, it should be added, is this because US planners have believed that, in a crisis, they could rely on an important contribution to the defence of the sea lanes from the South African Navy, the long-range patrolling capacities of which were never worth much, are now worth hardly anything at all and have indeed been publicly abandoned. (The SAN's 'blue water' force is now represented by three *Daphne*-class submarines and one *President*-class frigate.[15] Its only cruiser, the *President Kruger*, sank accidentally in 1982.) Having said this, such is the prominence given to the importance and vulnerability of the Cape Route in conservative demonology in the United States that this interest serves both as an ingredient of genuine concern over Southern Africa and as a convenient rationalisation to conceal less presentable motives in parts of Congress and official Washington.

The same sort of arguments apply to the strategic and economic interests of America and its allies in continuing access to the undoubted wealth of Southern Africa in non-fuel minerals, which a 1980 Senate study described as of 'significant, but not critical importance to the West'.[16] Thus the Rockefeller Foundation-funded Study Commission on US Policy Toward Southern Africa' observed that 'if widespread conflict broke out in Southern Africa or if a government hostile to the West took power in South Africa . . . stoppages in exports of these minerals, should they occur, are likely to be partial, intermittent, and short term (less than five years) in duration. Medium-term (five-to-ten-year) and long-term (more than ten-year) interruptions', the Commission concluded, 'appear unlikely'.[17]

In addition to these important but relatively invulnerable interests, the United States has an important but more exposed interest in relation to Southern Africa. This is the diplomatic and domestic political interest in avoiding a posture towards issues in the region which, in view of the strong feelings of African and (more recently) American blacks on the question of apartheid, are believed likely to lead to a deterioration in United States relations with OAU countries and – probably more importantly – to revive acute racial unrest in the United States itself.[18] (In practice American interests in Black Africa have not suffered markedly in those periods when Republican administrations have been accused of providing support for South Africa).[19] This interest in maintaining some distance between Washington and Pretoria does not necessarily conflict with America's other interests in South Africa, despite the claims of conservatives who regard the existing National Party regime as indispensable to the protection of these interests.

Among its less important but equally exposed interests in Southern Africa, the United States has other, economic, interests: investments and trading interests which, while considerably greater than those of the Soviet Union, are nevertheless small in aggregate terms. South Africa itself, the major location of these interests, has accounted annually for only about 1 per cent of US foreign trade and between 1 and 2 per cent of US direct investment overseas since the Second World War, and recently – for a mixture of political and commercial reasons – some major American corporations have been pulling out.[20] Moreover, foreign economic transactions are, in aggregate terms, relatively unimportant to the American economy.

The United States also has a strategic interest in access to intelligence on the region and its surrounding oceans (the Indian Ocean is probably of some importance as a prowling zone for American nuclear-missile-carrying submarines), and this is assiduously supplied by South Africa's Silvermine ground station.[21] However, in view of America's own enormous technical intelligence-gathering capacity – not to mention the increasing redundancy of far-flung and vulnerable ground stations – this can be no more than an interest in a back-up service.[22] Washington has a strategic interest, as well, in discouraging the unambiguous development of South Africa as a nuclear weapons state, because of its general interest in the avoidance of nuclear proliferation.

All of the American interests in Southern Africa detailed so far – important or less so, invulnerable or more exposed – are local interests. However, probably the most important American interest of all in Southern Africa is the diplomatic, cold-war interest in expelling Soviet influence from the region, in the same way that this was the cardinal US interest in the Middle East during the Nixon administration. Chalking up a major cold-war victory against Moscow, most dramatically by securing the removal of the Cuban troops from Angola, seems to be the major impulse behind American policy and is seen most obviously in the American attitude over the protracted negotiations for the independence of Namibia. Here, the United States, to the great relief of the South Africans, has 'linked' Namibian independence to the withdrawal of the Cubans from Angola. Furthermore, Congress in 1985 repealed the Clark Amendment, which in 1976 had been introduced in order to halt American support for UNITA. The Reagan administration subsequently renewed its backing for a military solution to the Angolan civil war. Partly to increase pressure on Angola, the United States also upgraded its military role in the Shaba province of Zaire.[23] In short, as Bowman has noted, the 'globalists' are in the ascendancy over the 'Africanists' in the determination of America's Southern Africa policy and have been since the second half of the Carter administration.[24]

Geoff R. Berridge

THE DEGREE OF INTEREST SYMMETRY AND COMPATIBILITY

It is extremely difficult to determine the extent of symmetry between Soviet and American interests in Southern Africa in terms of the value attached to them by each superpower. Instability in Southern Africa is now widespread and reflects problems which may well be as intractable as those in the Middle East. In such circumstances, it is not surprising that opinion in the United States, which has the more tangible interests in the region, should be deeply divided over the importance of these interests, the degree of their vulnerability to Soviet–Cuban attack, and the indispensability to their protection of the political status quo in Pretoria. Furthermore, while lists of Soviet interests in the region are confidently advanced by American analysts, some of whom clearly reflect one or other segment of official thinking, the very *intangibility* of most of these interests probably means that this confidence conceals considerable guesswork.

As for the state of mind of Soviet policy-makers, there is no certain way of telling how clear they are on their own or United States interests in the region. It seems likely, however, that the prism of ideology has imposed on Soviet thought about American interests a more coherent pattern than actually exists and one which emphasises the importance to the United States of its economic interests in Southern Africa.[25]

In short, in Southern Africa one superpower, the United States, seems to be unclear as to whether it has moderate or vital interests and a conception of its rival's stake which is partly speculative, while the other, the Soviet Union, probably has what it regards as only moderate interests with a fairly clear, ideologically framed picture of American interests in the region. It is impossible to sum this up neatly in Alexander George's terms, since a fluid or incoherent 'game structure' is a contradiction in terms.[26] On the other hand, America's main interests in the region are on the whole less vulnerable than those of its rival (though there is also dispute in Washington over this) and this is more important than the value of the interests concerned since, logically, a moderate but vulnerable interest is of more concern than a vital but invulnerable one.

How compatible are Soviet and American interests in Southern Africa? For reasons which are by now self-evident, this is just as difficult a question to answer. On the face of it, the superpowers seem to possess very few common interests in the region. Further thought, however, suggests five candidates – and perhaps not entirely trivial ones at that. First of all there is the acknowledged common interest in preventing South Africa from becoming an open nuclear weapons state, which was dramatised by the Soviet revelation, in August 1977, of the possibility of a South African nuclear test in the Kalahari Desert and the subsequent pressure applied on Pretoria by Washington with a view to preventing its occurrence. Secondly, there is the presumed common interest – in view of recent Soviet keenness to collaborate with the West against international terrorism – in dissuading the African National Congress (ANC) from resorting to terrorist methods (i.e., random attacks on civilians for political ends). Thirdly, there is the acknowledged common interest in Western-financed economic development in the Front Line States. This flows, on the one hand, from the inability of the Soviet bloc to help in this regard and its hope that Western capital will help to stabilise pro-Soviet regimes (especially those in Angola and Mozambique) at no cost,[27] and, on the other, from the hope of the Americans that Western economic support will lead either to the return of such regimes to the Western fold or to their adoption of a more genuine policy of non-alignment. Fourthly, there is the possible common interest in independence for Namibia. And last, but far from least, there is the certain common interest in the 'abolition of apartheid'.

Independence for Namibia under a SWAPO-dominated government, provided this is linked to the departure of Cuban combat troops from Angola as part of a package deal (which was first suggested by the incoming Reagan administration in 1981[28]), and irrespective of whether or not the Soviet Union had played a direct hand in events, *should* certainly suit the Soviet interest. This is so even though this 'linkage' proposal has been condemned by Moscow (although greater Soviet flexibility on this issue became apparent in 1988) and widely opposed in Africa as unacceptable interference in Angola's domestic affairs and inconsistent with Security Council Resolution 435 of 1978 on the procedures for achieving Namibia's independence (on which, incidentally, the Soviet Union abstained). On the one hand, Moscow could claim to have hastened Namibian independence by its support for the South West Africa People's Organization (SWAPO) and its general policy in Southern Africa, and might well gain a new partner in the region. On the other, the withdrawal of the Cubans would enable it to reduce its substantial subsidy of the Cuban economy and alleviate OAU suspicions of Soviet policy on the African continent. The Cuban troops themselves could be presented as no longer necessary since a major incentive for the incursion of South African Defence Forces into Angola (the destruction of SWAPO bases) would have been removed and UNITA's lines of supply to South Africa (though not, it is true, to Zaire) would have been cut.[29] In any case, it could be made clear that the Cubans would return – or that an Inter-African Force (of the kind seen after Shaba II) might intervene – if the MPLA regime were to come under renewed threat. It is interesting that Angola itself has accepted the principle of linkage.[30]

The Namibia–Angola linkage is rightly seen as suiting the American interest since, through its consummation, Washington could claim to have achieved a long-sought and widely approved diplomatic goal (Namibian independence), placed itself in a good position to compete with the Russians for influence in Windhoek, and removed 'the Cuban menace' from Southern Africa into the bargain.

It might be supposed that the claim that the superpowers share a perceived interest in the 'abolition of apartheid' is weakened by the vague practical implications of this slogan. However, a paper presented in Moscow in 1986 by Gleb Starushenko of the Soviet Union's Africa Institute strongly suggested that there may indeed be a great measure of common ground here. The analysis by Starushenko, a corresponding member of the USSR Academy of Sciences, was suffused by a fear that regional conflicts might lead to nuclear war. In relation to South Africa, it supported negotiations between the African National Congress (ANC) and the 'white bourgeoise' ('which is not tied to the chariot of apartheid'); cautioned against 'broad nationalization of capitalist property'; argued that pragmatism was strongly entrenched even among 'middle and lower strata' whites; favoured provision by the ANC of 'comprehensive guarantees for the white population' on the models of 'Kenia' (*sic*) and Zimbabwe; suggested a two-chamber parliament; and concluded by indicating a preference for a post-apartheid South Africa having 'a unitary system with autonomous components'.[31] Such a programme is not exactly a million miles away from the American position!

It might still be said, however, that the pursuit of an agreed superpower policy on the future of South Africa is complicated by the lack of any publicly extant geopolitical quid pro quo – comparable to the proposed departure of the Cubans from Angola in the Namibia negotiations – which the Russians could hand to the Americans to smooth acceptance of the collapse of National Party power by Washington conservatives. However, the fact that such quid pro quo have not yet been publicly canvassed does not mean to say that they could not be contrived. For example, in acknowledgement of the greater American interest in the security of the Cape Route, the Soviet Union could support the idea of a treaty of neutrality for post-apartheid South Africa comparable to the Austrian State Treaty (there is a strong Afrikaner neutralist tradition, as well as a likely disposition to support neutral*ism* on the part of the black population) or treaty-guaranteed rights over facilities at Simonstown and other South African ports for NATO vessels.

PATRON–CLIENT RELATIONS IN THE REGION

Whether or not the superpowers can cooperate to produce solutions in Namibia and South Africa or simply to avoid collision depends to some extent, of course, on the degree to which they can control their clients in the region. The Soviet Union's principal clients in Southern Africa are the MPLA government of Angola, the FRELIMO government of Mozambique, and the two militarily weak but nevertheless prestigious 'national liberation movements' – SWAPO, which operates against South African-controlled Namibia from bases in southern Angola, and the ANC, which has its headquarters in the Zambian capital, Lusaka, and conducts military activities against South Africa proper from bases in the neighbouring states, some with and some without the tacit blessing of their host governments.[32]

It is important to stress, however, that Soviet control of its 'clients' is far from complete. For example, in February 1984, to the great embarrassment of the Soviet Union, the Angolan government signed a non-aggression pact with South Africa, while in the following month the Mozambique government followed suit in the Nkomati Accord. The fact that these pacts have since crumbled – not through Soviet machinations – is beside the point.

The reasons for the weakness of Soviet control over its clients in the region are not difficult to identify. First of all, suspicion of Soviet motives on the part of almost all African politicians is at least as deep as suspicion of Western motives, and most of them share a strong attachment to non-alignment. The Angolan and Mozambique governments are stiffened in this regard by neighbouring leaders with high prestige in the non-aligned movement, Kenneth Kaunda of Zambia and Robert Mugabe of Zimbabwe. Secondly, the Soviet bloc has been manifestly incapable of providing the economic assistance so badly needed by Angola and Mozambique, and both have been turning for this increasingly to the West. (Of course, because neither SWAPO nor the ANC have as yet states to administer and are preoccupied with 'military struggle', the inability of Moscow to provide large-scale economic aid is not a weakness in its present relationship with them.) Thirdly, the Soviet bloc has no monopoly on the supply of military equipment or advice and in the latter half of the 1980s Mozambique accepted military advisers from Britain and Portugal, while Angola began purchasing weapons from Western Europe.[33] Fourthly, the Soviet Union does not have a monopoly on the supply of troops for internal security either. Mozambique, for example, whose need in this respect is particularly urgent in view of the extensive activities of the South African-backed Renamo 'bandits' (the Mozambique National Resistance) has, since July 1985, come to rely increasingly on the large and well-trained Zimbabwe army (plus a small complement of Tanzanian troops), especially for defence of the vital Beira Corridor. Following an agreement of December 1986, defence of the Nacala route by the Chissano government was assisted by troops from Malawi.[34] Fifthly, the Soviet Union cannot marshal military and economic power in the region comparable to that of South Africa. And, finally, it has no influence over the South African government nor even (since 1956) formal diplomatic relations with it; consequently, it cannot plausibly offer to put pressure on Pretoria in the interests of any of its clients.

As well as clients in Southern Africa, however loosely controlled they might be, the Soviet Union has a 'proxy' in the shape of Cuba, with its substantial armed forces stationed in Angola. The degree of control exercised by Moscow over Cuba's Angolan adventure is a vexed question, conservative opinion in Washington naturally holding that Castro plays a compliant role, but other observers being more inclined to allow some independence of action to the Cuban leader and to suggest, indeed, that it was Cuba which prodded a profoundly cautious Soviet leadership into the adventure in the first place.[35] Whatever the circumstances of the initial decision to enter Angola, it seems likely that it reflected a harmony of outlook between Moscow and Cuba: Castro is clearly not an unwilling servant. However, in view of the well-known dependence of Cuba on the Soviet Union for economic, diplomatic and, above all, military support, it is inconceivable that Castro would attempt to play a lone hand in Southern Africa. It seems unlikely, in particular, that he would decide to keep his troops in Angola if Moscow told him to get them out. It would appear no coincidence that multilateral talks on Angola, involving Cuban and South African as well as Angolan representatives, took place for the first time in 1988 just as the Soviet Union finally agreed to withdraw its troops from Afghanistan.

The United States, for its part, has tended to regard South Africa as its own – albeit, even by American standards, unusually embarrassing – 'client' in Southern Africa ever since the Nixon Doctrine advanced the idea that the United States should appoint and support regional 'deputy sheriffs' rather than employ direct force itself outside recognised American spheres of influence. However, it has from time to time been half-hearted, to say the least, in accepting South Africa as a client, and has only had very limited success in controlling the Republic's policies, foreign as well as domestic. Such internal changes as have occurred within South Africa are more likely to have been a response to domestic unrest than to American pressure, while the United States has failed to end South African prevarication over Namibia, has failed to halt the Republic's nuclear weapons' programme, and has failed to curb the ferocity of its regional 'de-stabilisation' policies – including even attacks on the capital of Western-inclined Botswana and American-owned oil installations in northern Angola.

America's inability to manipulate its South African 'client' has many sources. Firstly, there is the adequacy of the Republic's military strength relative to the threats which it believes it faces. Unlike Israel, South Africa does not need a constant supply of advanced heavy weapons from the United States or anyone else in order to protect its security. However, it is important to note that this may change because, as far as can be told, the South Africans cannot build jet fighters of their own without smuggling in components from abroad[36] and there is evidence that they are reluctant to commit their ageing squadrons in combat against Angola's modern Soviet-supplied fighters and air defence systems.[37] Secondly, there is the knowledge that South Africa has powerful friends as well as powerful enemies in Washington, with the constant promise which this provides that hostility from America is never likely to be pushed too far and, in any event, may tomorrow turn into discreet friendship. Thirdly, there is the Republic's well-developed siege economy, which makes it highly resistant to economic pressure. Fourthly, there are other states to which South Africa can turn for commercial, financial and military/technical assistance, such as Israel and Taiwan – though it is true that, on 19 March 1987, under pressure from the US Congress, the Israeli government announced that it would enter no *new* military contracts with South Africa.[38] And, amongst other factors, there is the ideological certainty which the ruling National Party has at any rate until recently displayed.

America's only other obvious client in Southern Africa is UNITA, to which 'covert' aid has been delivered, via Zaire and even South Africa itself, following Congressional repeal in 1985 of the 1976 Clark Amendment.[39] This may well have increased American influence over UNITA relative to that of South Africa, the movement's main backer.[40] At any rate Washington was successful – in the face of South African opposition – in persuading UNITA to offer the Angolan government talks on the reopening of the Benguela railway.[41]

It should also be noted here that there is a black group within South Africa itself which is a *potential* American client of some importance, and that is Chief Gatsha Buthelezi's powerful Zulu-based 'Inkatha' movement. This group is committed to a negotiated solution to the South African crisis and supports a free market economy; as a result, it is bitterly at odds with the ANC and the leftist umbrella group, the United Democratic Front (UDF). At the same time, Buthelezi has avoided identification with the South African government by refusing to accept 'independence' for KwaZulu and has been a prime mover in discussions for multiracial regional government in Natal. Though the tribal basis of his movement is a handicap, all of this makes Buthelezi a very attractive figure in the West and it is known that his contacts in the United States are good. If South Africa collapses into civil war, it is highly likely that Washington will back Buthelezi, especially if he forges an open alliance with moderate whites. Renamo, the movement of Mozambique 'contras', is not an American client, being controlled – to the extent that it is controlled by anybody – by the South African military and right-wing Portuguese who fled Mozambique following independence in 1975 (its headquarters are in Lisbon).

Geoff R. Berridge

THE UNLIKELIHOOD OF SUPERPOWER MILITARY CONFRONTATION

Apart from the risk of escalation, there are many reasons why direct superpower military confrontation in Southern Africa in the foreseeable future – even if South Africa itself were to collapse into civil war – is, to put it mildly, extremely unlikely. Soviet interests in the region are not of sufficient importance to warrant the undertaking of military risks, and these would be seen as high since Moscow appears to believe (incorrectly) that NATO stands behind the present South African government.[42] In this connection it is interesting to note that the defence provisions of its Treaties of Friendship and Cooperation with Angola and Mozambique are very vaguely worded,[43] and that East Germany – whose treaty with Mozambique is equally guarded[44] – has been delegated responsibility for the Southern African interests of the Warsaw Pact's Political Committee precisely in order to avoid provoking a NATO intervention.[45] Moreover, the Front Line States themselves have displayed great caution in responding to the kind of Soviet clumsiness which *might* have produced intervention by the Warsaw Pact.[46]

United States interests in the Front Line States, including the geopolitical interest in the withdrawal of the Cubans from Angola, are similarly not of sufficient importance to justify military intervention, while in South Africa itself America's main interests – minerals and the Cape Route – are rightly regarded as relatively invulnerable by at least some influential bodies of opinion in Washington. Besides, the National Party government is so unpopular in America, and among America's allies, that military intervention on its behalf would almost certainly provoke major domestic racial turmoil. Indeed, even in the extremely unlikely event that the Soviet Union, assuming the role in which the United States cast itself in over Korea – 'champion of international legality and of aroused world opinion' – proposed to intervene militarily against Pretoria, following a UN General Assembly Resolution calling upon members to do just that, America's most attractive option might be to side with Moscow rather than against it.[47]

Having said this, it is clear that Southern Africa – and especially Angola, which is of considerable historical significance as the occasion for the death of *détente* – is an irritant in superpower relations which could get worse and could, therefore, do with being soothed.

THE RULES OF THE GAME

There is limited evidence that the Soviet Union and the United States observe tacit procedural rules in regard to Southern Africa which are designed to prevent

218

their differences in the region escalating into a major crisis. Since the failed South African intervention in Angola in 1975–6 (itself partly a result of the refusal of US support), the United States has sought to restrain the Republic's military sorties into its neighbouring black states and, until the repeal of the Clark Amendment, denied 'covert' support to UNITA. Of course, for reasons already advanced, Washington has not been spectacularly successful in restraining the South African military machine but it has manifestly tried and, with the isolated exception of South African-surrounded Lesotho in January 1986, Pretoria has not risked provoking the Americans to the point of bringing down any of the governments of the neighbouring black states, or of creating new buffer states in, say, southern Angola or southern Mozambique, though this has long been within its grasp. As a result, the Soviet bloc and Cuban governments have not themselves been provoked into strengthening their military support for their regional clients to a point at which an increase in superpower tension would be inevitable.

For its part, the Soviet bloc has carefully kept its military advisers out of combat roles and ensured that the Cuban troops in Angola are kept behind a defensive line well above the Namibian frontier.[48] Indeed, in 1983, 'Castro instructed his troops in Angola not to engage South African forces in the south so as to avoid exacerbating East–West tensions at a particularly critical time in relations between the United States and the Soviet Union'.[49] In the same spirit, in 1977 and 1978, when successive invasions of the Shaba province of Zaire were launched by Katangan exiles based in Angola, and reportedly trained and equipped by the Cubans, Castro was at some pains to disown these actions and after the second of them, apparently collaborated with the Neto government of Angola to disarm the rebels.[50]

Of course, it cannot be assumed that because both superpowers, together with the Cubans and, even in some measure, the South Africans, have behaved with reasonable restraint since the Soviet–Cuban–MPLA victory in Angola in 1976, that this is a result of a norm implicitly upholding the regional status quo. For one thing, the United States has probably been more anxious to restrain South African 'destabilisation' tactics in order to preserve its own credentials as a regional mediator with the Front Line States, and to show that its policy of 'constructive engagement' with South Africa was working, than to avoid the possibility of an increase in tension with the Soviet Union. For another, not all of P. W. Botha's advisers appeared to be convinced that, quite apart from the American reaction, it would be in South Africa's interests to wage an all-out assault on Angola, Zimbabwe and Mozambique, where a combination of economic pressure, transport diplomacy and coercive bargaining has kept Marxist governments in a reasonably passive frame of mind towards the South African 'struggle'.

Nevertheless, in the light of norms of restraint in more dangerous areas of Third World superpower confrontation, such as the Middle East, it would be surprising if such rules were not also operating tacitly in Southern Africa. That the United States, at any rate, has been thinking expressly in these terms for some years is also evidenced by Kissinger's (albeit belated and unsuccessful) suggestion to Moscow, in late 1975, that the superpowers should not only agree to a withdrawal of Cuban and South African forces from the Angolan civil war but also cease military supplies to their respective clients engaged in the fighting.[51] Subsequently the Carter administration tried – equally unsuccess-fully – to persuade the Russians to leave Africa to the Africans, while its UN Ambassador, Andrew Young, somewhat contradictorily, described the Cubans as a 'stabilising' presence in African politics.[52] However, with the 'correlation of forces' now drastically unbalanced along the Angola–Namibia frontier and turning against it in the rest of Southern Africa, the Soviet Union may be more amenable to the observance of a regional norm of restraint.

SUPERPOWER CRISIS PREVENTION IN SOUTHERN AFRICA

What of more elaborate techniques of crisis prevention? Since the middle of the 1970s it has been American policy in Southern Africa to encourage the 'solution' of the region's major problems – Rhodesia, Namibia and apartheid – and thereby remove the opportunities for Soviet/Cuban intervention. During the Carter presidency, as already mentioned, it was hoped that, while solutions were being sought, superpower intervention could be minimised by persuading the Russians to agree to a policy of facilitating 'African solutions to African problems'.

However, the idea of a superpower 'no–go zone' as far as Southern Africa was concerned overlooked the formal responsibility of America's major NATO ally, Britain, for settling the Rhodesian problem, the disinclination of Moscow (which rightly saw Carter's suggestion as in large measure an attempt to make a virtue out of a necessity) to pass up opportunities for the expansion of its influence, and the enormous disparity of power between South Africa and the Front Line States, which meant that Pretoria could not be shifted from its entrenched positions in the absence of external pressure (or internal collapse). As a result, the Carter administration never abstained from diplomacy in Southern Africa itself (though it allowed Britain to take the lead in the Rhodesian negotiations) and, under Chester Crocker's direction during the Reagan period, the United States played a very active mediating role in the region. It mediated between South Africa on the one hand and Angola and Mozambique on the other in the non-aggression pacts signed in 1984, and it has been an active member of the Western Five's 'Contact Group' on Namibia. The Soviet Union has been resolutely excluded from this diplomacy by the United States, with the collusion of the

Front Line States (including Angola and Mozambique),[53] and in any case could not have aspired to a mediating role itself as a result of its absence of diplomatic relations with Pretoria.

Nevertheless, impaled on the contradiction between the requirements of its geopolitical desire to support the present South African regime, and its domestically prompted concern to push it in the direction of racial reform, and hampered by a traditional lack of State Department expertise on 'white Africa',[54] United States policy has so far failed. The Namibian independence negotiations were stalled until 1988–9; the Contact Group was disbanded in 1982. Constructive engagement has up to now failed to move the Botha government far enough on apartheid and, in September 1985, was abandoned in favour of minor sanctions which pleased no one and, alone, will not work because they are not remotely commensurate with the stakes at issue. South Africa's low-intensity wars on its frontiers continued and became possibly more dangerous with the military strengthening of Angola by the Soviet Union. Soviet influence itself, while diminishing perceptibly in Mozambique, remains strong in Angola. Moreover, the United States, which made the mistake from the beginning of refusing to recognise the MPLA government in Luanda (this was partly a function of American–Cuban relations) may have further compromised its ability to play the role of mediator in Angola – and indeed in the wider Southern African conflict – by resuming 'covert' aid to UNITA.[55] It thus behoves us to consider whether alternative superpower strategies are necessary or whether it might not be better for the Americans to fine tune their existing strategy and try again.

The idea of a superpower *no-go zone* in Southern Africa remains as much a non-starter today as it was when it was floated by President Carter. Unlike Antarctica, the region is too important to ignore and, unlike Iran, not so dangerous that lost opportunities are thought worth suffering in order to avoid the risk of swift escalation into direct superpower conflict. In any case, neither is such a proposal advisable since, as already mentioned, the disparity of power between South Africa and the Front Line States means that outside – and probably superpower – pressure on Pretoria is unavoidable if the region's problems are to be either solved or at least brought under control.

The possibility of minimising violence in the region by arms limitation techniques is also very low. This is principally because the mandatory UN arms embargo placed on South Africa in 1977 has encouraged the Republic to build up an impressive arms industry (though it is true that it is not as self-sufficient in armaments, especially in aircraft components, as it likes to make out), and also made it impossible for the Americans to offer the Russians any direct quid pro quo (other than another cessation of supplies to UNITA) in return for a halt to Soviet arms supplies to its own regional clients.

As for United Nations intervention in the region sanctioned by the superpowers via the Security Council – either with observer groups or peace-keeping forces in Hammarskjöld's virtually pacifist conception – this is obviously inappropriate within South Africa itself. In Namibia, as the Contact Group's protracted and finally abortive negotiations revealed, such an approach foundered before 1988–9 on the rock of the Republic's profound hostility to the UN,[56] its local military supremacy, its determination to exclude effective SWAPO participation from any constituent assembly elections,[57] and the inability of the United States to bring sufficient pressure to bear on Pretoria. In Angola and Mozambique none of the disputants have hitherto been inclined to take the idea of UN peacekeeping seriously, since all believed that they still had a good chance of prevailing – with outside help from other sources.

The idea of a superpower condominium in Southern Africa, i.e., the military imposition of solutions in the region by the superpowers acting in concert, preferably under UN auspices, is as appealing as it is unlikely – though it would be unwise to rule it completely impossible. Such a proposal was canvassed by Conor Cruise O'Brien in early 1986, though he posited its possibility on a degree of South African government brutality towards its black population comparable to that employed by the French Army against the Algerian nationalists in the 1950s.[58] Unlike economic sanctions, a superpower condominium would certainly have the great advantage of going straight to the heart of the matter – the need to destroy the military confidence of Afrikaner nationalism without wrecking the South African economy and what is left of the economies of the Front Line States. Unfortunately, O'Brien's precedents – Suez and Katanga – are hardly good ones, since superpower intervention in these cases never even approached the military threshold. Moreover, at Suez, the stakes were by no means as high for Britain, France and Israel as they are for Afrikaner nationalism today, and in Katanga, Tshombe's army was infinitely weaker than the South African Defence Force. Besides, neither of these instances approached anything like the prominence in American domestic politics of the South African problem. An American proposal to intervene by force against a white government involved in a brutal race war – especially if such an intervention was in collaboration with the Russians – would be likely to provoke as violent a white backlash in the United States as a pro-white intervention would a black one.

If ever a joint superpower intervention in Southern Africa were to get off the ground, therefore, at a minimum, certain conditions would have to be met. Firstly, there would not only have to be superpower consensus on the need for dramatic action of this kind but also a much lower temperature in the overall relationship between the superpowers: it is inconceivable that the Russians and the Americans could mount a joint military operation against the South Africans while still engaged in 'cold war' activities on other fronts, not least in the competition in nuclear arms. Secondly, Soviet influence throughout Southern Africa would need to be considerably greater than it is now, otherwise joint military intervention would entail the United States and its allies making a major and, thus, politically unacceptable sacrifice to the Soviet Union (unless requited via 'linkage' to some other area, which would admittedly be possible if the last mentioned condition existed). Thirdly, there would need to be in office in Washington a Republican president who combined enormous popularity with excellent anti-communist credentials and was not looking for a further term in office. And, finally, both superpowers would need to be fairly certain that the South Africans would not in some fashion resort to the use of nuclear weapons. In short, joint superpower military intervention in Southern Africa is, to put it mildly, highly unlikely.

For much the same reason, plus South African resistance, an international conference jointly presided over by the superpowers, in the style of that which has been canvassed for the Middle East, is unlikely to get off the ground, though Starushenko has implicitly suggested this by indicating that 'the peaceful settlement of the conflict might be expedited by resorting to the institution of international guarantees, the sides selecting the guarantors by agreement from among prestigious international organizations or individual states'.[59]

In the light of all this there seems little practical alternative to a continuation of the present regime: third-party mediation led by the United States with the assistance of the other Western states with interests in the region (especially Britain, West Germany and France), together with the observance of limited procedural rules designed to minimise superpower antagonisms. However, the United States should improve its mediator's credentials by severely restricting support for UNITA and opening relations with Luanda (these moves would also help the MPLA to get rid of the Cubans). In addition, Washington should pour more economic aid into the region – especially via the Southern African Development Coordination Conference (SADCC) – in order to increase its leverage over the Front Line States (and, thus, indirectly over SWAPO and the ANC) *and* make it more difficult for South Africa to destabilise their regimes. The 'linkage' between Namibian independence and the withdrawal of Cuban troops (not civilian personnel) from Angola should be maintained in order to carry along South Africa and conservative opinion in Washington, and a deadline should be set for Pretoria's agreement to this package deal, failure to meet which would result in the automatic introduction of rapidly escalating economic sanctions tied specifically to the Namibian question. (The threat of severe economic sanctions – secretly delivered – is much more likely to shift the South Africans over Namibia than over the issue of power within the Republic itself, which is the answer to the argument that after sanctions have brought down the National Party regime the Namibian problem will solve itself.[60]) With Namibia independent, probably under a 'pragmatic' SWAPO government, and the Cubans departed from Angola, conservative opinion in the West will have less incentive to support the present government in Pretoria.

In effect, this amounts to saying that the best way to prevent Southern Africa from being a serious irritant to superpower relations, both in the short and long terms, is to restore it to its earlier status as an internally stable, Western – not purely American – sphere of influence, albeit nominally non-aligned and tacitly accepted by the Soviet Union. This need not increase superpower tensions in the process of its achievement provided it is pursued slowly, with an emphasis on economic statecraft in relation to the Front Line States, and provided the Soviet Union can be made to appreciate that the regional interests which it shares with the United States – especially nuclear non-proliferation, independence for Namibia and the abolition of apartheid – will be advanced, as they certainly should be, by such a development.

NOTES

I am grateful for the comments on this paper of Jack Spence, John Day, Gareth Winrow and the members of the South African Workshop of the European Consortium for Political Research, Amsterdam, April 1987.
1 The significant role played by the German Democratic Republic in Southern Africa is emphasised by Christopher Coker in his *NATO, The Warsaw Pact and Africa* (Macmillan for RUSI: London, 1985).
2 Peter Clement, 'Moscow and Southern Africa', *Problems of Communism*, 34, March–April 1985, p. 45.
3 Private South African shipping source; information dated 23 December 1986.
4 Coker, *NATO, The Warsaw Pact and Africa*, p. 183.
5 G. R. Berridge, *The Politics of the South Africa Run: European Shipping and Pretoria* (Oxford: Clarendon Press, 1987), pp. 194–7.
6 Larry Bowman, 'The Strategic Importance of South Africa to the United States: An Appraisal and Policy Analysis', in O. Aluko and T. M. Shaw (eds.), *Southern Africa in the 1980s* (London: Allen & Unwin, 1985), pp. 139–40; and K. Booth, *Navies and Foreign Policy* (London: Croom Helm, 1977), p. 173.
7 J. E. Spence and G. R. Berridge, 'South Africa: The Road to Simonstown', in John W. Young (ed.), *The Foreign Policy of Churchill's Peacetime Administration* (Leicester University Press, forthcoming).
8 For example, Clement, 'Moscow and Southern Africa' p. 30; R. Legvold, 'The Soviet Threat to Southern Africa', in R. I. Rotberg and others, *South Africa and its Neighbours: Regional Security and Self-Interest* (Lexington, MA: D. C. Heath, 1985), pp. 27–30; David E. Albright, 'Moscow's African Policy of the 1970s', in Albright (ed.), *Africa and International Communism* (London: Macmillan, 1980), p. 49; and Kurt M. Campbell, *Soviet Policy Towards South Africa* (London: Macmillan, 1986), p. 165.
9 Clement, 'Moscow and Southern Africa' p. 30.
10 According to John A. Marcum, Angola 'uses upward from 50 per cent of its oil revenues of over $2 billion annually to purchase Soviet arms and to maintain Cuban troops and technicians . . .' 'United States Options in Angola', *CSIS Africa Notes*, 52 (20 December 1985), p. 4.
11 Polish Ocean Lines (Gdansk) and Deutsche Seereederei (Rostock) operate the Baltafrica service as members of this Conference. While it is true that the Soviet Baltestafrica service remains in opposition to the East African Conference, negotiations for its entry – which first took place in the second half of the 1970s – are once more in train, though not apparently proving very fruitful. Private London shipping source; information dated 5 March 1987.

12 Private South African shipping source; information dated 23 December 1986.

13 'South Africa: Strategy for Change', *Foreign Affairs*, 59, (Winter 1980–1) p. 346.

14 Coker, *Nato, The Warsaw Pact and Africa*, chapters 7 and 8.

15 *The Military Balance 1985–1986* (London: The International Institute for Strategic Studies, 1985), p. 106.

16 Quoted in Campbell, *Soviet Policy Towards South Africa*, p. 123.

17 *South Africa: Time Running Out*, Report of the Study Commission on US Policy Toward Southern Africa (Berkeley, CA: University of California Press, 1981), p. 392.

18 W. J. Foltz, 'United States Policy Toward South Africa: Is One Possible?' in G. J. Bender, J. S. Coleman and R. S. Sklar (eds.), *African Crisis Areas and US Foreign Policy* (Berkeley, CA: University of California Press, 1985), pp. 38–42.

19 *Ibid.* p. 37.

20 *Ibid.* p. 32.

21 William J. Foltz, 'United States Policy Toward Southern Africa: Economic and Strategic Constraints', *Political Science Quarterly*, 92, 1, (Spring 1977), pp. 56–8; and Dieter Braun, *The Indian Ocean: Region of Conflict or 'Peace Zone'*, trans. from the German by G. Geldart and K. Llanwarne (London: Hurst, 1983), p. 44; cf. Campbell, *Soviet Policy Towards South Africa*, p. 150.

22 Foltz, 'United States Policy Toward South Africa: Is One Possible?', p. 35; and J. T. Richelson and D. Ball, *The Ties That Bind* (London: Allen & Unwin, 1986).

23 The *Independent*, 24 March 1987.

24 'The Strategic Importance of South Africa to the United States', pp. 142–5.

25 This picture is qualified only slightly by Jerry Hough's study of Soviet thinking on the Third World and on US interests there: *The Struggle for the Third World: Soviet Debates and American Options* (Washington DC: Brookings, 1986), pp. 246–8.

26 See his 'Mechanisms for Moderating Superpower Competition', *AEI Foreign Policy and Defense Review*, 6, 1 (1986).

27 Arthur Jay Klinghoffer, 'The Soviet and Superpower Rivalry in Africa', in B. E. Ardinghaus (ed.) *African Security Issues* (Boulder, CO: Westview, 1984), p. 30. Insofar as Soviet bloc concurrence in the presence of Western multinationals in Southern Africa, as opposed to acceptance of Western aid for the region, is concerned, this is more readily forthcoming from certain East European countries than from Moscow itself; see Coker, *NATO, The Warsaw Pact and Africa*, pp. 187 and 202.

28 The *Economist*, 30 March 1985, p. 19.

29 This point is oddly overlooked by R. I. Rotberg in his otherwise penetrating analysis of the question: 'Namibia and the Crisis of Constructive Engagement', in G. J. Bender, J. S. Coleman and R. L. Sklar (eds.), *African Crisis Areas and US Foreign Policy*.

30 Marcum, 'United States Options in Angola', p. 4.

31 'Problems of Struggle against Racism, Apartheid and Colonialism in the [*sic*] South Africa', report presented to the II Soviet African conference 'For peace, cooperation and social progress', Moscow, 24–26 June 1986 (Moscow, 1986). I am grateful to Peter Shearman for a copy of this document.

32 On the history of Soviet backing of the ANC (and the SA Communist Party) see Campbell, *Soviet Policy Towards South Africa*, pp. 41–6.

33 Robert S. Jaster, 'South Africa and its Neighbours: The Dynamics of Regional Conflict', *Adelphi Paper*, 209 (London: International Institute for Strategic Studies, Summer 1986), p. 72.

34 President Chissano, speaking at Chatham House, 7 May 1987.

35 W. J. Foltz, 'Africa in Great-Power Strategy', in W. J. Foltz and H. S. Brewer (eds.) *Arms and the Africans* (New Haven, CT and London: Yale University Press, 1985), pp. 15–16.

36 Anthony Sampson, *Black & Gold: Tycoons, Revolutionaries and Apartheid* (London: Hodder & Stoughton, 1987), pp. 101–2.

37 Jaster, 'South Africa and its Neighbours', p. 66; and Lt Gen. D. J. Earp (Chief of the SA Air Force), 'The Role of Air Power in Southern Africa', in M. Hough and M. van der Merwe (eds.). *Contemporary Air Strategy*, Ad hoc Publication No 23 (Inst. for Strategic Studies, University of Pretoria, April 1986), pp. 27–52.

38 The *Economist*, 4 April 1987.

39 *The Times*, 21 November 1986 and 10 January 1987; The *Independent*, 28 March 1987.

40 Much of UNITA's cash, incidentally, has come from Saudi Arabia and other Gulf sources: Marcum, 'United States Options in Angola', p. 2.

41 The *Independent*, 29 April, 1987.

42 J. E. Spence, 'Soviet Relations with Africa', *Soviet Jewish Affairs*, 15, 1, 1985, p. 126.

43 The relevant clauses in the Angolan Treaty read as follows: 'VII. In the event of any situation arising that may create a danger to peace or disturb peace, the High Contracting Parties shall immediately establish contact with each other in order to coordinate their positions in the interests of removing the danger or restoring peace. . . . X. In the interests of strengthening the defence capability of the High Contracting Parties, they shall continue to promote co-operation in the military field on the basis of corresponding agreements concluded between them', *Africa Contemporary Record 1976–7*, p. C153. Similar clauses (IV and IX), with only insignificant differences in wording, appear in the Treaty with Mozambique; see *Africa Contemporary Record 1977–8*, pp. C17–18.

44 Its Treaty with Angola has no defence provisions at all; see *Against Racism, Apartheid and Colonialism: Documents Published by the GDR 1977–1982* (Dresden: Verlag Zeit im Bild, 1983), pp. 244–6 and 265–6 (Treaty with Mozambique). However, supplementary military agreements appear to have been negotiated by the GDR with both Angola and Mozambique, though their terms remain secret.

45 Coker, *NATO, The Warsaw Pact and Africa*, pp. 200–1.

46 *Ibid*, pp. 148–9.

47 Conor Cruise O'Brien, 'What Can Become Of South Africa?' *The Atlantic Monthly*, March 1986.

48 Jaster, 'South Africa and its Neighbours', p. 65.

49 Coker, *NATO, The Warsaw Pact and Africa*, p. 246.

50 G. Volska, 'Cuba', in T. H. Henriksen (ed.) *Communist Powers and Sub-Saharan Africa* (Stanford, CA: Hoover Institution Press, 1981), p. 68.

51 A. L. George, 'Missed Opportunities for Crisis Prevention: The War of Attrition and Angola', in A. L. George (ed.), *Managing US–Soviet Rivalry: Problems of Crisis Prevention* (Boulder, CA: Westview Press, 1983), pp. 211–19.

52 Volska, 'Cuba', p. 78.

53 Jaster, 'South Africa and its Neighbours', p. 73.

54 R. E. Bissell, *South Africa and the United States: The Erosion of an Influence Relationship* (New York: Praeger, 1982), p. 31.

55 Klinghoffer, 'The Soviet Union and Superpower Rivalry in Africa', p. 36.

56 On South African attitudes to the UN, see John Barratt, 'South African Diplomacy at the UN', in G. R. Berridge and A. Jennings (eds.), *Diplomacy at the UN* (London: Macmillan, 1985).

57 See Anthony Verrier, *International Peacekeeping: United Nations in a Troubled World* (Harmondsworth: Penguin Books, 1981), chapt. 8.

58 O'Brien 'What Can Become of South Africa?'

59 'Problems of Struggle against Racism, Apartheid and Colonialism in the [*sic*] South Africa'.

60 On the economic and strategic arguments for South African withdrawal to the 'Orange River Line' (from the National Party government's own point of view), see *African Contemporary Record 1983–4*, pp. B701–7.

12   The superpowers and Southeast Asia

Paikiasothy Saravanamuttu

In the developing world, the issue of contention for both superpowers is the belief that the internal political orientation of states could determine external affiliations in a manner prejudicial to their primary concern – a favourable global balance of power. Consequently, in the post-colonial era, the basic question of the political complexion and legitimacy of successor regimes in Southeast Asia has both attracted and been compounded by the competing attentions of extra-regional powers. This, in turn, suggests that fundamental to the analysis of superpower interests in the region and the prospects for crisis avoidance by them in the next decade, is the interaction between three sets of relationships – relations between superpowers, between local states themselves and between superpowers and local states.

The conflict and competition inherent in Soviet–American relations are also found in relations between local states in the region. Nevertheless, the relationship between the superpowers and local states does not readily fit the patron–client stereotype of conventional analysis. Neither is it characterised by an immutable congruence of interest. Furthermore, given that the issues at stake – political legitimacy, nation and state building – are of seminal importance in the development of the local states, even if techniques of crisis management and tacit agreement on spheres of interest were to be arrived at between the superpowers, such arrangements could be undermined by the independent actions or circumstances of the local states. Conventions of conduct derived from the past pattern of superpower involvement may, as a result, have to be revised and the process of revision itself could well be one that is punctuated by conflict and crisis. This, as will be argued, could be of particular relevance to Southeast Asia.

Because of the past pattern of superpower relations, an understanding can be said to have emerged between them, that the current, low level of conflict amongst the local states reflects *competition* rather than *conflict* in superpower relations. Accordingly, the prospects for *direct* confrontation between the superpowers in Southeast Asia remain low, with *indirect* confrontation being sustained through the interaction of local states. Therefore, the possibility of tensions between the local dynamics of nation–state building and the global imperatives escalating is of crucial significance.

The role of the People's Republic of China (PRC) is of central importance in this context. Its geographical position, historic role and influence, not just in the region but in all of Asia, plus its position in the global balance, mark it out for special attention. Neither superpower can ignore or control PRC policy, or assume a permanent congruence of interest with it. Both have experienced the PRC's hostility and recognise that manoeuvring against each other with Chinese support is preferable to doing so without it. In this respect, China is a constant factor in the Southeast Asian equation, with imperatives of its own and interests which are predominantly, though not exclusively, regional. Consequently, projections into the future about superpower relations have to incorporate assessments of the evolution of Chinese policy and the success of crisis avoidance and management techniques may well depend on Beijing's compliance.

Bearing these factors in mind, this chapter begins with a brief discussion of the historical context of superpower interest and involvement before analysing the present situation with particular attention to the potential for crises and their avoidance. Given that Indochina remains the scene of the most pervasive and persistent conflict in Southeast Asia and thereby best encapsulates the problem of security in the region, its three consecutive wars will serve as the major focus of analysis, although the situation in the Philippines will also be examined.

THE HISTORICAL CONTEXT OF SUPERPOWER INTERESTS (1945–1978)

The United States

On 8 September 1945, approximately a month after the conclusion of the Pacific War, a memorandum to President Truman from Under Secretary of State Joseph Grew and Assistant Secretary of State James Dunn identified US interests in Southeast Asia as follows:

These areas [Southeast Asia] are sources of products essential to both our wartime and peacetime economy. They are potentially important markets for American exports. They lie athwart the South Western approaches to the Pacific Ocean and have an important bearing on our security and the security of the Philippines. Their economic and political stability will be an important factor in the maintenance of peace in Asia.[1]

Whilst these intrinsic regional features underlie US interest in Southeast Asia up to the present, it is the extra-regional imperatives of containment that provide continuity to US policy by identifying interest in terms of an external communist threat. This meant that in the early post-war period, the US traditional espousal of national self-determination for the colonial territories was effectively dislodged by a burgeoning obsession with the perceived communist challenge. It was not so much the case that Washington denied legitimacy to nationalism in the developing world, but rather that the US sought to engraft upon it an overarching purpose – anti-communism. Accordingly, the US embarked upon a collision course with the forces of revolutionary change in the region, crystallised in its ill-fated preoccupation with the political destiny of Indochina.

Deriving its strategic unity from the containment doctrine with its core idea that security is indivisible, and re-inforced in its anti-communist conviction by· Mao's victory in China (1949), the Korean War (1950–3) and the fearful consequences these events portended for Japan's future, the US underwrote the French colonial effort in the First Indochina War (1945–54) against the nationalist-communist forces of Ho Chi Minh.[2] The French defeat, however, did not deflect the US from its avowed goal of a non-communist Indochina. More anxious than ever to avert the supposed 'domino' effect of communist expansion, the US pursued its containment objective with renewed vigour.

At the Geneva Conference (July 1954), convened to arrange the orderly transfer of power in Indochina, Washington managed to mitigate non-communist territorial losses. Vietnam was temporarily partitioned at the seventeenth parallel, and elections to reunify the country scheduled for July 1956. They were never held. Interpreting the temporary partition line as the permanent political and territorial boundary of a separate state and, more importantly, as the line of containment in Southeast Asia, the US entrenched the Ngo Dinh Diem regime in southern Vietnam. It also actively encouraged Diem's refusal to hold elections as scheduled.[3] A more enduring US commitment to containment in the region was symbolised in the Southeast Asia Treaty Organisation (SEATO), established under the Collective Defence Treaty, signed in Manila on 8 September 1954. The cumulative effect of these actions was the Second Indochina War (1960–75). This erupted at the end of the decade, when nationalist proponents of a revolutionary social order rose up with the help of their compatriots in the north against US-sponsored regimes in the south.

The obsolescence of the French dimension aside, US interests in the Second Indochina War were initially those that it had identified in the first. It saw a separate, non-communist, Vietnamese state as a necessary precondition for containment in Asia. Consequently, the belief in the direct correlation between the internal political orientation of a state, its external affiliations and the global balance of power, was reaffirmed in the Second Indochina War by the introduction of US troops in spring 1965. Entrapped by the apocalyptic assumptions underlying its expansive definition of threat, Washington prose-

cuted its Indochinese war without any understanding of Asian nationalism and
without reference to the opportunities presented by the Sino–Soviet split.
Furthermore, as it became more deeply involved, the US inflated the
importance of the war correspondingly and, in the hyperbole of the day,
presented South Vietnam as a pivotal member of the 'Free World'. Hence, when
the combined impact of the domestic political tensions generated by yet another
inconclusive war on the Asian mainland and Vietnamese resistance frustrated
Washington's experiment with nation-building and regional order in Southeast
Asia, the real casualty was the credibility of the containment doctrine.

Notwithstanding the Vietnam debacle, the US attempt to shape the political
destiny of Southeast Asia produced some dividends in the form of the avowedly
non-communist Association of Southeast Asian (ASEAN) states. Seen in these
terms, the legacy of containment in Southeast Asia is an enduring US stake in its
security.

Following Vietnam, the ASEAN states, disconcerted by the loss in the
credibility of US security guarantees, recognised that the change in their
strategic environment militated against over-reliance on Washington for their
security. Nevertheless, given their political and economic orientation, they
neither desired nor could afford to divorce themselves completely from the US.
Therefore, US *military retrenchment* from Indochina did not denote *political
disengagement* from Southeast Asia. For regional states the question remained as
to their exact position in the scale of Washington's geopolitical priorities and the
nature of commitment this entailed.

Some indication as to the US position was provided in the Guam or,
subsequently labelled, Nixon Doctrine, enunciated in 1969.[4] This was
essentially a damage limitation exercise, designed to reformulate the shattered
bases and instruments of foreign policy whilst at the same time avoiding a
detailed enumeration of geopolitical priorities. Nixon, following the decision to
de-Americanise the Vietnam War, did not wholly allay the fears of the ASEAN
states but, in the general propositions of the doctrine, went some way towards
assuaging their worst doubts. He served notice to the world that although the
United States would honour existing alliances, its future commitments were to
be determined by interests rather than the other way round, as had been the case
in the era of globalism. *Détente* with the communist states, implicitly
foreshadowed in the doctrine, was to be an indispensable component of this
strategic outlook. It was envisaged that *détente* would produce an understanding
with them that would obviate the *need* to fight another Vietnam war.
Complementing this was a concern with regional balances. The US would
provide its allies in local conflicts with arms, the deterrent power of its air and
naval strength, including nuclear protection, but would not deploy its own

troops. Consequently, by the onset of the Third Indochina war (December 1978), a transformation had taken place in the *means* the US would employ to secure its interests in Southeast Asia, whilst those interests, though demoted as a consequence, retained an enduring significance.

The Soviet Union

In the period up to the Third Indochina War, Soviet interests in Southeast Asia were interpreted in the idiom of Marxist–Leninist ideology and enhanced as a function of rival US and PRC activity.

Viewed initially in the wider context of promoting socialism in the developing world, Southeast Asia was not bestowed with especial significance. A number of constraining factors were responsible for this, namely, the pressing demands of the European situation, the limited reach of Soviet military capabilities and the rigidity of the prevailing Stalinist ideological orthodoxy. This is not to deny some Soviet interest during this period, simply to emphasise that the dimensions attributed to it by Washington were as much of the nature of a self-fulfilling prophecy on the part of the US as a consequence of independent Soviet action.

The class-based analysis of the developing world's revolutionary potential, and its animosity towards successor regimes not fully pledged to the socialist camp, was exemplified in Andrei Zhdanov's 22 September 1948 Comintern speech.[5] This marked out the Soviet approach to social change in the post-colonial world as paralleling US misconceptions of the nature of that process. However, Moscow soon realised that local communist parties in Southeast Asia were not on the verge of attaining power and it shifted attention away from local insurgency towards governments eager to establish political independence from the West. Another factor in this shift was the emergence of the PRC as the patron of the Southeast Asian Communist parties.

This new emphasis was more clearly demonstrated under Khrushchev, who attempted to exploit Afro–Asian solidarity and non-alignment to Soviet advantage. These efforts were nonetheless limited by the corresponding ability of the regional states to capitalise upon great power solicitations for their own ends and their lingering suspicion of the Soviet Union as a source of inspiration for internal revolt. The Soviet experience with Burma, which opted for neutrality and a non-provocative posture towards Beijing, illustrated the meagre gains from this approach, whilst relations with Sukarno's Indonesia revealed its accompanying risks. Before the mercurial Indonesian leader was overthrown by the army in 1965, he had distanced himself from the Soviets on account of their unwillingness to support his campaign of confrontation against Malaysia. Consequently, although it was the PRC that bore the brunt of the army's displeasure – Sukarno having aligned with the pro-Beijing PKI – Moscow reaped no benefit either from his downfall.

Relations with Hanoi also revealed a disjunction in interests. This created the impression that the Soviet preoccupation with extra-regional considerations could work to Vietnam's disadvantage. The disjunction was initially manifested at the 1954 Geneva Conference when Moscow's desire to secure France's rejection of the European Defence Community (EDC) Treaty overrode its efforts to translate Ho's military victory into permanent territorial gains. The PRC, too, at this time, seemed more eager to establish its international diplomatic credentials than to press relentlessly for Vietnamese advantage. After Geneva, Soviet pressure on Diem to realise the proposed electoral timetable was not applied in the measure required by Hanoi. More importantly, the latter's resort to arms was taken independently of Moscow and was at variance with Soviet perceptions of the correlation of forces. It coincided with the Sino–Soviet split, and Moscow's reluctance fully to endorse Hanoi's position is explicable in terms of the calculation that a national liberation struggle in Asia could enhance Beijing's reputation in the developing world. This was overturned, however, by the US intervention in 1965 which signalled to the Soviet Union that the future direction of the conflict augured well for Vietnamese reliance on Soviet material assistance. Notwithstanding this, during the war a divergence in interest was to be seen again when the US embarked upon *détente* with the Soviet Union. Despite the US mining of Haiphong harbour in May 1972, the Nixon–Brezhnev summit went ahead as planned. Not surprisingly, Vietnamese suspicion that superpower patronage, though indispensable, is not *necessarily* conducive to its regional goals, is discernible to this day.

The wider Soviet interest in Asia during the late 1960s and early 70s (and still not jettisoned) was to establish a collective security system, the details of which were kept deliberately vague on the grounds that these were to be agreed upon in consultation with the regional states. It was intended to exploit diminishing US power in Southeast Asia and at the same time contain the PRC. Nevertheless, given the track record of the superpowers, most states, including those, like India, who had cordial relations with the Soviet Union, cold-shouldered the proposal. In Southeast Asia, the ASEAN states, having declared in 1971 their long-term aim of creating a Zone of Peace, Freedom and Neutrality (ZOPFAN) in the region, expressed no interest in Moscow's proposal. However, during the course of the Vietnam War, the Soviet Union made some diplomatic inroads into the area which had hitherto eluded it. Diplomatic relations with Malaysia were established in April 1967, and the Philippines in June 1976. Further developments along these lines were constrained by the onset of the Third Indochina War.

CURRENT SUPERPOWER INTERESTS

Since the strategic environment of Southeast Asia is dominated by the Third Indochina War and more recently, by developments in the Philippines, the analysis of superpower relations must take account of them.

The Third Indochinese War resembles its predecessors in that it turns on the belief that the internal political orientation of a state has a direct bearing on its external affiliations and, as a consequence, on the global balance of power. What is distinctive about it, however, is that, at both the regional and extra-regional levels, the principal antagonists are the communist states. This does not mean that the US is not involved in the definite extra-regional dimension to the conflict, but that, in sharp contrast to the Second Indochina War, its involvement takes account of intra-communist differences. Crisis between the two super-powers can, in this sense, be avoided, as long as the prevailing pattern of conflict is sustained.

The indigenous sources of this conflict can be traced to the resurgence of ancient animosities between Kampuchea, China and Vietnam, which transcend considerations of a shared revolutionary ideology. In the wider global context it can be seen, alternatively, in terms either of Hanoi's insistence, partly underwritten by the Soviet Union, on treating Indochina as a single strategic unit under its patrimony, or of Chinese designs, expressed in the sustenance of Khmer nationalism and supported by the US and ASEAN, to contain Soviet–Vietnamese expansion and extend hegemony over the region.

The 25 December 1978 Vietnamese invasion of Kampuchea accomplished the overthrow of the murderous Pol Pot regime and the establishment in its place of the pro-Vietnamese People's Republic of Kampuchea under Heng Samrin. This had been preceded by numerous border incidents between the two states, dating from the US defeat in 1975, closer alignment between the Pol Pot regime and the PRC, consolidation of the Soviet–Vietnamese relationship (expressed in the November 1978 security treaty), as well as increasing tension between Vietnam and China over the former's treatment of its Chinese citizens in the south as part of a programme of economic restructuring along collectivist lines. Conse-quently, the Vietnam–Kampuchea conflict became entwined in the wider Sino–Soviet dispute, and the limited PRC military riposte in February 1979 to the Vietnamese invasion, following the normalisation of its relations with the US, confirmed the global alignments underpinning the Third Indochina War.

The importance of the situation in the Philippines stems from the enduring challenge posed to the Aquino government by the communist New People's Army and the implications this could have for the retention of the US bases at

Subic Bay and Clark Air Field. Were this challenge to be successful, and one of the largest US military installations abroad disbanded or dispersed, the psychological effect of this removal of power, if nothing else, could exacerbate tension, since it has been, in this form, a permanent feature of the strategic equation in the region.

The following section looks at current US and Soviet interests in the region, separately, in order to trace the continuity in interests and elucidate how the past pattern of superpower interaction has given rise to conventions of conduct which mitigate the probability of direct confrontation but, at the same time, facilitate competition. It also draws attention to the alignments that exemplify this competition and point to risks within them that could be detrimental to the interests the alignments are intended to serve.

The United States

As noted earlier, the Vietnam War did not constitute the obsolescence of US geopolitical and economic interests in Southeast Asia or the general perspective of containment through which they had been viewed. The *goals* of containment were retained, while the *means* were adjusted in the light of changed circumstances. In particular, the importance of regional states for the pursuit of US interests was emphasised – despite the humiliating reversal in Indochina, Washington maintained an interest in ensuring the prosperity and viability of non-communist Southeast Asia. This, in effect, had been one of the main justifications for the Vietnam War and, moreover, constituted in geo-strategic terms, a vital consideration in the projection of US power globally. Therefore, when the Third Indochina War and developments in Southwest Asia portended increased Soviet influence, Washington was sufficiently perturbed to reiterate its interest in maintaining the Southeast Asian balance of power so as to secure vital sea lanes of communication and commerce. Three years after the reunification of Vietnam, the US interest in Southeast Asia was defined by Assistant Secretary of State Richard Holbrooke in *realpolitik* terms. According to him, it was in Washington's interest 'not to allow any single power to achieve a preponderance of influence or military superiority in the region'.[6]

Commensurate with this formulation, the US has adopted a two-pronged strategy of containment to counter the increase in Soviet influence – directly at sea, through naval and air power concentrated in the Seventh Fleet; indirectly on land through increased aid to the ASEAN states and the non-communist Kampuchean resistance, as well as a tacit strategic alliance with the PRC. This strategy, which relies on low-level conflict to facilitate US interests *vis-à-vis* the Soviet Union, also contains tensions that could detract from the overall objective. Salient in this context is the possibility that the apparent coincidence of interest with the PRC could evolve in a manner in which Beijing's influence over the fortunes of the ASEAN states is unmatched by Washington's ability to moderate it. Indeed, the competitive engagement of the communist states has been institutionalised to such a degree that the influence of their ideological rivals is best served by preserving the ability to manoeuvre *against* the communist states as well as *between* them. Failure to sustain the flexibility necessitated by the classic balance-of-power doctrine could prejudice existing understandings between the superpowers regarding the boundaries within which interests are prosecuted. This could have grave consequences for crisis avoidance. In this connection, the ASEAN–PRC–US alignment in opposition to Vietnam's invasion of Kampuchea, and the opportunities available to the Soviet Union as a result, need closer inspection.

The US, ASEAN and the PRC

Formed in 1967 by states committed to a common political affinity with the West, ASEAN now comprises its original founders, Malaysia, Indonesia, Thailand, Singapore and the Philippines, plus Brunei. It was devised as an instrument of regional economic cooperation and not as a military–security alliance. Its constant reiteration of this distinction, and insistence on collective self-reliance in the military–security field, is premised primarily on the calculation that the combined might of its membership is insufficient to pose a credible deterrent or defence against hostile states. Consequently, ASEAN governments have emphasised collaborative security policies between members and endorsed a position of armed neutrality, as embodied in their 1976 Bali Summit Declaration of ASEAN Concord and the Treaty of Amity and Cooperation in Southeast Asia. This theme had been enunciated earlier in their 1971 proposal to establish a Zone of Peace, Freedom and Neutrality (ZOPFAN) in Southeast Asia. ZOPFAN, however, predicated as it is on the absence of extra-regional competition and congenial ASEAN–Indochinese relations, is beyond the realms of practicability at present; the intractability of the Third Indochina War suggests that it will remain so for the foreseeable future.

In response to this conflict, ASEAN has evolved into a diplomatic community bent on denying international recognition to the Heng Samrin regime, and as the regional conduit for assistance to the non-communist forces opposing it, namely, the Kampuchean People's National Liberation Front (KPNLF) under ex-Premier Son San, and former Head of State Sihanouk's Armee Nationale Sihanoukienne (ANS). Together with the Khmer Rouge, these groups form the Coalition Government of Democratic Kampuchea (CGDK) with Sihanouk as titular President.

ASEAN's opposition to Vietnam's occupation of Kampuchea arises out of its fear that even if Hanoi's ambitions do not extend beyond Indochina itself, as long as they remain, regional security will be mortgaged to oscillations in the Sino–Soviet conflict. This, in turn, requires a continuing US role to maintain the regional balance, thereby further retarding the prospects for a ZOPFAN.

ASEAN's dilemma is that although its members can agree on a broad definition of threat in the context of the communist/non-communist ideological divide, they disagree on the precise location and intensity of that threat. Hence, the correspondence of interest currently obtained with Beijing is not indicative of a unified strategic consensus which identifies the Soviet Union and Vietnam as the primary or exclusive danger. ASEAN's apprehension with respect to the PRC stems from Beijing's role as the patron of local communist parties in revolt against them as well as the PRC's hold over the approximately 20 million ethnic Chinese in the member states. Consequently, Indonesia is wary of China because of its role in the 1965 PKI *coup* attempt and, in the Indochinese context, feels a certain solidarity with Vietnam as another Asian state to have successfully resisted Western colonialism. Malaysian suspicions, on the other hand, stem from a delicate ethnic balance and the experience of communist insurgency. Therefore, Kuala Lumpur and Djakarta were willing to concede, in their 1980 Kuantan Declaration, that Hanoi has legitimate interests in Kampuchea. Bangkok, however, strenuously objects to this – its opposition being under-pinned by its position as the 'frontline' state in the Third Indochina War, whose security fears have to be accommodated if ASEAN is to maintain any degree of organisational cohesion for the duration of this conflict.

Thailand's fears arise from the loss of its traditional 'buffer' in Kampuchea, and consequent exposure to Vietnamese encroachments. Its vested interest in sustaining Khmer nationalism has led it to provide support and sanctuary to the CGDK opposition and, at the same time, made it vulnerable to Vietnamese border incursions. Whilst the coincidence of interest with the PRC this attests to has produced a Chinese guarantee to defend Thai territorial sovereignty, it has nevertheless been accompanied by reservations in other ASEAN capitals. Too intimate a relationship with Beijing, it is averred, could prove to be as risky as one that is too inimical. Even Singapore, which is particularly keen on containing Soviet influence in the area, is aware of this. As Premier Lee Kuan Yew observed after the February 1979 PRC military action,

Our dilemma is acute. If there had been no [Chinese] intervention, we would face Vietnamese supremacy, which in this case means Soviet supremacy. If the intervention is over successful, it means that in ten, fifteen years there will be an assertion of influence, perhaps not amounting to hegemony by a Communist power that has influence over all guerilla movements in the countries of Thailand, Malaysia, Singapore and Indonesia.[7]

Cognisant of this, the PRC has moved some way in allaying ASEAN fears about its long-term intent, but not gone far enough to eradicate ingrained suspicions. For instance, on the question of the ethnic Chinese, Beijing has declared itself opposed to dual nationality and encouraged integration within the ASEAN states. Those who have held on to Chinese citizenship are encouraged to do the same and, more importantly, the PRC has vowed to uphold the distinction it made between party–party links and government–government relations in favour of the latter.[8]

On the question of Kampuchea, too, there is a divergence between Chinese and ASEAN positions towards the CGDK. Whilst Beijing supports the Khmer Rouge because of its combat experience, not to mention past association, ASEAN favours the KPNLF and the ANS. Given its genocidal past, the Khmer Rouge is a diplomatic albatross in the ASEAN effort to extend diplomatic recognition to the Kampuchean opposition. Moreover, since Vietnam is adamantly opposed to any deal with the 'genocidal Pol Pot clique', and fearful that if it withdrew its troops the Khmer Rouge would seize power in Kampuchea, continued PRC sponsorship of the Khmer Rouge is an obstacle to ASEAN's preferred solution to the conflict – a negotiated settlement. In this respect, ASEAN is uneasy with Beijing's long-term strategy of attrition against Vietnam, with or without the KR.

The PRC believes that this strategy will succeed in the end because, unlike Hanoi's previous adversaries, it is a permanent presence in the region whose influence is secured by important historic and cultural ties, if nothing else. Therefore, Beijing discounts arguments that its 1979 punitive strike resulted in a 'distortion of strategic priorities', accounted for in the implications of the Soviet–Vietnamese relationship.[9] From Beijing's perspective, its regional and wider security goals are best served by the determination to prevail over Hanoi, which it sees both as a regional upstart and surrogate of Moscow. Deng Xiaoping, in response to Gorbachev's Vladivostok Asian Initiative (28 July 1986), pointed out that the main obstacle to a Sino–Soviet *rapprochement* is the Vietnamese occupation of Kampuchea. Consequently, for the foreseeable future, entrenched Chinese and Vietnamese positions, unmediated by Soviet leverage or a desire on Moscow' part to exert it – which will be addressed later – sustain the current *impasse* and ASEAN apprehensions.

Washington's response has been to assure the ASEAN states that its relationship with Beijing, in the context of superpower rivalry, will not develop at their expense. In accordance with this position, the US has repeatedly reaffirmed its security commitment to Thailand under the 1954 Manila Pact, conducted joint military exercises with Thai military forces and augmented Bangkok's military arsenal to include F16-A aircraft.[10] Indonesia, as well, has benefited from Washington's professed intention to augment ASEAN's military strength. The US also allocated $3.5 million in the 1986 International Security and Assistance Act for 'appropriate' aid to the non-communist CGDK forces.[11] This aid could include military assistance and was to be conveyed to its recipients via Bangkok. In addition, Washington was also reported to provide these forces with an additional $5 million in covert military aid.[12]

On the Kampuchean issue, the US studiously maintains that it supports the official ASEAN line i.e., withdrawal of Vietnamese troops and international supervision of elections to settle the question of sovereignty. That this position may be ultimately conditioned by long-term PRC interests prejudicial to ASEAN is dismissed in Washington by confidence in the ability to counter such a development, even if pre-emption proves unsuccessful.[13]

The role adopted by the US, as a consequence of its desire not to revise the Nixon Doctrine, is a supportive one: that of a 'balancer' unwilling to become embroiled as a direct protagonist. This is not to suggest that the US has only a casual interest in a conflict which it realises is inextricably connected to regional security. Rather, what can be inferred is that because of outstanding differences with Vietnam and residual acrimony between the two states, arising from the Second Indochina War, Washington realises its limitations as a mediator. Moreover, the US is confident that although the present conflict may consolidate Soviet influence, this at the same time underlines the relevance of US power for its containment. Furthermore, Washington has also intimated that in the event its efforts were insufficient or had to be reduced, it would turn to Tokyo rather than rely exclusively on Beijing. Commenting on US interests in Asia, if there were to be a Sino–Soviet *détente*, a senior Reagan Administration official remarked, 'We are relying more on allies than on friends who want to remain non-allies. China relations are not critical to us, Japanese relations are'.[14]

There are, of course, several factors that would have to be satisfied and obstacles removed, before Japan took on a military role to supplement its considerable economic one in Southeast Asia. Tokyo would have to reconsider its strictures on rearmament and ASEAN would have to overcome its residual bitterness towards Japan, dating from the Pacific War. Notwithstanding this, it must be conceded that there is a certain military and economic logic to this development, given Washington's enduring perception of Southeast Asia as being intimately connected to Japan's security. It will also mark Tokyo's recognition, in the post-war era, of the responsibilities this entails. Nevertheless, it does underline the argument that, however defined, US interests in Southeast Asia still require manipulation with the shadow if not the substance of military power to reconcile and mitigate underlying political differences.

US military power in Southeast Asia and the bases in the Philippines

Clark Field and Subic Bay in the Philippines, dating originally from the colonial period and retained under numerous agreements thereafter, are the largest and most comprehensive US military installations abroad. They have played a major part in ensuring US naval dominance over the sea-lanes of the region – the enduring importance of which has been reinforced by events in the Persian Gulf, the Soviet invasion of Afghanistan and the Soviet naval presence in Cam Ranh Bay. Concern over the bases – the current bases' agreement expires in 1991 – has been aroused by the political instability in the Philippines and led to debate about their indispensability to US naval strategy.

Whilst the Aquino government is pledged to respect the current agreement, it has not guaranteed indefinite retention; nor is it in a position to do so, given the periodic challenges to its rule. Recent developments suggest that the Philippines, citing a US rationale for the bases as a vital element of regional stability, is interested in persuading ASEAN to accept 'shared responsibility' for them.[15] However, apart from Thailand, the rest of ASEAN responded cautiously to this when the Philippino Foreign Secretary, Raul Manglapus aired the idea on a regional tour in November 1987 – even though, along with the PRC, they want the bases retained.

Challenges to the Aquino government aside, the bases' issue has long been a focus for nationalist dissent in the Philippines. Notwithstanding the previous arguments tying the bases to the Marcos dictatorship, opponents maintain that the bases constitute an invitation of threat, rather than insulation from it. Furthermore, the communist New Peoples Army (NPA), which poses a serious alternative to the existing political order, is committed to their withdrawal. It may well be the case that the bases are tied to the success of the Aquino government in serving out its term in office and effecting a peaceful transfer of power to a centrist successor. Any regime composed of the army and/or disaffected Marcos loyalists, is likely to be bedevilled by problems of legitimacy and to hasten a NPA victory. Mrs Aquino's success, it must be noted, requires substantial US support in the economic field, especially in the area of debt rescheduling. The other crucial or indeed *the* crucial ingredient in warding off the NPA challenge is land reform. The risk is that, given the prevailing orthodoxy, US assistance on debt may be curtailed by perceptions of too much progress on land reform. Ultimately, the issue will be settled by a calculation of the value of the bases, set against the prevailing political climate in the Philippines.[16]

There are those who contend that the bases are important but *not* indispensable to the US and could be relinquished. Incurring disaffection in the Philippines, it is averred, is an unacceptable political price to pay for them, in addition to the economic one demanded in rent by Manila. To these might be added the clauses in the new Philippino constitution containing strictures about nuclear weapons. The counter-argument is that a naval presence in the region is a necessity in the present strategic climate and that the current costs, just in excess of $1 billion spread over five years, compare favourably with the sum and time estimated for relocation – $3–4 billion and ten years respectively.[17] In addition, it is maintained that relocation to the possible alternatives in Palau, Guam and/or Tinian, would situate US forces at a greater distance from the Persian Gulf and require further deployments to preserve existing strength.

Consequently, it can be assumed that even if the Clark Field and Subic Bay bases were withdrawn, the direct strategy at sea would remain intact, despite expensive modifications. In this respect, the availability of options, and the determination of the US to maintain a regional naval presence, will mitigate the ill-effects of their removal. Crisis-avoidance considerations are pertinent, however, if the NPA were to attain power and transfer the bases to the Soviet Union. Whilst this cannot be ruled out, it is worth noting that one of the principal strengths of the NPA is that it does not rely on external sponsorship. Furthermore, the arrangements governing the bases rule out their direct use in the internal affairs of the host country. This consideration could militate against direct US intervention to forestall such an eventuality, and the desire not to repeat the Vietnam experience may result in a similar outcome, despite the 1951 US–Philippines security treaty. Alternatively, if these projections are over-turned and the US were to intervene to prevent a NPA victory, crisis avoidance between the two superpowers will depend on Soviet self-restraint and prudence – in effect a realisation by Moscow that even if the facilities at Cam Ranh Bay were conducive to a show of strength, its interests would be better served by allowing the US to become embroiled in another 'Vietnam'.

It can be assumed, therefore, that the current strategic balance in the region, effected in the main by past US intervention, has marked out for Washington a definite stake in the structure of regional security. Crisis avoidance, from Washington's point of view, depends on Soviet acceptance of this stake and the US ability to defend it without giving the impression of seeking to enlarge it.

The Soviet Union

Parallelling the US, current Soviet interest in Southeast Asia is the advancement of influence under the guise of containing its superpower rival. This can be broadly characterised as the Soviet objective of establishing itself as an 'Asia–Pacific' power – a characterisation which takes account of the economic inducements to ASEAN and Japan, outlined by Secretary Gorbachev in his speech on Asian security issues at Vladivostok in July 1986.[18] Like Washington, Moscow, too, has to contend with Beijing – a contest which has, at times, compared in its intensity with the earlier US–PRC enmity that compromised regional security for two decades. Both superpowers have a 'China card' to play, the availability and value of which they do not control.

For Moscow, the calculation is whether the prospects of better relations with the PRC and, possibly, ASEAN, at the expense of Vietnam, offset the gains presently obtained through its underwriting of Vietnamese regional policy. The optimum solution for Moscow, as underscored in the Vladivostok Initiative, would be to unite the Asian communist parties and demonstrate their benign intent to ASEAN, as a precursor to the acceptance of the Soviet Union as an 'Asia–Pacific Power'.[19] This could then lead, as mooted in the speech, to economic cooperation with Japan and ASEAN, and eventually to a Helsinki-type conference for Asia at Hiroshima – the revamped version, skeptics maintain, of the earlier collective security proposal. However, that Moscow may yet have to make a choice between sponsorship of Vietnamese regional ambitions and closer ties with Japan and ASEAN, as Deng's remarks indicate, attests to an irony – the advantages secured in 1978, through Vietnam joining the Council for Mutual Economic Assistance (CMEA), the friendship treaty and the acquisition of bases at Cam Ranh Bay and Da Nang soon after, amounted to an unprecented Soviet presence in Southeast Asia and, in turn, has shown up the limits of Soviet influence.

The Soviet Union and Vietnam

The Soviet–Vietnamese relationship has contained divergences of interest. It has developed in a manner which has inculcated a belief in fiercely independent Hanoi that extra-regional and inter-communist rivalry has so far been more conducive to its interests than cooperation. However, the importance attached to Kampuchea has isolated Vietnam and by breeding over-reliance, tantamount to dependence, on the Soviet Union for survival, runs the risk of compromising its independence as well.

The radically different interpretation given by Hanoi to the consequences of its obsession with Kampuchea is questioned by estimates of Soviet assistance varying from $1 million to $3.6 million a day.[20] It is also worth noting that, whilst Vietnam has entered into a security treaty with the Soviet Union in the Third Indochina War, it did not seek to do so in the Second, for national liberation. Consequently, as dependence has deepened, Hanoi has become more susceptible to Soviet pressure.

This, in the main, has been applied to economic reform, and the new leadership in Hanoi appears to be receptive to Gorbachev's admonishments on this score. Moscow's use of leverage on the Kampuchean issue can be detected, as well, in developments following the Vladivostok speech, although its public position has always been that its leverage is limited. The Heng Samrin regime has been encouraged to sponsor broad popular front proposals, similar to those mooted by Najibullah in Afghanistan. However, as Gorbachev acknowledged in the Vladivostok speech, with reference to Kampuchea, 'Much here, as in other problems in Southeast Asia, depends on normalisation of Chinese–Vietnamese relations.'[21]

The Soviets presumably hope that Beijing's commitment to the restoration of the *status quo antebellum*, or some approximation thereof, can be reversed, along with Hanoi's insistence on its gain through *force majeure*. In this respect, Soviet goals will have to be pursued according to a Chinese timetable, its leverage on Vietnam, though potentially considerable, being in practice constrained by the absence of other sources of influence in the region. Yet, Vietnam as a point of entry for Soviet influence in Southeast Asia may turn out to be a cul de sac.

The principal military advantage accruing to the Soviet Union from its relationship with Hanoi are the bases at Cam Ranh Bay and Da Nang. More comprehensive than Moscow's military facilities elsewhere in the developing world, they constitute the largest installations of their kind outside the Warsaw Pact and facilitate unprecedented displays of Soviet military power in the region by the Soviet Pacific Fleet. In April 1984, for example, Soviet marines were employed for the first time in exercises outside Soviet coastal waters. These manoeuvres, along the Vietnamese coast, involved the *Ivan Rogov* (the largest Soviet craft for amphibious assault capability) and the aircraft carrier *Minsk*.[22] This followed other seminal expressions of Soviet power in 1981 and 1982, when its anti-carrier warfare capability was demonstrated in Southeast Asian and northern Pacific waters.[23] As alarming to Western and ASEAN observers is the construction of a communications and electronic surveillance station in Vietnam to monitor PRC and US military activity and liaise with fleet headquarters at Vladivostok. According to the Far Eastern Economic Review (FEER), Soviet reconnaissance aircraft and electronic eavesdropping ships based in Vietnam entered the Gulf of Thailand to observe the summer 1984 US–Thai Cobra Gold military exercise. The 1984 manoeuvres were most probably related to a show of deterrent strength aimed at the PRC, in case the latter had decided on a second punitive strike against Vietnam. Reports indicate that when the 1984–5 Vietnamese dry-season offensive against the Kampuchean resistance did not occasion such a response, the Soviets halted their build-up at these bases.[24]

Nevertheless, because of deficiencies in the quality of these forces, the naval balance in the region is reported to favour the United States. Apprehensions that have been voiced over a Soviet wartime capability to obstruct the US Seventh Fleet's access to the Indian Ocean through the Malacca Straits may be unduly alarmist. This suggests that Soviet policy, shortcomings in military capability apart, is intent upon maritime peace in the area.[25] Its naval presence serves the function of protecting the Soviet commercial fleet and augmenting Moscow's stake in regional security. It does not, however, correspond with ASEAN's notion of the latter, as adumbrated in the ZOPFAN proposal, and could prove to be a liability in the long-term enhancement of Soviet influence. At present, though, it is not an impediment as such, to a Kampuchean settlement or Sino–Soviet *détente*. In 1985, Deng was reported to have presented Moscow with a *quid pro quo* – the PRC would overlook the bases if the Soviet Union prevailed upon Vietnam to withdraw from Kampuchea.[26]

Consequently, it would appear that the Soviet Union has not made the calculation outlined above, but premised its policy on the ability to manoeuvre around it. Rather than risk its alliance with Hanoi by exposing the divergence of interests between them on Kampuchea, Moscow proceeds on the assumption that the Vietnamese *fait accompli* there could eventually be accepted by the regional states – with minor modifications. Also incorporated in this is the possibility of the whole Kampuchean issue becoming less important. The announcement by Vietnam, in May 1988, that 50,000 troops would be withdrawn from Kampuchea and that the remaining troops would be placed under Kampuchean military control may support this possibility. Alternatively, although the existing evidence suggests otherwise, the Soviet Union may be confident in its ability to posit its economic cooperation and military security goals in Asia as the necessary preconditions for the solution of the Kampuchean conflict – in short, a reversal of the priorities favoured by the PRC and ASEAN. Either way, Moscow's policy is hampered by the prevailing perception of the Soviet Union as a revisionist power, overly reliant on military might to realise its goals. Having to labour against this enduring cold war strait-jacket, the Soviet Union has not been able to establish benign intent in the region. Its source of leverage – military power – is not particularly persuasive in this respect unless it is reduced. As the Vladivostok speech indicates, all that the Soviet Union has to offer in order to further its goals in Southeast Asia is reductions in military strength, depreciation of its asset, being the only Soviet currency with any credibility in the region.

Thus, whilst both superpowers rely on low-level tension to sustain their influence, the Soviet Union is doubly disadvantaged in not possessing the economic power of the US. In Southeast Asia it wants to play upon the North–South divide but is forced into playing within the East–West one for the same end. What seems assured is that Moscow cannot replace Washington's influence or exclude it in the near future, unless indigenous political change in Southeast Asia, or a considerable enhancement of Soviet economic power, militates otherwise, as Gorbachev realises.

Crisis avoidance, from Moscow's standpoint, relates more to the intensity of the Sino–Vietnamese conflict, which could test its treaty commitment to Hanoi, than it does to superpower relations in the region. Relaxation in Sino–Soviet tensions, and of both the Vietnamese and PRC positions on Kampuchea, of late, are propitious in this respect. Deterrent demonstrations of military power and respect for tacit 'spheres of influence', remain the instruments of crisis avoidance for the Soviet Union. They have been forged by the past pattern of conflict and consolidated by its continuation in the present.

CONCLUSION

This chapter has argued that the prospects for crisis avoidance in Southeast Asia crisis being interpreted as direct superpower military confrontation – are good. This is a continuation of the previous pattern of interaction, which produced a tacit acknowledgement of 'spheres of influence' in the region and allows for the possibility of a limited intervention on the part of either superpower in fulfilment of a treaty obligation. Whilst conflict has been ruled out, competition has replaced it.

As outlined earlier, as Washington is the repository of greater influence in the region, this is a formulation of the structure of regional security, which Moscow, at the very least, will insist upon. The Vladivostok speech must be seen in this light. The Soviet Union wants to be recognised as a legitimate and responsible power in the region, whose contribution to security is as non-provocative as it is necessary. A Helsinki-type conference for Asia will not in itself confirm this status, but constitute a necessary condition for it. However, the US, with its entrenched military and economic stake in the structure of regional security, sees no reason to make explicit, in institutionalised form, the existing conventions of superpower interaction. Consequently, superpower interests are facilitated by containment through experience, conventions of conduct that have been established by default and conflict to enable competition. The trend in the future seems to be a continuation of a low level of tension within broadly manageable bounds. It is not a recipe to be recommended in other parts of the developing world and, as noted at the outset, can be discredited by the dynamics of nation and state building. One cannot but conclude, as a consequence, that the surest recipe for superpower crisis avoidance, is a self-conscious policy of non-intervention in issues they, more often than not, prove either unwilling or unable to comprehend.

NOTES

1 Cited in Christopher Thorne, *Allies of a Kind* (Oxford: Oxford University Press, 1978), p. 464, from State Department file DS 851–G–01/9–844.
2 See in particular, Robert M. Blum, *Drawing the Line: The Origin of the American Containment Policy in East Asia* (New York, London: W. W. Norton and Company, 1982), and Michael Shaller, *The American Occupation of Japan: The Origins of the Cold War in Asia,* (Oxford: Oxford University Press, 1985), for an extended treatment of US policy in Southeast Asia at this time.
3 See in particular, Franklin B. Weinstein, *Vietnam's Unheld Elections* (Data Paper No 60, Southeast Asia Program, Dept of Asian Studies, Cornell University, Ithaca, NY, July 1966).
4 See Robert Litwak, *Detente and the Nixon Doctrine* (Cambridge: Cambridge University Press, 1984), for an extended treatment.
5 Leszek Buszynski, *Soviet Foreign Policy and Southeast Asia* (London: Croom Helm, 1986). The account of this early period of Soviet policy is taken from this source.
6 'US Policy in Asia: Changing Perspectives'. Address to the Western Governors' Conference in Honolulu, 16 June 1978. Cited in Michael Leifer, 'Conflict and Regional Order in Southeast Asia', *Adelphi Paper* 162 (London: International Institute for Strategic Studies), p. 17.
7 *Singapore Bulletin,* August 1979, quoted in Leifer 'Conflict and Regional Order in Southeast Asia', p. 16.
8 See Ji Guoxing, 'Current Security Issues in Southeast Asia', *Asian Survey* 26, 9 (September 1986).
9 Leifer, Conflict and Regional Order in Southeast Asia. pp. 13–16.
10 See Sheldon W. Simon, 'The Great Powers and Southeast Asia: Cautious Minuet or Dangerous Tango?', *Asian Survey,* 25, 9 (September 1985), pp. 923–5.
11 *Keesings Contemporary Archives,* 32, 6 (June 1986).
12 *Washington Post,* 8 July 1986.
13 This assessment is based on author interviews with State Dept and Pentagon officials in summer 1986.
14 *Far Eastern Economic Review* (FEER), 14 August 1986, p. 40.
15 *FEER,* 19 November 1987, pp. 28–9.
16 Observation based on author interviews with State Dept and Pentagon officials, summer 1986.
17 Figure cited in Simon, 'The Great Powers and Southeast Asia' p. 929 from US House of Representatives, Sub-Committee on Asian and Pacific Affairs, *Hearings: United States–Philippine Relations and the New Base and Aid Agreement,* 17, 23 and 28 June 1983. The figure of $1 billion is taken from The *Economist,* 9 November 1985.
18 See *FEER,* 14 August 1986, for a full report of this speech, also known as the Vladivostok Asian Initiative.
19 See *FEER,* 13 November 1986 for a 'stocktaking' of the implications of the speech.
20 See Gareth Porter in *Pacific Affairs,* 57, 1 (Spring 1984) for 'Hanoi's Strategic Perspective and the Sino-Vietnamese Conflict', pp. 7–25. See articles by Gerald Segal and Adam Forde in Robert Cassen (ed.) *Soviet Interests in the Third World* (London: Sage Publications, 1985), for the military and economic dimensions of the relationship.
21 *FEER,* 14 August 1986, p. 37.
22 Simon, 'The Great Powers and Southeast Asia', pp. 931–2.
23 *Ibid.,* from May 1983 CINPAC report, cited in F. A. Mediansky and Dianne Court, *The Soviet Union in Southeast Asia,* Canberra Papers on Strategy and Defence No. 29, (The Strategic and Defence Studies Centre, Research School of Pacific Studies, The Australian National University, 1984), p. 25.
24 *FEER,* 18 June 1987, pp. 34–35.
25 See Michael Leifer, 'The Security of the Sea-Lanes in Southeast Asia', in Robert O'Neill (ed.) *Security in East Asia* (International Institute for Strategic Studies, 1984).
26 *FEER,* 12 July 1985.

13   Crisis prevention: patterns and prospects

Roy Allison and Phil Williams

One implication of the analysis of regional trouble spots in preceding chapters is that superpower confrontations in the Third World are unlikely to be frequent in the 1990s. The typology offered by Alexander George, together with the detailed analyses of particular regions, suggests that Soviet–American competition carries considerable risks of confrontation only in those regions where interests are high and symmetrical. The Middle East clearly fits this description; but, in most other regions, Soviet and American interests are low or sufficiently asymmetrical to make it less likely – although certainly not impossible – that their rivalry will result in a direct confrontation.

Such a conclusion, however, should not lead to complacency for several reasons. In the first place, as Alexander George's chapter emphasises, superpower interests are not static. In areas where there is even a low degree of competitive engagement, there is considerable potential for both sides to raise the stakes. The danger is that each superpower will define its interests not in terms of the intrinsic importance of the region but in terms of the degree of involvement by the adversary – with the result that even areas of low importance can very rapidly take on much greater significance.

The second reason for caution is that Soviet–American crises in the 1990s may occur not because of intent or a deliberate challenge by one superpower to the other, but through inadvertence or the actions of states over which Moscow and Washington have only incomplete control. A theme running through all the chapters on regional competition is that Moscow and Washington are not in full control of their Third World clients. Consequently, the superpowers could, on occasion, find themselves locked on a collision course even though neither is actively seeking a direct military confrontation.

In past crises, the superpowers have displayed considerable skill and ingenuity in managing dangers and resolving differences. The Middle East Crisis of October 1973 was handled particularly well and never became as serious as the

246

Cuban Missile Crisis of 1962. Neither side tried to achieve a *fait accompli*, the crisis was relatively brief, and there was considerable flexibility in the American response to Soviet concerns. It is possible to argue that this was partly because it was the first crisis which had taken place in the era of nuclear parity, and that the United States had consequently become more cautious. Yet this is not entirely persuasive. As Richard Betts has argued, parity existed in the minds of American policy-makers even in the 1950s, and the advent of numerical parity in the 1970s did not bring about a major shift in American thinking about nuclear war.[1] It seems more plausible, therefore, to suggest that the management of the Middle East Crisis revealed that there has been a learning curve in the Soviet and American handling of direct confrontations. For all this, the events which led to the brief confrontation also revealed some of the more disturbing features of the kind of superpower crises in the Third World which could recur in the 1990s, and suggested that there are several aspects of such crises which could make them rather more intractable than might be expected.

One of the most important features of the Berlin Crises of 1948 and 1961, and the Cuban Missile Crisis of 1962 was their relatively simple structures. The bipolar confrontation, and the effective exclusion, for most purposes, of secondary actors, greatly simplified matters. This is not to deny that, on occasion, the actions of superpower clients could greatly complicate matters. In the Cuban Missile Crisis, for example, the Cuban shooting down of a U-2 plane almost provoked a United States air-strike against the SAM sites. The 1973 Crisis, however, was one in which the actions of the secondary actors were much more significant – and, in this respect, was far more typical of the kind of situation that seems likely to arise in the Third World in the future. Shoemaker and Spanier have encapsulated the complexity of such crises in the term 'bipolycentric crises'.[2] The management of these crises depends not only on the superpowers themselves behaving with restraint but also on their ability to impose restraints on allies and clients who have very different objectives and may be so preoccupied with the prospect of immediate gains that they are oblivious to the wider consequences of their actions.

The second, and closely related, difference between bipolar crises and bipolycentric crises is that the former were generally initiated as a result of deliberate decisions by one or both superpowers, whereas the latter are more likely to be precipitated by the actions of client states. If one of the superpowers is directly responsible for initiating a crisis, then it also retains the opportunity for a strategic withdrawal to allow a peaceful resolution. If the crisis has arisen primarily from the actions of others, ironically, the option of withdrawal or backing down may be less easy, and both Washington and Moscow may find that they are entangled to a much greater extent than they wish. An added complication is that although neither superpower is responsible for the actions of his ally he will be held accountable by the adversary, who will frame his own responses accordingly.

A third possible difference between bilateral crises and bipolycentric crises is that the former tended to be highly asymmetrical, whereas the stakes in the latter are rather more dynamic and uncertain. In bipolar crises the balance of interests clearly favoured one side or the other and this helped to determine the outcome. In the Cuban Missile Crisis, for example, American security interests were at stake in a way that the Soviet Union's were not. In the Berlin Crisis in 1961, the balance worked the other way and the United States did not challenge the erection of the Berlin Wall, although it vigorously reaffirmed its commitment to West Berlin itself. The danger with superpower confrontations in the Third World is that the balance of interests may be less obvious and more symmetrical and, even in circumstances where the initial stakes were very low, the superpowers may rapidly conclude that vital interests are at stake. The fluidity which makes the Third World an attractive arena for competition also makes it highly dangerous. The potential for miscalculation and misunderstanding about the limits of tolerable behaviour is very considerable.

The other possibility is that the superpowers will find themselves in a crisis in a region such as the Middle East where they both have a great deal at stake and where there are no asymmetries to structure the crisis in a way which makes it possible to settle very quickly on a peaceful solution. In this event the crisis would approximate closely to the models of the chicken game so beloved of strategic analysts and there would be an unprecedented premium on will, nerve and resolve, and on highly coercive bargaining tactics. It is not inconceivable that under the stress of a major crisis in which there are few structural guidelines both superpowers could commit themselves to such an extent that they deem withdrawal to be unacceptable.

Such an assessment clearly has elements of worst-case thinking and may exaggerate the dangers attendant upon bipolycentric crises. It may be that superpower confrontations in the Third World in the 1990s will prove more manageable and less dangerous than those which occurred between Washington and Moscow from the late 1940s to the early 1960s. Nevertheless, there are sufficient imponderables and uncertainties to give a worst-case analysis a degree of credibility, and to support the contention of Shoemaker and Spanier that the management of 'polycentric crises by the superpowers will be significantly more difficult than resolving bipolar crisis'.[3] Whereas past crises had both a simplicity and a relative transparency which made them manageable, future confrontations between the superpowers in the Third World could prove to be much more complicated. The relationships involved are likely to be 'greater in number and more complex: local state to local state, local state to each superpower, and patron to patron'.[4] Consequently, 'the number of opportunities for misperceptions, miscalculations and miscommunications' will rise accordingly.[5]

Such dangers are unlikely to compel the superpowers to remain aloof from regional conflicts in the Third World or to abandon their competition for geopolitical influence. Because this competition is potentially so dangerous, however, and direct confrontations so difficult to manage, the superpowers will want to take steps to ensure that crisis prevention remains as effective as possible.

In the past, there have been two major approaches to crisis prevention in the Third World – the development of tacit 'norms of competition' and the attempt, in the 1970s, to establish a more formal crisis-prevention regime. The strengths and weaknesses of these two broad approaches can now be considered. In view of the suggestions made in previous chapters for improving crisis prevention in particular regions, it is also necessary to consider the prospects for additional measures to prevent local conflicts developing into superpower crises.

TACIT NORMS OF COMPETITION

In some respects, the most important mode of crisis avoidance are the codes of conduct which have helped to contain Soviet and American tendencies towards confrontation for much of the post-war period. The Soviet–American competition for power and influence in the Third World is not entirely unregulated. Zbigniew Brzezinski, for example, has acknowledged that Soviet–American rivalry is mitigated by certain 'rudimentary rules of restraint' which provide 'a code of reciprocal behaviour guiding the competition, lessening the danger that it could become lethal'.[6]

Kenneth Waltz has indirectly challenged this interpretation of superpower competition, with his contention (developed in relation to the balance of power) that there is a crucial difference between identifying patterns of behaviour and imputing rules of behaviour. In his view it is crucial not to 'assume a necessary correspondence of motive and result and to infer rules for the actors from the results of their behaviour'.[7] One implication of this view is that constraint and restraint should not be confused with each other. What might appear to be restraint may reflect simply a lack of capability to undertake certain actions rather than a conscious decision to refrain from these actions because they are contrary to tacit understandings or codes of conduct. Furthermore, it is contended 'an orderliness abstracted from behaviour cannot guide behaviour'.[8] The problem with this argument, however, is that it ignores the role of precedent and downplays the likelihood that governments will so value the 'orderliness' that they will take conscious steps to maintain it. In short, although Waltz's objections are an important caution against reading too much into particular patterns of behaviour, they do not exclude the possibility of rules of behaviour.

This is especially the case in superpower relations 'which have provided ample scope for tacit regulation. Poised between bitter worldwide rivalry and the exigencies of at least minimal coexistence in the thermonuclear age, the Soviet Union and the United States have had extensive recourse to tacit rules of accommodation covering, first, regional involvement . . . and, second, the restraint of competition should regional curbs prove ineffective.'[9] These rules, or codes of behaviour, depend on three characteristics which differentiate them from patterns of behaviour – a degree of consciousness about the kinds of actions that are prohibited, an expectation of reciprocity in observing certain kinds of restraint, and a recognition that maintenance of this kind of restraint is, on balance, in the interests of the state, even though, in certain circumstances, it might work in favour of the adversary.

Such rules, of course, do not emerge fully fledged, but stem from practice and precedent. In this connection, Alexander George has argued very persuasively that 'norms of competition', whether of a tacit or verbalised character, 'can emerge during the course of superpower competition or reflect patterns of restraint that have emerged through past experience which the two sides find it useful to observe in new situations which arise'.[10] In other words, the 'norms of competition' develop through an evolutionary approach which codifies existing practice and builds incrementally upon it. The norms are not legal or quasi-legal, but are 'analogous to a "common law" which develops through experience and offers useful precedents or benchmarks'.[11] They are rules of prudence rather than of law or morality. Furthermore, they are rules which do not always work to the advantage of Third World states, which have different priorities, vulnerabilities and concerns. Nevertheless, their significance is difficult to over-estimate, as they provide a degree of predictability to what would otherwise be an even more uncertain and dangerous relationship.

The first rule of superpower behaviour is respect for each other's sphere of influence. This rule has an asymmetric quality in relation to geopolitical rivalry in that there exists no Soviet counterpart in the Third World itself to the American sphere of influence in Latin America, although Eastern Europe is clearly a Soviet sphere of influence. Nevertheless, it can be argued that Soviet leaders think in terms of an extended Soviet national security zone, which includes at least Afghanistan – although the decision to withdraw Soviet forces from this country makes such an assessment rather more problematic. Whatever the case, it is clear that the prospects for greater reliance on tacit agreements on spheres of influence elsewhere are not good. Much of the developing world is not clearly under the preponderant influence of either Moscow or Washington – and is anxious to retain its independence. A large and perhaps increasing number of countries will remain in such 'grey areas' where non-aligned nationalist impulses are strong. Even so, the United States can intervene directly in its sphere of influence without expecting more than verbal condemnation from the Soviet Union. Furthermore, as Raymond Cohen has pointed out, such condemnations are balanced by the acknowledgement that active counter-intervention by Moscow is out of the question.[12]

This is not to suggest that there is a complete abstinence by Moscow from involvement in America's sphere of influence. The Soviet–Cuban relationship complicates the situation and has encouraged American sensitivities about Soviet inroads into the Western hemisphere. Furthermore, there have been some Cuban and Soviet arms supplies to Nicaragua since the Sandinista revolution. Yet not too much should be made of this, as Moscow has been extremely circumspect in its relations with the Ortega government and has refused to undertake any extensive commitment to Nicaragua. If the norm of non-involvement (or at most low-intensity involvement) in the adversary's sphere of influence has been weakened, therefore, it has certainly not been subject to any fundamental challenge since the open defection of Cuba to the Soviet camp in the early 1960s.

The second rule of superpower competition is, in a sense, an extension of the first, and can be described as one of asymmetrical intervention outside the spheres of influence. If one side becomes militarily involved in a regional conflict, then the adversary tends to remain on the sidelines. This is fairly easy where there exists a clear asymmetry of interest, but is rather more problematic when there is greater equivalence. Problems can also arise, because the stakes are not always clear at the outset. Consequently a certain amount of superpower interaction in a regional conflict can be understood as a process of mutual clarification in an attempt to avoid deepening misunderstanding and compound miscalculation. Indeed, there has to be some working out of the rule as the situation evolves. By and large, however, if one side or the other intervenes directly then that is a signal to the adversary to stay out of the conflict. The American interventions in Korea and Vietnam, for example, were followed by Soviet inaction at least in terms of a direct response. It is true that massive arms supplies were delivered to North Vietnam and the Vietcong. Nevertheless, Moscow was scrupulous to avoid any action which would have challenged the United States directly and thereby precipitated a direct confrontation.

More recently, the Soviet Union took considerable pains to distance itself from US–Libyan conflict in 1986. During the skirmishes in March 1986, a Soviet Foreign Ministry spokesman made very clear that the Soviet Union had no intention of becoming involved. As he stated, 'we were not monitoring the situation, and were not taking part in the conflict in any way. The important thing now is to normalise the situation'.[13] Nor was the Soviet response very different some weeks later when the United States attacked Tripoli and Benghazi. Not only did the Soviet Union fail to offer anything more than a rhetorical denunciation of the United States, but it removed its personnel and ships from the area in response to American warnings of impending military action. Although Libya was an important regional client of the Soviet Union, it was not one which Moscow valued sufficiently to take the risk of confrontation inherent in any attempt to prevent the American attack. The United States presented its action as a retaliatory strike rather than an intervention. Nevertheless, the episode demonstrated the flexibility with which the super-powers are able to adapt or extend the basic tenets for crisis avoidance.

The converse of such unilateral American action, accompanied by Soviet acceptance of the situation, occurred in Afghanistan. Although substantial arms supplies were funnelled to the Afghans through Pakistan, which played a significant role in strengthening the resistance and thereby encouraging the Soviet decision to withdraw its forces, the United States consistently refrained from action likely to lead to a direct superpower clash. Indeed, even the initial American response in December 1979 and January 1980 was extremely circumspect. Although there was considerable outrage and much rhetoric on the part of the Carter Administration, the punitive sanctions that were imposed carried little risk. Diplomatic confrontation and denunciation were permissible, but the United States was not prepared to take action likely to provoke a military confrontation over a country which had effectively fallen under Soviet influence as a result of the 1978 *coup*.

Although this *coup* resulted from internal disaffection and was not engineered by the Soviet Union, Moscow had taken advantage of it to consolidate its relationship with Afghanistan. In contrast, the United States, during the period preceding the Soviet invasion of December 1979, followed a largely uncoordi-nated policy. On the one hand Washington issued a series of warnings to Moscow that it was seriously concerned about external intervention in Afghanistan. On the other, after the kidnapping and death of the American Ambassador in Kabul, the United States cut back sharply on economic aid, ended its small military training programme and withdrew the Peace Corps.[14] It was clear to Soviet leaders that the United States had no vital interests in Afghanistan, whereas in Moscow the growing turmoil on the border was seen as a direct and immediate threat to Soviet security interests. In these circumstances, American messages designed to deter Soviet intervention were irrelevant, if not meaningless. The Soviet Union understood this and, ultimately, so did the United States. When President Carter, in the aftermath of the invasion, sent a message to Brezhnev over the hot line suggesting that the invasion was 'a clear threat to the peace' this was clearly an exaggeration. In spite of the denunciations, the United States was prepared to acquiesce in the Soviet move.

When set against the previous Soviet acceptance of American interventions in areas which were not formally acknowledged as being clearly within the accepted spheres of influence, the Afghanistan experience suggests that where one side uses force and intervenes on a large scale it creates a temporary security zone which effectively prohibits the direct intervention of the other superpower. The very use of force is a good indication of just how vital the interests are, and places the onus for provoking a direct confrontation on the adversary.

In the aftermath of the Soviet invasion there was no chance of the United States responding militarily. At this stage Carter was already more concerned with forestalling any further move towards the Gulf than with Afghanistan. Indeed, the promulgation of the Carter Doctrine was designed to communicate to the Soviet Union that although the move against Afghanistan was tolerable, a similar move against Iran and into the Gulf was not, and would lead to a direct confrontation. This message was buttressed by the renewed emphasis placed by Washington on the ability to intervene rapidly in Southwest Asia. Yet the situation which has developed over Iran may well provide another form of crisis avoidance – what may be described as a mutual no-go area. If a particular country or region is disputed or of major importance to both the superpowers then the incentives for at least a tacit agreement on mutual non-intervention are very considerable. Something along these lines may well be in operation in relation to Iran, although it has not yet been put to the test. The real challenge would come in the event that Iran began to disintegrate, especially if one or other of the factions appealed for external support and intervention. Even without such appeals, major internal unrest would arouse anxieties in Moscow, given the common border with Iran, and might encourage the idea of some form of direct intervention in that country, despite the recent Soviet acknowledgement that intervention in Afghanistan was a political mistake. The United States might also feel compelled to act in order to forestall a Soviet invasion. The safest alternative to pre-emptive intervention, therefore, is either tacit or explicit agreement on a mutual non-intervention policy. Iran has to be acknowledged as a no-go area for both superpowers. This would endow it with a somewhat similar status and function as buffer states were given in the nineteenth century. Although such an arrangement demands considerable restraint and understanding, the fact that Iran acts as a buffer in both directions means that there would be a rough equality of sacrifice. This could well make it acceptable to both superpowers.

In the event that such an agreement has not been reached or cannot be sustained – and the analysis by Chubin casts some doubt upon the argument – the superpowers might still be able to avoid direct confrontation, simply through clarifying their intentions in a way which reinforces mutual deterrence. Even if

Iran is not accepted by either side as no-go area, therefore, neither superpower would be prepared to take the risks of going to war with the other. The problem with such an approach, as opposed to a tacit agreement on mutual noninvolvement, is that it would require considerable improvisation and clear communication of intent at a time when tensions would be running high, and when the possibilities of miscalculation would be significant. It would lie at that juncture of activity where crisis avoidance and crisis management phase into each other.

This is not surprising. The distinction between crisis avoidance and crisis management is not always very clear. Some activities which come under the heading of crisis management are essentially designed to avoid a more direct and dangerous confrontation between the superpowers, and could, therefore, be understood as coming within the present analysis. This is particularly important in relation to communication. Both superpowers accept the need in periods of regional conflict and local turbulence to maintain channels of communication and to clarify both intentions and actions. Direct communication has been used for clarification and for reassurance – most obviously during the Six Day War when, in the aftermath of the attack on the Liberty, the hot line was used to reassure Moscow about the movements of the Sixth Fleet. Consequently, it can be understood as a procedural norm which is crucial to effective crisis avoidance. By making clear in advance its intentions to initiate military action against Libya in 1986, for example, Washington effectively gave Moscow an opportunity to distance itself from Libya and ensure that Soviet personnel did not become victims of the American attack. In other words, the communication process is crucial to avoiding inadvertent crises.

These rules of the game are in many respects rather primitive. Nevertheless, they function with reasonable effectiveness and enable the superpowers to keep the risks of direct confrontation low and controllable. They are far from being absolute and neither superpower is wholly averse to a certain amount of rule bending or rule breaking when it believes that it can do this with impunity. There are also several developments which, paradoxically, challenge or subvert the general rules at one level but acknowledge the importance of crisis avoidance at another. Perhaps the most important of these is the use of proxies.

Both superpowers have developed proxy relationships which involve varying degrees of coordination between the superpower and Third World parties. Cuban involvement in the Third World, in particular, has been more extensive, overt and systematic than the policy of any equivalent state closely linked to the United States. Furthermore, Cuban support for Nicaragua, and its ideological commitment to revolution in Central America, arouse considerable consternation in the United States. Cuban foreign policy is governed to an appreciable extent by independent, radical and internationalist goals, yet Cuban activities are often attributed directly to Moscow's guiding hand, and are therefore regarded as an infringement of the American sphere of influence. At the same time, the fact that Cuban, rather than Soviet, military personnel or advisers are involved means that the risks of a direct superpower clash are reduced. Such proxy activities may challenge spheres of interest, but this is rendered possible precisely because the proxy states themselves command very limited resources. Consequently, although their actions challenge the rule, it is an indirect challenge and at a sufficiently low level to ensure that the validity of the rule itself is not endangered. In a sense, the activities of proxies can be dismissed as little more than diversionary since they are well below the threshold of provocation that would lead to direct superpower confrontation. Much the same can be said about the Reagan Administration's support for insurgencies against Marxist regimes. The support is indirect and, even where significant, is unlikely to provoke Soviet–American confrontation.

If the codes of conduct observed by the superpowers in the Third World are crude and simplistic, this very fact contributes to their effectiveness. Furthermore, because they are rules of prudence, unless there is a marked increase in the risk-taking propensity of one or other of the superpowers it is unlikely that they will be subjected to a frontal assault. There are, however, several other requirements that have to be met if the codes of conduct are to retain their validity as a guide to the behaviour of the superpowers in the Third World.

In order to be effective, rules have to demand sacrifices which are roughly equal. If there are major asymmetries and the principle of equality is seen to be lost then the codes of conduct will be seriously undermined. This does not mean that in every specific instance the rule has to constrain both sides equally. In one set of circumstances they may work to the advantage of the Soviet Union, while under different circumstances they will benefit the United States. The crucial requirement is simply that over the long term and under a variety of conditions, the rules appear to be equitable. Neither side will be overly concerned if a rule works against it in one instance so long as at other times or in other regions the rule works in its favour. Sacrifices are acceptable so long as they are balanced by compensations elsewhere which permit, in the long term, a rough equality of gains and losses.

The second requirement is that both superpowers have to accept the rules and be reasonably clear about the circumstances under which they apply. If extenuating circumstances exist which require deviations or departures from the rules then these too should be understood and acknowledged by both parties. Dangers may arise from either too rigid or too flexible an approach. A lack of flexibility renders the rules themselves vulnerable, since any action which breaches the rule will tend to be regarded as a direct challenge. On the other side, too much flexibility can also be damaging as it would render the rules irrelevant and meaningless. Nevertheless, it should be understood that shifts in relative power in particular regions may occur over time. If they are to retain their relevance the rules need to reflect such changes in the distribution of power rather than simply to ignore them.

The third requirement is that there has to be some penalty for non-compliance. At its most fundamental, each superpower must believe that violations of any significance will lead to a response in kind by the adversary. In other words, the more value each places on having the adversary behave in accordance with a particular kind of restraint, the greater the incentive to observe that rule oneself. Both must recognise that opportunistic behaviour based on 'myopic self interest' and the allure of short-term advantage, will damage the rule and therefore work against the mutual long-term interest in crisis avoidance. At the same time there must be a willingness to respond strongly to major breaches of the rule and to take steps to invoke sanctions against the transgressor. Reciprocity can be negative as well as positive.

The fourth requirement is that the rules be integrated into the broader set of foreign-policy activities, interests and commitments. Codes of conduct cannot exist apart from the underlying structure of power and interests in the superpower relationship. On the contrary, they grow out of and are intended to accentuate, ratify and strengthen the basic structure of interests and priorities of both superpowers. Consequently, both Washington and Moscow must ensure that their pronouncements and actions clarify, strengthen and sustain the rules. Commitments, for example, have to be based on underlying interests rather than made in a way which is not readily understandable or predictable to the adversary.

The fifth requirement is that the application of the rules be discriminate rather than global. In some geographic areas, a particular rule may apply, while in other regions the requirements and the prevailing code of conduct may be rather different. This pragmatic approach is actually far more effective than one based on the promulgation of universal norms which are often too general and lacking in precision. Indeed, a region by region analysis and a case by case assessment has a great deal to recommend it. Much will depend on the value the superpowers attach to their respective interests in the region, the clarity with which these interests are identified and the degree of symmetry between them.

The implication of all this is that the tacit codes of conduct which help to shape and constrain Soviet–American competition in the Third World have been and are likely to remain reasonably effective so long as both superpowers are concerned about the dangers of confrontation. Yet even norms of this kind suffer from certain disabilities. Some of the very characteristics that give them their strength and relevance also impose limits on their effectiveness. The fact that they 'leave players some room for flexibility in strategy and tactics . . . and can be readily adjusted to changing circumstances' is both a source of strength and of weakness.[15] Furthermore, the inevitable ambiguities that continue to exist, the lack of institutionalised procedures for their clarification and application to new situations, and the problems of transferring them from one region to another ensure that these 'norms of competition' cannot be a panacea.[16] Indeed, they can be undermined by a lack of symmetry in the approaches and assessments of the two superpowers. Moscow and Washington, at times, have been badly out of synchronisation in terms of both power and policies. Soviet assertiveness and activism in the 1970s was followed by a reassertion of American power in the 1980s – when the Soviet Union, for a variety of reasons, some unconnected with the American resurgence, sought a more regulated approach. In a fluctuating relationship of this kind the sacrifices and, therefore, the incentives for collaboration on crisis avoidance are rarely equal. The result has been that the more constrained of the two superpowers has tended to emphasise norms or 'codes of conduct' at a time when the adversary – calculating that the chances of being opposed and precipitating a direct confrontation are low – has had fewer incentives to accept them to anything like the same extent. There exists a further psychological dimension to this issue which militates against unilateral superpower restraint. As a Soviet analyst acknowledged pragmatically, 'as experience shows, it is very difficult for one side to show restraint when the other side is inclined to interpret such restraint as weakness which can and should be exploited'.[17]

These weaknesses in the tacit codes of conduct have not stopped them from providing a minimum framework for crisis avoidance. As suggested in the introduction, however, during the period of high *détente* in the early 1970s, the superpowers seemed to attach greater weight to a more formalised approach.

FORMAL CRISIS-PREVENTION REGIMES

During the 1970s the superpowers attempted to create a formal crisis-management regime through the Basic Principles of Relations Agreement signed in 1972 and the 1973 Agreement on the Prevention of Nuclear War. Yet this attempt to apply a contractual approach to international regimes was a dismal failure – and ended up exacerbating superpower relations rather than defusing or mitigating tensions. The problem is similar to that which occasionally surfaces in relation to strategic arms control: the existence of an agreement leads to much closer scrutiny of the adversary's actions and any violation, however minor, is treated as a major challenge both to the regime itself and to one's own interests and security. Paradoxically, this problem becomes all the more serious the more restrictive are the rules of the game. In this connection, the formal crisis-prevention regime of the 1970s was particularly demanding: it attempted to impose a degree of restrictiveness that was excessive. The stringency of the agreements did not allow for the fact that great powers will behave as such and that to expect otherwise is to foster illusions. In the end such illusions can only lead to the rejection of the formal agreements as inadequate. Modest ambitions and limited aims are essential, therefore, if formal rules are to be effective. This is all the more important because of the limited control the superpowers have over their allies.

The experience of the 1970s also revealed that creative ambiguity brings short-term agreement only at the expense of long-term acrimony. The superpowers need to confront their differences of approach openly and work within the limits of these differences. Obscuring or avoiding them in principle simply means that when they come to the fore in practice they have a much more disruptive impact on the relationship.

The allegations of bad faith which were made during the 1970s highlighted very clearly the problems, if not the futility, of establishing one code of conduct with global application. When this is combined with an emphasis on the proscription of certain activities (particularly when enshrined in ambiguous or general language) it invites violation. It is almost certainly far better to adopt a regional rather than global orientation which acknowledges that the prospects for superpower confrontation are far greater in some areas than others and focuses attention on these areas. A differentiated approach which takes account of regional variations as well as the sensitivities and concerns of the local actors themselves is likely to prove more sustainable than an indiscriminate global approach. Indeed, the chapters in this volume highlight the importance of regional dynamics and the need to take account of differences from one region to the next.

A suggestion for such an approach was made in 1982 by the US Committee on East–West Accord. This proposal called for the superpowers to negotiate 'a precise set of ground rules having to do with specific geography and a specific ban on direct or indirect use of combat forces in those areas'. It also suggested that the prohibition against the introduction of Soviet and American combat forces into specified regions be extended to include a ban on 'covert, paramilitary, or, so-called 'volunteer' combat forces'.[18] The difficulty with such a proposal, of course, is that it would not prohibit the transfer of weapons or the despatch of military advisers to the regions concerned. Furthermore, the threat of military intervention is one that the superpowers will be reluctant to renounce completely, despite their increased sensitivity to the possible costs of inter-vention even when the adversary remains aloof from the conflict.

Against this, Randall Forsberg has argued very forcefully that the super-powers should agree on a non-intervention regime in the Third World. The basic rationale for this is that the geopolitical competition between the superpowers does much to fuel the arms race, as both sides regard strategic advantage as a crucial asset if they become involved in regional confrontation. It is virtually impossible, therefore, to control the arms race without also doing something about Soviet–American competition in the Third World. Furthermore, with both superpowers having learned from experience that military interventions in the Third World are usually costly and sometimes futile, the creation of such a regime, it is argued, would formalise a growing trend towards non-intervention. The emphasis in Forsberg's proposal is on large-scale interventions such as Korea, Vietnam and Afghanistan. Yet, in a sense, such interventions do not pose a significant challenge to superpower efforts to prevent crises. As suggested above the norm of asymmetrical intervention ensures that direct military involvement by one side is accompanied by non-involvement on the part of the adversary. Alternatively, with countries like Iran, where both superpowers feel that they have vital interests at stake, there is a tacit acceptance that neither side can intervene without provoking a direct confrontation with the adversary – and that the country has become a mutual no-go zone. The tacit norm is given added potency by the deterrent effect that stems from the likelihood of counter-intervention. To the extent that this is effective, then the crisis-prevention rationale for a formal non-intervention regime is not compelling.

Forsberg also argues, however, that such a regime should ban 'all large scale foreign military presence, peacetime as well as wartime, noncombat as well as combat'.[19] The difficulty with this is that it requires the superpowers to give up positions of advantage in their peace-time competition. In essence, it demands a revolution in military thinking and contingency planning. This is unlikely to take place. Recognition of the difficulties attendant upon military intervention in Third World countries is one thing; relinquishing military facilities that facilitate power projection is another.

Forsberg, of course, is well aware of the difficulties but contends that without some sense of vision, it will be virtually impossible to reduce the existing level of competition. Nevertheless, question marks can be raised not only about the feasibility of such a regime but also about its desirability, at least in terms of crisis prevention. It is far from clear that a formal nonintervention regime would enhance the prospects for superpower crisis prevention in the Third World (although Forsberg herself argues very strongly that the strategic arms race itself is the main potential source of crises between the superpowers). In the present situation, the asymmetries of interest are both permissive and stabilising. They allow unilateral intervention while also helping to ensure that this does not result in the direct involvement of the adversary. With the establishment of a regime,

Roy Allison and Phil Williams

direct intervention by one superpower would be much more of a frontal challenge to the other. In a sense, a regime would nullify and obscure asymmetries of interest and endow any military action by the superpowers with greater significance than it really merits. This is not to suggest that the superpowers can afford to be complacent about the prospects for crisis prevention; it is simply to argue that the problem is not one that is best dealt with through formal agreements or regimes. If formal regimes have serious shortcomings, however, they are obtaining support across the political spectrum. In May 1988 a US–Soviet study group, which included former high-ranking US officials as well as prominent Soviet figures such as Georgi Arbatov, made proposals to end superpower military interventions in regional conflicts.[20]

Such an accord, however, is unlikely to be achieved very rapidly. In the meantime, therefore, it is necessary to consider other ways in which the informal codes of conduct outlined above can be augmented and the superpower capacity for crisis prevention enhanced.

ADDITIONAL CRISIS-PREVENTION MEASURES

Additional crisis-prevention measures are not a panacea. There are no simple solutions in the management of a mixed, complex and often highly ambivalent relationship between the superpowers. Nevertheless, it is clear that one of the deficiencies of the crisis-prevention regime of the 1970s was that it did not contain specific procedural injunctions or any mechanism for monitoring compliance or for airing grievances. These were important omissions. There was – and is – a clear need for procedures designed to facilitate crisis prevention. Although it has not been without its problems, the Standing Consultative Commission, which was set up to oversee the implementation of US–Soviet arms-control agreements, provides a useful model. Indeed, a new emphasis on procedural arrangements could greatly strengthen the existing 'norms of competition'. As Alexander George has pointed out, timely discussion of specific areas in which their interests diverge 'would offer the two superpowers opportunities to work out on a case-by-case basis useful patterns of restraint or agreements (tacit or explicit) tailored to the specific configuration of each area in which their interests clash and threaten to lead to a confrontation that neither desires'.[21] In other words, the procedural element would give the substantive rules both an immediacy and a continuing relevance that they might otherwise lack.

Perhaps the first of these is to formalise and regularise the kind of high-level consultations between American and Soviet officials on regional issues which began in the mid-1980s. In 1984 President Reagan proposed that the superpowers initiate discussions on regional issues at the expert level. As a result, Soviet and American delegations met in Vienna in February 1985 to discuss tensions in the Middle East. Although this meeting did not result in any new proposals for Middle East peace, it had an important symbolic impact and was followed by meetings to discuss Southern African issues and Afghanistan. These specialist meetings were the precursor of higher level discussions. In August 1986 an 'exchange of opinions' took place between A. Adamishin, the Soviet Deputy Minister of Foreign Affairs and Michael Armacost, United States Under Secretary of State, on regional conflicts and on possible ways to solve them peacefully.

These discussions were given considerable impetus by Soviet concerns about increasing tensions in the Persian Gulf. A Soviet commentator, analysing the growing crisis in the Gulf in June 1987, observed that 'during the exchange of views between the USSR and the USA on the problem of regional conflicts the sides were unanimous in their wish not to generate an atmosphere of Soviet–American confrontation in such crisis situations, but to exercise mutual restraint and settle anything that might have serious consequences'.[22] It appeared from this and other, similar, statements that Moscow had become more amenable to tacit or explicit understandings on mutual restraint in relation to regional conflicts. This was also evident in November 1987 when the pre-Summit talks in Geneva included discussions between Soviet Deputy Foreign Minister Yuri Vorontsov and Michael Armacost about the management of regional issues. The discussions, which covered Afghanistan, the Gulf War, the Arab–Israeli conflict, and Central America, lasted much longer than expected. At the Washington Summit in December 1987, the Soviet and American leaders spent more time discussing Afghanistan than any other issue apart from arms control. At the Moscow Summit in May–June 1988 Afghanistan was again prominent on the agenda, as was discussion over possible settlements for Angola and Kampuchea.

The implication of this is that, in the late 1980s, regional issues became a part of the superpower dialogue in a way that they had not been since the early 1970s. The importance of this was reinforced by dialogue at the non–official and semi-official level. In mid-February 1988, for example, the Dartmouth Conference – which had been in existence for several years and which pooled the expertise of Soviet and American academics and political figures – discussed various ways of resolving the conflicts in Afghanistan, southern Africa, and Central America as well as the impact of these regional conflicts on superpower relations.

Such interchanges could very usefully be developed. Private working meetings of the kind initiated during the mid-1980s provide an opportunity for each superpower to explore the adversary's concerns and objectives in ways which reduce the prospects for misunderstanding and miscalculation. Furthermore, regular private discussions between the Soviet and American governments on regional issues can not only help to correct misplaced images of each other but also, and perhaps even more importantly, enable the superpowers to gauge the nature and extent of each other's interests in what may be highly fluid and volatile conditions. The approach is less one of problem solving and more one of identifying potential flashpoints and the kinds of dangers that might be incurred. By their very existence such talks could help reduce these dangers. There is a strong case, therefore, for institutionalising the discussions and ensuring that they are held at regular intervals – perhaps as often as every three months – and at a sufficiently high level to ensure that they are taken seriously. Furthermore, they should be acknowledged as something which would not be derailed by changes of leadership, especially in Washington.

These meetings could be supplemented by the activities of nuclear-risk reduction centres in Washington and Moscow. The idea of such centres was enunciated initially by Senators Jackson, Nunn and Warner – but encountered considerable bureaucratic resistance. The result was that when the superpowers reached agreement in September 1987 on the establishment of such centres, the arrangements were rather more modest than the proponents had initially envisaged. If the responsibilities of the centres seem to be rather limited, however, there is still considerable scope for using the machinery which has been established as a basis for further improving the techniques and mechanisms for crisis prevention. Ideally, the centres would have an early warning function and the staff would play an important role in identifying issues and problems to be discussed either in the regular high-level consultations or, if necessary, in emergency meetings of senior Soviet and American officials.

An encouraging development – which suggests that further progress along these lines might be possible – was an understanding during a meeting between the Soviet and American ministers of defence in March 1988 over the usefulness of holding bilateral consultations 'to discuss questions of military activity and to elaborate principles for, and set up, an appropriate forum for the purpose of preventing incidents between USSR and US armed forces'.[23] Details of the framework of this new military forum were elaborated in July 1988.

These procedural mechanisms are not the only ways in which the prospects for superpower crisis prevention could be enhanced. Another possibility, which has by no means been exhausted, is that of self-regulating 'no-go zones'. Insofar as these have been recognised in the past it is either because the area was of such low value to both superpowers that they were able to ignore it or because – as with Iran – it was sufficiently important to both that neither could intervene without provoking the adversary into a counter-intervention. Yet it may be possible to extend such calculations to areas where the stakes are rather more uncertain.

Particular Third World regions could be either totally excluded from all forms of Soviet and American geopolitical competition or could be partially excluded through demilitarisation and denuclearisation. Nuclear free zones have long been advocated by the Non-Aligned Movement and many of the member states have declared themselves within such zones. It is likely, therefore, that any understandings between Moscow and Washington which prohibit the introduction of nuclear weapons into particular regions would receive the endorsement of many Third World states. The problem, of course, is that advance commitments of this kind are unlikely to be made, especially by the United States, not least because of the difficulties that would arise over monitoring and verification. All this is not to denigrate the idea of 'no-go zones' which, in some ways, would provide a limited and more modest version of the non-intervention regime proposed by Randall Forsberg. The idea is clearly one which merits careful consideration in both Washington and Moscow.

No-go zones would be most effective if accompanied by regional self-regulating mechanisms which would effectively limit both the opportunities and the incentives for superpower intervention. The Organisation for African Unity, the Andean Pact, the Arab League and ASEAN have all sought at times to arbitrate, contain, or defuse regional conflicts. These efforts have not always been supported by the superpowers. In Angola in 1975, for example, Washington was not very enthusiastic about the Alvor Accords and gave little support to OAU efforts to mediate amongst the competing factions. The result was to transform the Angolan civil war into a major geopolitical contest between the superpowers. To the extent that the superpowers have learned from such experiences, then it would make sense for them to support regional peace initiatives and to seek means to enhance the role of regional organisations. At the same time, it would be necessary to avoid giving the impression that such attempts are designed to bolster the position of one superpower at the expense of the other or the position of both superpowers at the expense of the regional states.

Regional bodies could also engage in third-party mediation between the superpowers or their clients. Such efforts would have the advantage that they would not provide unilateral advantage to either Moscow and Washington and would be more acceptable to the regional states themselves than anything which smacked of superpower condominium. Finally, the mediation opportunities which the United Nations can provide should not be ignored by the superpowers, especially in those instances where one (or both) of them seeks a face-saving formula to extricate itself from a regional conflict.

In contrast to these regional arrangements, broader schemes for crisis prevention appear to hold less promise. The exception is the non-proliferation regime, which continues to reflect the common interests of the two superpowers.

In contrast, the transfer of armaments and military technologies is likely to proceed without formal restraint – albeit not in a wholly unregulated manner. In a statement to the United Nations in June 1988, the Soviet foreign minister raised the issue of 'the intensive transfer of weapons into zones of increased confrontation' and called for restrictions on sales and supplies of conventional weapons.[24] It remains true, however, that formal restrictions on arms transfers would be strenuously opposed by domestic lobbies in both the United States and the Soviet Union as well as by many recipients of arms in the Third World. Moreover, the 'Discriminate Deterrence' report, prepared for the US Secretary of Defense and published in January 1988 by the Commission on Integrated Long Term Strategy (an extremely eminent group of former officials and advisers), recommended that greater use be made of military aid to Third World allies and more attention be devoted to developing 'cooperative forces' or proxies to challenge Soviet clients.[25]

Such proposals are the complete antithesis to those that are being developed here. They also highlight the need for a shift in attitudes. Without a profound transformation in thinking about the Third World, especially in Washington, the crisis-prevention measures outlined above are hardly likely to amount to much. Geopolitical competition in the Third World has become habitual for the superpowers: it is perpetuated and intensified by the perceptions, beliefs and calculations of those in power. Successful and sustained crisis prevention, therefore, requires not only improved procedures but also, still more important, a recognition that significant change can occur in the Third World without this necessarily working to the advantage of the adversary superpower. For the 'norms of competition' to be sustained and developed, and for the procedural injunctions to prove effective, they should be accompanied by a willingness not only to desensitise issues and cease imposing an East–West template on regional conflicts or domestic turbulence but also to place less emphasis on credibility. In a sense, there should be a reversion to the kind of approach advocated by US Secretary of State, Cyrus Vance in the late 1970s. Vance had a more differentiated and sophisticated assessment of the limits of geopolitical influence in the Third World than any of his contemporaries and realised that many of the gains made by the Soviet Union in the 1970s were likely to prove as ephemeral as many of those which had been made by the United States in the 1950s and 1960s. To concur with this is not to suggest that regional conflict or Third World turbulence is unimportant to the superpowers or that either can be indifferent to the actions of the other. It is simply to argue that they should not exaggerate the stakes involved. Such exaggeration may lead the superpowers to endow certain courses of action with symbolic importance and to commit themselves to policies which do not serve their underlying interests but may not easily be abandoned. A realistic appreciation of the limits of superpower influence will greatly facilitate the task of crisis prevention in the Third World. At the same time, it is important to recognise that cooperation will remain within limits and that it will accompany rather than supersede continued competition between the superpowers.

Such a conclusion is open to the criticism that it is extremely limited in its vision. Yet it starts from the assumption that there already exist rules of prudence which the superpowers are careful to observe. What is being proposed is that the superpowers take steps to deepen their understanding of these rules and minimise the prospects that they will be breached. Although this does not eliminate superpower competition for power and influence, a regulated competition is preferable to an unregulated one. In a world where crisis management is imperfect, efforts towards crisis prevention are essential.

NOTES

1 See R. Betts, *Nuclear Blackmail and Nuclear Balance* (Washington DC: The Brookings Institution, 1987).
2 C. S. Shoemaker and J. Spanier, *Patron-Client State Relationships* (New York: Praeger, 1984).
3 *Ibid.* p. 7.
4 *Ibid.* p. 8.
5 *Ibid.*
6 Z. Brzezinski, *Game Plan* (Boston, MA: Atlantic Monthly Press, 1986), p. 244.
7 See Kenneth Waltz, *Theory of International Politics* (London: Addison-Wesley, 1979), p. 120.
8 S. F. Nadel, quoted in *Ibid.* p. 121.
9 R. Cohen, *International Politics:. The Rules of the Game* (London: Longman, 1981), p. 55.
10 See Alexander L. George, 'US–Soviet Global Rivalry: Norms of Competition' in *Journal of Peace Research* 23, 3 (1986) pp. 248–62.
11 *Ibid.*
12 Cohen, *International Politics*, p. 56.
13 We are grateful to Nancy Adler for her discussion of the Soviet response in her unpublished paper, 'The USSR's Relations With Libya and Syria Since 1970'.
14 See R. Garthoff, *Detente and Confrontation* (Washington, DC: Brookings, 1985) p. 940.
15 See J. Gowa and N. H. Wessell, *Ground Rules: Soviet and American Involvement in Regional Conflicts* (Philadelphia, PA: Foreign Policy Research Institute, 1982), p. 3.
16 George, 'US–Soviet Global Rivalry: Norms of Competition', p. 249.
17 Trofimenko, 'The Third World and US–Soviet Competition', *Foreign Affairs* (Summer 1981) p. 1037.
18 See George, 'US–Soviet Global Rivalry: Norms of Competition', p. 248.
19 The analysis here draws heavily on R. Forsberg, 'Prospects for a Non-Intervention Regime', paper presented to the Conference on 'The Superpowers and Third World Security' Guernsey, 18–21 March 1987.
20 M. White, 'Joint Study Outlines End to Cold War' The *Guardian* 6 May 1988.
21 A. L. George, 'Toward a Soviet–American Crisis Prevention Regime: History and Prospects'. Chapter prepared in March 1986 for the project on US–Soviet Cooperation in Security Matters.
22 *Izvestiya* 4 June, 1987.
23 Press conference by USSR Minister of Defence, *Pravda*, 18 March 1988.
24 Statement by E. Shevardnadze at the third special session on disarmament of the United Nations General Assembly, *Tass* 8 June 1988, in *BBC Summary of World Broadcasts*, Soviet Union 0174 A1/3–4.
25 See *Discriminate Deterrence* (Washington, DC: Government Printing Office, Jan. 1988) p. 20.

Appendix 1 Basic Principles Agreement, 1972

BASIC PRINCIPLES OF RELATIONS BETWEEN THE UNITED STATES OF AMERICA
AND THE SOVIET SOCIALIST REPUBLICS

The United States of America and the Union of Soviet Socialist Republics:

Guided by their obligations under the Charter of the United Nations and by a desire to strengthen peaceful relations with each other and to place these relations on the firmest possible basis,

Aware of the need to make every effort to remove the threat of war and to create conditions which promote the reduction of tensions in the world and the strengthening of universal security and international co-operation,

Believing that the improvement of US–Soviet relations and their mutually advantageous development in such areas as economics, science and culture will meet these objectives and contribute to better mutual understanding and business-like co-operation, without in any way prejudicing the interests of third countries,

Conscious that these objectives reflect the interests of the peoples of both countries,

Have agreed as follows:

FIRST: They will proceed from the common determination that in the nuclear age there is no alternative to conducting their mutual relations on the basis of peaceful coexistence. Differences in ideology and in the social systems of the USA and the USSR are not obstacles to the bilateral development of normal relations based on the principles of sovereignty, equality, non–interference in internal affairs and mutual advantage.

SECOND: The USA and the USSR attach major importance to preventing the development of situations capable of causing a dangerous exacerbation of their relations. Therefore, they will do their utmost to avoid military confrontations and to prevent the outbreak of nuclear war. They will always exercise restraint in their mutual relations, and will be prepared to negotiate and settle differences by peaceful means. Discussions and negotiations on outstanding issues will be conducted in a spirit of reciprocity, mutual accommodation and mutual benefit.

Both sides recognize that efforts to obtain unilateral advantage at the expense of the other, directly or indirectly, are inconsistent with these objectives. The prerequisites for maintaining and strengthening peaceful relations between the USA and the USSR are the

266

recognition of the security interests of the parties based on the principle of equality and the renunciation of the use or threat of force.

THIRD: The USA and the USSR have a special responsibility, as do other countries which are permanent members of the United Nations Security Council, to do everything in their power so that conflicts or situations will not arise which would serve to increase international tensions. Accordingly, they will seek to promote conditions in which all countries will live in peace and security and will not be subject to outside interference in their internal affairs.

FOURTH: The USA and the USSR intend to widen the juridical basis of their mutual relations and to exert the necessary efforts so that bilateral agreements which they have concluded and multilateral treaties and agreements to which they are jointly parties are faithfully implemented.

FIFTH: The USA and the USSR reaffirm their readiness to continue the practice of exchanging views on problems of mutual interest and, when necessary, to conduct such exchanges at the highest level, including meetings between leaders of the two countries.

The two governments welcome and will facilitate an increase in productive contacts between representatives of the legislative bodies of the two countries.

SIXTH: The parties will continue their efforts to limit armaments on a bilateral as well as on a multilateral basis. They will continue to make special efforts to limit strategic armaments. Whenever possible, they will conclude concrete agreements aimed at achieving these purposes.

The USA and the USSR regard as the ultimate objective of their efforts the achievement of general and complete disarmament and the establishment of an effective system of international security in accordance with the purposes and principles of the United Nations.

SEVENTH: The USA and the USSR regard commercial and economic ties as an important and necessary element in the strengthening of their bilateral relations and thus will actively promote the growth of such ties. They will facilitate co-operation between the relevant organizations and enterprises of the two countries and the conclusion of appropriate agreements and contracts, including long-term ones.

The two countries will contribute to the improvement of maritime and air communications between them.

EIGHTH: The two sides consider it timely and useful to develop mutual contacts and co-operation in the fields of science and technology. Where suitable, the USA and the USSR will conclude appropriate agreements dealing with concrete co-operation in these fields.

NINTH: The two sides reaffirm their intention to deepen cultural ties with one another and to encourage fuller familiarization with each other's cultural values. They will promote improved conditions for cultural exchanges and tourism.

TENTH: The USA and the USSR will seek to ensure that their ties and co-operation in all the above-mentioned fields and in any others in their mutual interest are built on a firm and long-term basis. To give a permanent character to these efforts, they will establish in all fields where this is feasible joint commissions or other joint bodies.

ELEVENTH: The USA and the USSR make no claim for themselves and would not recognize the claims of anyone else to any special rights or advantages in world affairs.

They recognize the sovereign equality of all States.

The development of US–Soviet relations is not directed against third countries and their interests.

TWELFTH: The basic principles set forth in this document do not affect any obligations with respect to other countries earlier assumed by the USA and the USSR.

Appendix 2   Agreement on the Prevention of Nuclear War

AGREEMENT BETWEEN THE USSR AND THE USA ON THE PREVENTION OF
NUCLEAR WAR

22 JUNE 1973

The Union of Soviet Socialist Republics and the United States of America hereinafter referred to as the parties,

Guided by the objectives of strengthening world peace and international security,

Conscious that nuclear war would have devastating consequences for mankind,

Proceeding from the desire to bring about conditions in which the danger of an outbreak of nuclear war anywhere in the world would be reduced and ultimately eliminated,

Proceeding from their obligations under the Charter of the United Nations regarding the maintenance of peace, refraining from the threat or use of force, and the avoidance of war, and in conformity with the agreements to which either party has subscribed,

Proceeding from the basic principles of relations between the Union of Soviet Socialist Republics and the United States of America signed in Moscow on May 29, 1972,

Reaffirming that the development of relations between the Union of Soviet Socialist Republics and the United States of America is not directed against other countries and their interests,

Have agreed as follows:

Article 1

The Soviet Union and the United States agree that an objective of their policies is to remove the danger of nuclear war and of the use of nuclear weapons.

Accordingly, the parties agree that they will act in such a manner as to prevent the development of situations capable of causing a dangerous exacerbation of their relations, so as to avoid military confrontations, and to exclude the outbreak of nuclear war between them and between either of the parties and other countries.

Article 2

The parties agree, in accordance with Article 1 and Charter of the United Nations, to realize the objective stated in that Article, to proceed from the premise that each party will refrain from the threat or use of force against the other party, against the allies of the other party and against other countries in circumstances which may endanger international peace and security. The parties agree that they will be guided by these considerations in the formulation of their foreign policies and in their actions in the fields of international relations.

Article 3

The parties undertake to develop their relations with each other and with other countries in a way consistent with the purposes of this agreement.

Article 4

If at any time relations between the parties or between either party and other countries appear to involve the risk of a nuclear conflict, or if relations between countries not parties to this agreement appear to involve the risk of nuclear war between the USSR and the USA or between either party and other countries, the Soviet Union and the United States, acting in accordance with the provisions of this agreement, shall immediately enter into urgent consultations with each other and make every effort to avert this risk.

Article 5

Each party shall be free to inform the Security Council of the United Nations, the Secretary-General of the United Nations and the governments of allied or other countries of the progress and outcome of consultations initiated in accordance with Article 4 of this agreement.

Article 6

Nothing in this agreement shall affect or impair:
   (a) The inherent right of individual or collective self-defence as envisaged by Article 51 of the Charter of the United Nations,
   (b) The provisions of the Charter of the United Nations, including those relating to the maintenance or restoration of international peace and security, and,
   (c) The obligations undertaken by either party towards its allies or other countries in treaties, agreements and other appropriate documents.

Article 7

This agreement shall be of unlimited duration.

Article 8

This agreement shall enter into force upon signature.

Done at Washington on 22 June 1973, in two copies, each in the English and Russian languages, both texts being equally authentic.

Appendix 3 Brezhnev's Code of Conduct, 1981

The present American Administration, which thinks it sees the 'hand of Moscow' in all events taking place in the world, is always appealing to the USSR and its allies to agree to observe some sort of 'code of good behaviour' with regard to the young states of Africa, Asia and Latin America. Then, they say, the world will be calmer. What can be said to that? If they mean some sort of 'rules' which would perpetuate imperialist pillage and diktat with regard to the aforementioned states and the establishment of some sort of 'spheres of influence', then of course we shall never embark on such a thing. This is contrary to the principles of our policy.

At the same time, the USSR has always stood, and continues to do so, for the strict and complete observance of the principle of equality and the generally accepted norms of international law in relations between all states: such norms, for example, as are embodied in the UN Charter, the Helsinki Final Act or, let us say, in the well-known agreements of the 1970s between the USSR and USA – agreements which today, unfortunately, are being trampled on by the American authorities.

The application of these norms to relations with young states in three continents means, we believe, more or less the following, in the present situation:

Recognition of every people's right to decide itself on its internal affairs without interference from outside; rejection of attempts to establish any form of dominance or hegemony over them, or to include them in the 'sphere of interest' of any state.

Strict respect for the territorial integrity of these countries, and the inviolability of their frontiers; no outside support for any kind of separatist movements aimed at dismembering those countries.

Unconditional recognition of the right of each state of Africa, Asia and Latin America to equal participation in international life and to the development of relations with any country.

Complete and unconditional recognition of the sovereignty of those states over their own natural resources, as well as the recognition in practice of their complete equality in international economic relations; support for their efforts to eliminate remnants of colonialism and eradicate racism and apartheid in accordance with the well-known UN resolutions.

Respect for the non-aligned status chosen by the majority of the states of Africa, Asia and Latin America; abstention from attempts to draw them into military-political power blocs.

This is the code of conduct which we recognize and are always ready to observe, and we appeal to the USA, other permanent members of the UN Security Council and, of course, all other states, to do so as well. Then the world really will become more peaceful, and people will be able to look to the future with more confidence.
(Speech in Moscow on 27 April 1981.)

Index

Abbas, Mohammed, 135
Achille Lauro, hijacking of, 135
Adamishin, A. L., 19, 261
Afghanistan: and crisis prevention, 181–3;
  Geneva accord on, 19, 20; and Iraq, 153;
  and Pakistan, 168, 172, 178, 179, 180;
  People's Democratic Party (PDPA), 41,
  168, 173; Soviet invasion of, 11–12, 29,
  31–2, 95, 129, 153, 165, 166, 178; and the
  Soviet Union, 14, 30, 36, 70, 167–8, 172–3,
  180–1; and superpower confrontation, 174,
  175, 176; superpower discussions on, 184,
  261; and the United States, 71, 168, 169,
  178–80, 252–3; US support for Mujahidin,
  44, 45, 172, 178, 179, 180
Africa, 9, 58; and arms transfers, 98;
  Portuguese decolonisation in, 29; Southern
  Africa, 31, 32, 206–26; *see also* individual
  countries
Agreement on the Prevention of Nuclear War
  (1973), 7, 10, 107, 257, 269–71
aircraft: Soviet, 77–8
aircraft carriers, 76, 80, 86, 87
Algeria, 33
America, *see* Central America; Latin America;
  United States
Amin, Hafizullah, 173, 181
amphibious ships: Soviet, 76–7; United States,
  80
ANC (African National Congress), 213, 214,
  215, 217, 223
Andropov, Yuri, 41, 44, 132
Anglo–Russian Convention (1907), 144, 145
Angola: 1975–6 Civil War, 31, 35, 219; and
  Namibia, 213–14; and regional peace
  initiatives, 215, 263; and the Soviet Union,
  8, 30, 36, 37, 39, 41, 178, 191; Soviet/
  Cuban intervention in, 193, 206, 207, 208,
  213, 216, 218, 219, 220, 221, 223; and the
  United States, 44, 63

ANS (Armée Nationale Sihanoukienne), 235,
  237
apartheid: and Southern Africa, 210, 213, 214,
  221, 224
Arab states, 123; and the Soviet Union, 31;
  wars with Israel, 112–13, 121, 122, 123,
  124–6, 127, 254; *see also* individual
  countries
Arafat, Yasser, 132, 133, 134, 135, 138
Arbatov, Georgi, 51, 260
Argentina, 39, 70, 192
Arias peace plan, 204
Armacost, Michael, 261
arms control, 11, 44; maritime areas, 85–6;
  regional arms races, 14, 94–5; in Southern
  Africa, 221; strategic arms race, 259; talks,
  159
arms transfers, 11, 31, 71, 89–103; and Central
  America, 199; formal restraints on, 264; and
  the Gulf War, 157, 178; and Iran, 93, 99,
  100, 178, 195; in the Middle East, 139, 154;
  in Nicaragua, 251; South Africa, 216–17; in
  Southeast Asia, 251; in Southern Africa,
  215; in Southwest Asia, 168, 172, 183, 252;
  Soviet, 38–9
Aron, Raymond, 161
ASEAN (Association of South-East Asian
  Nations), 41, 76, 230, 232, 233, 234, 235–8,
  241, 243, 263
Asia: collective security proposals, 35, 45–6;
  see also individual countries
Assad, Hafiz, 125, 129, 135, 138
asymmetrical interests, 108–9, 250, 259; in
  Central America, 201, 203; in Southwest
  Asia, 169–70
asymmetrical intervention, 4, 251–6, 259
Attlee, Clement, 54

Baghdad Pact, 158
balance of power: shifts in, 2

275